Structure and Interpretation of Computer Programs

The MIT Electrical Engineering and Computer Science Series

Harold Abelson and Gerald Jay Sussman with Julie Sussman, *Structure and Interpretation of Computer Programs*, 1985

William Siebert, *Circuits, Signals, and Systems*, 1985

Structure and Interpretation of Computer Programs

Harold Abelson and Gerald Jay Sussman
with Julie Sussman

foreword by Alan J. Perlis

The MIT Press
Cambridge, Massachusetts   London, England

McGraw-Hill Book Company
New York   St. Louis   San Francisco   Montreal   Toronto

This book is one of a series of texts written by faculty of the Electrical Engineering and Computer Science Department at the Massachusetts Institute of Technology. It was edited and produced by The MIT Press under a joint production-distribution arrangement with the McGraw-Hill Book Company.

Ordering Information:

North America
Text orders should be addressed to the McGraw-Hill Book Company.
All other orders should be addressed to The MIT Press.

Outside North America
All orders should be addressed to The MIT Press or its local distributor.

Third printing, 1985

This book was set under the direction of the authors using the TEX typesetting system and was printed and bound by Halliday Lithograph in the United States of America.

Library of Congress Cataloging in Publication Data
Abelson, Harold.
    Structure and interpretation of computer programs.

    (The MIT electrical engineering and computer science series)
    Includes bibliography and index.
    1. Electronic digital computers—Programming.
2. LISP (Computer program language) I. Sussman, Gerald Jay. II. Sussman, Julie. III. Title. IV. Series
QA76.6.A255 1985   001.64'2   84-9688
ISBN 0-262-01077-1 (MIT Press)
ISBN 0-07-000-422-6 (McGraw-Hill)

This book is dedicated, in respect and admiration, to the spirit that lives in the computer.

"I think that it's extraordinarily important that we in computer science keep fun in computing. When it started out, it was an awful lot of fun. Of course, the paying customers got shafted every now and then, and after a while we began to take their complaints seriously. We began to feel as if we really were responsible for the successful, error-free perfect use of these machines. I don't think we are. I think we're responsible for stretching them, setting them off in new directions, and keeping fun in the house. I hope the field of computer science never loses its sense of fun. Above all, I hope we don't become missionaries. Don't feel as if you're Bible salesmen. The world has too many of those already. What you know about computing other people will learn. Don't feel as if the key to successful computing is only in your hands. What's in your hands, I think and hope, is intelligence: the ability to see the machine as more than when you were first led up to it, that you can make it more."

Alan J. Perlis

Contents

Foreword

Educators, generals, dieticians, psychologists, and parents program. Armies, students, and some societies are programmed. An assault on large problems employs a succession of programs, most of which spring into existence en route. These programs are rife with issues that appear to be particular to the problem at hand. To appreciate programming as an intellectual activity in its own right you must turn to computer programming; you must read and write computer programs—many of them. It doesn't matter much what the programs are about or what applications they serve. What does matter is how well they perform and how smoothly they fit with other programs in the creation of still greater programs. The programmer must seek both perfection of part and adequacy of collection. In this book the use of "program" is focused on the creation, execution, and study of programs written in a dialect of Lisp for execution on a digital computer. Using Lisp we restrict or limit not what we may program, but only the notation for our program descriptions.

Our traffic with the subject matter of this book involves us with three foci of phenomena: the human mind, collections of computer programs, and the computer. Every computer program is a model, hatched in the mind, of a real or mental process. These processes, arising from human experience and thought, are huge in number, intricate in detail, and at any time only partially understood. They are modeled to our permanent satisfaction rarely by our computer programs. Thus even though our programs are carefully handcrafted discrete collections of symbols, mosaics of interlocking functions, they continually evolve: we change them as our perception of the model deepens, enlarges, generalizes until the model ultimately attains a metastable place within still another model with which we struggle. The source of the exhilaration associated with computer programming is the continual unfolding within the mind and on the computer of mechanisms expressed as programs and the explosion of perception they generate. If art interprets our dreams, the computer executes them in the guise of programs!

For all its power, the computer is a harsh taskmaster. Its programs must be correct, and what we wish to say must be said accurately in every detail. As in every other symbolic activity, we become convinced of program truth through argument. Lisp itself can be assigned a semantics (another model, by the way), and if a program's function can be specified, say, in the predicate calculus, the proof methods of logic can be used to make an acceptable correctness argument. Unfortunately, as programs get large and complicated, as they almost always do, the adequacy, consistency, and correctness of the specifications themselves become open to doubt, so that complete formal arguments of correctness seldom accompany large programs. Since large programs grow from small ones, it is crucial that we develop an arsenal of standard program structures of whose correctness we have become sure—we call them idioms—and learn to combine them into larger structures using organizational techniques of proven value. These techniques are treated at length in this book, and understanding them is essential to participation in the Promethean enterprise called programming. More than anything else, the uncovering and mastery of powerful organizational techniques accelerates our ability to create large, significant programs. Conversely, since writing large programs is very taxing, we are stimulated to invent new methods of reducing the mass of function and detail to be fitted into large programs.

Unlike programs, computers must obey the laws of physics. If they wish to perform rapidly—a few nanoseconds per state change—they must transmit electrons only small distances (at most $1\frac{1}{2}$ feet). The heat generated by the huge number of devices so concentrated in space has to be removed. An exquisite engineering art has been developed balancing between multiplicity of function and density of devices. In any event, hardware always operates at a level more primitive than that at which we care to program. The processes that transform our Lisp programs to "machine" programs are themselves abstract models which we program. Their study and creation give a great deal of insight into the organizational programs associated with programming arbitrary models. Of course the computer itself can be so modeled. Think of it: the behavior of the smallest physical switching element is modeled by quantum mechanics described by differential equations whose detailed behavior is captured by numerical approximations represented in computer programs executing on computers composed of...!

It is not merely a matter of tactical convenience to separately identify the three foci. Even though, as they say, it's all in the head, this logical separation induces an acceleration of symbolic traffic between these foci whose richness, vitality, and potential is exceeded in human experience only by the evolution of life itself. At best, relationships between the foci are metastable. The computers are never large enough or fast enough. Each breakthrough in hardware technology leads to more massive programming enterprises, new organizational principles, and an enrichment of abstract models. Every reader should ask himself periodically "Toward what end, toward what end?"—but do not ask it too often lest you pass up the fun of programming for the constipation of bittersweet philosophy.

Among the programs we write, some (but never enough) perform a precise mathematical function such as sorting or finding the maximum of a sequence of numbers, determining primality, or finding the square root. We call such programs algorithms, and a great deal is known of their optimal behavior, particularly with respect to the two important parameters of execution time and data storage requirements. A programmer should acquire good algorithms and idioms. Even though some programs resist precise specifications, it is the responsibility of the programmer to estimate, and always to attempt to improve, their performance.

Lisp is a survivor, having been in use for about a quarter of a century. Among the active programming languages only Fortran has had a longer life. Both languages have supported the programming needs of important areas of application, Fortran for scientific and engineering computation and Lisp for artificial intelligence. These two areas continue to be important, and their programmers are so devoted to these two languages that Lisp and Fortran may well continue in active use for at least another quarter-century.

Lisp changes. The Scheme dialect used in this text has evolved from the original Lisp and differs from the latter in several important ways, including static scoping for variable binding and permitting functions to yield functions as values. In its semantic structure Scheme is as closely akin to Algol 60 as to early Lisps. Algol 60, never to be an active language again, lives on in the genes of Scheme and Pascal. It would be difficult to find two languages that are the communicating coin of two more different cultures than those gathered around these two languages. Pascal is for building pyramids—imposing, breathtaking, static structures built by armies pushing heavy blocks into place. Lisp is for building organisms—imposing, breathtaking, dynamic structures built by squads fitting fluctuating myriads of simpler organisms into place. The organizing principles used are the same in both cases, except for one extraordinarily important difference: The discretionary exportable functionality entrusted to the individual Lisp programmer is more than an order of magnitude greater than that to be found within Pascal enterprises. Lisp programs inflate libraries with functions whose utility transcends the application that produced them. The list, Lisp's native data structure, is largely responsible for such growth of utility. The simple structure and natural applicability of lists are reflected in functions that are amazingly nonidiosyncratic. In Pascal the plethora of declarable data structures induces a specialization within functions that inhibits and penalizes casual cooperation. It is better to have 100 functions operate on one data structure than to have 10 functions operate on 10 data structures. As a result the pyramid must stand unchanged for a millennium; the organism must evolve or perish.

To illustrate this difference, compare the treatment of material and exercises within this book with that in any first-course text using Pascal. Do not labor under the illusion that this is a text digestible at MIT only, peculiar to the breed found there. It is precisely what a serious book on programming Lisp must be, no matter who the student is or where it is used.

Note that this is a text about programming, unlike most Lisp books, which are used as a preparation for work in artificial intelligence. After all, the critical programming concerns of software engineering and artificial intelligence tend to coalesce as the systems under investigation become larger. This explains why there is such growing interest in Lisp outside of artificial intelligence.

As one would expect from its goals, artificial intelligence research generates many significant programming problems. In other programming cultures this spate of problems spawns new languages. Indeed, in any very large programming task a useful organizing principle is to control and isolate traffic within the task modules via the invention of language. These languages tend to become less primitive as one approaches the boundaries of the system where we humans interact most often. As a result, such systems contain complex language-processing functions replicated many times. Lisp has such a simple syntax and semantics that parsing can be treated as an elementary task. Thus parsing technology plays almost no role in Lisp programs, and the construction of language processors is rarely an impediment to the rate of growth and change of large Lisp systems. Finally, it is this very simplicity of syntax and semantics that is responsible for the burden and freedom borne by all Lisp programmers. No Lisp program of any size beyond a few lines can be written without being saturated with discretionary functions. Invent and fit; have fits and reinvent! We toast the Lisp programmer who pens his thoughts within nests of parentheses.

Alan J. Perlis
New Haven, Connecticut

Preface

A computer is like a violin. You can imagine a novice
trying first a phonograph and then a violin. The latter, he says, sounds terrible. That is the argument we
have heard from our humanists and most of our computer scientists. Computer programs are good, they
say, for particular purposes, but they aren't flexible.
Neither is a violin, or a typewriter, until you learn
how to use it.

Marvin Minsky, "Why Programming Is a Good Medium for Expressing Poorly-Understood and Sloppily-
Formulated Ideas"

"The Structure and Interpretation of Computer Programs" is the entry-
level subject in computer science at the Massachusetts Institute of Technology. It is required of all students at MIT who major in electrical
engineering or in computer science, as one-fourth of the "common core
curriculum," which also includes two subjects on circuits and linear systems
and a subject on the design of digital systems. We have been involved in the
development of this subject since 1978, and we have taught this material in
its present form since the fall of 1980 to between 600 and 700 students each
year. Most of these students have had little or no prior formal training in
computation, although many have played with computers a bit and a few
have had extensive programming or hardware-design experience.

Our design of this introductory computer-science subject reflects two
major concerns. First, we want to establish the idea that a computer
language is not just a way of getting a computer to perform operations
but rather that it is a novel formal medium for expressing ideas about
methodology. Thus, programs must be written for people to read, and only
incidentally for machines to execute. Second, we believe that the essential
material to be addressed by a subject at this level is not the syntax of particular programming-language constructs, nor clever algorithms for computing particular functions efficiently, nor even the mathematical analysis
of algorithms and the foundations of computing, but rather the techniques
used to control the intellectual complexity of large software systems.

Our goal is that students who complete this subject should have a good
feel for the elements of style and the aesthetics of programming. They
should have command of the major techniques for controlling complexity in

a large system. They should be capable of reading a 50-page-long program, if it is written in an exemplary style. They should know what not to read, and what they need not understand at any moment. They should feel secure about modifying a program, retaining the spirit and style of the original author.

These skills are by no means unique to computer programming. The techniques we teach and draw upon are common to all of engineering design. We control complexity by building abstractions that hide details when appropriate. We control complexity by establishing conventional interfaces that enable us to construct systems by combining standard, well-understood pieces in a "mix and match" way. We control complexity by establishing new languages for describing a design, each of which emphasizes particular aspects of the design and deemphasizes others.

Underlying our approach to this subject is our conviction that "computer science" is not a science and that its significance has little to do with computers. The computer revolution is a revolution in the way we think and in the way we express what we think. The essence of this change is the emergence of what might best be called *procedural epistemology*—the study of the structure of knowledge from an imperative point of view, as opposed to the more declarative point of view taken by classical mathematical subjects. Mathematics provides a framework for dealing precisely with notions of "what is." Computation provides a framework for dealing precisely with notions of "how to."

In teaching our material we use a dialect of the programming language Lisp. We never formally teach the language, because we don't have to. We just use it, and students pick it up in a few days. This is one great advantage of Lisp-like languages: They have very few ways of forming compound expressions, and almost no syntactic structure. All of the formal properties can be covered in an hour, like the rules of chess. After a short time we forget about syntactic details of the language (because there are none) and get on with the real issues—figuring out what we want to compute, how we will decompose problems into manageable parts, and how we will work on the parts. Another advantage of Lisp is that it supports (but does not enforce) more of the large-scale strategies for modular decomposition of programs than any other language we know. We can make procedural and data abstractions, we can use higher-order functions to capture common patterns of usage, we can model local state using assignment and data mutation, we can link parts of a program with streams and delayed evaluation, and we can easily implement embedded languages.

All of this is embedded in an interactive environment with excellent support for incremental program design, construction, testing, and debugging. We thank all the generations of Lisp wizards, starting with John McCarthy, who have fashioned a fine tool of unprecedented power and elegance.

Scheme, the dialect of Lisp that we use, is an attempt to bring together the power and elegance of Lisp and Algol. From Lisp we take the metalinguistic power that derives from the simple syntax, the uniform representation of programs as data objects, and the garbage-collected heap-allocated data. From Algol we take lexical scoping and block structure, which are gifts from the pioneers of programming-language design who were on the Algol committee. We wish to cite John Reynolds and Peter Landin for their insights into the relationship of Church's lambda-calculus to the structure of programming languages. We also recognize our debt to the mathematicians who scouted out this territory decades before computers appeared on the scene. These pioneers include Alonzo Church, Barkley Rosser, Stephen Kleene, and Haskell Curry.

Acknowledgments

We would like to thank the many people who have helped us develop this book and this curriculum.

Our subject is a clear intellectual descendant of "6.231," a wonderful subject on programming linguistics and the lambda-calculus taught at MIT in the late 1960s by Jack Wozencraft and Arthur Evans, Jr.

We owe a great debt to Robert Fano, who reorganized MIT's introductory curriculum in electrical engineering and computer science to emphasize the principles of engineering design. He led us in starting out on this enterprise and wrote the first set of subject notes from which this book evolved.

Much of the style and aesthetics of programming that we try to teach were developed in conjunction with Guy Lewis Steele Jr., who collaborated with Gerald Jay Sussman in the initial development of the Scheme language. In addition, David Turner, Peter Henderson, Dan Friedman, David Wise, and Will Clinger have taught us many of the techniques of the functional programming community that appear in this book.

Joel Moses taught us about structuring large systems. His experience with the Macsyma system for symbolic computation provided the insight that one should avoid complexities of control and concentrate on organizing the data to reflect the real structure of the world being modeled.

Marvin Minsky and Seymour Papert formed many of our attitudes about programming and its place in our intellectual lives. To them we owe the understanding that computation provides a means of expression for exploring ideas that would otherwise be too complex to deal with precisely. They emphasize that a student's ability to write and modify programs provides a powerful medium in which exploring becomes a natural activity.

We also strongly agree with Alan Perlis that programming is lots of fun and we had better be careful to support the joy of programming. Part of this joy derives from observing great masters at work. We are fortunate to have been apprentice programmers at the feet of Bill Gosper and Richard Greenblatt.

It is difficult to identify all the people who have contributed to the development of our curriculum. We thank all the recitation instructors and tutors who have worked with us over the past few years, especially Bill Siebert, Albert Meyer, Joe Stoy, and Randy Davis, who put in many extra hours on our subject. It is also hard to enumerate all the people who have made technical contributions to the development of the Scheme systems we use for instructional purposes. In addition to Guy Steele, principal wizards have included Chris Hanson, Joe Bowbeer, Jim Miller, and Guillermo Rozas. Others who have put in significant time are Richard

Stallman, Alan Bawden, Kent Pitman, Jon Taft, Neil Mayle, John Lamping, Gwyn Osnos, Tracy Larrabee, George Carrette, Soma Chaudhuri, Bill Chiarchiaro, Steven Kirsch, Leigh Klotz, Wayne Noss, Todd Cass, Patrick O'Donnell, Kevin Theobald, Daniel Weise, Kenneth Sinclair, Anthony Courtemanche, Henry M. Wu, and Andrew Berlin.

We are pleased that others are working on similar language implementations, and we hope that we will continue to learn from each other's activity. We want especially to draw attention to the work on "T" by Jon Rees, Kent Pitman, and others at Yale, and the work on "Scheme-311" by Mitch Wand, Will Clinger, Dan Friedman, and others at Indiana University.

Finally, we would like to thank all the people and organizations who have supported and encouraged this work, including Ira Goldstein and Joel Birnbaum at Hewlett-Packard Laboratories and Bob Kahn at DARPA.

Structure and Interpretation of Computer Programs

1

BUILDING ABSTRACTIONS
WITH PROCEDURES

> The acts of the mind, wherein it exerts its power over simple ideas, are chiefly these three: 1. Combining several simple ideas into one compound one, and thus all complex ideas are made. 2. The second is bringing two ideas, whether simple or complex, together, and setting them by one another so as to take a view of them at once, without uniting them into one, by which it gets all its ideas of relations. 3. The third is separating them from all other ideas that accompany them in their real existence: this is called abstraction, and thus all its general ideas are made.
>
> John Locke, *An Essay Concerning Human Understanding* (1690)

We are about to study the idea of a *computational process*. Computational processes are abstract beings that inhabit computers. As they evolve, processes manipulate other abstract things called *data*. The evolution of a process is directed by a pattern of rules called a *program*. People create programs to direct processes. In effect, we conjure the spirits of the computer with our spells.

A computational process is indeed much like a sorcerer's idea of a spirit. It cannot be seen or touched. It is not composed of matter at all. However, it is very real. It can perform intellectual work. It can answer questions. It can affect the world by disbursing money at a bank or by controlling a robot arm in a factory. The programs we use to conjure processes are like a sorcerer's spells. They are carefully composed from symbolic expressions in arcane and esoteric *programming languages* that prescribe the tasks that we want our processes to perform.

A computational process, in a correctly working computer, executes programs precisely and accurately. Thus, like the sorcerer's apprentice, the novice programmer must learn to understand and to anticipate the consequences of his conjuring. Even small errors (usually called *bugs* or *glitches*) in programs can have complex and unanticipated consequences.

Fortunately, learning to program is considerably less dangerous than learning sorcery, because the spirits we deal with are conveniently contained in a secure way. Real-world programming, however, requires care, expertise, and wisdom. A small bug in a computer-aided design program, for example, can lead to the catastrophic collapse of an airplane or a dam or the self-destruction of an industrial robot.

A master software engineer has the ability to organize programs so that he can be reasonably sure his processes will perform the tasks intended. He can visualize the behavior of his system in advance. He knows how to structure his programs so that unanticipated problems do not lead to catastrophic consequences, and when problems do arise he can debug his programs. Well-designed computational systems, like well-designed automobiles or nuclear reactors, are designed in a modular manner, so that the parts can be constructed, replaced, and debugged separately.

Programming in Lisp

We need an appropriate language for describing processes, and we will use for this purpose the programming language Lisp. Just as our everyday thoughts are usually expressed in our natural language (such as English, or French, or Japanese), and descriptions of quantitative phenomena are expressed with mathematical notations, our procedural thoughts will be expressed in Lisp. Lisp was invented in the late 1950s as a formalism for reasoning about the use of certain kinds of logical expressions, called *recursion equations*, as a model for computation. The language was conceived by John McCarthy and is based on his paper "Recursive Functions of Symbolic Expressions and Their Computation by Machine" (McCarthy 1960).

Despite its inception as a mathematical formalism, Lisp is a practical programming language. A Lisp *interpreter* is a machine that carries out processes described in the Lisp language. The first Lisp interpreter was implemented by McCarthy with the help of colleagues and students in the Artificial Intelligence Group of the MIT Research Laboratory of Electronics and in the MIT Computation Center.[1] Lisp, whose name is an acronym for LISt Processing, was designed to provide symbol-manipulating capabilities for attacking programming problems such as the symbolic differentiation and integration of algebraic expressions. It included for this purpose new data objects known as atoms and lists, which most strikingly set it apart from all other languages of the period.

Lisp was not the product of a concerted design effort. Instead, it evolved informally in an experimental manner in response to users' needs and to pragmatic implementation considerations. Lisp's informal evolution

---

1 The *Lisp 1 Programmer's Manual* appeared in 1960, and the *Lisp 1.5 Programmer's Manual* (see McCarthy 1965) was published in 1962. The early history of Lisp is described in McCarthy 1978.

has continued through the years, and the community of Lisp users has traditionally resisted attempts to promulgate any "official" definition of the language. This evolution, together with the flexibility and elegance of the initial conception, has enabled Lisp, which is the second oldest language in widespread use today (only Fortran is older), to continually adapt to encompass the most modern ideas about program design. Thus, Lisp is by now a family of dialects, which, while sharing most of the original features, may differ from one another in significant ways. The dialect of Lisp used in this book is called Scheme.[2]

Because of its experimental character and its emphasis on symbol manipulation, Lisp was at first very inefficient for numerical computations, at least in comparison with Fortran. Over the years, however, Lisp compilers have been developed that translate programs into machine code that can perform numerical computations as efficiently as code generated from any other high-level language. In spite of this, Lisp has not yet overcome its old reputation as a hopelessly inefficient language, and its use is still localized in a few research laboratories.

If Lisp is not a popular language, why are we using it as the framework for our discussion of programming? Because the language possesses unique features that make it an excellent medium for studying important programming constructs and data structures and for relating them to the linguistic features that support them. The most significant of these features is the fact that Lisp descriptions of processes, called *procedures*, can themselves be represented and manipulated as Lisp data. The importance of this is that there are powerful program-design techniques that rely on the ability to blur the traditional distinction between "passive" data and "active" processes. As we shall discover, Lisp's flexibility in handling procedures as data makes it one of the most convenient languages in existence for exploring these techniques. The ability to represent procedures as data also makes Lisp an excellent language for writing programs that must manipulate other programs as data, such as the interpreters and compilers that

2 The two dialects in which most major Lisp programs of the 1970s were written are MacLisp (Moon 1978; Pitman 1983), developed at the MIT Project MAC, and Interlisp (Teitelman 1974), developed at Bolt Beranek and Newman, Inc., and the Xerox Palo Alto Research Center. Portable Standard Lisp (Hearn 1969; Griss 1981) is another Lisp dialect designed to be easily portable between different machines, and is beginning to become widely available. MacLisp has also spawned a number of subdialects, such as Franz Lisp, which was developed at the University of California at Berkeley, and Zetalisp (Moon 1981), which is based on a special-purpose processor designed at the MIT Artificial Intelligence Laboratory to run Lisp very efficiently. Common Lisp, another Lisp dialect currently under development, is meant to serve as a standard for future production Lisp systems (Steele 1982). The Lisp dialect used in this book, called Scheme (Steele 1975), was invented in 1975 by Guy Lewis Steele Jr. and Gerald Jay Sussman of the MIT Artificial Intelligence Laboratory and later reimplemented for instructional use at MIT.

support computer languages. Above and beyond these considerations, programming in Lisp is great fun.

1.1 The Elements of Programming

A powerful programming language is more than just a means for instructing a computer to perform tasks. The language also serves as a framework within which we organize our ideas about processes. Thus, when we describe a language, we should pay particular attention to the means that the language provides for combining simple ideas to form more complex ideas. Every powerful language has three mechanisms for accomplishing this:

primitive expressions, which represent the simplest entities with which the language is concerned,

means of combination, by which compound expressions are built from simpler ones, and

means of abstraction, by which compound objects can be named and manipulated as units.

In programming, we deal with two kinds of objects: procedures and data. (Later we will discover that they are really not so distinct.) Informally, data is "stuff" that represents objects we want to manipulate, and procedures are descriptions of the rules for manipulating the data. Thus, any powerful programming language should be able to describe primitive data and primitive procedures and should have methods for combining and abstracting procedures and data.

In this chapter we will deal only with simple numerical data so that we can focus on the rules for building procedures.[3] In later chapters we will see that these same rules allow us to build procedures to manipulate compound data as well.

3 The characterization of numbers as "simple data" is a barefaced bluff. In fact, the treatment of numbers is one of the trickiest and most confusing aspects of any programming language. Some typical issues involved are these: Is there a difference between integers, such as 2, and "real" numbers, such as 2.00? Are the arithmetic operators used for integers the same as the operators used for real numbers? Does 6 divided by 2 produce 3, or 3.0? How large a number can we represent? How many decimal places of accuracy can we represent? Is the range of integers the same as the range of real numbers? Above and beyond these questions, of course, lies a collection of issues concerning roundoff and truncation errors—the entire science of numerical analysis. Since our focus in this book is on large-scale program design rather than on numerical techniques, we are going to ignore these problems. The Scheme dialect of Lisp, wherever possible, does not distinguish between integers and "real" numbers (for example, 3 is equal to 3.0). The numerical examples in this chapter will exhibit the usual roundoff behavior that one observes when using arithmetic operations that preserve a limited number of decimal places of accuracy in noninteger operations.

1.1.1 Expressions

One easy way to get started at programming is to examine some typical interactions with an interpreter for the Scheme dialect of Lisp. Imagine that you are sitting at a computer terminal, and that the interpreter has indicated that it is ready to serve you by displaying a *prompt*

```
==>
```

at the beginning of a blank line. If you respond to the prompt by typing an expression, the interpreter responds by displaying the result of its *evaluating* that expression.

One kind of primitive expression you might type is a number. (More precisely, the expression that you type consists of the numerals that represent the number in base 10.) If you present Lisp with a number

```
==> 486
```

the interpreter will respond by printing[4]

```
486
```

Expressions representing numbers may be combined with an expression representing a primitive procedure (such as + or *) to form a compound expression that represents the application of the procedure to those numbers. For example:

```
==> (+ 137 349)
486

==> (- 1000 334)
666

==> (* 5 99)
495

==> (/ 10 5)
2

==> (/ 10 6)
1.66667
```

---

4 Throughout this book, when we wish to emphasize the distinction between the input typed by the user and the response printed by the interpreter, we will show the latter in italic characters.

```
==> (+ 2.7 10)
```
12.7

Expressions such as these, formed by delimiting a list of expressions within parentheses, are called *combinations*. The leftmost element in the list is called the *operator*, and the other elements are called *operands*. The value of a combination is obtained by applying the procedure specified by the operator to the *arguments* that are the values of the operands.

The convention of placing the operator to the left of the operands is known as *prefix notation*, and it may be somewhat confusing at first because it departs significantly from the customary mathematical convention. Prefix notation has several advantages, however. One of them is that it can accommodate procedures that may take an arbitrary number of arguments, as in the following examples:

```
==> (+ 21 35 12 7)
```
75

```
==> (* 25 4 12)
```
1200

No ambiguity can arise, because the operator is always the leftmost element and the entire combination is delimited by the parentheses.

A second advantage of prefix notation is that it extends in a straightforward way to allow combinations to be *nested*, that is, to have combinations whose elements are themselves combinations:

```
==> (+ (* 3 5) (- 10 6))
```
19

There is no limit (in principle) to the depth of such nesting and to the overall complexity of the expressions that the Lisp interpreter can evaluate. It is we humans who get confused by still relatively simple expressions such as

```
(+ (* 3 (+ (* 2 4) (+ 3 5))) (+ (- 10 7) 6))
```

which the interpreter would readily evaluate to be 57. We can help ourselves by writing such an expression in the form

```
(+ (* 3
      (+ (* 2 4)
         (+ 3 5)))
   (+ (- 10 7)
      6))
```

following a formatting convention known as *pretty-printing*, in which each long combination is written so that the operands are aligned vertically. The resulting indentations display clearly the structure of the expression.[5]

Even with complex expressions, the interpreter always operates in the same basic cycle: It reads an expression from the terminal, evaluates the expression, and prints the result. This mode of operation is often expressed by saying that the interpreter runs in a *read-eval-print loop*. Observe in particular that it is not necessary to explicitly instruct the interpreter to print the value of the expression.

1.1.2 Naming and the Environment

A critical aspect of a programming language is the means it provides for using names to refer to computational objects. We say that the name identifies a *variable* whose *value* is the object.

In the Scheme dialect of Lisp, the operator for naming things is called define. Typing

```
==> (define size 2)
size
```

causes the interpreter to associate the value 2 with the name size. Notice that the interpreter responds to a define combination by printing the name being defined.[6]

Once the name size has been defined to be the number 2, we can refer to the value 2 by name:

```
==> size
2
```

---

5 Lisp systems typically provide features to aid the user in formatting expressions. Two especially useful features are one that automatically indents to the proper pretty-print position whenever a new line is started and one that highlights the matching left parenthesis whenever a right parenthesis is typed.

6 The symbol printed is actually the value of the define combination. In Lisp, one makes the convention that every expression has a value. This requirement may seem silly, but deviating from it would cause bothersome complications. It also meshes nicely with the read-eval-print mode in which the interpreter operates, since it ensures that the interpreter will have something to print in response to evaluating any expression. When there is no natural choice for the value to be returned as the result of an operation, language implementers choose a value by convention, as in the case of define. The conventions for choosing such values tend to be highly implementation-dependent, and it is dangerous practice to write programs that rely on them. (The convention that every Lisp expression must have a value, together with the old reputation of Lisp as an inefficient language, is the source of the quip by Alan Perlis that "Lisp programmers know the value of everything but the cost of nothing.")

```
==> (* 5 size)
```
10

Here are further examples of the use of `define`:

```
==> (define pi 3.14159)
```
pi

```
==> (define radius 10)
```
radius

```
==> (* pi (* radius radius))
```
314.159

```
==> (define circumference (* 2 pi radius))
```
circumference

```
==> circumference
```
62.8318

`Define` is our language's simplest means of abstraction, for it allows us to use simple names to refer to the results of compound operations, such as the `circumference` computed above. In general, computational objects may have very complex structures, and it would be extremely inconvenient to have to remember and repeat their details each time we want to use them. Indeed, complex programs are constructed by building, step by step, computational objects of increasing complexity. The interpreter makes this step-by-step program construction particularly convenient because name-object associations can be created incrementally in successive interactions. This feature encourages the incremental development and testing of programs and is largely responsible for the fact that a Lisp program usually consists of a large number of relatively simple procedures.

It should be clear that the possibility of associating values with symbols and later retrieving them means that the interpreter must maintain some sort of memory that keeps track of the name-object pairs. This memory is called the *environment* (more precisely the *global environment*, since we will see later that a computation may involve a number of different environments.)[7]

---

7 Chapter 3 will show that this notion of environment is crucial, both for understanding how the interpreter works and for implementing interpreters.

1.1.3 Evaluating Combinations

One of our goals in this chapter is to isolate issues about thinking procedurally. As a case in point, let us consider that, in evaluating combinations, the Lisp interpreter is itself following a procedure. For the expressions we have discussed so far, the evaluation process is described simply.

To evaluate a combination (other than a definition), do the following:

1. Evaluate the subexpressions of the combination.

2. Apply the procedure that is the value of the leftmost subexpression (the operator) to the arguments that are the values of the other subexpressions (the operands).

Even this simple rule illustrates some important points about processes in general. First, observe that step 1 dictates that in order to accomplish the evaluation process for a combination we must first perform the evaluation process on each element of the combination. Thus, the evaluation rule is recursive in nature; that is, it includes, as one of its steps, the need to invoke the rule itself.[8]

Notice how succinctly the idea of recursion can be used to express what, in the case of a deeply nested combination, would otherwise be viewed as a rather complicated process. For example, evaluating

```
(* (+ 2 (* 4 6))
   (+ 3 5 7))
```

requires that the evaluation rule be applied to four different combinations. We can obtain a picture of this process by representing the combination in the form of a tree, as shown in figure 1.1. Each combination is represented by a node, from which stem branches corresponding to the operator and the operands of the combination. The terminal nodes (that is, nodes with no branches stemming from them) represent either operators or numbers. Viewing evaluation in terms of the tree, we can imagine that the values of the operands percolate upward, starting from the terminal nodes and then combining at higher and higher levels. In general, we shall see that recursion is a very powerful technique for dealing with hierarchical, treelike objects. In fact, the "percolate values upward" form of the evaluation rule is an example of a general kind of process known as *tree accumulation*.

---

8 It may seem strange that the evaluation rule says, as part of step 1, that we should evaluate the leftmost element of a combination, which, at this point, can only be an operator representing a built-in primitive procedure such as + or *. We will see later that it is useful to be able to work with combinations whose operators are themselves compound expressions.

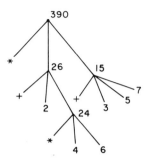

Figure 1.1
Tree representation, showing the value of each subcombination.

Next, observe that the repeated application of step 1 brings us to the point where we need to evaluate, not combinations, but primitive expressions such as numerals, built-in operators, or other names. We take care of the primitive cases by stipulating that

• the values of numerals are the numbers that they name,

• the values of built-in operators are the primitive machine instruction sequences that carry out the corresponding operations, and

• the values of other names are the objects associated with those names in the environment.

We may regard the second rule as a special case of the third one by imagining that symbols such as + and * are also included in the global environment, and are associated with the sequences of machine instructions that are their "values." The key point to notice is the role of the environment in determining the meaning of the symbols in the expressions. In an interactive language such as Lisp, it is meaningless to speak of the value of an expression such as (+ x 1) without specifying any information about the environment that would provide a meaning for the symbol x (or even for the symbol +). As we shall see in chapter 3, the general notion of the environment as providing a context in which evaluation takes place will play an important role in our understanding of program execution.

Finally, notice that define is an exception to the general evaluation rule given above. For instance, evaluating the expression (define x 3) does not apply define to two arguments, one of which is the value of the symbol x and the other of which is 3, since the purpose of the define is precisely to associate x with a value.

Such exceptions to the general evaluation rule are called *special forms*. Define is the only example of a special form that we have seen so far, but we will meet others shortly. Each special form has its own evaluation rule.

The special forms and their associated special evaluation rules constitute the syntax of the programming language. In comparison with most other programming languages, Lisp has a very simple syntax; that is, the evaluation rule for expressions can be described by a simple general rule together with specialized rules for a small number of special forms.[9]

1.1.4 Compound Procedures

We have identified in Lisp some of the elements that must appear in any powerful programming language:

Numbers and arithmetic operators are primitive data and procedures.

Nesting of combinations provides a means of combining operators.

Using `define` to associate names with values provides a limited means of abstraction.

Now we will learn about *procedure definitions*, a much more powerful abstraction technique by which a compound operation can be given a name and then referred to as a unit.

We begin by examining how to express the idea of "squaring." We might say, "To square something, multiply it by itself." This is expressed in our language as

```
(define (square x) (* x x))
```

We can understand this in the following way:

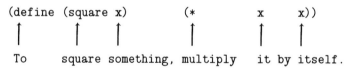

```
(define (square x)       (*        x       x))
```
```
   To    square something, multiply   it by itself.
```

We have here a *compound procedure*, which has been given the name `square`. It represents the operation of multiplying an entity by itself. The entity to be multiplied is given a local name, `x`, which plays the same role that a pronoun plays in natural language.

---

9 Special syntactic forms that are simply convenient alternative surface structures for things that can be written in more uniform ways are sometimes called *syntactic sugar*, to use a phrase coined by Peter Landin. In comparison with users of other languages, Lisp programmers, as a rule, are less concerned with matters of syntax. (By contrast, examine any Pascal manual and notice how much of it is devoted to descriptions of syntax.) This disdain for syntax is due partly to the flexibility of Lisp, which makes it easy to change surface syntax, and partly to the observation that many "convenient" syntactic constructs, which make the language less uniform, end up causing more trouble than they are worth when programs become large and complex. In the words of Alan Perlis, "Syntactic sugar causes cancer of the semicolon."

Evaluating the `define` form causes the specified procedure name to be associated with the corresponding procedure definition in the environment. The interpreter responds to `define` by printing the name of the procedure being defined:

```
==> (define (square x) (* x x))
square
```

The general form of a procedure definition is

```
(define (⟨name⟩ ⟨formal parameters⟩) ⟨body⟩)
```

The ⟨name⟩ is a symbol to be associated with the procedure definition in the environment.[10]   The ⟨formal parameters⟩ are the names used within the body of the procedure to refer to the corresponding arguments of the procedure. The ⟨body⟩ is an expression that will yield the value of the procedure application when the formal parameters are replaced by the actual arguments to which the procedure is applied.[11] The ⟨name⟩ and the ⟨formal parameters⟩ are grouped within parentheses, just as they would be in an actual call to the procedure being defined.

Having defined `square`, we can now use it:

```
==> (square 21)
441

==> (square (+ 2 5))
49

==> (square (square 3))
81
```

We can also use `square` as a building block in defining other procedures. For example, $x^2 + y^2$ can be expressed as

```
(+ (square x) (square y))
```

We can easily define a procedure `sum-of-squares` that, given any two numbers as arguments, produces the sum of their squares:

---

10 Throughout this book, we will describe the general syntax of expressions by using italic symbols delimited by angle brackets—e.g., ⟨name⟩—to denote the "slots" in the expression to be filled in when such an expression is actually used.

11 More generally, the body of the procedure can be a sequence of expressions. In this case, the interpreter evaluates each expression in the sequence in turn and returns the value of the final expression as the value of the procedure application.

```
(define (sum-of-squares x y)
  (+ (square x) (square y)))
```

```
==> (sum-of-squares 3 4)
```
25

Now we can use sum-of-squares as a building block in constructing further procedures:

```
(define (f a)
  (sum-of-squares (+ a 1) (* a 2)))
```

```
==> (f 5)
```
136

Defined procedures are used in exactly the same way as primitive procedures. Indeed, one could not tell by looking at the definition of sum-of-squares given above whether square was built into the interpreter or defined as a compound procedure.

1.1.5 The Substitution Model for Procedure Application

To evaluate a combination whose operator is a compound procedure, the interpreter follows much the same process as for combinations whose operators are primitive procedures, as we discussed in section 1.1.3. That is, the interpreter evaluates the elements of the combination and applies the procedure (which is the value of the operator of the combination) to the arguments (which are the values of the operands of the combination).

We can assume that the mechanism for applying primitive procedures to arguments is built into the interpreter. For compound procedures, the application process is as follows:

To apply a compound procedure to arguments, evaluate the body of the procedure with each formal parameter replaced by the corresponding argument.

To illustrate this process, let's evaluate the combination

```
(f 5)
```

where f is the procedure defined in section 1.1.4. We begin by retrieving the body of f:

```
(sum-of-squares (+ a 1) (* a 2))
```

Then we replace the formal parameter a by the argument 5:

```
(sum-of-squares (+ 5 1) (* 5 2))
```

Thus the problem reduces to the evaluation of a combination with two operands and an operator named sum-of-squares. Evaluating this combination involves three subproblems. We must evaluate the operator to get the procedure to be applied, and we must evaluate the operands to get the arguments. Now (+ 5 1) produces 6 and (* 5 2) produces 10, so we must apply the procedure sum-of-squares to 6 and 10. These values are substituted for the formal parameters x and y in the body of sum-of-squares, reducing the expression to

```
(+ (square 6) (square 10))
```

If we use the definition of square, this reduces to

```
(+ (* 6 6) (* 10 10))
```

which reduces by multiplication to

```
(+ 36 100)
```

and finally to

```
136
```

The process we have just described is called the *substitution model* for procedure application. It can be taken as a model that determines the "meaning" of procedure application, insofar as the procedures in this chapter are concerned. However, there are two points that should be stressed:

• The substitution model is a model that allows one to think about procedure application. Typical interpreters do not evaluate procedure applications by operating on the text of a procedure to substitute values for the formal parameters. In practice, the "substitution" is accomplished by using a local environment for the formal parameters. We will discuss this more fully in chapters 3 and 4 when we examine the implementation of an interpreter in detail.

• The substitution model is not powerful enough to describe all the procedures we will consider in this book. In particular, when we address in chapter 3 the use of procedures with so-called mutable data, we will see that the substitution model breaks down and must be replaced by a more complicated model of procedure application. On the other hand, substitution is a straightforward idea. It serves well for understanding all of the procedures in the first two chapters of this book, and indeed for understanding most of the procedures one normally encounters. The model is a good tool to use, so long as we bear in mind that it does have limitations.[12]

According to the model given in section 1.1.3, the interpreter first evaluates the arguments to a procedure and then applies the procedure to the evaluated arguments. This is not the only way to perform evaluation. An alternative evaluation model would first expand each procedure definition in terms of simpler and simpler procedures until it obtained an expression involving only primitive operators, and would then perform the evaluation. If we used this method, the evaluation of

(f 5)

would proceed according to the sequence of expansions

(sum-of-squares (+ 5 1) (* 5 2))

(+   (square (+ 5 1))   (square (* 5 2)))

(+   (* (+ 5 1) (+ 5 1))   (* (* 5 2) (* 5 2)))

followed by the reductions

(+   (* 6 6)   (* 10 10))

(+   36   100)

                    136

This gives the same answer as our previous evaluation model, but the process is different. In particular, the evaluations of (+ 5 1) and (* 5 2) are each performed twice here, corresponding to the reduction of the expression

(* x x)

with x replaced respectively by (+ 5 1) and (* 5 2).

12 Despite the fact that substitution is a "straightforward idea," it turns out to be surprisingly complicated to give a rigorous mathematical definition of the substitution process. The problem arises from the possibility of confusion between the names used for the formal parameters of a procedure and the (possibly identical) names used in the expressions to which the procedure may be applied. Indeed, there is a long history of erroneous definitions of *substitution* in the literature of logic and programming semantics. See Stoy 1977 for a careful discussion of substitution. And yet, from a formal mathematical perspective, substitution is much simpler to contend with rigorously than the more complete interpreter model we shall discuss in later chapters, which, at the current state of the art, seems hardly mathematically tractable at all.

This alternative "fully expand and then reduce" evaluation method is known as *normal-order evaluation*, in contrast to the "evaluate the arguments and then apply" method that the interpreter actually uses, which is called *applicative-order evaluation*. It can be shown that, for procedure applications that can be modeled using substitution (including all the procedures in the first two chapters of this book) and that yield legitimate values, normal-order and applicative-order evaluation produce the same value. (See exercise 1.3 for an instance of an "illegitimate" value where normal-order and applicative-order evaluation would not give the same result.) Most interpreters use applicative-order evaluation, partly because of the additional efficiency obtained from avoiding multiple evaluations of expressions such as those illustrated with (+ 5 1) and (* 5 2) above and, more significantly, because normal-order evaluation becomes much more complicated to deal with when we leave the realm of procedures that can be modeled by substitution, as we will do in chapter 3. On the other hand, normal-order evaluation can also be a useful technique. When we tackle "infinite data structures," we will use a method closely akin to normal-order evaluation.[13]

1.1.6 Conditional Expressions and Predicates

The expressive power of the class of procedures that we can define at this point is very limited. For instance, we cannot define a procedure that computes the absolute value of a number by testing whether the number is positive, negative, or zero and taking different actions in the different cases according to the rule

$$abs(x) = \begin{cases} x & \text{if } x > 0 \\ 0 & \text{if } x = 0 \\ -x & \text{if } x < 0 \end{cases}$$

This construct is called a *case analysis*, and there is a special form in Lisp for notating such a case analysis. It is called cond (which stands for "conditional"), and it is used as follows:

```
(define (abs x)
  (cond ((> x 0) x)
        ((= x 0) 0)
        ((< x 0) (- x)))))
```

---

13 In chapter 3 we will introduce the notion of delayed evaluation to provide various "intermediate grounds" between normal and applicative orders. We will also introduce call-by-need evaluation as a general technique for avoiding the multiple evaluations used in strict normal-order evaluation. See chapter 3, section 3.4.3.

The general form of a conditional expression is

```
(cond (⟨p₁⟩ ⟨e₁⟩)
      (⟨p₂⟩ ⟨e₂⟩)

      ⋮

      (⟨pₙ⟩ ⟨eₙ⟩)))
```

in which the arguments are pairs of expressions $(⟨p⟩ ⟨e⟩)$ called *clauses*. The first expression in each pair is a *predicate*—that is, an expression whose value is interpreted as either true or false. In Lisp, "false" is represented by the value of the distinguished symbol nil, and any other value is interpreted as "true." The symbol t is often used by convention as a symbol whose value is true.

Conditional expressions are evaluated as follows. The predicate $⟨p_1⟩$ is evaluated first. If its value is false, then $⟨p_2⟩$ is evaluated. If its value is also false, then $⟨p_3⟩$ is evaluated. This process continues until a predicate is found whose value is true (i.e., non-nil), in which case the interpreter returns the value of the corresponding *consequent expression* $⟨e⟩$ of the clause as the value of the conditional expression. If none of the $⟨p⟩$'s is found to be true, the cond returns a value of false.

The word *predicate* is also used for procedures that return true or false, as well as for expressions that evaluate to true or false. The absolute-value procedure abs makes use of the primitive predicates >, <, and =.[14] These take two numbers as arguments and test whether the first number is, respectively, greater than, less than, or equal to the second number, returning true or false accordingly.

Another way to write the absolute-value procedure is

```
(define (abs x)
  (cond ((< x 0) (- x))
        (else x)))
```

which could be expressed in English as "If x is less than zero return $-x$; otherwise return x." Else is a special symbol that can be used in place of the $⟨p⟩$ in the final clause of a cond. This causes the cond to return as its value the value of the corresponding $⟨e⟩$ whenever all previous clauses have been bypassed. In fact, any expression that always evaluates to a non-nil value could be used here.

Here is yet another way to write the absolute-value procedure:

14 **Abs** also uses the "minus" operator -, which, when used with a single operand, as in (- **x**), indicates negation.

```
(define (abs x)
  (if (< x 0)
      (- x)
      x))
```

This uses the special form `if`, a restricted type of conditional that can be used when there are precisely two cases in the case analysis. The general form of an `if` expression is

(if ⟨predicate⟩ ⟨consequent⟩ ⟨alternative⟩)

To evaluate an `if` expression, the interpreter first evaluates the ⟨predicate⟩ part of the expression. If the ⟨predicate⟩ evaluates to a true value, the interpreter then evaluates and returns the value of the ⟨consequent⟩. Otherwise it evaluates and returns the value of the ⟨alternative⟩.[15]

In addition to primitive predicates such as `<`, `=`, and `>`, there are logical composition operators, which enable us to construct compound predicates. The three most frequently used are these:

and   Takes an arbitrary number of arguments. If all of the arguments evaluate to true, the value of the `and` is true. Otherwise it is false.

or   Takes an arbitrary number of arguments. If all of the arguments evaluate to false, the value of the `or` is false. Otherwise it is true.

not   Takes a single argument. It returns true when the argument evaluates to false, and false otherwise.

For instance, the condition that a number x be in the range $5 < x < 10$ may be expressed as

(and (> x 5) (< x 10))

As another example, we can define a predicate to test whether one number is greater than or equal to another as

```
(define (>= x y)
  (or (> x y) (= x y)))
```

or, alternatively as

```
(define (>= x y)
  (not (< x y)))
```

---

[15] A minor difference between `if` and `cond` is that, in Scheme, the ⟨e⟩ part of each `cond` clause may be a sequence of expressions. If the corresponding ⟨p⟩ is found to be true, the expressions ⟨e⟩ are evaluated in sequence and the value of the final expression in the sequence is returned as the value of the `cond`. In an `if` combination, however, the ⟨consequent⟩ and ⟨alternative⟩ must be single expressions.

Exercise 1.1

Below is a sequence of expressions. What is the result printed by the interpreter in response to each expression? Assume that the sequence is to be evaluated in the order in which it is presented.

```
==> 10

==> (+ 5 3 4)

==> (- 9 1)

==> (/ 6 2)

==> (+ (* 2 4) (- 4 6))

==> (define a 3)

==> (define b (+ a 1))

==> (+ a b (* a b))

==> (= a b)

==> (if (and (> b a) (< b (* a b)))
        b
        a)

==> (cond ((= a 4) 6)
          ((= b 4) (+ 6 7 a))
          (else 25))
```

Exercise 1.2

Define a procedure that takes three numbers as arguments and returns the sum of the squares of the two larger numbers.

Exercise 1.3

Ben Bitdiddle has invented a test to determine whether the interpreter he is faced with is using applicative-order evaluation or normal-order evaluation. He defines the following two procedures:

```
(define (p) (p))

(define (test x y)
  (if (= x 0)
      0
      y))
```

Then he evaluates the expression

```
(test 0 (p))
```

What behavior will Ben observe with an interpreter that uses applicative-order evaluation? What behavior will he observe with an interpreter that uses normal-order evaluation? Explain your answer. (Assume that the evaluation rule for the special form if is the same whether the interpreter is using normal or applicative order: The predicate expression is evaluated first, and the result determines whether to evaluate the consequent or the alternative expression.)

1.1.7 Example: Square Roots by Newton's Method

Procedures, as introduced above, are much like ordinary mathematical functions—they specify a value that is determined by one or more parameters. But there is an important difference between mathematical functions and computer procedures. Procedures must be effective.

As a case in point, consider the problem of computing square roots. We can define the square-root function as

$$\sqrt{x} = \text{ the } y \text{ such that } y \geq 0 \text{ and } y^2 = x$$

This describes a perfectly legitimate mathematical function. We could use it to recognize whether one number is the square root of another, or to derive facts about square roots in general. On the other hand, the definition does not describe a procedure. Indeed, it tells us almost nothing about how to actually find the square root of a given number. It will not help matters to rephrase this definition in pseudo-Lisp:

```
(define (sqrt x)
  (the y (and (>= y 0)
              (= (square y) x))))
```

This only begs the question.

The contrast between function and procedure is a reflection of the general distinction between describing properties of things and describing how to do things, or, as it is sometimes referred to, the distinction between declarative knowledge and imperative knowledge. In mathematics we are usually concerned with declarative (what is) descriptions, whereas in computer science we are usually concerned with imperative (how to) descriptions.[16]

---

16 Declarative and imperative descriptions are intimately related, as indeed are mathematics and computer science. For instance, to say that the answer produced by a program is "correct" is to make a declarative statement about the program. There is a large amount of research aimed at establishing techniques for proving that programs are correct, and much of the technical difficulty of this subject has to do with negotiating

How does one compute square roots? The most common way is to use Newton's method of successive approximations, which says that whenever we have a guess y for the value of the square root of a number x, we can perform a simple manipulation to get a better guess (one closer to the actual square root) by averaging y together with x/y.[17] For example, we can compute the square root of 2 as follows. Suppose our initial guess is 1:

Guess	Quotient	Average
1	$\dfrac{2}{1} = 2$	$\dfrac{(2+1)}{2} = 1.5$
1.5	$\dfrac{2}{1.5} = 1.3333$	$\dfrac{(1.3333 + 1.5)}{2} = 1.4167$
1.4167	$\dfrac{2}{1.4167} = 1. .18$	$\dfrac{(1.4167 + 1.4118)}{2} = 1.4142$
1.4142	$\cdots$	$\cdots$

Continuing this process, we obtain better and better approximations to the square root.

Now let's formalize the process in terms of procedures. We start with a value for the radicand (the number whose square root we are trying to compute) and a value for the guess. If the guess is good enough for our purposes, we are done; if not, we must repeat the process with an improved guess. We write this basic strategy as a procedure:

```
(define (sqrt-iter guess x)
  (if (good-enough? guess x)
      guess
      (sqrt-iter (improve guess x)
                 x)))
```

A guess is improved by averaging it with the quotient of the radicand and the old guess:

---

the transition between imperative statements (from which programs are constructed) and declarative statements (which can be used to deduce things). In a related vein, an important current area in programming-language design is the exploration of so-called very high-level languages, in which one actually programs in terms of declarative statements. The idea is to make interpreters sophisticated enough so that, given "what is" knowledge specified by the programmer, they can generate "how to" knowledge automatically. This cannot be done in general, but there are important areas where progress has been made. In chapter 4 we shall implement such a language, a logic programming language used for information retrieval.

17 This square-root algorithm is actually a special case of Newton's method, which is a general technique for finding roots of equations. The square-root algorithm itself was developed by Heron of Alexandria in the first century A.D. We will see how to express the general Newton's method as a Lisp procedure in section 1.3.4.

```
(define (improve guess x)
  (average guess (/ x guess)))
```

where

```
(define (average x y)
  (/ (+ x y) 2))
```

We also have to say what we mean by "good enough." The following will do
for illustration, but it is not really a very good test. (See exercise 1.5.) The
idea is to improve the answer until it is close enough so that its square differs
from the radicand by less than a predetermined tolerance (here .001):[18]

```
(define (good-enough? guess x)
  (< (abs (- (square guess) x)) .001))
```

Finally, we need a way to get started. For instance, we can always guess
that the square root of any number is 1:

```
(define (sqrt x)
  (sqrt-iter 1 x))
```

If we type these definitions to the interpreter, we can use sqrt just as we
can use any procedure:

```
==> (sqrt 9)
```
3.0001

```
==> (sqrt (+ 100 37))
```
11.7047

```
==> (sqrt (+ (sqrt 2) (sqrt 3)))
```
1.7739

```
==> (square (sqrt 1000))
```
1000.0003

The sqrt program also illustrates that the simple procedural language we
have introduced so far is sufficient for writing any purely numerical program
that one could write in, say, Basic or Fortran. This might seem surprising,
since we have not included in our language any iterative (looping) constructs
that direct the computer to do something over and over again. Sqrt-iter,

---

18 We will give predicates names ending with question marks. This is just a stylistic
convention. As far as the interpreter is concerned, the question mark is just an ordinary
symbol.

on the other hand, demonstrates how iteration can be accomplished using no special construct other than the ordinary ability to call a procedure.[19]

Exercise 1.4

Alyssa P. Hacker doesn't see why if needs to be provided as a special form. "Why can't I just define it as an ordinary procedure in terms of cond?" she asks. Alyssa's friend Eva Lu Ator claims this can indeed be done, and she defines a new version of if:

```
(define (new-if predicate then-clause else-clause)
  (cond (predicate then-clause)
        (else else-clause)))
```

Eva demonstrates the program for Alyssa:

```
==> (new-if (= 2 3) 0 5)
5

==> (new-if (= 1 1) 0 5)
0
```

Delighted, Alyssa uses new-if to rewrite the square-root program:

```
(define (sqrt-iter guess x)
  (new-if (good-enough? guess x)
          guess
          (sqrt-iter (improve guess x)
                     x)))
```

What happens when Alyssa attempts to use this to compute square roots? Explain.

Exercise 1.5

The good-enough? test used in computing square roots will not be very effective for finding the square roots of very small numbers. Also, in real computers, arithmetic operations are almost always performed with limited precision. This makes our test inadequate for very large numbers. Explain these statements, with examples showing how the test fails for small and large numbers. An alternative strategy for implementing good-enough? is to watch how guess changes from one iteration to the next and to stop when the change is a very small fraction of the guess. Design a square-root procedure that uses this kind of end test. Does this work better for small and large numbers?

Exercise 1.6

Newton's method for cube roots is based on the fact that if y is an approximation to the cube root of x, then a better approximation is given by the value

19 Readers who are worried about the efficiency issues involved in using procedure calls to implement iteration should note the remarks on "tail recursion" in section 1.2.1.

$$\frac{x/y^2 + 2y}{3}$$

Use this formula to implement a cube-root procedure analogous to the square-root procedure. (In section 1.3.4 we will see how to implement Newton's method in general as an abstraction of these square-root and cube-root procedures.)

1.1.8 Procedures as Black-Box Abstractions

Sqrt is our first example of a process defined by a set of mutually defined procedures. Notice that the definition of sqrt-iter is *recursive*; that is, the procedure is defined in terms of itself. The idea of being able to define a procedure in terms of itself may be disturbing; it may seem unclear how such a "circular" definition could make sense at all, much less specify a well-defined process to be carried out by a computer. This will be addressed more carefully in section 1.2. But first let's consider some other important points illustrated by the sqrt example.

Observe that the problem of computing square roots breaks up naturally into a number of subproblems: how to tell whether a guess is good enough, how to improve a guess, and so on. Each of these tasks is accomplished by a separate procedure. The entire sqrt program can be viewed as a cluster of procedures (shown in figure 1.2) that mirrors the decomposition of the problem into subproblems.

The importance of this decomposition strategy is not simply that one is dividing the program into parts. After all, we could take any large program and divide it into parts—the first ten lines, the next ten lines, the next ten lines, and so on. Rather, it is crucial that each procedure accomplishes an identifiable task that can be used as a module in defining other procedures. For example, when we define the good-enough? procedure in terms of square, we are able to regard the square procedure as a "black box." We are not at that moment concerned with *how* the procedure computes its result, only with the fact that it computes the square. The details of how the square is computed can be suppressed, to be considered at a later time. Indeed, as far as the good-enough? procedure is concerned, square is not quite a procedure but rather an abstraction of a procedure, a so-called *procedural abstraction*. At this level of abstraction, any procedure that computes the square is equally good.

Thus, considering only the value, the following two procedures for squaring a number should be indistinguishable. Each takes a numerical argument and produces the square of that number as the value.[20]

20 It is not even clear which of these procedures is a more efficient implementation. This depends upon the hardware available. There are machines for which the "obvious" implementation is the less efficient. Consider a machine that has extensive tables of logarithms and antilogarithms stored in a very efficient manner.

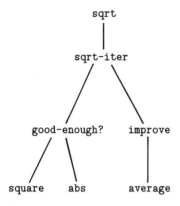

Figure 1.2
Procedural decomposition of the sqrt program

```
(define (square x) (* x x))
```

```
(define (square x)
  (exp (double (log x)))))
```

```
(define (double x) (+ x x))
```

So a procedure definition should be able to suppress detail. The user of the procedure may not have written the procedure himself, but may have obtained it as a black box to perform some function from another programmer. The user should not need to know how the procedure is implemented in order to use it.

Local names
One detail of a procedure's implementation that should not matter to the user of the procedure is the implementer's choice of names for the procedure's formal parameters. Thus, the following procedures should not be distinguishable:

```
(define (square x) (* x x))
```

```
(define (square y) (* y y))
```

This principle—that the meaning of a procedure should be independent of the parameter names used by its author—seems on the surface to be self-evident, but its consequences are profound. The simplest consequence is that the parameter names of a procedure must be local to the body of the procedure. For example, we used square in the definition of good-enough? in our square-root procedure:

```
(define (good-enough? guess x)
  (< (abs (- (square guess) x)) .001))
```

The intention of the author of good-enough? is to determine if the square of the first argument is within a given tolerance of the second argument. We see that the author of good-enough? used the name guess to refer to the first argument and x to refer to the second argument. The argument of square is guess. If the author of square used x (as he did above) to refer to that argument, we see that the x in good-enough? must be a different x than the one in square. Running the procedure square must not modify the value of x that is used by good-enough?, because that value of x may be needed by good-enough? after square is done computing.

If the parameters were not local to the bodies of their respective procedures, so that the x in square could be confused with the x in good-enough?, then the behavior of good-enough? would depend upon which version of square we used. Thus, square would not be the black box we desired.

A formal parameter of a procedure has a very special role in the procedure definition, in that it doesn't matter what name the formal parameter has. Such a name is called a *bound variable*, and we say that the procedure definition *binds* its formal parameters. A variable is bound in an expression if the meaning of the expression is unchanged when the variable is consistently renamed throughout the expression.[21] If a variable is not bound in an expression, we say that it is *free* in that expression. The set of expressions for which a binding defines a name is called the *scope* of that name. In a procedure definition, the bound variables declared as the formal parameters of the procedure have the body of the procedure as their scope.

In the definition of good-enough? above, guess and x are bound variables but <, -, abs, and square are free. The meaning of good-enough? should be independent of the names we choose for guess and x so long as they are distinct and different from <, -, abs, and square. (If we renamed guess to abs we would have introduced a bug by *capturing* the variable abs. It would have changed from free to bound.) The meaning of good-enough? is not independent of the names of its free variables, however. It surely depends upon the fact (external to this definition) that the symbol abs names a procedure for computing the absolute value of a number. Good-enough? will compute a different function if we substitute cos for abs in its definition.

---

21 The concept of consistent renaming is actually subtle and difficult to define formally. Famous logicians have made embarrassing errors here.

Internal definitions and block structure

We have one kind of name isolation available to us so far: The formal parameters of a procedure are local to the body of the procedure. The square-root program illustrates another way in which we would like to control the use of names. The existing program consists of separate procedures:

```
(define (sqrt x)
  (sqrt-iter 1 x))

(define (sqrt-iter guess x)
  (if (good-enough? guess x)
      guess
      (sqrt-iter (improve guess x) x)))

(define (good-enough? guess x)
  (< (abs (- (square guess) x)) .001))

(define (improve guess x)
  (average guess (/ x guess)))
```

The problem with this program is that the only procedure that is important to the user of sqrt is sqrt. The other procedures (sqrt-iter, good-enough?, and improve) only clutter up his mind. He may not define any other procedure called good-enough? as part of another program to work together with his square-root program, because sqrt needs it. The problem is especially severe in the construction of large systems by many separate programmers. For example, in the construction of a large library of numerical procedures, many numerical functions are computed as successive approximations and thus would have procedures named good-enough? and improve as auxiliary procedures. We would like to localize the subprocedures, hiding them inside sqrt so that sqrt could coexist with other successive approximations, each having its own private good-enough? procedure. To make this possible, we allow a procedure to have internal definitions that are local to that procedure. For example, in the square-root problem we can write

```
(define (sqrt x)
  (define (good-enough? guess x)
    (< (abs (- (square guess) x)) .001))
  (define (improve guess x)
    (average guess (/ x guess)))
  ;; continued on next page
```

```
(define (sqrt-iter guess x)
  (if (good-enough? guess x)
      guess
      (sqrt-iter (improve guess x) x)))
(sqrt-iter 1 x))
```

Such nesting of definitions, called *block structure*, is basically the right solution to the simplest name-packaging problem. But there is a better idea lurking here. In addition to internalizing the definitions of the auxiliary procedures, we can simplify them. Since x is bound in the definition of sqrt, the procedures good-enough?, improve, and sqrt-iter, which are defined internally to sqrt, are in the scope of x. Thus, it is not necessary to pass x explicitly to each of these procedures. Instead, we allow x to be a free variable in the internal definitions. Then x gets its value from the argument with which the enclosing procedure sqrt is called. This discipline is called *lexical scoping*.[22]

```
(define (sqrt x)
  (define (good-enough? guess)
    (< (abs (- (square guess) x)) .001))
  (define (improve guess)
    (average guess (/ x guess)))
  (define (sqrt-iter guess)
    (if (good-enough? guess)
        guess
        (sqrt-iter (improve guess))))
  (sqrt-iter 1))
```

From now on we will use block structure extensively to help us break up large programs into tractable pieces.[23] The idea of block structure originated with the programming language Algol 60. It appears in most advanced programming languages and is an important tool for helping to organize the construction of large programs.

22 Lexical scoping dictates that free variables in a procedure are taken to refer to variables in enclosing procedures; that is, they are looked up in the environment in which the procedure was defined. We will see how this works in detail in chapter 3 when we study environments and the detailed behavior of the interpreter.

23 Embedded definitions must come first in a definition. The management is not responsible for the consequences of running programs that intertwine definition and use.

1.2 Procedures and the Processes They Generate

We have now considered the elements of programming: We have used primitive arithmetic operations, combined these operations, and abstracted these composite operations by defining them as compound procedures. But that is not enough to enable us to say that we know how to program. Our situation is analogous to that of someone who has learned the rules for how the pieces move in chess but knows nothing of typical openings, tactics, or strategy. Like the novice chess player, we don't yet know the common patterns of usage in the domain. We lack the knowledge of which moves are worth making (which procedures are worth defining). We lack the experience to predict the consequences of making a move (executing a procedure).

The ability to visualize the consequences of the actions under consideration is crucial to becoming an expert programmer, just as it is in any synthetic, creative activity. In becoming an expert photographer, for example, one must learn how to look at a scene and know how dark each region will appear on a print for each possible choice of exposure and development conditions. Only then can one reason backward, planning framing, lighting, exposure, and development to obtain the desired effects. So it is with programming, where we are planning the course of action to be taken by a process and where we control the process by means of a program. To become experts, we must learn to visualize the processes generated by various types of procedures. Only after one has developed such a skill can one learn to reliably construct programs that exhibit the desired behavior.

A procedure is a pattern for the *local evolution* of a computational process. It specifies the evolution of a process in the same way that a differential equation describes the evolution of a physical system. At each instant, the change in state of a physical system is computed from its current state according to its equations of motion. At each step, the next state of the process is computed from its current state according to the rules of interpreting procedures. Much of the theory of differential equations is concerned with describing the overall, or *global*, behavior of a system whose local evolution has been specified by a differential equation. Similarly, we would like to be able to make statements about the overall behavior of a process whose local evolution has been specified by a procedure. This is very difficult to do in general, but we can at least try to describe some typical patterns of process evolution.

In this section we will examine some common "shapes" for processes generated by simple procedures. We will also investigate the rates at which

```
(factorial 6)
(* 6 (factorial 5))
(* 6 (* 5 (factorial 4)))
(* 6 (* 5 (* 4 (factorial 3))))
(* 6 (* 5 (* 4 (* 3 (factorial 2)))))
(* 6 (* 5 (* 4 (* 3 (* 2 (factorial 1))))))
(* 6 (* 5 (* 4 (* 3 (* 2 1)))))
(* 6 (* 5 (* 4 (* 3 2))))
(* 6 (* 5 (* 4 6)))
(* 6 (* 5 24))
(* 6 120)
720
```

Figure 1.3
A linear recursive process for computing 6!.

these processes consume the important computational resources of time and space. The procedures we will be considering are very simple. Their role is like that played by test patterns in photography: as oversimplified prototypical patterns, rather than practical examples in their own right.

1.2.1 Linear Recursion and Iteration

We begin by considering the factorial function, defined by

$$n! = n \cdot (n-1) \cdot (n-2) \cdots 3 \cdot 2 \cdot 1$$

There are many ways to compute factorials. One way is to make use of the observation that $n!$ is equal to n times $(n-1)!$ for any positive integer n:

$$n! = n \cdot \big((n-1) \cdot (n-2) \cdots 3 \cdot 2 \cdot 1\big) = n \cdot (n-1)!$$

Thus, we can compute $n!$ by computing $(n-1)!$ and multiplying the result by n. If we add the stipulation that $1!$ is equal to 1, this observation translates directly into a procedure:

```
(define (factorial n)
  (if (= n 1)
      1
      (* n (factorial (- n 1)))))
```

We can use the substitution model of section 1.1.5 to watch this procedure in action computing 6!, as shown in figure 1.3.

Now let's take a different perspective on computing factorials. We could describe a rule for computing $n!$ by specifying that we first multiply 1 by 2, then multiply the result by 3, then by 4, and so on until we reach n.

```
(factorial 6)
(fact-iter    1 1 6)
(fact-iter    1 2 6)
(fact-iter    2 3 6)
(fact-iter    6 4 6)
(fact-iter   24 5 6)
(fact-iter  120 6 6)
(fact-iter  720 7 6)
720
```

Figure 1.4
A linear iterative process for computing 6!.

More formally, we maintain a running product, together with a counter that counts from 1 up to n. We can describe the computation by saying that the counter and the product simultaneously change from one step to the next according to the rule

product ← counter · product

counter ← counter + 1

and stipulating that $n!$ is the value of the product when the counter exceeds n.

Once again, we can recast our description as a procedure for computing factorials:[24]

```
(define (factorial n)
  (fact-iter 1 1 n))

(define (fact-iter product counter max-count)
  (if (> counter max-count)
      product
      (fact-iter (* counter product)
                 (+ counter 1)
                 max-count)))
```

24 In a real program we would probably use the block structure introduced in the last section to hide the definition of fact-iter:

```
(define (factorial n)
  (define (iter product counter)
    (if (> counter n)
        product
        (iter (* counter product)
              (+ counter 1))))
  (iter 1 1))
```

We avoided doing this here so as to minimize the number of things to think about.

As before, we can use the substitution model to visualize the process of computing 6!, as shown in figure 1.4.

Compare the two processes. From one point of view, they seem hardly different at all. Both compute the same mathematical function on the same domain, and each requires a number of steps proportional to n to compute $n!$. Indeed, both processes even carry out the same sequence of multiplications, obtaining the same sequence of partial products. On the other hand, when we consider the "shapes" of the two processes, we find that they evolve quite differently.

Consider the first process. The substitution model reveals a shape of expansion followed by contraction, indicated by the arrow in figure 1.3. The expansion occurs as the process builds up a chain of *deferred operations* (in this case, a chain of multiplications). The contraction occurs as the arguments to each multiplication are evaluated and the multiplication is actually performed. This type of process, characterized by a chain of deferred operations, is called a *recursive process*. Carrying out this process requires that the interpreter keep track of the multiplications to be performed later on. In the computation of $n!$, the length of the chain of deferred operations, and hence the amount of information needed to keep track of it, grows linearly with n. Such a process is called a *linear recursive process*.

By contrast, the second process does not grow and shrink. At each step, all we need to keep track of, for any n, are the current values of the variables product, counter, and max-count. We call this an *iterative process*. In general, an iterative process is one whose state can be summarized by a fixed number of *state variables*, together with a fixed rule that describes how the state variables should be updated as the process moves from state to state and an (optional) end test that specifies conditions under which the process should terminate. In computing $n!$, the time required grows linearly with n. Such a process is called a *linear iterative process*.

The contrast between the two processes can be seen in another way. In the iterative case, the program variables provide a complete description of the state of the process at any point. If we stopped the computation between steps, all we would need to do to resume the computation is to supply the interpreter with the values of the three program variables. Not so with the recursive process. In this case there is some additional "hidden" information, maintained by the interpreter and not contained in the program variables, which indicates "where the process is" in negotiating the chain of deferred operations. The longer the chain, the more information must be maintained.[25]

In contrasting iteration and recursion, we must be careful not to confuse the notion of a recursive process with the notion of a recursive procedure. When we describe a procedure as recursive, we are referring to the syntactic fact that the procedure definition refers (either directly or indirectly) to the procedure itself. But when we describe a process as following a pattern that is, say, linearly recursive, we are speaking about how the process evolves, not about the syntax of how a procedure is written. It may seem disturbing that we refer to a recursive procedure such as `fact-iter` as generating an iterative process. However, the process really is iterative: Its state is captured completely by its three state variables, and an interpreter need keep track of only three variables in order to execute the process.

One reason that the distinction between process and procedure may be confusing is that interpreters for most common languages (including Algol, Pascal, and until recently most implementations of Lisp) are designed in such a way that the interpretation of any recursive procedure consumes an amount of memory that grows with the number of procedure calls, even when the process described is, in principle, iterative. As a consequence, these languages can describe iterative processes only by resorting to special-purpose "looping constructs" such as `do`, `repeat`, `until`, `for`, and `while`. The interpreter we shall consider in chapter 5 (section 5.2) does not share this defect. It will execute an iterative process in constant space, even if the iterative process is described by a recursive procedure. An interpreter with this property is called *tail-recursive*. With a tail-recursive interpreter, iteration can be expressed using the ordinary procedure call mechanism, so that special iteration constructs are useful only as syntactic sugar.[26]

Exercise 1.7

Each of the following two procedures defines a method for adding two positive integers in terms of the more primitive operators `1+`, which increments its argument by 1, and `-1+`, which decrements its argument by 1.

25 When we discuss the implementation of procedures on register machines in chapter 5, we will see that any iterative process can be realized "in hardware" as a machine that has a fixed set of registers and no auxiliary memory. In contrast, realizing a recursive process requires a machine that uses an auxiliary data structure known as a *stack*.

26 Tail recursion has long been known as a compiler optimization trick. A coherent semantic basis for tail recursion was provided by Carl Hewitt (1977), who explained it in terms of the "message-passing" model of computation that we shall discuss in chapter 3. Inspired by this, Gerald Jay Sussman and Guy Lewis Steele Jr. (see Steele 1975) constructed a tail-recursive interpreter for Scheme. Steele later showed how tail recursion is a consequence of the natural way to compile procedure calls (Steele 1977).

```
(define (+ a b)
  (if (= a 0)
      b
      (1+ (+ (-1+ a) b))))
(define (+ a b)
  (if (= a 0)
      b
      (+ (-1+ a) (1+ b))))
```

Using the substitution model, illustrate the process generated by each procedure in evaluating (+ 4 5). Are these processes iterative or recursive?

Exercise 1.8

The following procedure computes a mathematical function called Ackermann's function.

```
(define (A x y)
  (cond ((= y 0) 0)
        ((= x 0) (* 2 y))
        ((= y 1) 2)
        (else (A (- x 1)
                 (A x (- y 1))))))
```

What are the values of the following expressions?

(A 1 10)

(A 2 4)

(A 3 3)

Consider the following procedures, where A is the procedure defined above:

(define (f n) (A 0 n))

(define (g n) (A 1 n))

(define (h n) (A 2 n))

(define (k n) (* 5 n n))

Give concise mathematical definitions for the functions computed by the procedures f, g, and h for positive integer values of n. For example, (k n) computes $5n^2$.

1.2.2 Tree Recursion

Another common pattern of computation is called *tree recursion*. As an example, consider computing the sequence of Fibonacci numbers, in which each number is the sum of the preceding two:

0, 1, 1, 2, 3, 5, 8, 13, 21, ...

In general, the Fibonacci numbers can be defined by the rule

$$\text{Fib}(n) = \begin{cases} 0 & \text{if } n = 0 \\ 1 & \text{if } n = 1 \\ \text{Fib}(n-1) + \text{Fib}(n-2) & \text{otherwise} \end{cases}$$

We can immediately translate this definition into a recursive procedure for computing Fibonacci numbers:

```
(define (fib n)
  (cond ((= n 0) 0)
        ((= n 1) 1)
        (else (+ (fib (- n 1))
                 (fib (- n 2))))))
```

Consider the pattern of this computation. To compute (fib 5), we compute (fib 4) and (fib 3). To compute (fib 4), we compute (fib 3) and (fib 2). In general, the evolved process looks like a tree, as shown in figure 1.5. Notice that the branches split into two at each level (except at the bottom); this reflects the fact that the fib procedure calls itself twice each time it is invoked.

This procedure is instructive as a prototypical tree recursion, but it is a terrible way to compute Fibonacci numbers because it does so much redundant computation. Notice in figure 1.5 that the entire computation of (fib 3)—almost half the work—is duplicated. In fact, it is not hard to show that the number of times the procedure will compute (fib 1) or (fib 0) (the number of leaves in the above tree, in general) is precisely Fib(n + 1). To get an idea of how bad this is, one can show that the value of Fib(n) grows exponentially with n. More precisely (see exercise 1.14), Fib(n) is the closest integer to $\phi^n/\sqrt{5}$, where

$$\phi = (1 + \sqrt{5})/2 \approx 1.6180$$

is the *golden ratio*, which satisfies the equation

$$\phi^2 = \phi + 1$$

Thus, the process takes an amount of time that grows exponentially with the input. On the other hand, the space required grows only linearly with the input, because we need keep track only of which nodes are above us in the tree at any point in the computation. In general, the time required by

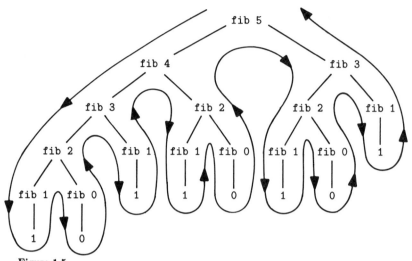

Figure 1.5
The tree-recursive process generated in computing (fib 5).

a tree-recursive process will be proportional to the number of nodes in the tree, while the space required will be proportional to the maximum depth of the tree.

We can also formulate an iterative process for computing the Fibonacci numbers. The idea is to use a pair of integers a and b, initialized to 1 and 0, and to repeatedly apply the simultaneous transformations

$$a \leftarrow a + b$$

$$b \leftarrow a$$

It is not hard to show that, after applying this transformation n times, a and b will be equal, respectively, to Fib(n) and Fib($n-1$). Thus, we can compute Fibonacci numbers iteratively using the procedure

```
(define (fib n)
  (fib-iter 1 0 n))

(define (fib-iter a b count)
  (if (= count 0)
      b
      (fib-iter (+ a b) a (- count 1))))
```

This second method for computing Fib(n) is a linear iteration. The difference in time required by the two methods—one linear in n, one growing as fast as Fib(n) itself—is enormous, even for small inputs.

One should not conclude from this that tree-recursive processes are use-less. When we consider processes that operate on hierarchically structured data rather than numbers, we will find that tree recursion is a natural and powerful tool.[27]   But even in numerical operations, tree-recursive processes can be useful in helping us to understand and design programs. For in-stance, although the first fib procedure is much less efficient than the second one, it is more straightforward, being little more than a translation into Lisp of the definition of the Fibonacci sequence. To formulate the iterative algorithm required noticing that the computation could be recast as an iteration with three state variables.

Example: Counting change

It takes only a bit of cleverness to come up with the iterative Fibonacci algorithm. In contrast, consider the following problem: How many different ways can we make change of $1.00, given half-dollars, quarters, dimes, nickels, and pennies? More generally, can we write a procedure to compute the number of ways to change any given amount of money?

This problem has a simple solution as a recursive procedure. Suppose we think of the types of coins available as arranged in some order. Then the following relation holds:

Number of ways to change amount a using n kinds of coins =

> Number of ways to change amount a using all but the first kind of coin

+ Number of ways to change amount $a - d$ using all n kinds of coins, where d is the denomination of the first kind of coin.

To see why this is true, observe that the ways to make change can be divided into two groups: those that do not use any of the first kind of coin, and those that do. Therefore, the total number of ways to make change for some amount is equal to the number of ways to make change for the amount without using any of the first kind of coin, plus the number of ways to make change assuming that we do use the first kind of coin. But the latter number is equal to the number of ways to make change for the amount that remains after using a coin of the first kind.

Thus, we can recursively reduce the problem of changing a given amount to the problem of changing smaller amounts using fewer kinds of coins.

---

27 An example of this was hinted at in section 1.1.3: The interpreter itself evaluates expressions using a tree-recursive process.

Consider this reduction rule carefully, and convince yourself that we can use it to describe an algorithm if we specify the following degenerate cases:[28]

- If a is exactly 0, we should count that as 1 way to make change.
- If a is less than 0, we should count that as 0 ways to make change.
- If n is 0, we should count that as 0 ways to make change.

We can easily translate this description into a recursive procedure:

```
(define (count-change amount)
  (cc amount 5))

(define (cc amount kinds-of-coins)
  (cond ((= amount 0) 1)
        ((or (< amount 0) (= kinds-of-coins 0)) 0)
        (else (+ (cc (- amount
                        (first-denomination kinds-of-coins))
                     kinds-of-coins)
                 (cc amount
                     (- kinds-of-coins 1))))))

(define (first-denomination kinds-of-coins)
  (cond ((= kinds-of-coins 1) 1)
        ((= kinds-of-coins 2) 5)
        ((= kinds-of-coins 3) 10)
        ((= kinds-of-coins 4) 25)
        ((= kinds-of-coins 5) 50)))
```

(The first-denomination procedure takes as input the number of kinds of coins available and returns the denomination of the first kind. Here we are thinking of the coins as arranged in order from smallest to largest, but any order would do as well.) We can now answer our original question about changing a dollar:

```
==> (count-change 100)
292
```

Count-change generates a tree-recursive process with redundancies similar to those in our first implementation of fib. (It will take quite a while for that 292 to be computed.) On the other hand, it is not so obvious how to design a better algorithm for computing the result, and we leave

---

28 For example, work through in detail how the reduction rule applies to the problem of making change for 10 cents using pennies and nickels.

this problem as a challenge (exercise 1.9). The observation that a tree-recursive process may be highly inefficient but often easy to specify and understand has led people to propose that one could get the best of both worlds by designing a "smart compiler" that could transform tree-recursive procedures into more efficient procedures that would compute the same result.[29]

Exercise 1.9

Design a procedure that evolves an iterative process for solving the change-counting problem. For simplicity, you may wish to start by considering only two or three kinds of coins.

1.2.3 Orders of Growth

The previous examples illustrate that processes can differ considerably in the rates at which they consume computational resources of time and space. One convenient way to describe this difference is to use the notion of *order of growth* to obtain a gross measure of the resources required by a process as the inputs become larger.

Let n be a parameter that measures the size of the problem, and let $R(n)$ be the amount of resources the process requires for a problem of size n. In our previous examples we took n to be the number for which a given function is to be computed, but there are other possibilities. For instance, if our goal is to compute an approximation to the square root of a number, we might take n to be the number of digits accuracy required. For matrix multiplication we might take n to be the number of rows in the matrices. In general there are a number of properties of the problem with respect to which it will be desirable to analyze a given process. Similarly, $R(n)$ might measure the time required to complete the computation, the number of internal storage registers used, the number of elementary machine operations performed, and so on.

We say that $R(n)$ has order of growth $O(f(n))$, written $R(n) = O(f(n))$ (pronounced "oh of $f(n)$"), if there is some constant K independent of n

---

[29] This idea is not as outlandish as it may appear at first sight. One approach to coping with redundant computations is to arrange matters so that we automatically construct a table of function values as they are computed. Each time we are asked to compute the function on some input, we first look to see if the value is already stored in the table, in which case we avoid performing the redundant computation. This strategy, known as *tabulation* or *memoization*, can be implemented in a straightforward way. Tabulation can sometimes be used to transform processes that require exponential time (such as count-change) into processes whose space and time requirements grow linearly with the input. See exercise 3.27 of chapter 3.

such that

$$R(n) \leq K\, f(n)$$

for any sufficiently large value of n. For instance, with the linear recursive process for computing factorial described in section 1.2.1 the number of steps grows proportionally to the input n. Thus, the time required for this process grows as $O(n)$. We also saw that the space required grows as $O(n)$. For the iterative factorial, the required time is still $O(n)$ but the space is $O(1)$—that is, constant.[30] The tree-recursive Fibonacci computation requires time $O(\phi^n)$ and space $O(n)$.

Orders of growth provide only a crude description of the behavior of a process. For example, a process requiring n steps and a process requiring $1000n$ steps are both considered to have $O(n)$ order of growth.[31] On the other hand, order of growth provides a useful indication of how we may expect the behavior of the process to change as we change the size of the input. For an $O(n)$ process, doubling the size will roughly double the amount of resources used. For an exponential process, each increment in input size will multiply the resource utilization by a constant factor. In the remainder of section 1.2, we will examine two algorithms whose order of growth is logarithmic, so that doubling the input size increases the resource requirement by a constant amount.

Exercise 1.10

Draw the tree illustrating the process generated by the count-change procedure of section 1.2.2 in making change for 11 cents. What are the orders of growth of the space and time used by this process as the amount to be changed increases?

---

30 These statements mask a great deal of oversimplification. For instance, when we identify process steps with "time" we are making the assumption that the amount of time needed to perform, say, a multiplication is independent of the size of the numbers to be multiplied, which is false if the numbers are sufficiently large. Similar remarks hold for the estimates of space. Like the design and description of a process, the analysis of a process can be carried out at various levels of abstraction.

31 Another drawback of order notation is that it provides only an upper bound on the growth. Because of the inequality sign in the definition, any process with order of growth $f(n)$ will also have order of growth $g(n)$ for any function g that grows faster than f. For example, any $O(n)$ process is also $O(n^2)$. Thus, strictly speaking, we should interpret the equation $R(n) = O(f(n))$ to mean that $R(n)$ grows at most as fast as $f(n)$. In more careful analyses of resource utilization, one also considers estimates which say that $R(n)$ grows at least as fast as $f(n)$. This is expressed as "$R(n)$ has order of growth $\Omega(f(n))$," written $R(n) = \Omega(f(n))$ (pronounced "big omega of $f(n)$"), which is defined to mean that there is some constant K independent of n such that $R(n) \geq K f(n)$ for any sufficiently large value of n. In addition, the notation $R(n) = \theta(f(n))$ is used to mean that $R(n) = O(f(n))$ and $R(n) = \Omega(f(n))$, or, roughly, that $R(n)$ grows exactly as fast as $f(n)$.

1.2.4 Exponentiation

Consider the problem of computing the exponential of a given number. We would like a procedure that takes as arguments a base b and a positive integer exponent n and computes b^n. One way to do this is via the recursive definition

$$b^n = b \cdot b^{n-1}$$

$$b^0 = 1$$

which translates readily into the procedure

```
(define (expt b n)
  (if (= n 0)
      1
      (* b (expt b (- n 1))))))
```

This is a linear recursive process, with time and space requirements $O(n)$. Just as with factorial, we can readily formulate an equivalent linear iteration:

```
(define (expt b n)
  (exp-iter b n 1))

(define (exp-iter b counter product)
  (if (= counter 0)
      product
      (exp-iter b
                (- counter 1)
                (* b product)))))
```

This version requires time $O(n)$ and space $O(1)$.

We can compute exponentials in fewer steps by using the idea of successive squaring. For instance, rather than computing b^8 as

$$b \cdot b \cdot b \cdot b \cdot b \cdot b \cdot b \cdot b$$

we can compute it using three multiplications:

$$b^2 = b \cdot b$$

$$b^4 = (b^2)^2$$

$$b^8 = (b^4)^2$$

This method works fine for exponents that are powers of 2. We can also take advantage of successive squaring in computing exponentials in general if we use the rule

$$b^n = (b^{n/2})^2 \qquad \text{if } n \text{ is even}$$
$$b^n = b \cdot b^{n-1} \qquad \text{if } n \text{ is odd}$$

We can express this method as a procedure:

```
(define (fast-exp b n)
  (cond ((= n 0) 1)
        ((even? n) (square (fast-exp b (/ n 2))))
        (else (* b (fast-exp b (- n 1))))))
```

where the predicate to test whether an integer is even is defined in terms of the primitive procedure `remainder` by

```
(define (even? n)
  (= (remainder n 2) 0))
```

The process evolved by `fast-exp` grows logarithmically with n in both space and time. To see this, observe that computing b^{2n} using `fast-exp` requires only one more multiplication than computing b^n. The size of the exponent we can compute therefore doubles (approximately) with every new multiplication we are allowed. Thus, the number of multiplications required for an exponent of n grows about as fast as the logarithm of n to the base 2. The process has $O(\log n)$ growth.[32]

The difference between $O(\log n)$ growth and $O(n)$ growth becomes striking as n becomes large. For example, `fast-exp` for $n = 1000$ requires only 14 multiplications.[33] It is also possible to use the idea of successive squaring to devise an iterative algorithm that computes exponentials in logarithmic time, although, as is often the case with iterative algorithms, this is not written down so straightforwardly as the recursive algorithm.[34]

32 More precisely, the number of multiplications required is equal to 1 less than the log base 2 of n plus the number of ones in the binary representation of n. This total is always less than twice the log base 2 of n. The arbitrary constant K in the definition of order notation implies that, for a logarithmic process, the base to which logarithms are taken does not matter, so all such process are described as $O(\log n)$.

33 You may wonder why anyone would care about raising numbers to the 1000th power. See section 1.2.6.

34 This iterative algorithm is ancient. It appears in the Hindu *Chandah-sutra* by Acharya Pingala, written before 200 B.C. See Knuth 1969, section 4.6.3, for a full discussion and analysis of this and other methods of exponentiation.

Exercise 1.11

Design a procedure that evolves an iterative exponentiation process that uses successive squaring and works in logarithmic time, as does fast-exp. (Hint: Using the observation that $(b^{n/2})^2 = (b^2)^{n/2}$, keep, along with the exponent n and the base b, an additional state variable a, and define the state transformation in such a way that the product ab^n is unchanged from state to state. At the beginning of the process a is taken to be 1, and the answer is given by the value of a at the end of the process. In general, the technique of defining an *invariant quantity* that remains unchanged from state to state is a powerful way to think about the design of iterative algorithms.)

Exercise 1.12

The exponentiation algorithms in section 1.2.4 are based on performing exponentiation by means of repeated multiplication. In a similar way, one can perform integer multiplication by means of repeated addition. The following multiplication procedure (in which it is assumed that our language can only add, not multiply) is analogous to the expt procedure:

```
(define (* a b)
  (if (= b 0)
      0
      (+ a (* a (- b 1))))))
```

This algorithm takes time linear in b. Now suppose we include, together with addition, the operations double, which doubles an integer, and halve, which divides an (even) integer by 2. Using these, design a multiplication procedure analogous to fast-exp that works in logarithmic time.

Exercise 1.13

Using the results of exercises 1.11 and 1.12, devise a procedure that generates an iterative process for multiplying two integers in terms of adding, doubling, and halving and works in logarithmic time.[35]

Exercise 1.14

Prove that Fib(n) is the closest integer to $\phi^n/\sqrt{5}$, where $\phi = (1 + \sqrt{5})/2$. (Hint: Let $\psi = (1 - \sqrt{5})/2$. Use induction and the definition of the Fibonacci numbers (see section 1.2.2) to prove that Fib(n) = $(\phi^n - \psi^n)/\sqrt{5}$.) Using this fact, devise a procedure that computes Fibonacci numbers in logarithmic time. (Assume that there are primitive procedures floor and ceiling that return, respectively, the closest integers below and above their argument.) Explain why this method is not likely to be practical for computing Fib(n) unless n is fairly small.

[35] This algorithm, which is sometimes known as the "Russian peasant method" of multiplication, is ancient. Examples of its use are found in the Rhind Papyrus, one of the two oldest mathematical documents in existence, written about 1700 B.C. (and copied from an even older document) by an Egyptian scribe named A'h-mose.

1.2.5 Greatest Common Divisors

The greatest common divisor (GCD) of two integers a and b is defined to be the largest integer that evenly divides both a and b. For example, the GCD of 16 and 28 is 4. In chapter 2, when we investigate how to implement rational-number arithmetic, we will need to be able to compute GCDs in order to reduce rational numbers to lowest terms. (To reduce a rational number to lowest terms, we must divide both numerator and denominator by their GCD. For example, 16/28 reduces to 4/7.) One way to find the GCD of two integers is to factor them and search for common factors, but there is a famous algorithm that is much more efficient.

The idea of the algorithm is based on the observation that, if r is the remainder when a is divided by b, then the common divisors of a and b are precisely the same as the common divisors of b and r. Thus, we can use the equation

$$\text{GCD}(a, b) = \text{GCD}(b, r)$$

to successively reduce the problem of computing a GCD to the problem of computing the GCD of smaller and smaller pairs of integers. For example,

$$\text{GCD}(206, 40) = \text{GCD}(40, 6) = \text{GCD}(6, 4) = \text{GCD}(4, 2) = \text{GCD}(2, 0) = 2$$

reduces GCD(206,40) to GCD(2,0), which is 2. It is possible to show that starting with any two positive integers and performing repeated reductions will always eventually produce a pair where the second number is 0. Then the GCD is the other number in the pair. This method for computing the GCD is known as *Euclid's Algorithm*.[36]

It is easy to express Euclid's Algorithm as a procedure:

```
(define (gcd a b)
  (if (= b 0)
      a
      (gcd b (remainder a b))))
```

This generates an iterative process, whose number of steps grows as the logarithm of the numbers involved.

The fact that the number of steps required by Euclid's Algorithm has logarithmic growth bears an interesting relation to the Fibonacci numbers:

---

36 Euclid's Algorithm is so called because it appears in Euclid's *Elements* (Book 7, ca. 300 B.C.). According to Knuth (1969), it may be considered the oldest known nontrivial algorithm. The ancient Egyptian method of multiplication (exercise 1.13) is surely older, but, as Knuth explains, Euclid's algorithm is the oldest known to have been presented as a general algorithm, rather than as a set of illustrative examples.

Lamé's Theorem: If Euclid's Algorithm requires k steps to compute the GCD of some pair, then the smaller number in the pair must be greater than or equal to the kth Fibonacci number.[37]

We can use this theorem to get an order-of-growth estimate for Euclid's Algorithm. Let n be the smaller of the two inputs to the procedure. If the process takes k steps, then we must have $n \geq \text{Fib}(k) \approx \phi^k$. Therefore the number of steps k must be less than the logarithm (to the base ϕ) of n. Hence, the order of growth is $O(\log n)$.

Exercise 1.15

The process that a procedure generates is of course dependent on the rules used by the interpreter. As an example, consider the iterative gcd procedure given above, which has logarithmic growth. Suppose we were to interpret this procedure using normal-order evaluation, as discussed in section 1.1.5. (The normal-order-evaluation rule for if is described in exercise 1.3.) Using the substitution method (for normal order), illustrate the process generated in evaluating (gcd 206 40). In general, what is the order of growth in time resources for gcd using normal-order evaluation? (Assume that the time required is proportional to the number of remainder operations performed.)

1.2.6 Example: Testing for Primality

This section describes two methods for checking the primality of an integer n, one with order of growth $O(\sqrt{n})$, and a "probabilistic" algorithm with order of growth $O(\log n)$. The related exercises at the end of this section suggest programming projects based on these algorithms.

---

37 This theorem was proved in 1845 by Gabriel Lamé, a French mathematician and engineer known chiefly for his contributions to mathematical physics. To prove the theorem, we consider pairs (a_k, b_k), where $a_k \geq b_k$, for which Euclid's Algorithm terminates in k steps. The proof is based on the claim that, if $(a_{k+1}, b_{k+1}) \to (a_k, b_k) \to (a_{k-1}, b_{k-1})$ are three successive pairs in the reduction process, then we must have $b_{k+1} \geq b_k + b_{k-1}$. To verify the claim, consider that a reduction step is defined by applying the transformation $a_{k-1} = b_k$, $b_{k-1} = $ remainder of a_k divided by b_k. The second equation means that $a_k = q b_k + b_{k-1}$ for some positive integer q. And since q must be at least 1 we have $a_k = q b_k + b_{k-1} \geq b_k + b_{k-1}$. But in the previous reduction step we have $b_{k+1} = a_k$. Therefore, $b_{k+1} = a_k \geq b_k + b_{k-1}$. This verifies the claim. Now we can prove the theorem by induction on k, the number of steps that the algorithm requires to terminate. The result is true for $k = 1$, since this merely requires that b be at least as large as $\text{Fib}(1) = 1$. Now, assume that the result is true for all integers less than or equal to k and establish the result for $k + 1$. Let $(a_{k+1}, b_{k+1}) \to (a_k, b_k) \to (a_{k-1}, b_{k-1})$ be successive pairs in the reduction process. By our induction hypotheses, we have $b_{k-1} \geq \text{Fib}(k - 1)$ and $b_k \geq \text{Fib}(k)$. Thus, applying the claim we just proved together with the definition of the Fibonacci numbers gives $b_{k+1} \geq b_k + b_{k-1} \geq \text{Fib}(k) + \text{Fib}(k - 1) = \text{Fib}(k + 1)$, which completes the proof of Lamé's Theorem.

Searching for divisors

Since ancient times, mathematicians have been fascinated by problems concerning prime numbers, and many people have worked on the problem of determining ways to test if numbers are prime. One way to test if a number is prime is to find the number's divisors. The following program finds the smallest integral divisor (greater than 1) of a given number n. It does this in a straightforward way, by testing n for divisibility by successive integers starting with 2.

```
(define (smallest-divisor n)
  (find-divisor n 2))

(define (find-divisor n test-divisor)
  (cond ((> (square test-divisor) n) n)
        ((divides? test-divisor n) test-divisor)
        (else (find-divisor n (+ test-divisor 1)))))

(define (divides? a b)
  (= (remainder b a) 0))
```

We can test whether a number is prime as follows: n is prime if and only if n is its own smallest divisor.

```
(define (prime? n)
  (= n (smallest-divisor n)))
```

The end test for find-divisor is based on the fact that if n is not prime it must have a divisor less than or equal to $\sqrt{n}$.[38] This means that the algorithm need only test divisors between 1 and $\sqrt{n}$. Consequently, the number of steps required to identify n as prime will have order of growth $O(\sqrt{n})$.

The Fermat test

The $O(\log n)$ primality test is based on a result from number theory known as Fermat's Little Theorem.

Fermat's Little Theorem: If n is a prime number and a is any positive integer less than n, then a raised to the nth power is congruent to a modulo n.

(Two numbers are said to be *congruent modulo n* if they both have the

---

38 If d is a divisor of n, then so is n/d. But d and n/d cannot both be greater than $\sqrt{n}$.

same remainder when divided by n. The remainder of a number a when divided by n is also referred to as the *remainder of a modulo n*, or simply as *a modulo n*.)

If n is not prime, then, in general, most of the numbers $a < n$ will not satisfy the above relation. This leads to the following algorithm: Given a number n, pick a random number $a < n$ and compute the remainder of a^n modulo n. If the result is not equal to a, then n is certainly not prime. If it is a, then chances are good that n is prime. Now pick another random number a and test it with the same method. If it also satisfies the equation, then we can be even more confident that n is prime. By trying more and more values of a, we can increase our confidence in the result. This algorithm is known as the Fermat test.

To implement the Fermat test, we need a procedure that computes the exponential of a number modulo another number:

```
(define (expmod b e m)
  (cond ((= e 0) 1)
        ((even? e)
         (remainder (square (expmod b (/ e 2) m))
                    m))
        (else
         (remainder (* b (expmod b (- e 1) m))
                    m))))
```

This is very similar to the **fast-exp** procedure of section 1.2.4. It uses successive squaring, so that the number of steps grows logarithmically with the exponent.[39]

The Fermat test is performed by choosing at random a number a between 2 and $n - 1$ inclusive and checking whether the remainder modulo n of the nth power of a is equal to a. The random number a is chosen using the procedure **random**, which is included as a primitive in Scheme. Random returns a nonnegative integer less than its input. Hence, to obtain a random number between 2 and $n - 1$, we call **random** with an input of $n - 2$ and add 2 to the result:

---

39 The reduction steps in the cases where the exponent e is greater than 1 are based on the fact that, for any integers x, y, and m, we can find the remainder of x times y modulo m by computing separately the remainders of x modulo m and y modulo m, multiplying these, and then taking the remainder of the result modulo m. For instance, in the case where e is even, we compute the remainder of $b^{e/2}$ modulo m, square this, and take the remainder modulo m. This technique is useful because it means we can perform our computation without ever having to deal with numbers much larger than m. (Compare exercise 1.20.)

```
(define (fermat-test n)
  (define a (+ 2 (random (- n 2)))))
  (= (expmod a n n) a))
```

The following procedure runs the test a given number of times, as specified by a parameter. Its value is true if the test succeeds every time, and false otherwise.

```
(define (fast-prime? n times)
  (cond ((= times 0) t)
        ((fermat-test n)
         (fast-prime? n (- times 1)))
        (else nil)))
```

Note that `fast-prime?` will return immediately if it ever finds (`fermat-test n`) to be false.

Probabilistic methods

The Fermat test differs in character from most familiar algorithms, in which one computes an answer that is guaranteed to be correct. Here, the answer obtained is only probably correct. More precisely, if n ever fails the Fermat test, we can be certain that n is not prime. But the fact that n passes the test, while an extremely strong indication, is still not a guarantee that n is prime. What we would like to say is that for any number n, if we perform the test enough times and find that n always passes the test, then the probability of error in our primality test can be made as small as we like.

Unfortunately, this assertion is not quite correct. There do exist numbers that fool the Fermat test: numbers n that are not prime and yet have the property that a^n is congruent to a modulo n for all integers $a < n$. Such numbers are extremely rare, so the Fermat test is quite reliable in practice. Nevertheless, the possibility of error still exists, and because of this mathematicians tended until recently to regard the Fermat test as a good way of showing that a number is not prime, but not an adequate method of showing that a number is prime.[40]

Over the past few years, mathematicians have discovered variations of the Fermat test that cannot be fooled. In these tests, as with the Fermat method, one tests the primality of an integer n by choosing a random integer $a < n$ and checking the value of some quantity $F(a, n)$ that can be computed in logarithmic time. (See exercise 1.22 for an example of such a

---

40 Numbers that fool the Fermat test are called Carmichael numbers, and little is known about them other than that they are extremely rare. There are 16 Carmichael numbers below 100,000. The smallest few are 561, 1105, 1729, 2465, 2821, and 6601.

test.) On the other hand, in contrast with the Fermat test, one can prove that, for any n, $F(a, n)$ will not have the right value for most of the integers $a < n$ unless n is prime. This means that if n passes the test for some random choice of a we know that the chances are better than even that n is prime. If n passes the test for two random choices of a, the odds are better than 4 to 1 that n is prime. By running the test with more and more randomly chosen values of a we can make the probability of error as small as we like.

The difference between these methods and the Fermat test is not significant for practical purposes.[41] On the other hand, the existence of tests for which one can prove that the chance of error becomes arbitrarily small sparked interest in algorithms of this type, which have come to be known as *probabilistic algorithms*. There is currently a great deal of research activity in this area, and probabilistic algorithms have been fruitfully applied to many fields.[42]

Exercise 1.16

Use the `smallest-divisor` procedure of section 1.2.6 to find the smallest divisor of each of the following numbers: 199, 1999, 19999.

Exercise 1.17

Most Lisp implementations include a primitive called `runtime` which returns an integer that specifies the amount of time the system has been running (measured, for example, in microseconds). The following `timed-prime-test` procedure, when called with an integer n, prints n and checks to see if n is prime. If n is prime, the procedure prints three asterisks followed by the number of microseconds used in performing the test.

```
(define (timed-prime-test n)
  (define start-time (runtime))
  (define found-prime? (prime? n)))
```

[41] In testing primality of very large numbers chosen at random, the chance of stumbling upon a value that fools the Fermat test is less than the chance that cosmic radiation will cause the computer to make an error in carrying out a "correct" algorithm. Considering an algorithm to be inadequate for the first reason but not for the second illustrates the difference between mathematics and engineering.

[42] One of the most striking applications of probabilistic prime testing has been to the field of cryptography. Although it is now computationally infeasible to factor an arbitrary 200-digit number, the primality of such a number can be checked in a few seconds with the Fermat test. This fact forms the basis of a technique for constructing "unbreakable codes" suggested by Rivest, Shamir, and Adelman (1977). Because of this and related developments, the study of prime numbers, once considered the epitome of a topic in "pure" mathematics to be studied only for its own sake, now turns out to have important practical applications to cryptography, electronic funds transfer, and information retrieval.

```
(define elapsed-time (- (runtime) start-time))
(print n)
(cond (found-prime?
       (print " *** ")
       (print elapsed-time))))
```

Using this procedure, write a procedure `search-for-primes` that checks the primality of consecutive odd integers in a specified range. Use your procedure to find the three smallest primes larger than 1000; larger than 10,000; larger than 100,000; larger than 1,000,000. Note the time needed to test each prime. Since the testing algorithm has order of growth of $O(\sqrt{n})$, you should expect that testing for primes around 10,000 should take about $\sqrt{10}$ times as long as testing for primes around 1000. Do your timing data bear this out? How well do the data for 100,000 and 1,000,000 support the $\sqrt{n}$ prediction?

Exercise 1.18

The `smallest-divisor` procedure described in section 1.2.6 is doing lots of needless testing, for after it checks to see if the number is divisible by 2 there is no point in its checking to see if it is divisible by any larger even numbers. This suggests that the values used for `test-divisor` should not be 2, 3, 4, 5, 6, 7,..., but rather 2, 3, 5, 7, 9, ... To implement this change, define a procedure `next` that returns 3 if its input is equal to 2 and otherwise returns its input plus 2. Modify the `smallest-divisor` procedure to use `(next test-divisor)` instead of `(+ test-divisor 1)`. With `timed-prime-test` incorporating this modified version of `smallest-divisor`, run the test for each of the 12 primes found in exercise 1.17. Since this modification halves the number of test steps, you should expect it to run about twice as fast. Is this expectation confirmed? If not, what is the observed ratio of the speeds of the two algorithms, and how do you explain the fact that it is different from 2?

Exercise 1.19

Modify the `timed-prime-test` procedure of exercise 1.17 to use `fast-prime?` (the Fermat method), and test each of the 12 primes you found in that exercise. Since the Fermat test has $O(\log n)$ growth, how would you expect the time to test primes near 1,000,000 to compare with the time needed to test primes near 1000? Do your data bear this out? Can you explain any discrepancy you find?

Exercise 1.20

Alyssa P. Hacker complains that we went to a lot of extra work in writing `expmod`. After all, she says, since we already know how to compute exponentials, we could have simply written

```
(define (expmod base exp m)
  (remainder (fast-exp base exp) m))
```

Is she correct? Would this procedure serve as well for our fast prime tester? Explain.

Exercise 1.21

Louis Reasoner is having great difficulty doing exercise 1.19. His `fast-prime?` test seems to run more slowly than his `prime?` test. Louis calls his friend Eva Lu Ator over to help. When they examine Louis's code, they find that he has rewritten the `expmod` procedure to use an explicit multiplication, rather than calling `square`:

```
(define (expmod b e m)
  (cond ((= e 0) 1)
        ((even? e)
         (remainder (* (expmod b (/ e 2) m)
                       (expmod b (/ e 2) m))
                    m))
        (else
         (remainder (* b (expmod b (- e 1) m))
                    m))))
```

"I don't see what difference that could make," says Louis. "I do," says Eva. "By writing the procedure like that, you have transformed the $O(\log n)$ process into an $O(n)$ process." Explain.

Exercise 1.22

One of the variants of the Fermat test that cannot be fooled was discovered by Solovay and Strassen (1977). It proceeds by choosing a random number $a < n$, checking that $\mathrm{GCD}(a, n) = 1$, and then computing a number-theoretic quantity called the Jacobi symbol: $J(a, n)$, which is equal to ± 1. If n is prime, then $J(a, n)$ is always congruent modulo n to $a^{(n-1)/2}$ for any a such that $\mathrm{GCD}(a, n) = 1$. If n is not prime, then it can be proved that this relation does not hold for at least half the numbers $a < n$. Thus, if we find that the relation holds for some randomly chosen a, we can assert that the chances are better than even that n is prime. The Jacobi symbol can be computed by using the reductions

$$
J(a, n) = \begin{cases} 1 & \text{if } a = 1 \\ J(a/2, n) \cdot (-1)^{(n^2-1)/8} & \text{if } a \text{ is even} \\ J(\mathrm{remainder}(n, a), a) \cdot (-1)^{(a-1)(n-1)/4} & \text{otherwise} \end{cases}
$$

Implement the Solovay-Strassen test as a procedure that runs in $O(\log n)$ time.

1.3 Formulating Abstractions with Higher-Order Procedures

We have seen that procedures are, in effect, abstractions that describe compound operations on numbers independent of the particular numbers.

For example, when we

```
(define (cube x) (* x x x))
```

we are not talking about the cube of a particular number, but rather about a method for obtaining the cube of any number. Of course we could get along without ever defining this procedure, by always writing expressions such as

```
(* 3 3 3)
(* x x x)
(* y y y)
```

and never mentioning cube explicitly. This would place us at a serious disadvantage, forcing us to work always at the level of the particular operations that happen to be primitives in the language (multiplication, in this case) rather than in terms of higher-level operations. Our programs would be able to compute cubes, but our language would lack the ability to express the concept of cubing. One of the things we should demand from a powerful programming language is the ability to build abstractions by assigning names to common patterns and then to work in terms of the abstractions directly. Procedures provide this ability. This is why all but the most primitive programming languages include mechanisms for defining procedures.

Yet even in numerical processing we will be severely limited in our ability to create abstractions if we are restricted to procedures whose parameters must be numbers. Often the same programming pattern will be used with a number of different procedures. To express such patterns as concepts, we will need to construct procedures that can accept procedures as arguments or return procedures as values. Procedures that manipulate procedures are called *higher-order procedures*. This section shows how higher-order procedures can serve as powerful abstraction mechanisms, vastly increasing the expressive power of our language.

1.3.1 Procedures as Parameters

Consider the following three procedures. The first computes the sum of the integers from a through b:

```
(define (sum-integers a b)
  (if (> a b)
      0
      (+ a (sum-integers (+ a 1) b))))
```

The second computes the sum of the cubes of the integers in the given range:

```
(define (sum-cubes a b)
  (if (> a b)
      0
      (+ (cube a) (sum-cubes (+ a 1) b))))
```

The third computes the sum of a sequence of terms in the following series, which converges to $\pi/8$ (very slowly):[43]

$$\frac{1}{1 \cdot 3} + \frac{1}{5 \cdot 7} + \frac{1}{9 \cdot 11} + \cdots$$

```
(define (pi-sum a b)
  (if (> a b)
      0
      (+ (/ 1 (* a (+ a 2))) (pi-sum (+ a 4) b))))
```

These three procedures clearly share a common underlying pattern. They are for the most part identical, differing only in the name of the procedure, the function of a used to compute the term, and the function that provides the next value of a. We could generate each of the procedures by filling in slots in the same template:

```
(define (⟨name⟩ a b)
  (if (> a b)
      0
      (+ (⟨term⟩ a)
         (⟨name⟩ (⟨next⟩ a) b))))
```

The presence of such a common pattern is strong evidence that there is a useful abstraction waiting to be brought to the surface. Indeed, mathematicians long ago identified the abstraction of *summation of a series* and invented "sigma notation," for example

$$\sum_{n=a}^{b} f(n) = f(a) + \cdots + f(b),$$

to express this concept. The power of sigma notation is that it allows mathematicians to deal with the concept of summation itself rather than

---

43 This formula, usually written in the equivalent form $\frac{\pi}{4} = 1 - \frac{1}{3} + \frac{1}{5} - \frac{1}{7} + \cdots$, is due to Leibniz.

only with particular sums—for example, to formulate general results about sums that are independent of the particular series being summed.

Similarly, as program designers, we would like our language to be powerful enough so that we can write a procedure that expresses the concept of summation itself rather than only procedures that compute particular sums. We can do so readily in our procedural language by taking the common template shown above and transforming the "slots" into formal parameters:

```
(define (sum term a next b)
  (if (> a b)
      0
      (+ (term a)
         (sum term (next a) next b))))
```

Notice that sum takes as its arguments the upper and lower bounds a and b together with the procedures term and next. We can use sum just as we would any procedure. For example, we can use it to define sum-cubes:

```
(define (sum-cubes a b)
  (sum cube a 1+ b))
```

Using this, we can compute the sum of the cubes of the integers from 1 to 10:

```
==> (sum-cubes 1 10)
3025
```

We could also define pi-sum in the same way:

```
(define (pi-sum a b)
  (define (pi-term x)
    (/ 1 (* x (+ x 2))))
  (define (pi-next x)
    (+ x 4))
  (sum pi-term a pi-next b))
```

Using these procedures, we could get an approximation to π:

```
==> (* 8 (pi-sum 1 1000))
3.13592
```

Once we have sum, we can use it as a building block in formulating further concepts. For instance, the definite integral of a function f between the limits a and b can be approximated numerically using the formula

$$\int_a^b f = \left[f\left(a + \frac{dx}{2}\right) + f\left(a + dx + \frac{dx}{2}\right) + f\left(a + 2dx + \frac{dx}{2}\right) + \cdots \right] dx$$

for small values of dx. We can express this directly as a procedure:

```
(define (integral f a b dx)
  (define (add-dx x) (+ x dx))
  (* (sum f (+ a (/ dx 2)) add-dx b)
     dx))
```

```
==> (integral cube 0 1 .01)
0.249987492
```

```
==> (integral cube 0 1 .001)
0.250000063
```

(The exact value of the integral of cube between 0 and 1 is 1/4.)

Exercise 1.23

Simpson's Rule is a more accurate method of numerical integration than the method illustrated above. Using Simpson's Rule, the integral of a function f between a and b is approximated as

$$\frac{h}{3}[y_0 + 4y_1 + 2y_2 + 4y_3 + 2y_4 + \cdots + 2y_{n-2} + 4y_{n-1} + y_n]$$

where $h = (b-a)/n$, for some even integer n, and $y_k = f(a+kh)$. (Increasing n increases the accuracy of the approximation.) Define a procedure that takes as arguments f, a, b, and n and returns the value of the integral, computed using Simpson's Rule.

Exercise 1.24

The sum procedure above generates a linear recursion. The procedure can be rewritten so that the sum is performed iteratively. Show how to do this by filling in the missing expressions in the following definition:

```
(define (sum term a next b)
  (define (iter a result)
    (if ⟨??⟩
        ⟨??⟩
        (iter ⟨??⟩
              ⟨??⟩)))
  (iter ⟨??⟩ ⟨??⟩))
```

Exercise 1.25[44]

The sum procedure is only the simplest of a vast number of similar abstractions that can be captured as higher-order procedures. Write an analogous procedure called product that returns the product of the values of a function at points over a given range. Write the procedure in two forms, one that generates a recursive process and one that generates an iterative process. Show how to define factorial in terms of product. Also use product to compute approximations to π using the formula[45]

$$\frac{\pi}{4} = \frac{2 \cdot 4 \cdot 4 \cdot 6 \cdot 6 \cdot 8 \cdots}{3 \cdot 3 \cdot 5 \cdot 5 \cdot 7 \cdot 7 \cdots}$$

Exercise 1.26

Show that sum (section 1.3.1) and product (exercise 1.25) are both special cases of a still more general notion called accumulate that combines a collection of terms, using some general accumulation function:

(accumulate combiner null-value term a next b)

Accumulate takes as arguments the same term and range specifications as sum and product, together with a combiner procedure (of two arguments) that specifies how the current term is to be combined with the accumulation of the preceding terms and a null-value that specifies what initial value to use when the terms run out. Write accumulate (in both recursive and iterative forms) and show how sum and product can both be defined as simple calls to accumulate.

Exercise 1.27

You can obtain an even more general version of accumulate (exercise 1.26) by introducing the notion of a *filter* on the terms to be combined. That is, combine only those terms derived from values in the range that satisfy a specified condition. The resulting filtered-accumulate abstraction takes the same arguments as accumulate, together with an additional predicate of one argument that specifies the filter. Write filtered-accumulate as a procedure. Show how to express the following using filtered-accumulate:

a. the sum of the squares of the prime numbers in the interval a to b (assuming that you have a prime? predicate already written)

b. the product of all the positive integers $i < n$ such that $\text{GCD}(i, n) = 1$.

---

44 The intent of exercises 1.25–1.27 is to demonstrate the expressive power that is attained by using an appropriate abstraction to consolidate many seemingly disparate operations. However, though accumulation and filtering are elegant ideas, our hands are somewhat tied in using them at this point since we do not yet have data structures to provide suitable means of combination for these abstractions. We will return to these ideas in chapter 3 when we study data structures called *streams*. Streams are interfaces that allow us to combine filters and accumulators to build even more powerful abstractions. We will see in section 3.4.2 how these methods really come into their own as a powerful and elegant approach to designing programs.

45 This formula was discovered by the seventeenth-century English mathematician John Wallis.

1.3.2 Constructing Procedures Using Lambda

In using sum as in section 1.3.1, it seems terribly awkward to have to define trivial procedures such as pi-term and pi-next just so we can use them as inputs to our higher-order procedure. Rather than define pi-next and pi-term (even if in a local environment), it would be more convenient to have a way to directly specify "the procedure that returns its input incremented by 4" and "the procedure that returns the reciprocal of its input times its input plus 2." We can do this by introducing the special form lambda, which can be thought of as a "define anonymous." Using lambda we can describe what we want as

```
(lambda (x) (+ x 4))
```

and

```
(lambda (x) (/ 1 (* x (+ x 2))))
```

Then our pi-sum procedure can be expressed without defining any auxiliary procedures as

```
(define (pi-sum a b)
  (sum (lambda (x) (/ 1 (* x (+ x 2))))
       a
       (lambda (x) (+ x 4))
       b))
```

Again using lambda, we can write the integral procedure without having to define the auxiliary procedure add-dx:

```
(define (integral f a b dx)
  (* (sum f
          (+ a (/ dx 2))
          (lambda (x) (+ x dx))
          b)
     dx))
```

In general, lambda is used to define procedures in the same way as define, except that no name is specified for the procedure being defined:

```
(lambda (⟨formal-parameters⟩) ⟨body⟩)
```

The resulting procedure is just as much a procedure as one that is created using define. The only difference is that it has not been associated with any name in the environment. In fact,

```
(define (plus4 x) (+ x 4))
```

is equivalent to

```
(define plus4 (lambda (x) (+ x 4)))
```

Like any expression that has as its value a Lisp procedure, a `lambda` form can be used as the operator in a combination such as

```
==> ((lambda (x y z) (+ x y (square z))) 1 2 3)
12
```

or, more generally, in any context where we would normally use a procedure name.[46]

Using `let` to define local variables

Another use of `lambda` is in defining local variables. We often need local variables in our procedures other than those that have been bound as formal parameters. For example, suppose we wish to compute the function

$$f(x,y) = x(1+xy)^2 + y(1-y) + (1+xy)(1-y),$$

which we could also express as

$$a = 1 + xy,$$

$$b = 1 - y,$$

$$f(x,y) = xa^2 + yb + ab.$$

In writing a procedure to compute f, we would like to include as local variables not only x and y but also the names of intermediate quantities like a and b. One natural way to accomplish this is to `define` these expressions locally:

```
(define (f x y)
  (define a (+ 1 (* x y)))
  (define b (- 1 y))
  (+ (* x (square a))
     (* y b)
     (* a b)))
```

---

[46] It would be clearer and less intimidating to people learning Lisp if a name more obvious than `lambda`, such as `make-procedure`, were used. But the convention is firmly entrenched. The notation is adopted from the λ calculus, a mathematical formalism introduced by the mathematical logician Alonzo Church (1941). Church developed the λ calculus to provide a rigorous foundation for studying the notions of function and function application. The λ calculus has become a basic tool for mathematical investigations of the semantics of programming languages.

An alternative is to use an auxiliary procedure to bind the local variables instead of defining them:

```
(define (f x y)
  (define (f-helper a b)
    (+ (* x (square a))
       (* y b)
       (* a b)))
  (f-helper (+ 1 (* x y))
            (- 1 y)))
```

Of course, we could use a lambda expression to specify an anonymous procedure for binding our local variables. The body of f then becomes a single call to that procedure:

```
(define (f x y)
  ((lambda (a b)
     (+ (* x (square a))
        (* y b)
        (* a b)))
   (+ 1 (* x y))
   (- 1 y)))
```

This construct is so useful that there is a special form called let to make its use more convenient. Using let, the f procedure could be written as

```
(define (f x y)
  (let ((a (+ 1 (* x y)))
        (b (- 1 y)))
    (+ (* x (square a))
       (* y b)
       (* a b))))
```

The general form of let is

$$(\texttt{let} \ ((\langle var_1 \rangle \ \langle exp_1 \rangle)$$
$$(\langle var_2 \rangle \ \langle exp_2 \rangle)$$
$$\vdots$$
$$(\langle var_n \rangle \ \langle exp_n \rangle))$$
$$\langle body \rangle)$$

which can be thought of as saying

let $\langle var_1 \rangle$ have the value $\langle exp_1 \rangle$ and
  $\langle var_2 \rangle$ have the value $\langle exp_2 \rangle$ and
  $\vdots$
  $\langle var_n \rangle$ have the value $\langle exp_n \rangle$
in $\langle body \rangle$

The first part of the let expression is a list of name-expression pairs. When the let is evaluated, each name is associated with the value of the corresponding expression. The body of the let is evaluated in a local environment that includes these names as local variables. The way this happens is that the let expression is interpreted as an alternate syntax for

```
((lambda (⟨var₁⟩...⟨varₙ⟩)
    ⟨body⟩)
 ⟨exp₁⟩
   ⋮
 ⟨expₙ⟩))
```

No new mechanism is required in the interpreter in order to provide local variables. Let is simply syntactic sugar for the underlying lambda.

A let construct (or the equivalent lambda expression) is often preferable to define for making local variables for several reasons, among them the following.

• With define, the scope of the name being defined is the entire environment in which the define is executed. In contrast, the scope of a variable specified by a let expression is the body of the let. Consequently, let allows one to construct expressions that bind variables as locally as possible to where they are to be used. For example, in an environment in which x is bound to 5, the value of the expression

```
(+ (let ((x 3))
     (+ x (* x 10)))
   x)
```

is 38. Here, the x in the body of the let is bound to 3, so the value returned by the let is 33. On the other hand, the x that is the second argument to the outermost + is still bound to 5.

• In a let expression the variables are bound simultaneously, using values computed outside the let, rather than being bound in sequence. This makes a difference when the expressions that provide the values for the let local variables depend upon variables having the same names as the let variables themselves. For example, in an environment where x is bound to 2 the expression

```
(let ((x 3) (y (+ x 2)))
  (* x y))
```

will have the value 12 because, inside the body of the let, x will be bound to 3 and y will be bound to 4 (which is the original x plus 2). In contrast, evaluating the sequence

```
(define x 3)
(define y (+ x 2))
(* x y)
```

will result in 15 as the value of the last expression, since x will be bound to 3 and y will then be bound to 5.

Exercise 1.28

Suppose we define the procedure

```
(define (f g)
  (g 2))
```

Then we have

```
==> (f square)
4

==> (f (lambda (z) (* z (+ z 1))))
6
```

What happens if we (perversely) ask the interpreter to evaluate the combination (f f)? Explain.

1.3.3 Procedures as General Methods

We introduced compound procedures in section 1.1.4 as a mechanism for abstracting useful numerical operations so as to make them independent of the particular numbers involved. With higher-order procedures, such as the integral procedure of section 1.3.1, we began to see a more powerful kind of abstraction: procedures used to express general methods of computation, independent of the particular mathematical functions involved. In this section we discuss two more elaborate examples—general methods for finding zeroes and maxima of functions—and show how these methods can be expressed directly as procedures.

Finding roots of equations by the half-interval method

The *half-interval method* is a simple but powerful technique for finding roots of an equation $f(x) = 0$, where f is a continuous function. The idea is that, if we are given points a and b such that $f(a) < 0 < f(b)$, then f must have at least one zero between a and b. To locate a zero, let x be the average of a and b and compute $f(x)$. If $f(x) > 0$, then f must have a zero between a and x. If $f(x) < 0$, then f must have a zero between x and b. Continuing in this way, we can identify smaller and smaller intervals on which f must have a zero. When we reach a point where the interval is small enough, the process stops. Since the interval of uncertainty is reduced by half at each step of the process, the number of steps required grows as $O(\log(L/T))$, where L is the length of the original interval and where T is the error tolerance (that is, the size of the interval we will consider "small enough").

Here is a procedure that implements this strategy:

```
(define (search f neg-point pos-point)
  (let ((midpoint (average neg-point pos-point)))
    (if (close-enough? neg-point pos-point)
        midpoint
        (let ((test-value (f midpoint)))
          (cond ((positive? test-value)
                 (search f neg-point midpoint))
                ((negative? test-value)
                 (search f midpoint pos-point))
                (else midpoint))))))
```

We assume that we are initially given the function f together with points at which its values are negative and positive. We first compute the midpoint of the two given points. Next we check to see if the given interval is small enough, and if so we simply return the midpoint as our answer. Otherwise, we compute as a test value the value of f at the midpoint. If the test value is positive, then we continue the process with a new interval running from the original negative point to the midpoint. If the test value is negative, we continue with the interval from the midpoint to the positive point. Finally, there is the possibility that the test value is 0, in which case the midpoint is itself the root we are searching for.

To test whether the endpoints are "close enough" we can use a procedure similar to the one used in section 1.1.7 for computing square-roots:

```
(define (close-enough? x y)
  (< (abs (- x y)) .001))
```

Finally, we can use the search procedure in a procedure that takes as inputs the function and the two endpoints. This checks to see which of the endpoints has a negative function value and which has a positive value, and calls the search procedure accordingly. If the function has the same sign on the two given points, the half-interval method cannot be used, in which case the procedure signals an error.[47]

```
(define (half-interval-method f a b)
  (let ((a-value (f a))
        (b-value (f b)))
    (cond ((and (negative? a-value) (positive? b-value))
           (search f a b))
          ((and (negative? b-value) (positive? a-value))
           (search f b a))
          (else
           (error "Values are not of opposite sign" a b)))))
```

The following example uses the half-interval method to approximate π as the root between 2 and 4 of $\sin x = 0$:

```
==> (half-interval-method sin 2 4)
3.14111328
```

Here is another example, using the half-interval method to search for a root of the equation $x^3 - 2x - 3 = 0$ between 1 and 2:

```
==> (half-interval-method (lambda (x)
                            (- (* x x x) (* 2 x) 3))
                          1
                          2)
1.8931
```

Finding the maximum of a unimodal function

Suppose we are given a function f defined on some interval and we wish to find, to within a tolerance T, the point on the interval at which f attains its maximum value. One straightforward way to do this is to evaluate the function at points along the interval that are evenly spaced a distance T apart and pick the one that has the maximum value. This *exhaustive search* procedure requires evaluating the function at $O(L/T)$ points, where

---

47 This can be accomplished using the **error** primitive, which takes as arguments a number of items that are printed as error messages.

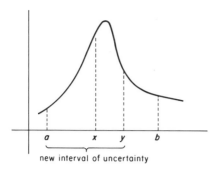

new interval of uncertainty

Figure 1.6
Searching for the maximum of a unimodal function

L is the length of the interval. This is surely not a very effective method if T is small. Fortunately, for many classes of functions, there are much better techniques for locating the maximum. The method we shall discuss here applies to functions that are *unimodal*; that is, functions that are known to have only one "bump" on the interval in question. More formally, a unimodal function f with a maximum on an interval from a to b has the property that there is some point m on the interval such that f is increasing between a and m and decreasing between m and b.

For unimodal functions, there is a process that will find the maximum using $O(\log(L/T))$ function evaluations. The idea is to evaluate f at two intermediate points x and y on the interval (with $x < y$). Then if $f(x)$ is greater than $f(y)$ we can assert that the maximum must lie on the interval between a and y, while if $f(x)$ is less than $f(y)$ we can assert that the maximum lies between x and b. Thus, if we choose x and y to lie toward the middle of the interval, we can with two function evaluations cut the interval of uncertainty roughly in half, as shown in figure 1.6. Repeatedly performing this cutting will produce an interval of size smaller than T in $O(\log(L/T))$ steps.

But we can be cleverer yet. Notice that we need to compare the function value at two intermediate points x and y in order to reduce the interval. Thus, each reduction step requires that we find the value of the function at two intermediate points. Suppose, however, that we could arrange things so that we could guarantee that one of the intermediate values had already been generated by the previous reduction step. Then each new reduction step would require only one new function evaluation. If the function is difficult to compute, this would represent a substantial savings, making our search twice as efficient.

One way to accomplish this, known as the *golden section method*, is to choose the intermediate points x and y to lie at certain fixed fractions along the interval. That is, we always choose x to lie at a fraction p of the way from a to b, and y to lie at a fraction q of the way from a to b:

$$x - a = p(b - a),$$

$$y - a = q(b - a).$$

The reason this is called the golden section method is that we choose the fraction q to be

$$q = (\sqrt{5} - 1)/2 \approx 0.618,$$

which is precisely the reciprocal of the golden ratio, which describes the order of growth of the Fibonacci numbers. The number p is chosen to be q^2. If we always use this rule to choose the intermediate values x and y, then we can guarantee that one of the intermediate values to be chosen for the next round will be either the x or the y for the current round.[48]

In summary, we carry out the golden section method by choosing as our two intermediate points a point y that lies a fraction of the way from a to b equal to 1 over the golden ratio, and a point x that lies at a fraction of 1 over the golden ratio squared. If $f(x) > f(y)$, then the new interval of uncertainty is from a to y, x will serve as the "y point" for this interval, and we should compute a new "x point." If $f(x) < f(y)$, then the new interval of uncertainty is from x to b, y will serve as the "x point" for this interval, and we should compute a new "y point." In either case, the interval of uncertainty is reduced to at most .618 of its previous length. We repeat the process, reducing the interval over and over, until the endpoints are close enough for our purposes, in which case we can return any intermediate point on the interval (say, x).

48 Here is a proof of this fact: Suppose that $f(x) > f(y)$. Then our new interval of uncertainty will run from a to y. If we want to use our old x as the intermediate value that lies a fraction q of the way from a to y, then we should have $x - a = q(y - a)$, or
$$p(b - a) = q(y - a) = q^2(b - a),$$
which implies that $p = q^2$. Now consider the other case, where $f(x) < f(y)$. Then our new interval will run from x to b. If we want to use our old y as the intermediate point at a fraction p of the distance along this interval, we should have $y - x = p(b - x)$, or
$$(y - a) - (x - a) = p[(b - a) - (x - a)],$$
or, substituting for $x - a$ and $y - a$,
$$q(b - a) - p(b - a) = p[(b - a) - p(b - a)].$$
This reduces to
$$q - p = p - p^2.$$
Combining this with the relation $p = q^2$ that we derived above yields
$$q - q^2 = q^2 - q^4,$$
which simplifies to
$$1 = q^2 + q.$$
The number q that satisfies this relation is the reciprocal of the golden ratio.

The golden section method can be implemented as an iterative process described by the following procedure reduce, which maintains state variables for a, x, y, b, and the values of f at x and y.

```
(define (reduce f a x y b fx fy)
  (cond ((close-enough? a b) x)
        ((> fx fy)
         (let ((new (x-point a y)))
           (reduce f a new x y (f new) fx)))
        (else
         (let ((new (y-point x b)))
           (reduce f x y new b fy (f new))))))
```

Notice (and this is the whole point of the method) that we have to compute the value of f at only one new point on each iteration. The new points are computed at the appropriate ratio along the interval. The procedures to do this take as arguments the endpoints of the new interval:

```
(define (x-point a b)
  (+ a (* golden-ratio-squared (- b a))))

(define (y-point a b)
  (+ a (* golden-ratio (- b a))))
```

where the golden-ratio constants are computed by

```
(define golden-ratio
  (/ (- (sqrt 5) 1) 2))

(define golden-ratio-squared (square golden-ratio))
```

Finally, we initialize the process with a procedure that takes as inputs the function we wish to maximize and the endpoints of the interval in question and calls reduce after setting up the initial x and y points of the interval:

```
(define (golden f a b)
  (let ((x (x-point a b))
        (y (y-point a b)))
    (reduce f a x y b (f x) (f y))))
```

As a test, we can use our procedure to approximate π as twice the maximum point $\pi/2$ of the sine function on the interval 0 to 3:

```
==> (* 2 (golden sin 0 3))
3.14143
```

Exercise 1.29

When we introduced the golden section method for finding the maximum of a function on an interval, we also mentioned the brute-force method of evaluating the function at evenly spaced points along the interval and choosing the largest value. Assuming you have a procedure max that returns the larger of its two inputs, show how a brute-force search for the maximum value can be implemented as a single call to accumulate (exercise 1.26).

Exercise 1.30

In finding the maximum of a unimodal function, how much faster is the golden section method than the brute-force method of evaluating the function at equally spaced points along the interval and choosing the largest? In particular, suppose we want to find the maximum point of a function on the interval from 0 to 1 with an accuracy to within .001. How many function evaluations would be required using brute force? How many using the golden section method?

Exercise 1.31

A number x is called a *fixed point* of a function f if x satisfies the equation $f(x) = x$. For some functions f (the cosine function is an example) we can locate a fixed point by beginning with an initial guess and applying f repeatedly,

$$f(x), f(f(x)), f(f(f(x))), \ldots$$

until the value does not change very much. Using this idea, design a procedure fixed-point that takes as inputs a function and an initial guess and produces an approximation to a fixed point of the function. Test your procedure by evaluating the expression (fixed-point cos 1) to produce a fixed point of the cosine function.

1.3.4 Procedures as Returned Values

The previous examples show how the ability to pass procedures as parameters significantly enhances the expressive power of our programming language. We obtain even more expressive power if we have the ability to create procedures whose returned values are themselves procedures.

Consider the statement "The derivative of x^3 is $3x^2$." This says that the derivative of the function whose value at x is x^3 is another function, namely the function whose value at x is $3x^2$. In particular, "derivative" itself can be regarded as an operator that, when applied to a function f, returns another function Df. To describe "derivative" we can say that, if f is a function and dx is some number, then the derivative Df of f is the function whose value at any number x is given (in the limit of small dx) by

$$Df(x) = \frac{f(x + dx) - f(x)}{dx} .$$

Using `lambda`, we can express the derivative formula as the procedure

```
(lambda (x)
  (/ (- (f (+ x dx)) (f x))
     dx))
```

where `dx` is some small number.

Going further, we can express the idea of derivative itself as the procedure

```
(define (deriv f dx)
  (lambda (x)
    (/ (- (f (+ x dx)) (f x))
       dx)))
```

This is a procedure that takes as its argument a procedure `f` and returns as its value a procedure (produced by the `lambda`) that, when applied to a number `x`, will produce an approximation to the derivative of `f` at `x`.

We can use our `deriv` procedure as follows to approximate the derivative of the cube function at 5 (whose exact value is 75):

```
==> ((deriv cube .001) 5)
75.015
```

The operator of the combination above is itself a combination, because the procedure to be applied to 5 is the value of `deriv` applied to `cube`.

Newton's method for arbitrary functions

We can use `deriv` to build a procedure that implements Newton's method for finding the roots of a differentiable function. This method says that, if y is an approximation to a root of the function f, then a better approximation is given by

$$y - \frac{f(y)}{Df(y)} .$$

This generalizes the formula that we used in section 1.1.7 for computing square roots.[49]   Now, however, we are trying to compute not only square

---

[49] Newton's method does not always converge to an answer, but it can be shown that in favorable cases each iteration of the Newton formula doubles the number-of-digits accuracy of the approximation to the root. In such cases, Newton's method will converge much more rapidly than the half-interval method. In the case of square roots (which is a favorable case for Newton's method), we are trying to find a zero of the function $y^2 - x$. If we use the fact that the derivative of this function is $2y$, and a little algebra, the above formula reduces to $\frac{1}{2}(y + x/y)$, which is the formula we used in section 1.1.7.

roots but roots of any function. It is a general method, like the half-interval method we described in section 1.3.3.

We can implement Newton's method as a straightforward generalization of the square-root program of section 1.1.7. As before, we start with an initial guess and improve it until it is good enough:

```
(define (newton f guess)
  (if (good-enough? guess f)
      guess
      (newton f (improve guess f))))
```

Improving the guess is done using the formula given above:

```
(define (improve guess f)
  (- guess (/ (f guess)
              ((deriv f .001) guess))))
```

Finally, a guess is good enough when the value of the function at that point is very small:

```
(define (good-enough? guess f)
  (< (abs (f guess)) .001))
```

Having defined these procedures, we can now try Newton's method with any function. For example, we can approximate the value of x for which x is equal to $\cos x$, starting with an initial guess of 1:

```
==> (newton (lambda (x) (- x (cos x))) 1)
0.7391
```

The idea of procedures as returned values may take some getting used to, or may seem little more than a mathematical trick. However, the increase in expressive power in a language that can return procedure values is enormous, because this means that we can compute not only with particular procedures but also with procedures that can evolve in response to the ongoing computation. This ability lies at the root of some powerful programming techniques that will be discussed in later chapters.[50]

Exercise 1.32

If f is a numerical function and n is a positive integer, then we can form the nth repeated application of f, which is defined to be the function whose value at

50 In chapter 2 (section 2.1.3) we shall see that in a language that allows procedures as returned values there is, in principle, no need to include any additional machinery for handling data structures, although Lisp implementations do include such machinery for efficiency reasons. Moreover, we shall see that allowing procedures as returned values enables us to deal with infinite data structures via the technique of stream processing, to be introduced in chapter 3.

x is $f(f(\ldots(f(x))\ldots))$. For example, if $f(x) = x + 1$, then the nth repeated application of f is the function g where $g(x) = x + n$. If f is the operation of squaring a number, then the nth repeated application of f is the function that raises its argument to the 2^nth power. Write a procedure that takes as inputs a procedure that computes f and a positive integer n and returns the procedure that computes the nth repeated application of f. For example, your procedure should be able to be used as follows:

```
==> ((repeated square 2) 5)
625
```

Exercise 1.33

The idea of *smoothing* a function is an important concept in signal processing. If f is a function and dx is some small value, then the smoothed version of f is the function whose value at a point x is the average of $f(x - dx)$, $f(x)$, and $f(x + dx)$. Write a procedure smooth that takes as input a procedure that computes f and returns a procedure that computes the smoothed f. It is sometimes valuable to repeatedly smooth a function (that is, smooth the smoothed function, and so on) to obtained the *n-fold smoothed function*. Show how to generate the n-fold smoothed function of any given function using smooth and repeated from exercise 1.32.

Exercise 1.34

Define a procedure cubic that can be used together with the newton procedure in expressions of the form

(newton (cubic a b c) 1)

to approximate roots (starting with an initial guess of 1) to the cubic $x^3 + ax^2 + bx + c$.

Exercise 1.35

Newton's method is an example of a still more general computational strategy known as *iterative improvement*. An iterative improvement says that, to compute something, we start with an initial guess for the answer, test if the guess is good enough, and otherwise improve the guess and continue the process using the improved guess as the new guess. Write a procedure iterative-improve that takes two procedures as arguments: a method for telling whether a guess is good enough and a method for improving a guess. Iterative-improve should return as its value a procedure that takes a guess as argument and keeps improving the guess until it is good enough. Express Newton's method using the iterative-improve procedure. Also, show how the fixed-point search (exercise 1.31) can be expressed as an iterative improvement.

2

BUILDING ABSTRACTIONS WITH DATA

> We now come to the decisive step of mathematical
> abstraction: we forget about what the symbols stand
> for.... [The mathematician] need not be idle; there
> are many operations which he may carry out with
> these symbols, without ever having to look at the
> things they stand for.
>
> Hermann Weyl, *The Mathematical Way of Thinking*

We concentrated in chapter 1 on computational processes and on the role of
procedures in program design. We saw how to use primitive data (numbers)
and primitive operators (arithmetic operators), how to combine procedures
to form compound procedures through composition, conditionals, and the
use of parameters, and how to abstract procedures by using **define**. We
saw that a procedure can be regarded as a local pattern for the evolution
of a process, and we classified, reasoned about, and performed simple
algorithmic analyses of some common patterns for processes as embodied in
procedures. We also saw that higher-order procedures enhance the power
of our language by enabling us to manipulate, and thereby to reason in
terms of, general methods of computation. This is much of the essence of
programming.

In this chapter we are going to look at more complex data. All the procedures in chapter 1 operate on simple numerical data, and simple data are
not sufficient for many of the problems we wish to address using computation. Programs are typically designed to model complex phenomena, and
more often than not one must construct computational objects that have
several parts in order to model real-world phenomena that have several
aspects. Thus, whereas our focus in chapter 1 was on building abstractions
by combining procedures to form compound procedures, we turn in this
chapter to another key aspect of any programming language: the means
it provides for building abstractions by combining data objects to form
compound data.

Why do we want compound data in a programming language? For the
same reasons that we want compound procedures: to elevate the conceptual
level at which we can design our programs, to increase the modularity of

our designs, and to enhance the expressive power of our language. Just as the ability to define procedures enables us to deal with processes at a higher conceptual level than that of the primitive operations of the language, the ability to construct compound data objects enables us to deal with data at a higher conceptual level than that of the primitive data objects of the language.

Consider the task of designing a system to perform arithmetic with rational numbers. We could imagine an operator +rat that takes two rational numbers as arguments and produces their sum. In terms of simple data, a rational number can be thought of as two integers: a numerator and a denominator. Thus, we could design a program in which each rational number would be reflected by two integers (a numerator and a denominator) and where +rat would be implemented by two procedures (one producing the numerator of the sum and one producing the denominator). But this would be awkward, because we would then need to explicitly keep track of which numerators corresponded to which denominators. In a system intended to perform many operations on many rational numbers, such bookkeeping details would clutter the programs substantially, to say nothing of what they would do to our minds. It would be much better if we could "glue together" a numerator and denominator to form a pair—a *compound data object*—that our programs could manipulate in a way that would be consistent with regarding a rational number as a single conceptual unit.

The use of compound data also enables us to increase the modularity of our programs. If we can manipulate rational numbers directly as objects in their own right, then we can separate the part of our program that deals with rational numbers per se from the details of how rational numbers may be represented as pairs of integers. The general technique of isolating the parts of a program that deal with how data objects are represented from the parts of a program that deal with how data objects are used is a powerful design methodology called *data abstraction*. We will see how data abstraction makes programs much easier to design, maintain, and modify.

The use of compound data leads to a real increase in the expressive power of our programming language. Consider the idea of forming a "linear combination" $ax+by$. We might like to write a procedure that would accept a, b, x, and y as arguments and return the value of $ax + by$. This presents no difficulty if the arguments are to be numbers, because we can readily define the procedure

```
(define (linear-combination a b x y)
  (+ (* a x) (* b y)))
```

But suppose we are not concerned only with numbers. Suppose we would like to express, in procedural terms, the idea that one can form linear combinations whenever addition and multiplication are defined—for rational numbers, complex numbers, polynomials, or whatever. We could express this as a procedure of the form

```
(define (linear-combination a b x y)
  (add (mul a x) (mul b y)))
```

where add and mul are not the primitive procedures + and * but rather more complex things that will perform the appropriate operations for whatever kinds of data we pass in as the arguments a, b, x, and y. The key point is that the only thing linear-combination should need to know about a, b, x, and y is that the operators add and mul will perform the appropriate manipulations. From the perspective of the procedure linear-combination, it is irrelevant what a, b, x, and y are and even more irrelevant how they might happen to be represented in terms of more primitive data. This same example shows why it is important that our programming language provide the ability to manipulate compound objects directly: Without this, there is no way for a procedure such as linear-combination to pass its arguments along to add and mul without having to know their detailed structure.[1]

We begin this chapter by implementing the rational-number arithmetic system mentioned above. This will form the background for our discussion of compound data and data abstraction. As with compound procedures, the main issue to be addressed is that of abstraction as a technique for coping with complexity, and we will see how data abstraction enables us to erect suitable *abstraction barriers* between different parts of a program.

We will see that the key to forming compound data is that a programming language should provide some kind of "glue" so that data objects can be combined to form more complex data objects. There are many possible kinds of glue. Indeed, we will discover how to form compound data using no special "data" operations at all, only procedures. This will

1 The ability to directly manipulate procedures provides an analogous increase in the expressive power of a programming language. For example, in section 1.3.1 we introduced the sum procedure, which takes a procedure term as a parameter and computes the sum of the values of term over some specified interval. In order to define sum, it is crucial that we be able to speak of a procedure such as term as an entity in its own right, without regard for how term might be expressed with more primitive operations. Indeed, if we did not have the notion of "a procedure," it is doubtful that we would ever even think of the possibility of defining an operation such as sum. Moreover, insofar as performing the summation is concerned, the details of how term may be constructed from more primitive operations are irrelevant.

further blur the distinction between "procedure" and "data," which was already becoming tenuous toward the end of chapter 1. We will also explore some conventional techniques for representing sequences, trees, and symbolic expressions and apply these techniques to symbolic differentiation, the representation of sets, and the encoding of information. Next we will take up the problem of working with data that may be represented differently by different parts of a program. Complex numbers, for example, can be represented in either rectangular or polar form, and for some applications it may be desirable to be able to use both representations without sacrificing the ability to work in terms of abstract "complex numbers." This leads to the problem of implementing *generic operators* (such as add and mul, alluded to above), which must operate on many different types of data. Maintaining modularity in the presence of generic operators requires more powerful abstraction barriers than can be erected with simple data abstraction alone, and we introduce *data-directed programming* as a powerful design technique for coping with this complexity.

To illustrate the power of this approach to system design, we close the chapter by applying what we have learned to the implementation of a package for performing symbolic arithmetic on polynomials, in which the coefficients of the polynomials can be integers, rational numbers, complex numbers, and even other polynomials.

2.1 Introduction to Data Abstraction

When we discussed procedures in section 1.1.8, we noted that a procedure used as an element in creating a more complex procedure could be regarded not only as a collection of particular operations but also as a procedural abstraction. That is, the details of how the procedure was implemented could be suppressed, and the particular procedure itself could be replaced by any other procedure with the same overall behavior. In other words, we could make an abstraction that would separate the way the procedure would be used from the details of how the procedure would be implemented in terms of more primitive procedures. The analogous notion for compound data is called *data abstraction*. Data abstraction is a methodology that enables us to isolate how a compound data object is used from the details of how it is constructed from more primitive data objects.

The basic idea of data abstraction is to structure the programs that are to use compound data objects so that they operate on "abstract data." That is, our programs should use data in such a way as to make no assumptions about the data that are not strictly necessary for performing the task at hand. At the same time, a "concrete" data representation is defined independent of the programs that use the data. The interface between these two parts of our system will be a set of procedures, called *selectors* and *constructors*, that implement the abstract data in terms of the concrete representation. To illustrate this technique, we will consider how to design a set of procedures for manipulating rational numbers.

2.1.1 Example: Arithmetic Operators for Rational Numbers

Suppose we want to do arithmetic with rational numbers. We want to be able to add, subtract, multiply, and divide them and to test whether two rational numbers are equal.

Let us begin by assuming that we already have a way of constructing a rational number from a numerator and a denominator. We also assume that, given a rational number, we have a way of extracting or selecting its numerator and its denominator. Let us further assume that the constructor and selectors are available as procedures:

(make-rat $\langle n \rangle$ $\langle d \rangle$) returns the rational number whose numerator is the integer $\langle n \rangle$ and whose denominator is the integer $\langle d \rangle$.

(numer $\langle x \rangle$) returns the numerator of the rational number $\langle x \rangle$.

(denom $\langle x \rangle$) returns the denominator of the rational number $\langle x \rangle$.

We are using here a powerful strategy of synthesis: wishful thinking. We haven't yet said how a rational number is represented, or how the procedures numer, denom, and make-rat should be implemented. Even so, if we did have these three procedures, we could then add, subtract, multiply, divide, and test equality by using the following relations:

$$\frac{n_1}{d_1} + \frac{n_2}{d_2} = \frac{n_1 d_2 + n_2 d_1}{d_1 d_2},$$

$$\frac{n_1}{d_1} - \frac{n_2}{d_2} = \frac{n_1 d_2 - n_2 d_1}{d_1 d_2},$$

$$\frac{n_1}{d_1} \cdot \frac{n_2}{d_2} = \frac{n_1 n_2}{d_1 d_2},$$

$$\frac{n_1/d_1}{n_2/d_2} = \frac{n_1 d_2}{d_1 n_2},$$

$$\frac{n_1}{d_1} = \frac{n_2}{d_2} \text{ if and only if } n_1 d_2 = n_2 d_1.$$

We can express these rules as Lisp procedures:

```
(define (+rat x y)
  (make-rat (+ (* (numer x) (denom y))
               (* (denom x) (numer y)))
            (* (denom x) (denom y))))

(define (-rat x y)
  (make-rat (- (* (numer x) (denom y))
               (* (denom x) (numer y)))
            (* (denom x) (denom y))))

(define (*rat x y)
  (make-rat (* (numer x) (numer y))
            (* (denom x) (denom y))))

(define (/rat x y)
  (make-rat (* (numer x) (denom y))
            (* (denom x) (numer y))))

(define (=rat x y)
  (= (* (numer x) (denom y))
     (* (numer y) (denom x))))
```

Now we have the operators on rational numbers defined in terms of the selector and constructor procedures numer, denom, and make-rat. But we haven't yet defined these. What we need is some way to glue together a numerator and a denominator to form a rational number.

Pairs

To enable us to implement the more concrete level of our data abstraction, our language provides a compound structure called a *pair*, which can be constructed with the primitive procedure cons. This procedure takes two arguments and returns a compound data object that contains the two arguments as parts. Given a pair, we can extract the parts using the primitive procedures car and cdr.[2] Thus, we can use cons, car, and cdr as follows:

```
==> (define x (cons 1 2))
x
```

---

2 The name cons stands for "construct." The names car and cdr relate to the original implementation of Lisp on the IBM 704. That machine had an addressing scheme that allowed one to reference the "address" and "decrement" parts of a memory location. Car stands for "contents of address register" and cdr (pronounced "could-er") stands for "contents of decrement register."

```
==> (car x)
1

==> (cdr x)
2
```

Notice that a pair is a real data object that can be given a name and manipulated, just like any data object. Moreover, cons can be used to form pairs whose elements are pairs, and so on:

```
==> (define x (cons 1 2))
x

==> (define y (cons 3 4))
y

==> (define z (cons x y))
z

==> (car (car z))
1

==> (car (cdr z))
3
```

In section 2.2 we will see how this ability to combine pairs means that pairs can be used as general-purpose building blocks to create all sorts of complex data structures. The single compound-data primitive *pair*, implemented by the procedures cons, car, and cdr, is the only glue we need. Data objects constructed from pairs are called *list-structured* data.

Representing rational numbers

Pairs offer a natural way to complete the rational-number system. Simply represent a rational number as a pair of two integers: a numerator and a denominator. Then make-rat, numer, and denom are readily implemented as follows:

```
(define (make-rat n d) (cons n d))

(define (numer x) (car x))

(define (denom x) (cdr x))
```

Also, in order to display the results of our computations, we can choose
to print a rational number by printing the numerator, a slash, and the
denominator:[3]

```
(define (print-rat x)
  (newline)
  (princ (numer x))
  (princ "/")
  (princ (denom x)))
```

Now we can try our rational-number functions:

```
==> (define one-half (make-rat 1 2))
one-half

==> (print-rat one-half)
1/2

==> (define one-third (make-rat 1 3))
one-third

==> (print-rat (+rat one-half one-third))
5/6

==> (print-rat (*rat one-half one-third))
1/6

==> (print-rat (+rat one-third one-third))
6/9
```

As the final example shows, our rational-number implementation does not
reduce rational numbers to lowest terms. We can remedy this by changing make-rat. If we have a gcd procedure like the one in section 1.2.5
that produces the greatest common divisor of two integers, we can use gcd
to reduce the numerator and the denominator to lowest terms before constructing the pair:

---

3 Print and princ are the Scheme procedures for printing data. They are similar, except
that print starts a new line for printing and terminates its output with a space, whereas
princ does not. We implement print-rat using princ because we want the numerator,
the slash, and the denominator to be printed on the same line. The Scheme procedure
newline starts a new line for printing. (Normally, print does this automatically.)

```
(define (make-rat n d)
  (let ((g (gcd n d)))
    (cons (/ n g) (/ d g))))
```

Now we have

```
==> (print-rat (+rat one-third one-third))
```
2/3

as desired. This modification was accomplished by changing the constructor make-rat without changing any of the procedures that implement the actual operators such as +rat and *rat.

Exercise 2.1

This version of make-rat is not quite correct; make-rat might be called with negative values for n and d, and the gcd procedure of section 1.2.5 was defined to work only with positive integers. Define a better version of make-rat that handles both positive and negative arguments. Make-rat should normalize the sign so that if the rational number is positive, both the numerator and denominator are positive, and if the rational number is negative, only the numerator is negative.

2.1.2 Abstraction Barriers

Before continuing with more examples of compound data and data abstraction, let us consider some of the issues raised by the rational-number example. We defined the rational-number operators in terms of a constructor make-rat and selectors numer and denom. In general, the underlying idea of data abstraction is to identify for each type of data object a basic set of operators in terms of which all manipulations of data objects of that type will be expressed, and then to use only those operators in manipulating the data.

We can envision the structure of our system as shown in figure 2.1. The thick horizontal lines represent *abstraction barriers* that isolate different "levels" of the system. Programs that use rational numbers manipulate them solely in terms of the operators supplied "for public use" by the rational-number package: +rat, -rat, *rat, /rat, and =rat. These, in turn, are implemented solely in terms of the constructor and selectors make-rat, numer, and denom, which themselves are implemented in terms of pairs. The details of how pairs are implemented are irrelevant to the rest of the rational-number package so long as pairs can be manipulated by the use of cons, car, and cdr. In effect, procedures at each level are the interfaces that define the abstraction barriers and connect the different levels.

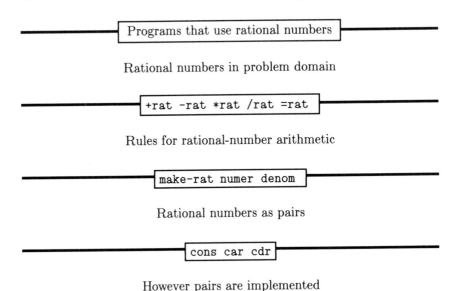

Figure 2.1
Data-abstraction barriers in the rational-number package.

This simple idea has many advantages. One advantage is that it makes programs much easier to maintain and to modify. Any complex data structure can be represented in a variety of ways with the primitive data structures provided by a programming language. Of course, the choice of representation influences the programs that operate on it; thus, if the representation were to be changed at some later time, all such programs might have to be modified accordingly. This task could be time-consuming and expensive in the case of large programs unless the dependence on the representation were to be confined by design to a very few program modules.

For example, an alternate way to address the problem of reducing rational numbers to lowest terms is to perform the reduction whenever we access the parts of a rational number, rather than when we construct it. This leads to different constructor and selector procedures:

```
(define (make-rat n d)
  (cons n d))

(define (numer x)
  (let ((g (gcd (car x) (cdr x))))
    (/ (car x) g)))
```

```
(define (denom x)
  (let ((g (gcd (car x) (cdr x))))
    (/ (cdr x) g)))
```

The difference between this implementation and the previous one lies in when we compute the gcd. If we examine rational numbers often, it would be better to compute the gcd once in constructing them. If not, we may be better off waiting until access time or even print time to compute the gcd. In any case, when we change from one representation to the other the operators +rat, -rat, and so on do not have to be modified at all.

Constraining the dependence on the representation to a few interface procedures helps us to design programs as well as to modify them, because it allows us to maintain the flexibility to consider alternate implementations. To continue with our simple example, suppose we are designing a rational-number package and we can't decide initially whether to perform the gcd at construction time or at selection time. The data-abstraction methodology gives us a way to defer that decision without losing the ability to make progress on the rest of the system.

Exercise 2.2

Consider the problem of representing line segments on a two-dimensional plane. Each segment is represented as a pair of points: a starting point and an ending point. Define a constructor make-segment and selectors start-point and end-point that define the representation of segments in terms of points. Furthermore, a point can be represented as a pair of numbers: the x coordinate and the y coordinate. Accordingly, specify a constructor make-point and selectors x-coord and y-coord that define this representation. Finally, using your selectors and constructors, define a procedure midpoint that takes a line segment as argument and returns the midpoint (the point whose coordinates are the average of the coordinates of the endpoints).

2.1.3 What Is Meant by Data?

We began the rational-number implementation in section 2.1.1 by implementing the rational-number operators +rat, -rat, and so on in terms of three unspecified procedures: make-rat, numer, and denom. At that point, we could think of the operators as being defined in terms of data objects (numerators, denominators, and rational numbers) whose behavior was specified by the latter three procedures.

But exactly what is meant by *data*? It is not enough to say "whatever is implemented by the given selectors and constructors," for clearly any arbitrary three procedures could not serve as an appropriate basis for the rational-number implementation. We need to guarantee that, if we construct a rational number x from a pair of integers n and d, extracting the numerator and the denominator of x and forming the quotient should yield a rational number equal to n/d. In other words, make-rat, numer, and denom must satisfy the condition that, for any integers n and d, if x is (make-rat n d), then

$$\frac{(\texttt{numer x})}{(\texttt{denom x})} = \frac{n}{d}.$$

In fact, this is the only condition make-rat, numer, and denom must fulfill in order to form a suitable basis for a rational-number representation. In general, we can think of data as defined by some collection of selectors and constructors, together with specified conditions that these procedures must fulfill in order to be a valid representation.[4]

This point of view can serve to define not only "high-level" data objects, such as rational numbers, but lower-level objects as well. Consider the notion of a pair, which we used in order to define our rational numbers. We never actually said what a pair was, only that the language supplied operators cons, car, and cdr for operating on pairs. But the only thing we need to know about these three operators is that if we glue two objects together using cons we can retrieve the objects using car and cdr. That is, the operators satisfy the condition that, for any objects x and y, if z is (cons x y) then (car z) is x and (cdr z) is y. Indeed, we mentioned that these three operators are included as primitives in our language. However, any triple of procedures that satisfies the above condition can be used as

---

4 Surprisingly, this idea is very difficult to formulate rigorously. In fact, despite an enormous amount of work in programming-language semantics, the notion of a data object, which is so important and pervasive in modern programming practice, does not have a completely satisfactory mathematical treatment. There are two approaches to giving such a treatment. One approach, pioneered by C. A. R. Hoare (1972), is known as the method of *abstract models*. It formalizes the "procedures plus conditions" specification as outlined in the rational-number example above. Note that the condition on the rational-number representation was stated in terms of facts about integers (equality and division). In general, abstract models define new kinds of data objects in terms of previously defined types of data objects. Assertions about data objects can therefore be checked by reducing them to assertions about previously defined data objects. Another approach, introduced by J. Guttag (1977), is called *algebraic specification*. It regards the "operators" as elements of an abstract algebraic system whose behavior is specified by axioms that correspond to our "conditions," and uses the techniques of abstract algebra to check assertions about data objects. Both methods are surveyed in the paper by Liskov and Zilles (1975). These methods work well for simple examples, but they become very complex and even break down in complicated situations and they have difficulties in dealing with "mutable" data objects such as will be introduced in the next chapter. Resolving these difficulties is an active area of research.

the basis for implementing pairs. This point is illustrated strikingly by the fact that we could implement cons, car, and cdr without using any data structures at all but only using procedures. Here are the definitions:

```
(define (cons x y)
  (define (dispatch m)
    (cond ((= m 0) x)
          ((= m 1) y)
          (else (error "Argument not 0 or 1 -- CONS" m))))
  dispatch)

(define (car z) (z 0))

(define (cdr z) (z 1))
```

This is an extremely convoluted use of procedures, and it corresponds to nothing like our intuitive notion of what data should be. Nevertheless, all we need to do to show that this is a valid way to represent pairs is to verify that these procedures satisfy the condition given above.

The subtle point to notice is that the value returned by (cons x y) is a procedure—namely the internally defined procedure dispatch, which takes one argument and returns either x or y depending on whether the argument is 0 or 1. Correspondingly, (car z) is defined to apply z to 0. Hence, if z is the procedure formed by (cons x y), then z applied to 0 will yield x. Thus, we have shown that (car (cons x y)) yields x, as desired. Similarly, (cdr (cons x y)) applies the procedure returned by (cons x y) to 1, which returns y. Therefore, this procedural implementation of pairs is a valid implementation, and if we access pairs using only cons, car, and cdr we cannot distinguish this implementation from one that uses "real" data structures.

The point of this is not that our language works this way (Lisp systems implement pairs directly, for efficiency reasons) but that it could work this way. The above representation, although obscure, is a perfectly adequate way to represent pairs, since it fulfills the only conditions that pairs need to fulfill. As an interesting sidelight, we see that the ability to manipulate procedures as objects automatically provides the ability to represent compound data. This may seem a curiosity now, but procedural representations of data will play a central role in our programming repertoire. This style of programming is often called *message passing*, and we will be using it as a basic tool in chapter 3 when we address the issues of modeling and simulation.

Exercise 2.3

Given the following procedural representation, verify that (car (cons x y))
yields x for any objects x and y.

```
(define (cons x y)
  (lambda (m) (m x y)))

(define (car z)
  (z (lambda (p q) p)))
```

What is the corresponding definition of cdr? (Hint: To verify that this works,
make careful use of the substitution model of section 1.1.5.)

Exercise 2.4

Show that we can represent pairs of nonnegative integers using only numbers and
arithmetic operations if we represent the pair a and b as the integer that is the
product $2^a 3^b$. Give the corresponding definitions of the procedures cons, car,
and cdr.

Exercise 2.5

In case representing pairs as procedures wasn't mind-boggling enough, consider
that, in a language that can manipulate procedures, we can get by without
numbers (at least insofar as nonnegative integers are concerned) by implementing
0 and the operation of adding 1 as

```
(define zero (lambda (f) (lambda (x) x)))

(define (1+ n)
  (lambda (f) (lambda (x) (f ((n f) x)))))
```

This representation is known as *Church numerals*, after its inventor Alonzo
Church, the logician who invented the λ calculus.

Define one and two directly (not in terms of zero and 1+). (Hint: Use substitution to evaluate (1+ zero)). Give a direct definition of the addition operator +
(without introducing any auxiliary procedures).

2.1.4 Example: Interval Arithmetic

Alyssa P. Hacker is designing a system to help people solve engineering
problems. One feature she wants to provide in her system is the ability
to manipulate inexact quantities (such as measured parameters of physical
devices) with known precision, so that when computations are done with
such approximate quantities the results will be numbers of known precision.

Electrical engineers will be using Alyssa's system to compute electrical
quantities. It is sometimes necessary for them to compute the value of

a parallel equivalent resistance R_p of two resistors R_1 and R_2 using the formula

$$R_p = \frac{1}{1/R_1 + 1/R_2}.$$

Resistance values are usually known only up to some tolerance guaranteed by the manufacturer of the resistor. For example, if you buy a resistor labeled "6.8 ohms with 10% tolerance" you can only be sure that the resistor has a resistance between $6.8 - 0.68 = 6.12$ and $6.8 + 0.68 = 7.48$ ohms. Thus, if you have a 6.8-ohm 10% resistor in parallel with a 4.7-ohm 5% resistor, the resistance of the combination can range from about 2.58 ohms (if the two resistors are at the lower bounds) to about 2.97 ohms (if the two resistors are at the upper bounds).

Alyssa's idea is to implement "interval arithmetic" as a set of primitive arithmetic operators for combining "intervals" (objects that represent the range of possible values of an inexact quantity). The result of adding, subtracting, multiplying, or dividing two intervals is itself a new interval representing the range of the result.

Alyssa postulates the existence of an abstract object called an "interval" that has two endpoints: a lower bound and an upper bound. She also presumes that, given the endpoints of an interval, she can construct the interval using the data constructor `make-interval`. Alyssa first writes `intadd` for adding two intervals. She reasons that the minimum value the sum could be is the sum of the two lower bounds and the maximum value it could be is the sum of the two upper bounds:

```
(define (intadd x y)
  (make-interval (+ (lower-bound x) (lower-bound y))
                 (+ (upper-bound x) (upper-bound y))))
```

Alyssa also works out the product of two intervals by finding the minimum and the maximum of the products of the bounds and using them as the bounds of the resulting interval. (Min and max are primitives that find the minimum or maximum of any number of arguments.)

```
(define (intmul x y)
  (let ((p1 (* (lower-bound x) (lower-bound y)))
        (p2 (* (lower-bound x) (upper-bound y)))
        (p3 (* (upper-bound x) (lower-bound y)))
        (p4 (* (upper-bound x) (upper-bound y))))
    (make-interval (min p1 p2 p3 p4)
                   (max p1 p2 p3 p4))))
```

To divide two intervals, Alyssa multiplies the first by the reciprocal of the second. Note that the bounds of the reciprocal interval are the reciprocal of the upper bound and the reciprocal of the lower bound, in that order.

```
(define (intdiv x y)
  (intmul x
          (make-interval (/ 1 (upper-bound y))
                         (/ 1 (lower-bound y)))))
```

Exercise 2.6

Alyssa's program is incomplete because she has not specified the implementation of the interval abstraction. Here is a definition of the constructor make-interval:

```
(define (make-interval a b) (cons a b))
```

Complete the implementation by defining selectors upper-bound and lower-bound.

Exercise 2.7

Using reasoning analogous to Alyssa's, describe how the difference of two intervals may be computed. Define a corresponding subtraction procedure, called intsub.

Exercise 2.8

The *width* of an interval is the difference between its upper and lower bounds. The width is a measure of the uncertainty of the number specified by the interval. For some arithmetic operators the width of the result of combining two intervals is a function only of the widths of the argument intervals, whereas for others the width of the combination is not a function of the widths of the argument intervals. Show that the width of the sum (or difference) of two intervals is a function only of the widths of the intervals being added (or subtracted). Give examples to show that this is not true for multiplication or division.

Exercise 2.9

Ben Bitdiddle, an expert systems programmer, looks over Alyssa's shoulder and comments that it is not clear what it means to divide by an interval that spans zero. Modify Alyssa's code to check for this condition and to signal an error if it occurs.

Exercise 2.10

In passing, Ben also cryptically comments: "By testing the signs of the endpoints of the intervals passed to intmul, it is possible to break intmul into nine cases, only one of which requires more than two multiplications." Rewrite `intmul` using Ben's suggestion.

After debugging her program, Alyssa shows it to a potential user, who complains that her program solves the wrong problem. He wants a program that can deal with numbers represented as a center value and an additive tolerance; for example, he wants to work with intervals such as 3.5 ± 0.15 rather than $[3.35, 3.65]$. Alyssa returns to her desk and fixes this problem by supplying an alternate constructor and alternate selectors:

```
(define (center-width c w)
  (make-interval (- c w) (+ c w)))

(define (center i)
  (/ (+ (lower-bound i) (upper-bound i)) 2))

(define (width i)
  (/ (- (upper-bound i) (lower-bound i)) 2))
```

Unfortunately, most of Alyssa's users are engineers. Real engineering situations usually involve measurements with only a small uncertainty, measured as the ratio of the width of the interval to the midpoint of the interval. Engineers usually specify percentage tolerances on the parameters of devices, as in the resistor specifications given earlier.

Exercise 2.11

Define a constructor `make-center-percent` that takes a center and a percentage tolerance and produces the desired interval. You must also define a selector `percent` that produces the correct percentage tolerance for a given interval. The `center` selector is the same as the one shown above.

Exercise 2.12

Show that under the assumption of small percentage tolerances there is a simple formula for the approximate percentage tolerance of the product of two intervals in terms of the tolerances of the factors. You may simplify the problem by assuming that all numbers are positive.

After considerable work, Alyssa P. Hacker delivers her finished system. Several years later, after she has forgotten all about it, she gets a frenzied call from an irate user. It seems that the user has noticed that the formula for parallel resistors can be written in two algebraically equivalent ways:

$$\frac{R_1 R_2}{R_1 + R_2}$$

and

$$\frac{1}{1/R_1 + 1/R_2} .$$

The user has written the following two programs, each of which computes the parallel-resistors formula differently:

```
(define (par1 r1 r2)
  (intdiv (intmul r1 r2)
          (intadd r1 r2)))

(define (par2 r1 r2)
  (let ((one (make-interval 1 1)))
       (intdiv one
               (intadd (intdiv one r1)
                       (intdiv one r2)))))
```

The user complains that Alyssa's program gives different answers for the two ways of computing. This is a serious complaint.

Exercise 2.13

Demonstrate that the user is right. Investigate the behavior of the system on a variety of expressions. Make some intervals A and B, and use them in computing the expressions A/A and A/B. You will get the most insight by using intervals whose width is a small percentage of the center value. Examine the results of the computation in center-percent form.

Exercise 2.14

Eva Lu Ator, another user, has also noticed the different intervals computed by different but algebraically equivalent expressions. She says that a formula to compute with intervals using Alyssa's system will produce tighter error bounds if it can be written in such a form that no variable that represents an uncertain number is repeated. Thus, she says, par2 is a "better" program for parallel resistances than par1. Is she right? Why?

Exercise 2.15

Explain, in general, why equivalent algebraic expressions may lead to different answers. Can you devise an interval-arithmetic package that does not have this shortcoming, or is this task impossible? (Warning: This problem is very difficult.)

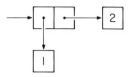

Figure 2.2
Box-and-pointer representation of (cons 1 2).

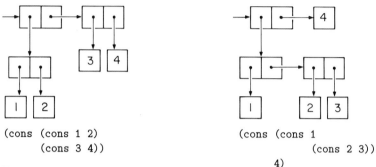

(cons (cons 1 2)   (cons (cons 1
     (cons 3 4))   (cons 2 3))
                                                             4)

Figure 2.3
Two ways to combine 1, 2, 3, and 4 using pairs.

2.2 Hierarchical Data

As we have seen, pairs provide a primitive "glue" that we can use to construct compound data objects. Figure 2.2 shows a standard way to visualize a pair—in this case, the pair formed by (cons 1 2). In this representation, which is called *box-and-pointer notation*, each object is shown as a *pointer* to a box. The box for a primitive object contains a representation of the object. For example, the box for a number contains a numeral. The box for a pair is actually a double box, the left part containing (a pointer to) the car of the pair and the right part containing the cdr.

It was already mentioned that cons can be used to combine not only numbers but other pairs as well. (You made use of this fact, or should have, in doing exercise 2.2.) As a consequence, pairs provide a universal building block from which we can construct all sorts of data structures. Figure 2.3 shows two ways to use pairs to combine the numbers 1, 2, 3, and 4.

In general, pairs enable us to represent *hierarchical* data—data made up of parts, which themselves are made up of parts, and so on. As figure 2.3 indicates, we can use pairs to combine data in many different ways, and we begin this section by exploring some conventional techniques for using pairs to represent sequences and trees. Next, we will augment the repre-

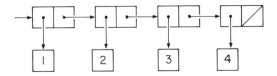

Figure 2.4
The sequence 1, 2, 3, 4 represented as a sequence of pairs.

sentational power of our language by introducing *symbolic expressions*—
data whose elementary parts can be arbitrary symbols rather than only
numbers. We will then explore various alternatives for representing sets
of objects. We will find that, just as a given numerical function can be
computed by many different computational processes, there are many ways
in which a given data structure can be represented in terms of simpler
objects, and the choice of representation can have significant impact on
the time and space requirements of processes that manipulate the data. We
will also investigate Huffman encoding as a clever use of trees to implement
efficient codes.

2.2.1 Representing Sequences

One of the useful structures we can build with pairs is a *sequence*—an
ordered collection of data objects. There, are, of course, many ways to
represent sequences in terms of pairs. One particularly straightforward
representation is illustrated in figure 2.4, where the sequence 1, 2, 3, 4 is
represented as a sequence of pairs. The car of each pair is the corresponding
item in the sequence, and the cdr of the pair is the next pair in the sequence.
The cdr of the final pair signals the end of the sequence by pointing
to a distinguished element, represented in box-and-pointer diagrams as a
diagonal line and in Lisp programs as the value of the symbol nil. This
sequence is constructed by nested cons operations:

```
(cons 1
      (cons 2
            (cons 3
                  (cons 4 nil))))
```

Such a sequence of pairs, formed by nested conses, is called a *list*,[5] and
Lisp provides a primitive called list to help in constructing lists. The
above sequence could be produced by (list 1 2 3 4). In general,

(list $\langle a_1 \rangle$ $\langle a_2 \rangle$ ... $\langle a_n \rangle$)

---

5 The term *list structure* refers to any data structure made out of pairs, not just to lists.

is equivalent to

(cons ⟨a₁⟩ (cons ⟨a₂⟩ (cons ... (cons ⟨aₙ⟩ nil) ...))).

Lisp conventionally prints lists by printing the sequence of elements, enclosed in parentheses. Thus, the data object in figure 2.4 is printed as (1 2 3 4):

```
==> (define 1-through-4 (list 1 2 3 4))
1-through-4
```

```
==> 1-through-4
(1 2 3 4)
```

Be careful not to confuse the expression (list 1 2 3 4) with the list (1 2 3 4), which is the result obtained when the expression is evaluated. Attempting to evaluate the list (1 2 3 4) as an expression would signal an error when the interpreter tried to apply the procedure 1 to arguments 2, 3, and 4.

We can think of car as selecting the first item in the list, and of cdr as selecting the sublist consisting of all but the first item. Nested applications of car and cdr can be used to extract the second, third, and subsequent items in the list.[6] The constructor cons adds a new item to the beginning of a list.

```
==> (car 1-through-4)
1
```

```
==> (cdr 1-through-4)
(2 3 4)
```

```
==> (car (cdr 1-through-4))
2
```

```
==> (cons 10 1-through-4)
(10 1 2 3 4)
```

The value of nil, used to terminate the chain of pairs, can be thought of

---

[6] Since nested applications of car and cdr are cumbersome to write, Lisp provides abbreviations for them—for instance,

(cadr ⟨arg⟩) = (car (cdr ⟨arg⟩))

The names of all such procedures start with c and end with r. Each a between them stands for a car operator and each d for a cdr operator, to be applied in the same order in which they appear in the name. The names car and cdr persist because simple combinations like cadr are pronounceable.

as a sequence of no elements, the *empty list*. Indeed, *nil* is a contraction of
the Latin word for nothing.[7]

List operations

The use of pairs to represent sequences of elements as lists is accompanied
by conventional programming techniques for manipulating lists by successively "cdring down" the lists. For example, the procedure nth takes as
arguments a number n and a list and returns the nth item of the list. It
is customary to number the elements of the list beginning with 0. The
method for computing nth is the following:

- For $n = 0$, nth should return the car of the list.

- Otherwise, nth should return the $(n-1)$st item of the cdr of the list.

```
(define (nth n x)
  (if (= n 0)
      (car x)
      (nth (- n 1) (cdr x))))
```

```
==> (define squares (list 1 4 9 16 25))
squares
```

```
==> (nth 3 squares)
16
```

Often we cdr down the whole list. To aid in this, Lisp includes a primitive
predicate null?, which tests whether its argument is the empty list. Here
is a typical procedure length, which returns the number of items in a list:

```
(define (length x)
  (if (null? x)
      0
      (+ 1 (length (cdr x)))))
```

```
==> (define odds (list 1 3 5 7))
odds
```

```
==> (length odds)
4
```

---

7 Recall from section 1.1.6 that the value of nil is returned by a predicate to indicate
"false." This mixing of logical operations with list operations is sometimes convenient
but more often leads to programming errors. People who do not like Lisp regard this
feature as one of their favorite things not to like.

The `length` procedure implements a simple recursive plan. The reduction step is:

• The `length` of any list is 1 plus the `length` of the `cdr` of the list.

This is applied successively until we reach the base case:

• The `length` of the empty list is 0.

We could also compute `length` in an iterative style:

```
(define (length x)
  (define (length-iter a count)
    (if (null? a)
        count
        (length-iter (cdr a) (+ 1 count))))
  (length-iter x 0))
```

Another conventional programming technique is to "cons up" an answer list while cdring down a list. The procedure `append` takes two lists as arguments and combines their elements to make a new list:

```
==> (append squares odds)
```
(1 4 9 16 25 1 3 5 7)

```
==> (append odds squares)
```
(1 3 5 7 1 4 9 16 25)

Append is also implemented using a recursive plan. To append lists `x` and `y`, do the following.

• If `x` is the empty list, then the result is just `y`.

• Otherwise, append the `cdr` of `x` and `y` and cons the `car` of `x` onto the result:

```
(define (append x y)
  (if (null? x)
      y
      (cons (car x) (append (cdr x) y))))
```

Exercise 2.16

Define a procedure `last` that returns the list that contains only the last element of a given (nonempty) list:

```
==> (last squares)
```
(25)

Exercise 2.17

Define a procedure `reverse` that takes a list as argument and returns a list of the same elements in reverse order:

```
==> (reverse squares)
(25 16 9 4 1)
```

Exercise 2.18

One very common programming technique is to apply a given procedure to each item in a list by cdring down the list and consing up an answer. Suppose you want a procedure `square-list` that, when given a list of numbers, returns a list of the squares of those numbers.

```
==> (define 1-through-4 (list 1 2 3 4))
1-through-4

==> (square-list 1-through-4)
(1 4 9 16)
```

Fill in the missing expressions to complete the definition of `square-list`:

```
(define (square-list x)
  (if (null? x)
      nil
      (cons (square ⟨??⟩)
            (square-list ⟨??⟩)))))
```

Exercise 2.19

Louis Reasoner tries to rewrite the `square-list` procedure of exercise 2.18 as an iteration:

```
(define (square-list x)
  (define (iter list answer)
    (if (null? list)
        answer
        (iter (cdr list)
              (cons (square (car list))
                    answer))))
  (iter x nil))
```

Unfortunately, defining `square-list` this way produces the answer list in the reverse order of the one desired. Why?

Louis then tries to fix his bug by interchanging the arguments to `cons`:

```
(define (square-list x)
  (define (iter list answer)
    (if (null? list)
        answer
        (iter (cdr list)
              (cons answer
                    (square (car list)))))))
  (iter x nil))
```

This doesn't quite work either. Explain.

Exercise 2.20

We can improve on exercise 2.18 by following the method of section 1.3 to introduce a higher-order procedure that expresses the general operation of applying a
procedure to every item in a list and returning the list of results. This procedure,
traditionally called mapcar, is used as follows:

```
==> (mapcar square 1-through-4)
(1 4 9 16)
```

```
==> (mapcar 1+ 1-through-4)
(2 3 4 5)
```

Give an appropriate definition of mapcar.[8]

Exercise 2.21

Consider the change-counting program of section 1.2.2. It would be nice to be
able to change the currency used by the program easily, so that we could compute
the number of ways to change a British pound, for example. As the program is
written, the knowledge of the currency is distributed partly into the procedure
first-denomination and partly into the procedure count-change (which knows
that there are five different kinds of U.S. coins). It would be nicer to be able to
supply a list of coins to be used for making change.

We want to rewrite the essential procedure, cc, so that its second argument,
kinds-of-coins, is a list of coins to use rather than an integer specifying which
coins to use. We could then have lists that defined each kind of currency:

```
(define us-coins (list 50 25 10 5 1))
```

```
(define uk-coins (list 100 50 20 10 5 2 1 .5))
```

We could then call cc as follows:

```
==> (cc 100 us-coins)
292
```

---

8 Mapcar barely hints at the expressive power to be gained by combining higher-order
procedures with hierarchical data. We will have much more to say about this in chapter
3 (section 3.4.2).

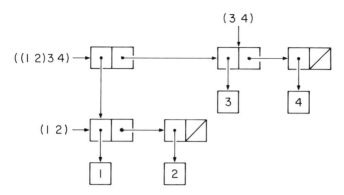

Figure 2.5
Structure formed by (cons (list 1 2) (list 3 4)).

To do this will require changing the program cc somewhat. It will still have the same form, but it will access its second argument differently, as follows:

```
(define (cc amount kinds-of-coins)
  (cond ((= amount 0) 1)
        ((or (< amount 0) (no-more? kinds-of-coins)) 0)
        (else (+ (cc (- amount (first-denomination kinds-of-coins))
                     kinds-of-coins)
                 (cc amount
                     (except-first-denomination kinds-of-coins))))))
```

Define the procedures first-denomination, except-first-denomination, and no-more? in terms of the primitive operators on list structures. Does the order of the list kinds-of-coins affect the answer produced by cc? Why or why not?

2.2.2 Representing Trees

The representation of sequences in terms of lists generalizes naturally to enable us to represent sequences whose elements may themselves be sequences. For example, we can regard the object

```
==> (cons (list 1 2) (list 3 4))
```
((1 2) 3 4)

as a list of three items, the first of which is itself the list (1 2). Indeed, this is suggested by the form in which the result is printed by the interpreter. Figure 2.5 shows the representation of this structure in terms of pairs.

Another way to think of sequences whose elements are sequences is as *trees*. The elements of the sequence are the branches of the tree, and elements that are themselves sequences are subtrees. Figure 2.6 shows the structure in figure 2.5 viewed as a tree.

((1 2) 3 4)

Figure 2.6
The pair structure in figure 2.5, viewed as a tree.

Exercise 2.22

Suppose we evaluate the combination (list 1 (list 2 (list 3 4))). Give the result printed by the interpreter, the corresponding box-and-pointer structure, and the interpretation of this as a tree (as in figure 2.6).

Exercise 2.23

Give combinations of cars and cdrs that will pick 7 from each of the following lists:

(1 (2 3 (5 7) 9))

((7))

(1 (2 (3 (4 (5 (6 7))))))

Exercise 2.24

Suppose we define x and y to be two lists:

(define x (list 1 2 3))

(define y (list 4 5 6))

What result is printed by the interpreter in response to evaluating each of the following expressions:

(append x y)

(cons x y)

(list x y)

Recursion is a natural tool for dealing with tree structures, since we can often reduce operations on trees to operations on their branches, which reduce in turn to operations on the branches of the branches, and so on, until we reach the leaves of the tree. To aid in writing recursive procedures on trees, Lisp provides the primitive predicate atom?, which tests whether its argument is *atomic* (i.e., not a pair). As an example, compare the length procedure of section 2.2.1 with the countatoms procedure, which returns the total number of atoms at all levels of a tree:

```
==> (define x (cons (list 1 2) (list 3 4)))
x

==> (length x)
3

==> (countatoms x)
4

==> (list x x)
((((1 2) 3 4) ((1 2) 3 4))

==> (length (list x x))
2

==> (countatoms (list x x))
8
```

To implement countatoms, recall the recursive plan for computing length:

- Length of a list x is 1 plus length of (cdr x).
- Length of the empty list is 0.

Countatoms is similar. The value for the empty list is the same:

- Countatoms of the empty list is 0.

But in the reduction step, where we strip off the car of the list, we must take into account that (car x) may itself be a list whose atoms we need to count. Thus, the appropriate reduction step is

- (countatoms x) = (countatoms (car x)) + (countatoms (cdr x)).

Finally, if we keep taking successive cars of cars we eventually get down to atoms, so we need another base case:

- Countatoms of an atom is 1.

Here is the complete procedure:[9]

```
(define (countatoms x)
  (cond ((null? x) 0)
        ((atom? x) 1)
        (else (+ (countatoms (car x))
                 (countatoms (cdr x)))))))
```

---

9 The order of the first two clauses in the cond matters, since the empty list satisfies both null? and atom?. (The empty list is an atom because it is not a pair.)

Exercise 2.25

Modify your `reverse` procedure of exercise 2.17 to produce a procedure `deep-reverse` that takes a list as argument and returns as its value the list with its elements reversed and with all sublists deep-reversed as well. For example,

```
==> (define x (cons (list 1 2) (list 3 4)))
x

==> x
((1 2) 3 4)

==> (reverse x)
(4 3 (1 2))

==> (deep-reverse x)
(4 3 (2 1))
```

Exercise 2.26

Write a procedure `fringe` that takes a list as argument and returns a list whose elements are all the atoms appearing in the original list or any of its sublists, arranged in left-to-right order. (That is, given a tree, `fringe` returns the list of leaves of the tree.) For example,

```
==> (define x (cons (list 1 2) (list 3 4)))
x

==> (fringe x)
(1 2 3 4)

==> (fringe (list x x))
(1 2 3 4 1 2 3 4)
```

Exercise 2.27

A binary mobile consists of two branches, a left branch and a right branch. Each branch is a rod of a certain length, from which hangs either a weight or another binary mobile. We can represent a binary mobile using compound data by constructing it from two branches (for example, using `list`):

```
(define (make-mobile left right)
  (list left right))
```

A branch is constructed from a `length` (which must be a number) together with a `structure`, which may be either a number (representing a simple weight) or another mobile:

```
(define (make-branch length structure)
  (list length structure))
```

a. Supply the corresponding selectors left-branch and right-branch, which return the branches of a mobile, and branch-length and branch-structure, which return the components of a branch.

b. Using your selectors, define a procedure total-weight that returns the total weight of a mobile.

c. A mobile is said to be *balanced* if the torque applied by its top-left branch is equal to that applied by its top-right branch (that is, if the length of the left rod multiplied by the weight hanging from that rod is equal to the corresponding product for the right side) and if each of the submobiles hanging off its branches is balanced. Design a predicate that tests whether a binary mobile is balanced.

d. Suppose we change the representation of mobiles so that the constructors are now

```
(define (make-mobile left right)
  (cons left right))
```

and

```
(define (make-branch length structure)
  (cons length structure))
```

How much do you need to change your programs to convert to the new representation?

2.2.3 Symbols and the Need for Quote

All the compound data objects we have used so far were constructed ultimately from numbers. Now we extend the representational capability of our language by introducing the ability to work with arbitrary symbols as data. If we can form compound data using as atoms not only numbers but also arbitrary symbols, we can have lists such as

```
(a b c d)
(23 45 17)
((Charles 33) (Leonard 31) (Carolyn 27))
```

Lists containing symbols can look just like the expressions of our language:

```
(* (+ 23 45) (+ x 9))
```

```
(define (factorial n) (if (= n 1) 1 (* n (factorial (- n 1)))))
```

In order to manipulate symbols we need a new element in our language: the ability to *quote* a data object. Suppose we want to construct the list (a b). We can't accomplish this with (list a b), because the interpreter will think that we mean to combine in a list the *values* of a and b rather than the symbols themselves. This issue is well known in the context of natural languages, where words and sentences may be regarded either as semantic entities or as character strings (syntactic entities). The common practice in natural languages is to use quotation marks to indicate that a word or a sentence is to be treated literally as a string of characters. For instance, the first letter of "John" is clearly "J." If we tell somebody "say your name aloud," we expect to hear that person's name. However, if we tell somebody "say 'your name' aloud," we expect to hear the words "your name." Note that we are forced to nest quotation marks to describe what somebody else might say.[10]

We can follow this same practice to identify lists and atoms that are to be treated as data objects rather than as expressions to be evaluated. However, our format for quoting differs from that of natural languages in that we place a quotation mark (traditionally, the single quote symbol ') only at the beginning of the object to be quoted. We can get away with this in Lisp syntax because we rely on blanks and parentheses to delimit objects. Thus, the meaning of the single quote character is to quote the next object.[11]

Now we can distinguish between symbols and their values:

```
==> (define a 1)
a

==> (define b 2)
b

==> (list a b)
(1 2)
```

---

10 Allowing quote in a language wreaks havoc with the ability to reason simply about the language, because it destroys the notion that equals can be substituted for equals. For example, 3 is $1 + 2$, but the word "three" is not "one plus two." More significant, quote gives us a way to build expressions that manipulate other expressions (as we will see when we write an interpreter in chapter 4). But allowing statements in a language that talk about other statements in that language makes it very difficult to maintain any coherent principle of what "equals can be substituted for equals" should mean. For example, if we know that the evening star is the morning star, then from the statement "the evening star is Venus" we can deduce "the morning star is Venus." However, given that "John knows that the evening star is Venus" we cannot infer that "John knows that the morning star is Venus."

11 The single quote is different from the double quote we have been using to enclose character strings to be printed. Whereas the single quote can be used to denote lists or symbols, the double quote is used only with character strings. In Scheme, the only use for character strings is as items to be printed.

```
==> (list 'a 'b)
(a b)

==> (list 'a b)
(a 2)
```

Quotation also allows us to type in compound objects, using the conventional printed representation for lists:[12]

```
==> (car '(a b c))
a

==> (cdr '(a b c))
(b c)
```

One additional primitive used in manipulating symbols is eq?, which takes two symbols as arguments and tests whether they are the same.[13] Using eq?, we can implement a useful procedure called memq. This takes two arguments, a symbol and a list. If the symbol is not contained in the list (i.e., is not eq? to any item in the list), then memq returns the empty list. Otherwise, it returns the sublist of the list beginning with the first occurrence of the symbol:

```
(define (memq item x)
  (cond ((null? x) '())
        ((eq? item (car x)) x)
        (else (memq item (cdr x)))))
```

---

12 Strictly, our use of the quotation mark violates the general rule that all compound expressions in our language should be represented as combinations. We can recover this consistency by introducing a special form quote, which serves the same purpose as the quotation mark. Thus, we would type (quote a) instead of 'a, and we would type (quote (a b c)) instead of '(a b c). This is precisely how the interpreter works. The quotation mark is just a single-character abbreviation for wrapping the next complete expression with quote to form (quote ⟨expression⟩). This is important because it maintains the principle that any expression seen by the interpreter can be manipulated as a data object. For instance, we could construct the expression

(car '(a b c)) = (car (quote (a b c)))

as

(list 'car (list 'quote '(a b c)))

13 We can consider two symbols to be "the same" if they consist of the same characters in the same order. Such a definition skirts a deep issue that we are not yet ready to address: the meaning of "sameness" in a programming language. We will return to this in chapter 3 (section 3.1.2.).

For example,

(memq 'apple '(pear banana prune))

returns the empty list, whereas

(memq 'apple '(x (apple sauce) y apple pear))

returns (apple pear).

Exercise 2.28

What would the interpreter print in response to evaluating each of the following expressions?

(list 'a 'b 'c)

(list (list 'george))

(cdr '((x1 x2) (y1 y2)))

(cadr '((x1 x2) (y1 y2)))

(atom? (car '(a short list)))

(memq 'red '((red shoes) (blue socks)))

(memq 'red '(red shoes blue socks))

Exercise 2.29

Two lists are said to be equal? if they contain equal elements arranged in the same order. For example,

(equal? '(this is a list) '(this is a list))

is true, but

(equal? '(this is a list) '(this (is a) list))

is false. To be more precise, we can define equal? recursively in terms of the basic eq? equality of symbols by saying that a and b are equal? if they are both symbols and the symbols are eq?, or if they are both lists such that (car a) is equal? to (car b) and (cdr a) is equal? to (cdr b). Using this idea, implement equal? as a procedure.[14]

14 In practice, Lisp programmers use equal? to compare lists that contain numbers as well as symbols. Numbers are atomic data items (they are not pairs), but in most dialects of Lisp they are not considered symbols. The question whether two numerically equal numbers (as tested by =) are also eq? is highly implementation-dependent. A better definition of equal? would also stipulate that if a and b are both numbers, then a and b are equal? if they are numerically equal.

Exercise 2.30

Eva Lu Ator types to the interpreter the expression

`(car ''abracadabra)`

To her surprise, the interpreter prints back quote. Explain. What would be printed in response to

`(cdddr '(this list contains '(a quote)))`

2.2.4 Example: Symbolic Differentiation

As an illustration of symbol manipulation and a further illustration of data abstraction, consider the design of a procedure that performs symbolic differentiation of algebraic expressions. We would like the procedure to take as arguments an algebraic expression and a variable and to return the derivative of the expression with respect to the variable. For example, if the arguments to the procedure are $ax^2 + bx + c$ and x, the procedure should return $2ax + b$. Symbolic differentiation is of special historical significance in Lisp. It was one of the motivating examples behind the development of a computer language for symbol manipulation. Furthermore, it marked the beginning of the line of research that led to the development of powerful systems for symbolic mathematical work, which are currently being used by a growing number of applied mathematicians and physicists.

In developing the symbolic-differentiation program, we will follow the same strategy of data abstraction that we followed in developing the rational-number system of section 2.1.1. That is, we will first define a differentiation algorithm that operates on abstract objects such as "sums," "products," and "variables" without worrying about how these are to be represented. Only afterward will we address the representation problem.

The differentiation program with abstract data

In order to keep things simple, we will consider a very simple symbolic-differentiation program that handles expressions that are built up using only the operations of addition and multiplication with two arguments. Differentiation of any such expression can be carried out by applying the following reduction rules:

$$\frac{dc}{dx} = 0 \text{ for } c \text{ a constant or a variable different from } x,$$

$$\frac{dx}{dx} = 1,$$

$$\frac{d(u+v)}{dx} = \frac{du}{dx} + \frac{dv}{dx},$$

$$\frac{d(uv)}{dx} = u\left(\frac{dv}{dx}\right) + v\left(\frac{du}{dx}\right).$$

Observe that the latter two rules are recursive in nature. That is, to obtain the derivative of a sum we first find the derivatives of the addends and add them. Each of the addends may in turn be an expression that needs to be decomposed. Decomposing into smaller and smaller pieces will eventually produce pieces that are either constants or variables, whose derivatives will be either 0 or 1.

To embody these rules in a procedure we indulge in a little wishful thinking, as we did in designing the rational-number implementation. If we had a means for representing algebraic expressions, we should be able to tell whether an expression is a sum, a product, a constant, or a variable. We should be able to get the parts of an expression (e.g., for a sum we want to be able to extract the addend and the augend), and we should be able to construct expressions from parts. Let us assume that we already have procedures to implement the following selectors, constructors, and predicates:

(constant? $\langle e \rangle$)   Is $\langle e \rangle$ a constant?

(variable? $\langle e \rangle$)   Is $\langle e \rangle$ a variable?

(same-variable? $\langle v1 \rangle$ $\langle v2 \rangle$) Are $\langle v1 \rangle$ and $\langle v2 \rangle$ the same variable?

(sum? $\langle e \rangle$)   Is $\langle e \rangle$ a sum?

(product? $\langle e \rangle$)   Is $\langle e \rangle$ a product?

(addend $\langle e \rangle$)   Addend of the sum $\langle e \rangle$.

(augend $\langle e \rangle$)   Augend of the sum $\langle e \rangle$.

(multiplier $\langle e \rangle$)   Multiplier of the product $\langle e \rangle$.

(multiplicand $\langle e \rangle$)   Multiplicand of the product $\langle e \rangle$.

(make-sum $\langle a1 \rangle$ $\langle a2 \rangle$)   Construct the sum of $\langle a1 \rangle$ and $\langle a2 \rangle$.

(make-product $\langle m1 \rangle$ $\langle m2 \rangle$) Construct the product of $\langle m1 \rangle$ and $\langle m2 \rangle$.

Using these operators, we can express the differentiation rules as the following procedure:

```
(define (deriv exp var)
  (cond ((constant? exp) 0)
        ((variable? exp)
         (if (same-variable? exp var) 1 0))
        ((sum? exp)
         (make-sum (deriv (addend exp) var)
                   (deriv (augend exp) var)))
        ((product? exp)
         (make-sum
           (make-product (multiplier exp)
                         (deriv (multiplicand exp) var))
           (make-product (deriv (multiplier exp) var)
                         (multiplicand exp))))))
```

This procedure incorporates the complete differentiation algorithm. Since it is expressed in terms of abstract data, it will work no matter how we choose to represent algebraic expressions, as long as we design a proper set of selectors and constructors. This is the issue we must address next.

Representing algebraic expressions

We can imagine many ways to use list structure to represent algebraic expressions. For example, we could use lists of symbols that mirror the usual algebraic notation, representing $ax + b$ as the list (a * x + b). However, one especially straightforward choice is to use the same parenthesized prefix notation that Lisp uses for combinations; that is, to represent $ax + b$ as (+ (* a x) b). Then our data representation for the differentiation problem is as follows:

• The constants are numbers, identified by the primitive predicate number?:

```
(define (constant? x) (number? x))
```

• The variables are symbols, identified by the primitive predicate symbol?:

```
(define (variable? x) (symbol? x))
```

• Two variables are the same if the symbols representing them are eq?:

```
(define (same-variable? v1 v2)
  (and (variable? v1) (variable? v2) (eq? v1 v2)))
```

• Sums and products are constructed as lists:

```
(define (make-sum a1 a2) (list '+ a1 a2))

(define (make-product m1 m2) (list '* m1 m2))
```

• A sum is a list whose first element is the symbol +:

```
(define (sum? x)
  (if (not (atom? x)) (eq? (car x) '+) nil))
```

• The addend is the second item of the sum list:

```
(define (addend s) (cadr s))
```

• The augend is the third item of the sum list:

```
(define (augend s) (caddr s))
```

• A product is a list whose first element is the symbol *:

```
(define (product? x)
  (if (not (atom? x)) (eq? (car x) '*) nil))
```

• The multiplier is the second item of the product list:

```
(define (multiplier p) (cadr p))
```

• The multiplicand is the third item of the product list:

```
(define (multiplicand p) (caddr p))
```

Thus, we need only combine these with the algorithm as embodied by deriv
in order to have a working symbolic-differentiation program. Let us look
at some examples of its behavior:

```
==> (deriv '(+ x 3) 'x)
(+ 1 0)

==> (deriv '(* x y) 'x)
(+ (* x 0) (* 1 y))

==> (deriv '(* (* x y) (+ x 3)) 'x)
(+ (* (* x y) (+ 1 0))
   (* (+ (* x 0) (* 1 y))
      (+ x 3)))
```

The program produces answers that are correct; however, they are unsim-
plified. It is true that

$$\frac{d(xy)}{dx} = x \cdot 0 + 1 \cdot y,$$

but we would like the program to know that $x \cdot 0 = 0$, $1 \cdot y = y$, and $0 + y = y$. The answer for the second example should have been simply y. As the third example shows, this becomes a serious issue when the expressions are complex.

Our difficulty is much like the one we encountered with the rational-number implementation: we haven't reduced answers to lowest form. To accomplish the rational-number reduction, we needed to change only the constructors and the selectors of the implementation. We can adopt a similar strategy here. We won't change deriv at all. Instead, we will change make-sum so that, if both summands are numbers, make-sum will add them and return their sum. Also, if one of the summands is 0, then make-sum will return the other summand.

```
(define (make-sum a1 a2)
  (cond ((and (number? a1) (number? a2)) (+ a1 a2))
        ((number? a1) (if (= a1 0) a2 (list '+ a1 a2)))
        ((number? a2) (if (= a2 0) a1 (list '+ a1 a2)))
        (else (list '+ a1 a2))))
```

Similarly, we will change make-product to build in the rules that 0 times anything is 0 and 1 times anything is the thing itself:

```
(define (make-product m1 m2)
  (cond ((and (number? m1) (number? m2)) (* m1 m2))
        ((number? m1)
         (cond ((= m1 0) 0)
               ((= m1 1) m2)
               (else (list '* m1 m2))))
        ((number? m2)
         (cond ((= m2 0) 0)
               ((= m2 1) m1)
               (else (list '* m1 m2))))
        (else (list '* m1 m2))))
```

Here is how this version works on our three examples:

```
==> (deriv '(+ x 3) 'x)
1

==> (deriv '(* x y) 'x)
y
```

```
==> (deriv '(* (* x y) (+ x 3)) 'x)
(+ (* x y) (* y (+ x 3)))
```

Although this is quite an improvement, the third example shows that there is still a long way to go before we get a program that puts expressions into a form that we might agree is "simplest." The problem of algebraic simplification is quite complex because, among other reasons, a form that may be simplest for one purpose may not be for another.

Exercise 2.31

Show how to extend the basic differentiator to handle more kinds of expressions. For instance, implement the differentiation rule

$$\frac{d(u^n)}{dx} = nu^{n-1}\left(\frac{du}{dx}\right)$$

by adding a new clause to the `deriv` program and extending the interface to the data by defining appropriate procedures `exponentiation?`, `base`, `exponent`, and `make-exponentiation`. (You may use the symbol `**` to denote the exponentiation operator.)

Exercise 2.32

Suppose we want to modify the differentiation program so that it works with ordinary mathematical notation, in which + and * are infix rather than prefix operators. Since the differentiation program is defined in terms of abstract data, we can modify it to work with different representations of expressions solely by changing the predicates, selectors, and constructors that define the representation of the algebraic expressions on which the differentiator is to operate.

a. Show how to do this in order to differentiate algebraic expressions presented in infix form, such as (x+(3*(x+(y+2)))). This is not difficult if we assume that + and * always take two arguments and that expressions are fully parenthesized.

b. The problem becomes substantially harder if we allow standard algebraic notation, such as (x+3*(x+y+2)), which drops unnecessary parentheses and assumes that multiplication is done before addition. Can you design appropriate predicates, selectors, and constructors for this notation such that our derivative program still works?

2.2.5 Example: Representing Sets

In the previous examples we built representations for two kinds of compound data objects: rational numbers and algebraic expressions. In one of these examples we had the choice of simplifying (reducing) the expressions at either construction time or selection time, but other than that the choice of a representation for these structures in terms of lists was straightforward.

When we turn to the representation of sets, the choice of a representation is not so obvious. Indeed, there are a number of possible representations, and they differ significantly from one another in several ways.

Informally, a set is simply a collection of distinct objects. To give a more precise definition we can employ the method of data abstraction. That is, we define "set" by specifying the operators that are to be used on sets. These operators are union-set, intersection-set, element-of-set?, and adjoin-set. Element-of-set? is a predicate that determines whether a given element is a member of a set. Adjoin-set takes an object and a set as arguments and returns a set that contains the elements of the original set and also the adjoined element. Union-set computes the union of two sets, which is the set containing each element that appears in either argument. Intersection-set computes the intersection of two sets, which is the set containing only elements that appear in both arguments. We will use the empty list to represent the empty set. From the viewpoint of data abstraction, we are free to design any representation that implements these operators in a way consistent with the interpretations given above.[15]

Sets as unordered lists

One way to represent a set is as a list of its elements where no element appears more than once. The empty set is represented by the empty list. In this representation, element-of-set? is similar to the procedure memq of section 2.2.3. It uses equal? instead of eq? so that the set elements need not be symbols:

```
(define (element-of-set? x set)
  (cond ((null? set) nil)
        ((equal? x (car set)) t)
        (else (element-of-set? x (cdr set)))))
```

15 If we want to be more formal, we can specify "consistent with the interpretations given above" to mean that the operators satisfy a collection of rules such as these:

• For any set S and any object x,

(element-of-set? x (adjoin-set x S))

is true (informally: "Adjoining an object to a set produces a set that contains the object").

• For any sets S and T and any object x,

(element-of-set? x (union-set S T))

is equal to

(or (element-of-set? x S) (element-of-set? x T))

(informally: "The elements of (union S T) are the elements that are in S or in T").

• For any object x,

(element-of-set? x '())

is false (informally: "No object is an element of the empty set").

Using this, we can write `adjoin-set`. If the object to be adjoined is already in the set, we just return the set. Otherwise, we use `cons` to add the object to the list that represents the set:

```
(define (adjoin-set x set)
  (if (element-of-set? x set)
      set
      (cons x set)))
```

For `intersection-set` we can use a recursive strategy. If we know how to form the intersection of the set2 and the `cdr` of set1, we only need to decide whether to include the `car` of set1 in this. But this depends on whether (`car` set1) is also in set2. Here is the resulting procedure:

```
(define (intersection-set set1 set2)
  (cond ((or (null? set1) (null? set2)) '())
        ((element-of-set? (car set1) set2)
         (cons (car set1)
               (intersection-set (cdr set1) set2)))
        (else (intersection-set (cdr set1) set2))))
```

Exercise 2.33

Give the analogous implementation of `union-set`.

In designing a representation, one of the issues we should be concerned with is efficiency. Consider the time required by our set operations. Since most of these use `element-of-set?`, the speed of this operation has a major impact on the efficiency of the set implementation as a whole. Now, in order to check whether an object is a member of a set, `element-of-set?` may have to scan the entire set. (In the worst case, the object turns out not to be in the set.) Hence, if the set has n elements, `element-of-set?` might take up to n steps. Thus, the time required grows as $O(n)$. The time required by `adjoin-set`, which uses this operation, also grows as $O(n)$. For `intersection-set`, which does an `element-of-set?` check for each element of set1, the time required grows as the product of the sizes of the sets involved, or $O(n^2)$ for two sets of size n. The same will be true of `union-set`.

Exercise 2.34

We specified that a set would be represented as a list with no duplicate elements. Now suppose we allow duplicates. For instance, the set $\{1, 2, 3\}$ could be represented as the list (2 3 2 1 3 2 2). Design procedures `element-of-`

`set?`, `adjoin-set`, `union-set`, and `intersection-set` that operate on this representation. How does the efficiency of each compare with the corresponding procedure for the nonduplicate representation? Are there applications for which you would use this representation in preference to the nonduplicate one?

Sets as ordered lists

One way to speed up our set operations is to change the representation so that the set elements are listed in increasing order. To do this, we need some way to compare two objects so that we can say which is bigger. For example, we could compare symbols lexicographically, or we could agree on some method for assigning a unique number to an object and then compare the elements by comparing the corresponding numbers. To keep our discussion simple, we will consider only the case where the set elements are numbers, so that we can compare elements using > and <. We will represent a set of numbers by listing its elements in increasing order. Whereas our first representation above allowed us to represent the set $\{1, 3, 6, 10\}$ by listing the elements in any order, our new representation allows only the list (1 3 6 10).

One advantage of ordering shows up in `element-of-set?`: In checking for the presence of an item, we no longer have to scan the entire set. If we reach a set element that is larger than the item we are looking for, then we know that the item is not in the set:

```
(define (element-of-set? x set)
  (cond ((null? set) nil)
        ((= x (car set)) t)
        ((< x (car set)) nil)
        (else (element-of-set? x (cdr set)))))
```

How much time does this save? In the worst case, the item we are looking for may be the largest one in the set, so the number of steps is the same as for the unordered representation. On the other hand, if we search for items of many different sizes we can expect that sometimes we will be able to stop searching at a point near the beginning of the list and that other times we will still need to examine most of the list. On the average we should expect to have to examine about half the number of items in the set. Thus, the average time required will be about $n/2$. This is still $O(n)$ growth, but it does save us, on the average, a factor of 2 in time over the previous implementation.

Exercise 2.35

Give an implementation of `adjoin-set` using the ordered representation. By analogy with `element-of-set?` show how to take advantage of the ordering to produce a procedure that requires on the average about half as many recursions as with the unordered representation. Compare them by counting conses.

We obtain a more impressive speedup when we consider intersection-set. In the unordered representation this operation required time $O(n^2)$, because we performed a complete scan of set2 for each element of set1. But with the ordered representation, we can use a more clever method. Begin by comparing the initial elements, x1 and x2, of the two sets. If x1=x2, then that gives an element of the intersection, and the rest of the intersection is the intersection of the cdrs of the two sets. Suppose, however, that x1 is less than x2. Since x2 is the smallest element in set2, we can immediately conclude that x1 cannot appear anywhere in set2 and hence is not in the intersection. Hence, the intersection is equal to the intersection of set2 with the cdr of set1. Similarly, if x2 is less than x1, then the intersection is given by the intersection of set1 with the cdr of set2. Here is the procedure:

```
(define (intersection-set set1 set2)
  (if (or (null? set1) (null? set2))
      '()
      (let ((x1 (car set1)) (x2 (car set2)))
        (cond ((= x1 x2)
               (cons x1
                     (intersection-set (cdr set1)
                                       (cdr set2))))
              ((< x1 x2)
               (intersection-set (cdr set1) set2))
              ((< x2 x1)
               (intersection-set set1
                                 (cdr set2)))))))
```

To estimate the time required by this process, observe that at each step we reduce the intersection problem to computing intersections of smaller sets—removing the first element from set1 or set2 or both. Thus, the number of steps required is at most the sum of the sizes of set1 and set2, rather than the product of the sizes as with the unordered representation. This is $O(n)$ growth rather than $O(n^2)$—a considerable speedup, even for sets of moderate size.

Exercise 2.36

Give the analogous $O(n)$ implementation of union-set for sets implemented as ordered lists.

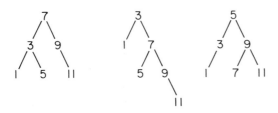

Figure 2.7
Various binary trees that represent the set $\{1, 3, 5, 7, 9, 11\}$.

Sets as binary trees

We can do better than the ordered-list representation by arranging the set elements in the form of a tree. Each node of the tree holds one element of the set, called the "entry" at that node, and a link to each of two other (possibly empty) nodes. The "left" link points to elements smaller than the one at the node, and the "right" link to elements greater than the one at the node. Figure 2.7 shows some trees that represent the set $\{1, 3, 5, 7, 9, 11\}$. The same set may be represented by a tree in a number of different ways. The only thing we require for a valid representation is that all elements in the left subtree be smaller than the node entry and that all elements in the right subtree be larger.

The advantage of the tree representation is this: Suppose we want to check whether a number x is contained in a set. We begin by comparing x with the entry in the top node. If x is less than this, we know that we need only search the left subtree; if x is greater, we need only search the right subtree. Now, if the tree is "balanced," each of these subtrees will be about half the size of the original. Thus, in one step we have reduced the problem of searching a tree of size n to searching a tree of size $n/2$. Since the size of the tree is halved at each step, we should expect that the number of steps needed to search a tree of size n grows as $O(\log n)$.[16] For large sets, this will be a significant speedup over the previous representations.

We can represent trees by using lists. Each node will be a list of three items: the entry at the node, the left subtree, and the right subtree. A left or a right subtree of the empty list will indicate that there is no subtree connected there. We can describe this representation by the following procedures:[17]

16 Halving the size of the problem at each step is the distinguishing characteristic of logarithmic growth, as we saw with the fast-exponentiation algorithm of section 1.2.4 and the half-interval search method of section 1.3.3.

17 We are representing sets in terms of trees, and trees in terms of lists—in effect, a data abstraction built upon a data abstraction. We can regard the procedures entry, left-branch, right-branch, and make-tree as a way of isolating the abstraction of "a binary tree" from the particular way we might wish to represent such a tree in terms of lists.

```
(define (entry tree) (car tree))

(define (left-branch tree) (cadr tree))

(define (right-branch tree) (caddr tree))

(define (make-tree entry left right)
  (list entry left right))
```

Now we can write the element-of-set? procedure using the strategy
described above:

```
(define (element-of-set? x set)
  (cond ((null? set) nil)
        ((= x (entry set)) t)
        ((< x (entry set))
         (element-of-set? x (left-branch set)))
        ((> x (entry set))
         (element-of-set? x (right-branch set)))))
```

Adjoining an item to a set is implemented similarly and also requires
$O(\log n)$ steps. To adjoin an item x, we compare x with the node entry to
determine whether x should be added to the right or to the left branch,
and having adjoined x to the appropriate branch we piece this newly
constructed branch together with the original entry and the other branch.
If x is equal to the entry, we just return the original set. If we are asked to
adjoin x to an empty tree, we generate a tree that has x as the entry and
null right and left branches. Here is the procedure:

```
(define (adjoin-set x set)
  (cond ((null? set) (make-tree x '() '()))
        ((= x (entry set)) set)
        ((< x (entry set))
         (make-tree (entry set)
                    (adjoin-set x
                                (left-branch set))
                    (right-branch set)))
        ((> x (entry set))
         (make-tree (entry set)
                    (left-branch set)
                    (adjoin-set x
                                (right-branch set))))))
```

For large sets, the tree representation is much more efficient than the ordered or unordered lists for searching and adjoining new elements. For computing intersections, however, it turns out that there is no general way to proceed other than to use the same strategy we used in the unordered-list representation. That is, we scan to see if each element in set1 is in set2, and if so we adjoin it to an intersection set that we accumulate. Since the search requires time roughly equal to the logarithm of the number of items in set2, and since we must do this operation for each element in set1, the total time required grows as the size of set1 times the logarithm of the size of set2, or $O(n \log n)$ if the two sets are comparable in size. This is still much better than the unordered-list representation, but not quite as good as the ordered-list representation. Since a typical set implementation is likely to do much more searching than intersection, the tree representation is usually to be preferred.

Exercise 2.37

How does the tree representation of sets compare with other representations on set-union problems?

There is an additional problem with the tree implementation. The claim that searching the tree can be performed in logarithmic time rests on the assumption that the tree is "balanced," i.e., that the left and the right subtree of every tree have approximately the same number of elements, so that each subtree contains about half the elements of its parent. But how can we be certain that the trees we construct will be balanced? Even if we start with a balanced tree, adding elements with adjoin-set may produce an unbalanced result. Since the position of a newly adjoined element depends on how the element compares with the items already in the set, we can expect that if we add elements "randomly" the tree will tend to be balanced on the average. But this is not a guarantee. For example, if we start with an empty set and adjoin the numbers 1 through 7 in sequence we end up with the highly unbalanced tree shown in figure 2.8. In this tree all the left subtrees are empty, and so it has no advantage over a simple ordered list. One way to solve this problem is to define an operation that transforms an arbitrary tree into a balanced tree with the same elements. Then we can perform this transformation after every few adjoin-set operations to keep our set in balance. There are also other ways to solve this problem, most of which involve designing new data structures for which searching and insertion both can be done in $O(\log n)$ steps.[18]

18 Examples of such structures include *heaps*, *2–3 trees*, and *AVL-trees*. There is a large literature on data structures that is devoted to this problem.

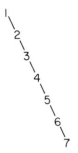

Figure 2.8
Unbalanced tree produced by adjoining 1 through 7 in sequence.

Sets and information retrieval

We have examined options for using lists to represent sets and have seen how the choice of representation for a data object can have a large impact on the performance of the programs that use the data. Another reason for concentrating on sets is that the techniques discussed here appear again and again in applications involving information retrieval.

Consider a data base containing a large number of individual records—for example, personnel files for a company, or the transactions in an accounting system. A typical data-management system spends a large amount of time accessing or modifying the data in the records and therefore requires an efficient method for accessing records. This is done by identifying a part of each record to serve as an identifying *key*. A key can be anything that uniquely identifies the record. For a personnel file, it might be an employee's social security number. For an accounting system, it might be a transaction number. Whatever the key is, when we define the record as a data structure we should include a **key** selector procedure that retrieves the key associated with a given record.

Now we represent the data base as a set of records. To locate the record with a given key we use a procedure lookup, which takes as arguments a key and a data base and which returns the record that has that key, or nil if there is no such record. Lookup is implemented in almost the same way as element-of-set?. For example, if the set of records is implemented as an unordered list, we could use

```
(define (lookup given-key set-of-records)
  (cond ((null? set-of-records) nil)
        ((equal? given-key (key (car set-of-records)))
         (car set-of-records))
        (else (lookup given-key (cdr set-of-records)))))
```

Of course, there are better ways to represent large sets than as unordered lists. Information-retrieval systems in which records have to be "randomly accessed" are typically implemented by a tree-based method, such as the binary tree representation discussed previously. In the designing of such a system the methodology of data abstraction can be a great help. The designer can create an initial implementation using a simple, straightforward representation such as unordered lists. This will be unsuitable for the eventual system, but it can be useful in providing a "quick and dirty" data base with which to test the rest of the system. Later on, the data representation can be modified to be more sophisticated. If the data base is accessed in terms of abstract selectors and constructors, this change in representation will not require any changes to the rest of the system.

Exercise 2.38

Give an implementation of the lookup procedure for the case where the set of records is structured as a binary tree, ordered by the numerical values of the keys.

2.2.6 Example: Huffman Encoding Trees

This section provides practice in the use of list structure and data abstraction to manipulate sets and trees. The application is to methods for representing data as sequences of ones and zeros (bits). For example, the ASCII standard code used to represent text in computers encodes each character as a sequence of seven bits. Using seven bits allows us to distinguish 2^7, or 128, possible different characters. In general, if we want to distinguish N different symbols, we will need to use $\log_2 N$ bits per symbol. If all our messages are made up of the eight symbols A, B, C, D, E, F, G, and H, we can choose a code with three bits per character, for example

A 000	C 010	E 100	G 110
B 001	D 011	F 101	H 111

With this code, the message

BACADAEAFABBAAAGAH

is encoded as the string of 54 bits

001000010000011000100000101000010010000000000110000111

Codes such as ASCII and the A-through-H code above are known as *fixed-length* codes, because they represent each symbol in the message with the same number of bits. It is sometimes advantageous to use *variable-length* codes, in which different symbols may be represented by different numbers of bits. For example, Morse code does not use the same number of dots and dashes for each letter of the alphabet. In particular, E, the most frequent letter, is represented by a single dot. In general, if our messages are such that some symbols appear very frequently and some very rarely, we can encode data more efficiently (i.e., using fewer bits per message) if we assign shorter codes to the frequent symbols. Consider the following alternative code for the letters A through H:

A 0	C 1010	E 1100	G 1110
B 100	D 1011	F 1101	H 1111

With this code, the same message as above is encoded as the string

100010100101101100011010100100000111001111

This string contains 42 bits, so it saves more than 20% in space in comparison with the fixed-length code shown above.

One of the difficulties of using a variable-length code is knowing when you have reached the end of a symbol in reading a sequence of zeros and ones. Morse code solves this problem by using a special *separator code* (in this case, a pause) after the sequence of dots and dashes for each letter. Another solution is to design the code in such a way that no complete code for any symbol is the beginning (or *prefix*) of the code for another symbol. Such a code is called a *prefix code*. In the example above, A is encoded by 0 and B is encoded by 100, so no other symbol can have a code that begins with 0 or with 100.

In general, we can attain significant savings if we use variable-length prefix codes that take advantage of the relative frequencies of the symbols in the messages to be encoded. One particular scheme for doing this is called the Huffman encoding method, after its discoverer, David Huffman. A Huffman code can be represented as a binary tree whose leaves are the symbols that are encoded. At each nonleaf node of the tree there is a set containing all the symbols in the leaves that lie below the node. In addition, each symbol at a leaf is assigned a frequency number, and each nonleaf node contains a weight that is the sum of all the frequencies of the leaves lying below it. The weights are not used in the encoding or the decoding process. We will see below how they are used to help construct the tree.

Figure 2.9 shows the Huffman tree for the A-through-H code given above. The frequency numbers at the leaves indicate that the tree was designed for messages in which A appears with relative frequency 8, B with relative frequency 3, and the other letters each with relative frequency 1.

Given a Huffman tree, we can find the encoding of any symbol by starting at the root and moving down until we reach the leaf that holds the symbol. Each time we move down a left branch we add a 0 to the code, and each

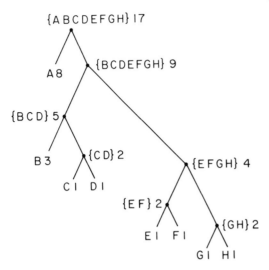

Figure 2.9
A Huffman encoding tree.

time we move down a right branch we add a 1. (We decide which branch to
follow by testing to see which branch either is the leaf node for the symbol
or contains the symbol in its set.) For example, starting from the root of
the tree in figure 2.9, we arrive at the leaf for D by following a right branch,
then a left branch, then a right branch, then a right branch; hence, the
code for D is 1011.

To decode a bit sequence using a Huffman tree, we begin at the root and
use the successive zeros and ones of the bit sequence to determine whether
to move down the left or the right branch. Each time we come to a leaf, we
have generated a new symbol in the message, at which point we start over
from the root of the tree to find the next symbol. For example, suppose we
are given the tree above and the sequence 10001010. Starting at the root,
we move down the right branch, (since the first bit of the string is 1), then
down the left branch (since the second bit is 0), then down the left branch
(since the third bit is also 0). This brings us to the leaf for B, so the first
symbol of the decoded message is B. Now we start again at the root, and
we make a left move because the next bit in the string is 0. This brings
us to the leaf for A. Then we start again at the root with the rest of the
string 1010, so we move right, left, right, left and reach C. Thus, the entire
message is BAC.

Generating Huffman trees
Given an "alphabet" of symbols and their relative frequencies, how do we
construct the "best" code? (In other words, which tree will encode messages
with the fewest bits?) Huffman gave an algorithm for doing this and showed

that the resulting code is indeed the best variable-length code for messages where the relative frequency of the symbols matches the frequencies with which the code was constructed. We will not prove this optimality of Huffman codes here, but we will show how Huffman trees are constructed.[19]

The algorithm for generating a Huffman tree is very simple. The idea is to arrange the tree so that the symbols with the lowest frequency appear farthest away from the root. Begin with the set of leaf nodes, together with their frequencies, as determined by the initial data from which the code is to be constructed. Now find two leaves with the lowest frequencies and merge them to produce a node that has these two nodes as its left and right branches. The weight of the new node is the sum of the two frequencies. Remove the two leaves from the original set and replace them by this new node. Now continue this process. At each step, merge two nodes with the smallest weights, removing them from the set and replacing them with a node that has these two as its left and right branches. The process stops when there is only one node left, which is the root of the entire tree. Here is how the Huffman tree of figure 2.9 was generated:

Initial leaves	{(A 8) (B 3) (C 1) (D 1) (E 1) (F 1) (G 1) (H 1)}
Merge	{(A 8) (B 3) ({C D} 2) (E 1) (F 1) (G 1) (H 1)}
Merge	{(A 8) (B 3) ({C D} 2) ({E F} 2) (G 1) (H 1)}
Merge	{(A 8) (B 3) ({C D} 2) ({E F} 2) ({G H} 2)}
Merge	{(A 8) (B 3) ({C D} 2) ({E F G H} 4)}
Merge	{(A 8) ({B C D} 5) ({E F G H} 4)}
Merge	{(A 8) ({B C D E F G H} 9)}
Final merge	{(({A B C D E F G H} 17)}

The algorithm does not always specify a unique tree, because there may not be unique smallest-weight nodes at each step. Also, the choice of the order in which the two nodes are merged (i.e., which will be the right branch and which will be the left branch) is arbitrary.

Representing Huffman trees

In the following exercises we will work with a system that uses Huffman trees to encode and decode messages and generates Huffman trees according to the algorithm outlined above. We will begin by discussing how trees are represented.

Leaves of the tree are represented by a list consisting of the symbol `leaf`, the symbol at the leaf, and the weight:

---

[19] See Hamming (1980) for a discussion of the mathematical properties of Huffman codes.

```
(define (make-leaf symbol weight)
  (list 'leaf symbol weight))

(define (leaf? object)
  (eq? (car object) 'leaf))

(define (symbol-leaf x) (cadr x))

(define (weight-leaf x) (caddr x))
```

A general tree will be a list of a left branch, a right branch, a set of symbols, and a weight. The set of symbols will be simply a list of the symbols, rather than some more sophisticated set representation. When we make a tree by merging two nodes, we obtain the weight of the tree as the sum of the weights of the nodes, and the set of symbols as the union of the symbols for the nodes. Since our symbol sets are represented as lists, we can form the union by using the append procedure we defined in section 2.2.1:

```
(define (make-code-tree left right)
  (list left
        right
        (append (symbols left) (symbols right))
        (+ (weight left) (weight right))))
```

If we make a tree in this way, we have the following selectors:

```
(define (left-branch tree) (car tree))

(define (right-branch tree) (cadr tree))

(define (symbols tree)
  (if (leaf? tree)
      (list (symbol-leaf tree))
      (caddr tree)))

(define (weight tree)
  (if (leaf? tree)
      (weight-leaf tree)
      (cadddr tree)))
```

The procedures symbols and weight must do something slightly different depending on whether they are called with a leaf or a general tree. These procedures are simple examples of *generic operators* (operators that can handle more than one kind of data), about which we will have much more to say in section 2.3.

The decoding procedure

The following procedure implements the decoding algorithm specified above. It takes as arguments a list of zeros and ones, together with a Huffman tree.

```
(define (decode bits tree)
  (decode-1 bits tree tree))
```

The procedure decode-1 takes three arguments: the list of bits, the tree, and the current position in the tree. It keeps moving "down" the tree, choosing a left or a right branch according to whether the next bit in the list is a zero or a one. (This is done with the procedure choose-branch.) When it reaches a leaf, it returns the symbol at that leaf as the next symbol in the message (consing it onto the rest of the message) and proceeds to decode the rest of the message, starting at the root of the tree.

```
(define (decode-1 bits tree current-branch)
  (if (null? bits)
      '()
      (let ((next-branch
              (choose-branch (car bits) current-branch)))
        (if (leaf? next-branch)
            (cons (symbol-leaf next-branch)
                  (decode-1 (cdr bits) tree tree))
            (decode-1 (cdr bits) tree next-branch)))))

(define (choose-branch bit branch)
  (cond ((= bit 0) (left-branch branch))
        ((= bit 1) (right-branch branch))
        (else (error "bad bit -- CHOOSE-BRANCH" bit))))
```

Note the error check in the final clause of choose-branch, which complains if the procedure finds something other than a zero or a one in the input data.

Sets of weighted elements

In our representation of trees, each nonleaf node contains a set of symbols, which we have represented as a simple list. However, the tree-generating algorithm discussed above requires that we also work with sets of leaves and trees, successively merging the two smallest items. Since we will be required to repeatedly find the smallest item in a set, it is convenient to use an ordered representation for this kind of set.

We will represent a set of leaves and trees as a list of elements, arranged
in increasing order of weight. The following `adjoin-set` procedure for
constructing sets is similar to the one described in exercise 2.35; however,
items are compared by comparing their weights, and the element being
added to the set is never already in it.

```
(define (adjoin-set x set)
  (cond ((null? set) (list x))
        ((< (weight x) (weight (car set))) (cons x set))
        (else (cons (car set)
                    (adjoin-set x (cdr set))))))
```

The following procedure takes as its argument a list of symbol-frequency
pairs such as `((A 4) (B 2) (C 1) (D 1))` and constructs an initial ordered set of leaves, ready to be merged according to the Huffman algorithm:

```
(define (make-leaf-set pairs)
  (if (null? pairs)
      '()
      (let ((pair (car pairs)))
        (adjoin-set (make-leaf (car pair)      ;symbol
                               (cadr pair))     ;frequency
                    (make-leaf-set (cdr pairs))))))
```

Exercise 2.39

Define an encoding tree and a sample message:

```
(define sample-tree
  (make-code-tree (make-leaf 'A 4)
                  (make-code-tree (make-leaf 'B 2)
                                  (make-code-tree
                                   (make-leaf 'D 1)
                                   (make-leaf 'C 1)))))
```

```
(define sample-message '(0 1 1 0 0 1 0 1 0 1 1 1 0))
```
Use the decode procedure to decode the message, and give the result.

Exercise 2.40

The encode procedure takes as arguments a message and a tree and produces the
list of bits that gives the encoded message.

```
(define (encode message tree)
  (if (null? message)
      '()
      (append (encode-symbol (car message) tree)
              (encode (cdr message) tree))))
```

Encode-symbol is a procedure, which you must write, that returns the list of bits that encodes a given symbol according to a given tree. You should design encode-symbol so that it signals an error if the symbol is not in the tree at all. Test your procedure by encoding the result you obtained in exercise 2.39 with the sample tree and seeing whether it is the same as the original sample message.

Exercise 2.41

The following procedure takes as its argument a list of symbol-frequency pairs (where no symbol appears in more than one pair) and generates a Huffman encoding tree according to the Huffman algorithm.

```
(define (generate-huffman-tree pairs)
  (successive-merge (make-leaf-set pairs)))
```

Make-leaf-set is the procedure given above that transforms the list of pairs into an ordered set of leaves. Successive-merge is the procedure you must write, using make-code-tree to successively merge the smallest-weight elements of the set until there is only one element left, which is the desired Huffman tree. (This procedure is slightly tricky, but not really complicated. If you find yourself designing a complex procedure, then you are almost certainly doing something wrong. You can take significant advantage of the fact that we are using an ordered set representation.)

Exercise 2.42

The following eight-symbol alphabet with associated relative frequencies was designed to efficiently encode the lyrics of 1950s rock songs. (Note that the "symbols" of an "alphabet" need not be individual letters.)

A	2	NA	16
BOOM	1	SHA	3
GET	2	YIP	10
JOB	2	WAH	1

Generate a corresponding Huffman tree, and use it to encode the following message:

Get a job
Sha na na na na na na na na
Get a job
Sha na na na na na na na na
Wah yip yip yip yip yip yip yip yip
Sha boom

How many bits are required for the encoding? What is the smallest number of bits that would be needed to encode this song if we used a fixed-length code for the eight-symbol alphabet?

Exercise 2.43

Suppose we have a Huffman tree for an alphabet of N symbols, and that the relative frequencies of the symbols are $1, 2, 4, \ldots, 2^{N-1}$. Sketch the tree for $N=5$; for $N=10$. In such a tree (for general N) how may bits are required to encode the most frequent symbol? the least frequent symbol?

Exercise 2.44

Consider the encoding procedure that you designed in exercise 2.40. What is the order of growth in the number of steps needed to encode a symbol? Be sure to include the number of steps needed to search the symbol list at each node encountered. To answer this question in general is difficult. Consider the special case where the relative frequencies of the N symbols are as described in exercise 2.43, and give the order of growth (as a function of N) of the number of steps needed to encode the most frequent and least frequent symbols in the alphabet.

2.3 Multiple Representations for Abstract Data

We have introduced data abstraction, a methodology for structuring systems in such a way that much of a program can be specified independent of the choices involved in implementing the data objects that the program manipulates. For example, we saw in section 2.1.1 how to separate the designing of a program that uses rational numbers from the implementation of rational numbers in terms of the computer language's primitive mechanisms for constructing compound data. The key idea was to erect an abstraction barrier—in this case, the selectors and constructors for rational numbers (make-rat, numer, denom)—that isolates the way rational numbers are used from their underlying representation in terms of list structure. A similar abstraction barrier isolates the details of the procedures that perform rational arithmetic (+rat, -rat, *rat, and /rat) from the "higher-level" procedures that use rational numbers. The resulting program has the structure shown in figure 2.1.

These data-abstraction barriers are powerful tools for controlling complexity. By isolating the underlying representations of data objects, we can divide the task of designing a large program into smaller tasks that can be performed separately. But the kind of data abstraction we have presented is not yet powerful enough. In a large system it may not make sense to speak of "the underlying representation" of a data object. To take a simple example, complex numbers may be represented in two almost equivalent ways: in rectangular form (real and imaginary parts) and in polar form (magnitude and angle). Sometimes rectangular form is more appropriate and sometimes polar form is more appropriate. Indeed, it is

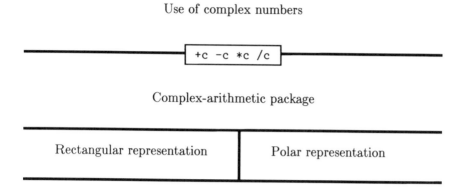

Figure 2.10
Data-abstraction barriers in the complex-number system.

perfectly plausible to imagine a system in which complex numbers are represented in both ways and in which the operators for manipulating complex numbers will work with either representation.

Now we will learn how to cope with data that may be represented in different ways by different parts of a program. This requires constructing *generic operators*—procedures that can operate on data that may be represented in more than one way. Our main technique for building generic operators will be to work in terms of data objects that have *manifest types*, that is, data objects that include explicit information about how they are to be processed. We will also discuss *data-directed* programming, a powerful and convenient implementation strategy for systems of generic operators.

We begin with the simple complex-number example. We will see how manifest types and data-directed style enable us to design separate rectangular and polar representations for complex numbers while maintaining the notion of an abstract "complex-number" data object. We will accomplish this by defining arithmetic operators for complex numbers (+c, -c, *c, and /c) in terms of generic selectors that access parts of a complex number independent of how the number is represented. The resulting complex-number system, as shown in figure 2.10, contains two different kinds of abstraction barriers. The "horizontal" abstraction barriers play the same role as the ones in figure 2.1. They isolate "higher-level" operations from "lower-level" representations. In addition, there is a "vertical" barrier that gives us the ability to separately design and install alternative representations.

In section 2.4 we will show how to use manifest types and data-directed style to develop a generic arithmetic package. This provides operators (add, mul, and so on) that can be used to manipulate all sorts of "numbers" and

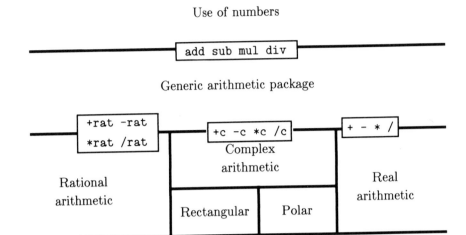

Figure 2.11
Generic arithmetic system.

can be easily extended when a new kind of number is needed. Figure 2.11 shows the structure of the system we shall build. Notice the abstraction barriers. From the perspective of someone using "numbers," there is a single operator add that operates on whatever numbers are supplied. In fact, add is a "generic interface" that allows the separate real-arithmetic, rational-arithmetic, and complex-arithmetic packages to be accessed uniformly by programs that use numbers. Moreover, any individual arithmetic package (such as the complex package) may itself be accessed through generic operators (such as +c) that combine packages designed for different representations. Of particular importance to the system designer is the fact that one can design the individual arithmetic packages separately and combine them to produce a generic arithmetic package by using data-directed style as a conventional interface.

2.3.1 Representations for Complex Numbers

We will develop a system that performs arithmetic operations on complex numbers as a simple but somewhat unrealistic example of a program that uses generic operators. We begin by discussing two plausible representations for complex numbers as ordered pairs: rectangular form (real part and imaginary part) and polar form (magnitude and angle).[20]   Section

---

[20] In actual computational systems, rectangular form is preferable to polar form most of the time because of roundoff errors in conversion between rectangular and polar form. This is why the complex-number example is unrealistic. Nevertheless, it provides a clear illustration of the design of a system using generic operators and a good introduction to the more substantial systems to be developed later in this chapter.

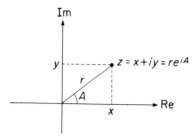

Figure 2.12
Complex numbers as vectors.

2.3.2 will show how both representations can be made to coexist in a single system through the use of manifest types and generic operators, and section 2.3.3 will introduce data-directed programming as a technique for organizing systems that use generic operators.

Like rational numbers, complex numbers are naturally represented as ordered pairs. The set of complex numbers can be thought of as a two-dimensional space with two orthogonal axes, the "real" axis and the "imaginary" axis. (See figure 2.12.) From this point of view, the complex number $z = x + iy$ (where $i^2 = -1$) can be thought of as the vector whose real coordinate is x and whose imaginary coordinate is y. Addition of complex numbers reduces in this representation to addition of coordinates:

$$\text{Real-part}(z_1 + z_2) = \text{Real-part}(z_1) + \text{Real-part}(z_2)$$
$$\text{Imaginary-part}(z_1 + z_2) = \text{Imaginary-part}(z_1) + \text{Imaginary-part}(z_2)$$

When multiplying complex numbers, it is more natural to think in terms of representing a complex number in polar form, as a magnitude and an angle, as shown in figure 2.12. The product of two complex numbers is the vector obtained by nstretching one complex number by the length of the other and then rotating it through the angle of the other:

$$\text{Magnitude}(z_1 \cdot z_2) = \text{Magnitude}(z_1) \cdot \text{Magnitude}(z_2)$$
$$\text{Angle}(z_1 \cdot z_2) = \text{Angle}(z_1) + \text{Angle}(z_2)$$

Thus, there are two different representations for complex numbers, which are appropriate for different operations. Yet, from the viewpoint of someone writing a program that uses complex numbers, the principle of data abstraction suggests that all the operations for manipulating complex numbers should be available regardless of which representation is used by the computer. For example, it is often useful to be able to find the magnitude of a complex number that is specified by rectangular coordinates. Similarly, it is often useful to be able to determine the real part of a complex number that is specified by polar coordinates.

To design such a system, we can follow the same data-abstraction strategy we followed in designing the rational-number package in section 2.1.1. Assume that the operators on complex numbers are implemented in terms of the following four selectors: `real-part`, `imag-part`, `magnitude`, and `angle`. Also assume that we have two procedures for constructing complex numbers: `make-rectangular` returns a complex number with given real and imaginary parts, and `make-polar` returns a complex number with given magnitude and angle. These procedures have the property that, for any complex number z, both

```
(make-rectangular (real-part z) (imag-part z))
```

and

```
(make-polar (magnitude z) (angle z))
```

produce complex numbers that are equal to z.

Using these constructors and selectors, we can implement complex-number arithmetic using the "abstract data" specified by the constructors and selectors, just as we did for rational numbers in section 2.1.1. As shown in the formulas above, we can add and subtract complex numbers in terms of real and imaginary parts while multiplying and dividing complex numbers in terms of magnitudes and angles:

```
(define (+c z1 z2)
  (make-rectangular (+ (real-part z1) (real-part z2))
                    (+ (imag-part z1) (imag-part z2))))

(define (-c z1 z2)
  (make-rectangular (- (real-part z1) (real-part z2))
                    (- (imag-part z1) (imag-part z2))))

(define (*c z1 z2)
  (make-polar (* (magnitude z1) (magnitude z2))
              (+ (angle z1) (angle z2))))

(define (/c z1 z2)
  (make-polar (/ (magnitude z1) (magnitude z2))
              (- (angle z1) (angle z2))))
```

To complete the complex-number package, we must choose a representation and we must implement the constructors and selectors in terms of the primitive numbers and the primitive list structure. There are two obvious possible choices. We can represent a complex number in "rectangular form" as a pair (real part, imaginary part) or in "polar form" as a pair (magnitude, angle). Which shall we choose?

If we represent a complex number in rectangular form, then selecting the real and imaginary parts is straightforward, as is constructing a complex number with given real and imaginary parts. To find the magnitude and the angle, or to construct a complex number with a given magnitude and angle, we use the relations

$$x = r\ \cos A, \qquad r = \sqrt{x^2 + y^2},$$

$$y = r\ \sin A, \qquad A = \arctan(y, x),$$

which relate the real and imaginary parts (x, y) to the magnitude and the angle (r, A).[21] This leads to the following selectors and constructors:

```
(define (make-rectangular x y) (cons x y))

(define (real-part z) (car z))

(define (imag-part z) (cdr z))

(define (make-polar r a)
  (cons (* r (cos a)) (* r (sin a))))

(define (magnitude z)
  (sqrt (+ (square (car z)) (square (cdr z)))))

(define (angle z)
  (atan (cdr z) (car z)))
```

On the other hand, we may choose to implement our complex numbers in polar form. If so, then selecting the magnitude and angle will be straightforward but we will have to use trigonometry to find the real and imaginary parts. Here is the corresponding set of procedures:

```
(define (make-rectangular x y)
  (cons (sqrt (+ (square x) (square y)))
        (atan y x)))
```

21 The arctangent function referred to here is defined so as to take two arguments y and x and to return the angle whose tangent is y/x. The signs of the arguments determine the quadrant of the angle.

```
(define (real-part z)
  (* (car z) (cos (cdr z))))

(define (imag-part z)
  (* (car z) (sin (cdr z))))

(define (make-polar r a) (cons r a))

(define (magnitude z) (car z))

(define (angle z) (cdr z))
```

The discipline of data abstraction ensures that the implementation of the complex-number-arithmetic operators +c, -c, *c, and /c is independent of which representation we choose.

2.3.2 Manifest Types

One way to view data abstraction is as an application to program design of the "principle of least commitment." By setting up selectors and constructors as an abstraction barrier, we can defer to the last possible moment the choice of a concrete representation for our data objects and thus retain maximum flexibility in our system design. In fact, the principle of least commitment can be carried to further extremes than we have seen so far. If we desire, we can maintain the ambiguity of representation even after we have designed the selectors and constructors, electing to represent some complex numbers in polar form and some in rectangular form. However, if both kinds of representations are included in a single system we will need some way to distinguish data in polar form from data in rectangular form. Otherwise, if we were asked, for instance, to find the magnitude of the pair $(3, 4)$, we wouldn't know whether to answer 5 (interpreting the number in rectangular form) or 3 (interpreting the number in polar form). A straightforward way to accomplish this distinction is to include a "type"—in this case, rectangular or polar—as part of each complex number. Then when we need to manipulate a complex number we can use the type to decide which selector to apply.

A data object that has a type that can be recognized and tested is said to have *manifest type*. In order to manipulate typed data, we will assume that we have two procedures, type and contents, that extract from a data object the type and the actual contents (the polar or rectangular coordinates, in the case of a complex number). We will also postulate a procedure, attach-type, that takes a type and contents and produces a typed data object. A straightforward way to implement this is to use ordinary list structure:

```
(define (attach-type type contents)
  (cons type contents))

(define (type datum)
  (if (not (atom? datum))
      (car datum)
      (error "Bad typed datum -- TYPE" datum)))

(define (contents datum)
  (if (not (atom? datum))
      (cdr datum)
      (error "Bad typed datum -- CONTENTS" datum)))
```

Using these procedures, we can define predicates rectangular? and polar?, which recognize polar and rectangular numbers, respectively:

```
(define (rectangular? z)
  (eq? (type z) 'rectangular))

(define (polar? z)
  (eq? (type z) 'polar))
```

Now we modify the constructors for complex numbers to include the type as part of the number. To construct a complex number in rectangular form, given real and imaginary parts, we use

```
(define (make-rectangular x y)
  (attach-type 'rectangular (cons x y)))
```

To construct a complex number in polar form, given magnitude and angle, we use[22]

```
(define (make-polar r a)
  (attach-type 'polar (cons r a)))
```

Our abstract selectors for typed complex numbers are now defined in terms of the appropriate selectors for the untyped complex numbers. We can use the type of a complex number to select the appropriate procedures for dealing with numbers of the given type. These procedures can be

---

[22] In our previous implementation, we also included operations for constructing a rectangular number from a magnitude and angle and for constructing a polar number from real and imaginary parts. These are unnecessary in the new system we are designing.

divided into two "packages," one for handling rectangular form and the
other for polar form. We use contents to get at the bare, untyped datum.

```
(define (real-part z)
  (cond ((rectangular? z)
         (real-part-rectangular (contents z)))
        ((polar? z)
         (real-part-polar (contents z)))))

(define (imag-part z)
  (cond ((rectangular? z)
         (imag-part-rectangular (contents z)))
        ((polar? z)
         (imag-part-polar (contents z)))))

(define (magnitude z)
  (cond ((rectangular? z)
         (magnitude-rectangular (contents z)))
        ((polar? z)
         (magnitude-polar (contents z)))))

(define (angle z)
  (cond ((rectangular? z)
         (angle-rectangular (contents z)))
        ((polar? z)
         (angle-polar (contents z)))))
```

As the underlying procedures in each of the packages for handling untyped complex numbers we can use the selectors defined in the previous
section, after renaming each procedure so as to avoid name conflicts. Here
are the selectors for the rectangular representation:

```
(define (real-part-rectangular z) (car z))

(define (imag-part-rectangular z) (cdr z))

(define (magnitude-rectangular z)
  (sqrt (+ (square (car z))
           (square (cdr z)))))

(define (angle-rectangular z)
  (atan (cdr z) (car z)))
```

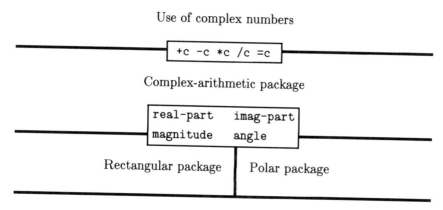

Figure 2.13
Structure of the generic complex-arithmetic system.

The selectors for the polar representation are

```
(define (real-part-polar z)
  (* (car z) (cos (cdr z))))

(define (imag-part-polar z)
  (* (car z) (sin (cdr z))))

(define (magnitude-polar z) (car z))

(define (angle-polar z) (cdr z))
```

The resulting complex-number system has the structure shown in figure 2.13. Notice that the system can be decomposed into three relatively independent parts: the complex-number-arithmetic package, the rectangular-representation package, and the polar-representation package. Each of these packages could have been designed without any knowledge of the others. For instance, the polar and rectangular packages could have been written separately, by two separate people, and then both could have been used as underlying representations by a third programmer implementing the complex-arithmetic procedures +c, -c, *c, and /c in terms of the abstract constructor/selector interface.

Since each data object is "tagged" with its type, the selectors can operate on the data in a generic manner. That is, each selector may be defined to have a behavior that depends upon the particular type of data it is applied to. Notice the general mechanism for interfacing the separate packages: Within a given representation package (say, the polar package) a complex number is an untyped pair (magnitude, angle). When a generic selector operates on a number of polar type, it strips off the type and passes the untyped contents on to the polar package. Conversely, when a number is constructed and "exported" from the polar package, it is given a manifest type so that it can be appropriately recognized by the higher-level procedures. This discipline of stripping off and attaching types as data objects are passed from level to level can be an important organizational strategy, as we shall see in section 2.4.

Although this way of organizing generic operators is very valuable, there are two weak points in our system. One is that the generic interface procedures (real-part, imag-part, magnitude, and angle) must "know about" all the different representations. In the following section we will introduce data-directed programming, a technique that can be used to deal with this problem. Another weakness of our system is that although the separate packages can be designed separately, we have to make sure that no two procedures in the entire system have the same name. This is why we appended the package name to each selector procedure (e.g., real-part-polar) in the example above.[23]

2.3.3 Data-Directed Programming

The use of manifest types and generic operators is a powerful tool for obtaining modularity in system design, but the techniques we have available at this moment are too weak to solve really large-scale problems. For example, suppose someone designed a new package, using a new representation for complex numbers, and asked us to interface this with our complex-number system. We would need to identify this new representation with a type, and then add a clause to each of the generic interface procedures (real-part, imag-part, magnitude, and angle) to check for the new type and access the appropriate selector in the new package. This is not much of a problem for the complex-number system as it stands, but suppose there were not two but hundreds of different representations for complex numbers. And suppose that there were many generic selectors to be maintained in the abstract-data interface. Suppose, in fact, that no one programmer knew all the interface procedures or all the representations. Although this is not likely to be the case with systems that perform arithmetic, the problem is

---

23 There are more elegant ways to handle name conflict. In chapter 3 we will see how environments serve as contexts that determine the meaning of names in expressions. We will exploit this idea in section 4.3 to show how each package can be structured as a separate environment, with its own local names.

Types

		Polar	Rectangular
	real-part	real-part-polar	real-part-rectangular
Operators	imag-part	imag-part-polar	imag-part-rectangular
	magnitude	magnitude-polar	magnitude-rectangular
	angle	angle-polar	angle-rectangular

Figure 2.14
Table of operators for complex-number system.

real and must be addressed in programs such as large-scale data-base-management systems and symbolic-algebra systems. What we need is a means for modularizing the system design even further. This is provided by the programming technique known as *data-directed programming*.

To understand how data-directed programming works, begin with the observation that whenever we deal with a number of generic operators that are common to a number of different types we are, in effect, dealing with a two-dimensional table that contains the possible operators on one axis and the possible types on the other axis. The entries in the table are the procedures that implement each operator for each type of operand presented. In the complex-number system developed in the previous section, the correspondence between operator name, data type, and actual procedure was spread out among the various conditional clauses in the generic interface procedures. But the same information could have been organized in a table, as shown in figure 2.14. Data-directed programming is the technique of designing programs to work with such a table directly. Previously, we implemented the mechanism that interfaces the complex-arithmetic package with the two representation packages as a set of procedures. Here we will implement the interface as a single procedure that looks up the combination of the operator and type in the table to find the correct procedure to apply, and then applies it to the contents of the operand. If we do this, then to add a new representation package to the system we need not change any existing procedures; we need only add new entries to the table.

To implement this plan, assume that we have two procedures, put and get, for manipulating the operator-and-type table:

(put ⟨*type*⟩ ⟨*op*⟩ ⟨*item*⟩) installs ⟨*item*⟩ in the table entry indexed by ⟨*type*⟩ and ⟨*op*⟩.

(get ⟨*type*⟩ ⟨*op*⟩) looks up the ⟨*type*⟩, ⟨*op*⟩ entry in the table and returns the item found there. If no item is found, get returns nil.

For now, we can assume that put and get are primitive operators included in our language. In chapter 3 (section 3.3.3) we will see how to implement these and other operations for manipulating tables.

Here is how the data-directed system works. The programmer who defined the rectangular representation package could install it in the complex-arithmetic system by adding entries to the table that tell the system how to operate on rectangular numbers:

```
(put 'rectangular 'real-part real-part-rectangular)
(put 'rectangular 'imag-part imag-part-rectangular)
(put 'rectangular 'magnitude magnitude-rectangular)
(put 'rectangular 'angle angle-rectangular)
```

(The ⟨item⟩ entries in the table are the actual procedures that are to be applied, not the names of the procedures.) Meanwhile, another programmer could work on the polar-form definitions, independent of his colleague, and the completed definitions could be similarly interfaced with the complex-number package:

```
(put 'polar 'real-part real-part-polar)
(put 'polar 'imag-part imag-part-polar)
(put 'polar 'magnitude magnitude-polar)
(put 'polar 'angle angle-polar)
```

The complex-arithmetic package itself accesses the table by means of a general "operator" procedure called operate, which applies a generic operator to an object by looking in the table under the name of the operator and the type of the object and applying the resulting procedure if one is present:

```
(define (operate op obj)
  (let ((proc (get (type obj) op)))
    (if (not (null? proc))
        (proc (contents obj))
        (error "Operator undefined for this type -- OPERATE"
               (list op obj)))))
```

Using operate, we can define our generic interface procedures as follows:

```
(define (real-part obj) (operate 'real-part obj))
(define (imag-part obj) (operate 'imag-part obj))
(define (magnitude obj) (operate 'magnitude obj))
(define (angle obj) (operate 'angle obj))
```

These procedures do not have to be changed at all if a new representation is added to the system.

The general strategy of checking the type of a datum and calling an appropriate procedure is called *dispatching on type,* and data-directed programming is an extremely flexible way to organize the dispatch. This kind of "conventional interface" can be used to combine packages for representations that were constructed separately. This technique is used regularly by expert programmers to enhance the extensibility and the modularity of their systems.

Exercise 2.45

Section 2.2.4 described a program that performs symbolic differentiation:

```
(define (deriv exp var)
  (cond ((constant? exp) 0)
        ((variable? exp)
         (if (same-variable? exp var) 1 0))
        ((sum? exp)
         (make-sum (deriv (addend exp) var)
                   (deriv (augend exp) var)))
        ((product? exp)
         (make-sum
           (make-product (multiplier exp)
                         (deriv (multiplicand exp) var))
           (make-product (deriv (multiplier exp) var)
                         (multiplicand exp))))
        ⟨ more rules can be added here⟩
        ))
```

We can regard this program as performing a dispatch on the "type" of the expression to be differentiated. In this situation the "type" tag of the datum is the algebraic operator symbol (such as +) and the operation being performed is deriv. We can transform this program into data-directed style by rewriting the basic derivative procedure as

```
(define (deriv exp var)
  (cond ((constant? exp) 0)
        ((variable? exp)
         (if (same-variable? exp var) 1 0))
        (else ((get (operator exp) 'deriv) (operands exp) var))))

(define (operator exp) (car exp))

(define (operands exp) (cdr exp))
```

a. Explain what was done above. Why can't we assimilate the constant? and same-variable? predicates into the data-directed dispatch?

b. Write the procedures for derivatives of sums and products, and the auxiliary code required to install them in the table used by the program above.

c. Choose any additional differentiation rule that you like, such as the one for exponents, and install it in this data-directed system.

d. In this simple algebraic manipulator the type of an expression is the algebraic operator that binds it together. Suppose, however, we indexed the procedures in the opposite way, so that the dispatch line looked like

```
((get 'deriv (operator exp)) (operands exp) var)
```

What corresponding changes to the derivative system are required?

Exercise 2.46

Insatiable Enterprises, Inc., is a highly decentralized conglomerate company consisting of a large number of independent divisions located all over the world. The company's computer facilities have just been interconnected by means of a clever network interfacing scheme that makes the entire network appear to any user to be a single computer. Insatiable's president, in her first attempt to exploit the ability of the network to extract administrative information from division files, is dismayed to discover that, although all the division files have been implemented as data structures in Lisp, the particular data structure used varies from division to division. A meeting of division managers is hastily called to search for a strategy to integrate the files that will satisfy headquarters' needs while preserving the existing autonomy of the divisions.

Show how such a strategy can be implemented with data-directed programming. As an example, suppose that each division's personnel records consist of a single file, which contains a set of records keyed on employees' names. The structure of the set varies from division to division. Furthermore, each employee's record is itself a set (structured differently from division to division) that contains information keyed under identifiers such as address and salary. In particular:

• Implement for headquarters a get-record procedure that retrieves a specified employee's record from a specified personnel file. The procedure should be applicable to any division's file. Explain how the individual divisions' files should be structured. In particular, what type information must be supplied?

• Implement for headquarters a get-salary procedure that returns the salary information from a given employee's record from any division's personnel file. How should the record be structured in order to make this operation work?

• Implement for headquarters a find-employee-record procedure that searches all the divisions' files for the record of a given employee and returns the record. Assume that this procedure takes as arguments an employee's name and a list of all the divisions' files.

• When Insatiable takes over a new company, what changes must be made in order to incorporate the new personnel information into the central system?

Message passing

The key idea of data-directed programming is to handle generic operators in programs by dealing explicitly with operator-and-type tables, such as the table in figure 2.14. The more traditional style of programming, which we used in section 2.3.2, organized the required dispatching on type by having each operator take care of its own dispatching. In effect, this style of programming decomposes the operator-and-type table into rows, with each generic operator procedure representing a row of the table.

An alternate implementation strategy is to decompose the table into columns and, instead of using "intelligent operators" that dispatch on data types, to work with "intelligent data objects" that dispatch on operator names. We can do this by arranging things so that a data object, such as a rectangular number, is represented as a procedure that takes as input the required operation name and performs the operation indicated. In such a discipline, make-rectangular could be written as

```
(define (make-rectangular x y)
  (define (dispatch m)
    (cond ((eq? m 'real-part) x)
          ((eq? m 'imag-part) y)
          ((eq? m 'magnitude)
           (sqrt (+ (square x) (square y))))
          ((eq? m 'angle) (atan y x))
          (else
           (error "Unknown op -- MAKE-RECTANGULAR" m))))
  dispatch)
```

The corresponding operate procedure, which applies a generic operation to a data object, now simply feeds the operation's name to the data object and lets the object do the work:

```
(define (operate op obj) (obj op))
```

Note that the "data object" returned by make-rectangular is a procedure—the internal dispatch procedure. This is the procedure that is invoked when operate requests an operation to be performed.

This style of programming is called *message passing*. The name comes from the image that a data object is an entity that receives the requested operation name as a "message." We have already seen an example of message passing in section 2.1.3, where we saw how cons, car, and cdr could be defined with no data objects but only procedures. Here we see that message passing is not a mathematical trick but a useful technique for organizing systems with generic operators. In the remainder of this chapter we will continue to use data-directed programming, rather than message passing, to discuss generic arithmetic operators. In chapter 3 we will return to message passing, and we will see that it can be a powerful tool for structuring simulation programs.

Exercise 2.47

Implement the constructor make-polar in message-passing style. Your procedure should be analogous to the make-rectangular procedure given above.

Exercise 2.48

As a large system with generic operators evolves, new types of data objects or new operators may be needed. For each of the three organizational strategies—"conventional" style (as in section 2.3.2), data-directed style, and message-passing-style—describe the changes that must be made to a system in order to add new types or new operators. Which organization would be most appropriate for a system in which new types must often be added? Which would be most appropriate for a system in which new operators must often be added?

2.4 Systems with Generic Operators

In the previous section, we saw how to design systems in which data objects can be represented in more than one way. The key idea is to link the package that specifies the data operations to the several packages that implement the various representations by means of generic interface procedures. Now we will see how to use this same idea not only to define operators that are generic over different representations but also to define operators that are generic over different kinds of operands.

We will consider how to design a set of arithmetic operators that work on "all different kinds of numbers." We have already seen several different packages of arithmetic operators: the primitive arithmetic (+, -, *, /) built into our language, the rational-number arithmetic (+rat, -rat, *rat, /rat) that we implemented in section 2.1.1, and the generic complex-number arithmetic that we implemented in section 2.3.3. We will now use data-directed techniques to construct a package of arithmetic operators that incorporates all the arithmetic systems we have already constructed. Moreover, our operators will be "extensible" in the sense that, if later we come up with a new class of "numbers," we can easily add these to the system without changing any of the programs we have already written.

2.4.1 Generic Arithmetic Operators

The task of designing generic arithmetic operators is analogous to that of designing the generic complex-number operators. We would like, for instance, to have a generic addition operator add that would act like ordinary primitive addition + on ordinary numbers, like +rat on rational numbers, and like +c on complex numbers. We can implement add, and

the other generic arithmetic operators, by following the same strategy that
we used in section 2.3.3 to implement the generic selectors for complex
numbers. We will attach a manifest type to each kind of number and cause
the generic operator to dispatch to an appropriate package according to
the data type of its arguments.

We begin by installing a package for handling "ordinary numbers," that
is, the primitive numbers of our language. We will refer to these as type
number. The arithmetic operators in this package are essentially the primitive arithmetic:

```
(define (+number x y)
   (make-number (+ x y)))

(define (-number x y)
   (make-number (- x y)))

(define (*number x y)
   (make-number (* x y)))

(define (/number x y)
   (make-number (/ x y)))
```

Here make-number is a procedure that attaches an appropriate manifest
type to its argument:

```
(define (make-number n)
   (attach-type 'number n))
```

The next step is to link the operators in the package to the generic
operators add, sub, mul, and div. We do this with data-directed programming, just as in section 2.3.3. As before, we place the procedures in a table,
indexed under the data type and the name of the generic operator:

```
(put 'number 'add +number)
(put 'number 'sub -number)
(put 'number 'mul *number)
(put 'number 'div /number)
```

The generic operators are defined as follows:

```
(define (add x y) (operate-2 'add x y))
(define (sub x y) (operate-2 'sub x y))
(define (mul x y) (operate-2 'mul x y))
(define (div x y) (operate-2 'div x y))
```

As with the complex-number selectors, our generic arithmetic operators will use a general "operate" procedure that dispatches according to the type of the argument. However, whereas the selectors for complex numbers were operators with one argument, our generic arithmetic operators are operators with two arguments. Hence, we cannot use the same `operate` procedure as before (section 2.3.3). Instead we use the following procedure to perform the dispatch:

```
(define (operate-2 op arg1 arg2)
  (let ((t1 (type arg1)))
    (if (eq? t1 (type arg2))
        (let ((proc (get t1 op)))
          (if (not (null? proc))
              (proc (contents arg1) (contents arg2))
              (error
               "Operator undefined on this type -- OPERATE-2"
               (list op arg1 arg2))))
        (error "Operands not of same type -- OPERATE-2"
               (list op arg1 arg2)))))
```

`Operate-2` verifies that the two operands have the same type and, if so, dispatches to the procedure that was installed in the table for the given type and operator. If there is no such procedure, then `operate-2` signals an error.

If the two operands do not have the same type, `operate-2` signals an error. This is not really the correct thing to do. For instance, if we try to add the (primitive) number 3 to the (complex) number $2 + 4i$, `operate-2` will complain that the types do not match. And yet we should expect a "reasonable" system to produce the answer $5 + 4i$. On the other hand, it turns out that arranging for this kind of "reasonable" behavior opens an enormous can of worms concerning the interactions among data of different types. We will duck this issue now and return to it in section 2.4.2.

Exercise 2.49

In defining the package for handling ordinary numbers, we defined operators +number, -number, and so on, which were essentially nothing more than calls to the primitive operators +, -, etc. It was not possible to use the primitives of the language directly because our manifest type system requires that each data object have a type attached to it. In fact, however, Lisp implementations do have a type system, which they use internally. Primitive predicates such as symbol? and number? determine whether data objects have particular types.

Modify the definitions of type, contents, and attach-type from section 2.3.2 so that our generic system takes advantage of the internal type system. That is to say, the system should work as before except that ordinary numbers should be represented simply as numbers rather than as pairs whose car is the symbol number.

Interfacing the complex-number package

Now that the framework of the generic arithmetic system is in place, it is easy to incorporate the complex-number package. We begin by writing a procedure that attaches the type complex to complex numbers, so they can be recognized outside of the complex package:

```
(define (make-complex z)
  (attach-type 'complex z))
```

We next define the complex-arithmetic operators to be calls to our generic complex-number-representation operators:

```
(define (+complex z1 z2) (make-complex (+c z1 z2)))
(define (-complex z1 z2) (make-complex (-c z1 z2)))
(define (*complex z1 z2) (make-complex (*c z1 z2)))
(define (/complex z1 z2) (make-complex (/c z1 z2)))
```

Finally, we install the complex-arithmetic operators in the appropriate positions in the operator table, so that the generic arithmetic operators will dispatch correctly:

```
(put 'complex 'add +complex)
(put 'complex 'sub -complex)
(put 'complex 'mul *complex)
(put 'complex 'div /complex)
```

What we have here is a two-level type system. A typical complex number such as the number constructed by

```
(make-complex (make-rectangular 3 4))
```

would be represented as shown in figure 2.15. The outer type (complex) is used to direct the number to the complex package. Once within the complex package, the next type (rectangular) is used to direct the number to the rectangular package. Strictly, rectangular and polar are not types of numbers at all but types for the contents of a complex number. In a large and complicated system there might be many levels, each interfaced with the next by means of generic operators. As a data object is passed "downward," the outer type that is used to direct it to the appropriate package is stripped off (by applying contents) and the next level of type becomes visible to be used for further dispatching.

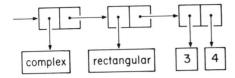

Figure 2.15
The object constructed by (make-complex (make-rectangular 3 4)).

Exercise 2.50

When we evaluate the expression

```
(add (make-complex (make-rectangular 3 4))
     (make-complex (make-polar 5 1)))
```

what are the actual arguments sent to +c? What happened to the symbol complex? Where was it stripped off?

Finally, observe that the operators real-part, imag-part, magnitude, and angle are available only inside the complex-number package—they are defined only for data objects of type rectangular or polar. On the other hand, it is easy to "export" these operators from the package, so that they can be applied directly to objects of type complex and be automatically redispatched to the right representation type. We simply install the operators in the table under type complex:

```
(put 'complex 'real-part real-part)
(put 'complex 'imag-part imag-part)
(put 'complex 'magnitude magnitude)
(put 'complex 'angle angle)
```

Exercise 2.51

Describe in detail why this exporting method works. As an example, trace through all the procedures called in evaluating the expression (magnitude z) where z is the object shown in figure 2.15. In particular, how many times is operate invoked? What procedure is dispatched to in each case?

Exercise 2.52

The rational-arithmetic package of section 2.1.1 can be easily incorporated into our generic arithmetic system. Make the necessary additions and modifications to the package to make it compatible with the conventions of the generic arithmetic system. Install it.

Exercise 2.53

Define a generic equality operator equ? that tests the equality of two numbers and install it as an operator in the generic arithmetic package. It should work for ordinary numbers, rational numbers, and complex numbers.

Exercise 2.54

Define and install in the generic arithmetic package a generic operator =zero? that tests if its argument is zero. This operator should work for ordinary numbers, rational numbers, and complex numbers.

2.4.2 Combining Operands of Different Types

We have seen how to define a unified arithmetic system that encompasses ordinary numbers, complex numbers, rational numbers, and any other type of number we might decide to invent, but we have ignored an important issue. The operators we have defined so far treat the different data types as being completely independent. Thus, there are separate packages for adding, say, two ordinary numbers, or two complex numbers. What we have not yet considered is the fact that it is meaningful to define operations that cross the type boundaries, such as the addition of a complex number to an ordinary number. We have gone to great pains to introduce barriers between parts of our programs so that they can be developed and understood separately. We would like to introduce the new operations in some carefully controlled way, so that we can support the cross-type operations without seriously violating our module boundaries.

One way to handle cross-type operations is to design a different operator for each possible pair of types for which the operation is valid. For instance, we could have addition operations +number-complex (which adds an ordinary number to a complex number), +rational-complex, and so on. Then we could arrange these in a three-dimensional table that indexes the appropriate procedure under the name of the generic operator, the type of the first argument, and the type of the second argument. Support for such a table could be introduced into the operate-2 procedure of section 2.4.1.

This three-dimensional-table method allows us to combine numbers of different types, but at an enormous price. If there are n different types in our system, we need in general to design n^2 different versions of each generic operator. In such a system, the cost of introducing a new type is not just the construction of the package of operators for that type but also the construction and installation of the procedures that implement the cross-type operations. This can easily be much more code than is needed to define the operators on the type itself. If our system includes not only binary operators but also operators on three, four, or more arguments that may have different types, the penalty for introducing a new type is even more severe.

Coercion

In the general situation of completely unrelated operations acting on completely unrelated types, the method of using a three-dimensional table to handle operands of different types, cumbersome though it may be, is the best that one can hope for. Fortunately, we can usually do better, by taking advantage of additional structure that may be latent in our type system. Often the different data types are not completely independent, and there may be ways by which objects of one type may be viewed as being of another type. This process is called *coercion*. For example, if we are asked to arithmetically combine an ordinary number with a complex number, we can view the ordinary number as a complex number whose imaginary part is zero. This transforms the problem to that of combining two complex numbers, which can be handled in the ordinary way by the complex-arithmetic package.

In general, we can implement this idea by designing coercion procedures that transform an object of one type into an equivalent object of another type. Here is a typical coercion procedure, which transforms a given ordinary number to a complex number with that real part and zero imaginary part:

```
(define (number->complex n)
  (make-complex (make-rectangular (contents n) 0)))
```

We install these coercion procedures in a special coercion table, indexed under the names of the two types:

```
(put-coercion 'number 'complex number->complex)
```

(We assume that there are procedures put-coercion and get-coercion available for manipulating this table.) Generally some of the slots in the table will be empty, because it is not generally possible to coerce an arbitrary data object of each type into all other types. For example, there is no way to coerce an arbitrary complex number to an ordinary number, so there will be no general complex->number procedure included in the table.

Once the coercion table has been set up, we can handle coercion in a data-directed manner by modifying the operate-2 procedure given in section 2.4.1 as follows. When asked to operate on two objects obj1 and obj2, we first check to see if they have the same type. If so, we dispatch to the procedure for handling that type, just as before. If the types are different, we check the coercion table to see if objects of type 1 can be coerced to type 2. If so, we coerce obj1 and try the operation again. If objects of type 1 cannot in general be coerced to type 2, we try the coercion the other way around to see if there is a way to coerce obj2 to the type of obj1. Finally, if there is no known way to coerce either type to the other type, we give up. Here is the procedure:

```
(define (operate-2 op obj1 obj2)
  (let ((t1 (type obj1)) (t2 (type obj2)))
    (if (eq? t1 t2)
        (let ((proc (get t1 op)))
          (if (not (null? proc))
              (proc (contents obj1) (contents obj2))
              (error
                "Operator undefined on this type -- OPERATE-2"
                (list op obj1 obj2))))
        (let ((t1->t2 (get-coercion t1 t2))
              (t2->t1 (get-coercion t2 t1)))
          (cond ((not (null? t1->t2))
                 (operate-2 op (t1->t2 obj1) obj2))
                ((not (null? t2->t1))
                 (operate-2 op obj1 (t2->t1 obj2)))
                (else
                 (error
                   "Operands not of same type -- OPERATE-2"
                   (list op obj1 obj2)))))))))
```

This coercion scheme for binary operators has many advantages over the method of using an unstructured three-dimensional table, as outlined above. Although we still need to write coercion procedures to relate the types (possibly n^2 procedures for a system with n types), we need to write only one procedure for each pair of types rather than a different procedure for each pair of types and each generic operator.[24]   What we are counting on here is the fact that the appropriate transformation between types depends only on the types themselves, not on the operator to be applied.

On the other hand, there may be applications for which our coercion scheme is not general enough. Even when neither of the objects to be combined can be converted to the type of the other it may still be possible to perform the operation by converting both objects to a third type. In

[24] If we are clever, we can usually get by with fewer than n^2 coercion procedures. For instance, if we know how to convert from type 1 to type 2 and from type 2 to type 3, then we can use this knowledge to convert from type 1 to type 3. This can greatly decrease the number of coercion procedures we need to supply explicitly when we add a new type to the system. If we are willing to build the required amount of sophistication into our system, we can have it search the "graph" of relations among types and automatically generate those coercion procedures that can be inferred from the ones that are supplied explicitly.

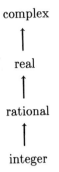

complex

real

rational

integer

Figure 2.16
A tower of types.

order to deal with such complexity and still preserve modularity in our programs, it is usually necessary to build systems that take advantage of still further structure in the relations among types, as we discuss next.

Hierarchies of types
The coercion scheme presented above relied on the existence of natural relations between pairs of types. Often there is more "global" structure in how the different types relate to each other. For instance, suppose we are building a generic arithmetic system to handle integers, rational numbers, real numbers, and complex numbers. In such a system, it is quite natural to regard an integer as a special kind of rational number, which is in turn a special kind of real number, which is in turn a special kind of complex number. What we actually have is a so-called *hierarchy of types*, in which, for example, integers are a *subtype* of rational numbers (i.e., any operator that can be applied to a rational number can automatically be applied to an integer). Conversely, we say that rational numbers form a *supertype* of integers. The particular hierarchy we have here is of a very simple kind, in which each type has at most one supertype and at most one subtype. Such a structure, called a *tower*, is illustrated in figure 2.16.

If we have a tower structure, then we can greatly simplify the problem of adding a new type to the hierarchy, for we need only specify how the new type is embedded in the next supertype above it and how it is the supertype of the type below it. For example, if we want to add an integer to a complex number, we need not explicitly define a special coercion procedure `integer->complex`. Instead, we define how an integer can be transformed into a rational number, how a rational number is transformed into a real number, and how a real number is transformed into a complex number. We then allow the system to transform the integer into a complex number through these steps and then add the two complex numbers.

We can redesign our `operate-2` procedure in the following way: For each type, we need to supply a `raise` operator, which "raises" objects of that type one level in the tower. Then when the system is required to operate on two objects of different types it can successively raise the lower type until the two objects are at the same level in the tower. (Exercise 2.56 concerns the details of implementing such a strategy.)

Another advantage of a tower is that we can easily implement the notion that every type "inherits" all operations defined on a supertype. For instance, if we do not supply a special procedure for finding the real part of an integer, we should nevertheless expect that `real-part` will be defined for integers by virtue of the fact that integers are a subtype of complex numbers. In a tower, we can arrange for this to happen by a simple modification to the `operate` procedure given in section 2.3.3: If the required operator is not directly defined for the type of the object given, we `raise` the object to its supertype and try again. We thus crawl up the tower, transforming our operand as we go, until we either find a level at which the desired operation can be performed or hit the top (in which case we give up).

Yet another advantage of a tower over a more general hierarchy is that it gives us a simple way to "lower" a data object to the simplest representation. For example, if we add $2 + 3i$ to $4 - 3i$, it would be nice to obtain the answer as the integer 6 rather than as the complex number $6 + 0i$. Exercise 2.57 discusses a way to implement such a lowering operation. (The trick is that we need a general way to distinguish those objects that can be lowered, such as $6 + 0i$, from those that cannot, such as $6 + 2i$.)

Inadequacies of hierarchies

If the data types in our system can be naturally arranged in a tower, this greatly simplifies the problems of dealing with generic operators on different types, as we have seen. Unfortunately, this is usually not the case. Figure 2.17 illustrates a more complex arrangement of mixed types, this one showing relations among different types of geometric figures. We see that, in general, a type may have more than one subtype. Triangles and quadrilaterals, for instance, are both subtypes of polygons. In addition, a type may have more than one supertype. For example, an isosceles right triangle may be regarded either as an isosceles triangle or as a right triangle. This multiple-supertypes issue is particularly thorny, since it means that there is no unique way to "raise" a type in the hierarchy. Finding the "correct" supertype in which to apply an operator to an object may involve considerable searching through the entire type network on the part of a procedure such as `operate`. Since there generally are multiple subtypes for

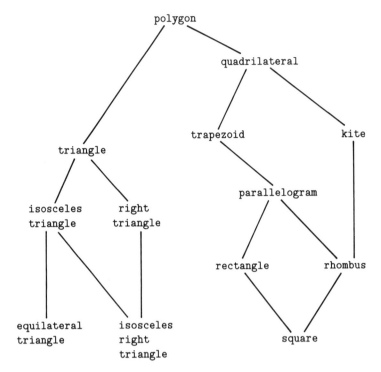

Figure 2.17
Relations among types of geometric figures.

a type, there is a similar problem in coercing a value "down" the type hierarchy. Dealing with large numbers of interrelated types while still preserving modularity in the design of large systems is very difficult, and is an area of much current research.

Exercise 2.55

Suppose you are designing a generic arithmetic system for dealing with the following tower of types: integer, rational, real, complex. For each type (except complex), design a procedure that raises objects of that type one level in the tower. Show how to install a generic `raise` operator that will work for each type (except complex).

Exercise 2.56

Using the `raise` operator of exercise 2.55, modify the `operate-2` procedure so that it coerces its two arguments to have the same type by the method of successive raising, as discussed in this section. You will need to devise a way to test which of two types is higher in the tower. Do this in a manner that is "compatible" with the rest of the system and will not lead to problems in adding new levels to the tower.

Exercise 2.57

This section mentioned a method for "simplifying" a data object in a tower of types by lowering it in the tower as far as possible. Design a procedure `drop` that accomplishes this for the tower described in exercise 2.55. The key is to decide, in some general way, whether an object can be lowered. For example, the complex number $1.5 + 0i$ can be lowered as far as `real`, the complex number $1 + 0i$ can be lowered as far as `integer`, and the complex number $2 + 3i$ cannot be lowered at all. Here is a plan for determining whether an object can be lowered: Begin by defining a generic operator `project` that "pushes" an object down in the tower. For example, projecting a complex number would involve throwing away the imaginary part. Then a number can be dropped if, when we `project` it and `raise` the result back to the type we started with, we end up with something equal to what we started with. Show how to implement this idea in detail, by writing a `drop` procedure that drops an object as far as possible. You will need to design the various projection operations[25] and install `project` as a generic operator in the system. You will also need to make use of a generic equality operator, such as described in exercise 2.53. Finally, use `drop` to rewrite `operate-2` from exercise 2.56 so that it "simplifies" its answers.

Exercise 2.58

Suppose we want to include in the package complex numbers whose real parts, imaginary parts, magnitudes, and angles can be either ordinary numbers, rational numbers, or other numbers we might wish to add to the system. Describe and implement the changes to the system needed to accommodate this. You will have to define operators such as `sine` and `cosine` that are generic over ordinary numbers and rational numbers.

2.4.3 Example: Symbolic Algebra

The manipulation of symbolic algebraic expressions is a complex process that illustrates many of the hardest problems that occur in the design of large-scale systems. An algebraic expression, in general, can be viewed as a hierarchical structure, a tree of operators applied to operands. We can construct algebraic expressions by starting with a set of primitive objects, such as constants and variables, and combining these by means of algebraic operators, such as addition and multiplication. As in other languages, we form abstractions that enable us to refer to compound objects in simple terms. Typical abstractions in symbolic algebra are ideas such as linear combination, polynomial, rational function, or trigonometric function. We can regard these as compound "types," which are often useful for directing the processing of expressions. For example, we could describe the

---

25 A real number can be projected to an integer using the `floor` or the `ceiling` primitive. These return the closest integer below or above an argument, respectively.

expression

$$x^2 \sin(y^2 + 1) + x \cos 2y + \cos(y^3 - 2y^2)$$

as a polynomial in x with coefficients that are trigonometric functions of polynomials in y whose coefficients are integers.

We will not attempt to develop a complete algebraic-manipulation system here. Such systems are exceedingly complex programs, embodying deep algebraic knowledge and elegant algorithms. What we will do is look at a simple but important part of algebraic manipulation: the arithmetic of polynomials. We will illustrate the kinds of decisions the designer of such a system faces, and how to apply the ideas of abstract data and generic operators to help organize this effort.

Arithmetic on polynomials

Our first task in designing a system for performing arithmetic on polynomials is to decide just what a polynomial is. Polynomials are normally defined relative to certain variables (the *indeterminates* of the polynomial). For simplicity, we will restrict ourselves to polynomials having just one indeterminate (*univariate polynomials*).[26] Usually we define a polynomial to be a sum of terms, each of which is either a coefficient, a power of the indeterminate, or a product of a coefficient and a power of the indeterminate. A coefficient is defined as an algebraic expression that is not dependent upon the indeterminate of the polynomial. For example,

$$5x^2 + 3x + 7$$

is a simple polynomial in x, and

$$(y^2 + 1)x^3 + (2y)x + 1$$

is a polynomial in x whose coefficients are polynomials in y.

Already we are skirting some thorny issues. Is the first of these polynomials the same as the polynomial $5y^2 + 3y + 7$, or not? A reasonable answer might be "yes, if we are considering a polynomial purely as a mathematical function, but no, if we are considering a polynomial to be a syntactic form." The second polynomial is algebraically equivalent to a polynomial in y whose coefficients are polynomials in x. Should our system recognize this, or not? Furthermore, there are other ways to represent a polynomial—for example, as a product of factors, or (for a univariate polynomial) as the set of roots, or as a listing of the values of the polynomial at a specified set

---

26 On the other hand, we will allow polynomials whose coefficients are themselves polynomials in other variables. This will give us essentially the same representational power as a full multivariate system, although it does lead to coercion problems, as discussed below.

of points.[27]   We can finesse these questions by deciding that in our algebraic-manipulation system a "polynomial" will be a particular syntactic
form, not its underlying mathematical meaning.

Now we must consider how we go about doing arithmetic on polynomials.
In this simple system, we will consider only addition and multiplication.
Moreover, we will insist that two polynomials to be combined must have
the same indeterminate.

We will approach the design of our system by following the familiar
discipline of data abstraction. We will assume that a polynomial consists
of a variable and a collection of terms, and that we have selectors `variable`
and `term-list` that extract those parts from a polynomial. All arithmetic
is actually done on the term lists; the variable is just an extension of the
type of the polynomial used to check for legitimate polynomial operations.
We will also suppose that we have a constructor `make-polynomial` that
assembles a polynomial from a given variable and a term list.

The following procedures are the entry points to our polynomial-mani-
pulation package:

```
(define (+poly p1 p2)
  (if (same-variable? (variable p1) (variable p2))
      (make-polynomial (variable p1)
                       (+terms (term-list p1)
                               (term-list p2)))
      (error "Polys not in same var -- +POLY" (list p1 p2))))

(define (*poly p1 p2)
  (if (same-variable? (variable p1) (variable p2))
      (make-polynomial (variable p1)
                       (*terms (term-list p1)
                               (term-list p2)))
      (error "Polys not in same var -- *POLY" (list p1 p2))))
```

We can now use data-directed programming to install these new procedures
in our generic arithmetic system:

```
(put 'polynomial 'add +poly)
(put 'polynomial 'mul *poly)
```

---

[27] For univariate polynomials, giving the value of a polynomial at a given set of points
can be a particularly good representation. This makes polynomial arithmetic extremely
simple. To obtain, for example, the sum of two polynomials represented in this way,
we need only add the values of the polynomials at corresponding points. To transform
back to a more familiar representation, we can use the Lagrange interpolation formula,
which shows how to recover the coefficients of a polynomial of degree n given the values
of the polynomial at $n + 1$ points.

Polynomial addition is performed termwise. Terms of the same order (i.e., with the same power of the indeterminate) must be combined. This is done by forming a new term of the same order whose coefficient is the sum of the coefficients of the addends. Terms in one addend for which there are no terms of the same order in the other addend are simply accumulated into the sum polynomial being constructed.

In order to manipulate term lists, we will assume that we have a constructor `the-empty-termlist` that returns an empty term list and a constructor `adjoin-term` that adjoins a new term to a term list. We will also assume that we have a predicate `empty-termlist?` that tells if a given term list is empty, a selector `first-term` that extracts the highest-order term from a term list, and a selector `rest-terms` that returns all but the highest term. Given a term, we will suppose that we have two selectors `order` and `coeff` that return, respectively, the order and the coefficient of the term. These operators allow us to consider both terms and term lists as data abstractions, whose concrete representations we can worry about separately.

Here is the procedure that constructs the term list for the sum of two polynomials:[28]

```
(define (+terms L1 L2)
  (cond ((empty-termlist? L1) L2)
        ((empty-termlist? L2) L1)
        (else
         (let ((t1 (first-term L1)) (t2 (first-term L2)))
           (cond ((> (order t1) (order t2))
                  (adjoin-term t1
                               (+terms (rest-terms L1) L2)))
                 ((< (order t1) (order t2))
                  (adjoin-term t2
                               (+terms L1 (rest-terms L2))))
                 (else
                  (adjoin-term (make-term (order t1)
                                          (add (coeff t1)
                                               (coeff t2)))
                               (+terms (rest-terms L1)
                                       (rest-terms L2)))))))))
```

---

[28] This operation is very much like the ordered union-set operation we developed in exercise 2.36. In fact, if we think of the terms of the polynomial as a set ordered according to the power of the indeterminate, then the program that produces the term list for a sum is almost identical to union-set.

The most important point to note here is that we used the generic addition operator add to add together the coefficients of the terms being combined. This has powerful consequences, as we will see below.

In order to multiply two term lists, we multiply each term of the first list by all the terms of the other list, repeatedly using the procedure *-term-by-all-terms, which multiplies a given term by all terms in a given term list. The resulting polynomials (one for each term of the first list) are accumulated into a sum. Multiplying two terms forms a term whose order is the sum of the orders of the factors and whose coefficient is the product of the coefficients of the factors:

```
(define (*terms L1 L2)
  (if (empty-termlist? L1)
      (the-empty-termlist)
      (+terms (*-term-by-all-terms (first-term L1) L2)
              (*terms (rest-terms L1) L2))))

(define (*-term-by-all-terms t1 L)
  (if (empty-termlist? L)
      (the-empty-termlist)
      (let ((t2 (first-term L)))
        (adjoin-term (make-term (+ (order t1) (order t2))
                                (mul (coeff t1) (coeff t2)))
                     (*-term-by-all-terms t1
                                          (rest-terms L))))))
```

This is really all there is to polynomial addition and multiplication. Notice that, since we operate on terms using the generic operators add and mul, our polynomial package is automatically able to handle any type of coefficient that is known about by the generic arithmetic package. If we include a coercion mechanism such as one of those discussed in section 2.4.2, then we also are automatically able to handle operations on polynomials of different coefficient types, such as

$$\left[3x^2 + (2 + 3i)x + 7\right] \cdot \left[x^4 + \frac{2}{3}x^2 + (5 + 3i)\right].$$

Because we installed the polynomial addition and multiplication operators +poly and *poly in the generic arithmetic system as the add and mul operators for type polynomial, our system is also automatically able to handle polynomial operations such as

$$[(y+1)x^2 + (y^2+1)x + (y-1)] \cdot [(y-2)x + (y^3+7)].$$

The reason is that when the system tries to combine coefficients, it will dispatch through add and mul. Since the coefficients are themselves polynomials (in y), these will be combined using +poly and *poly. The result is a kind of "data-directed recursion" in which, for example, a call to *poly will result in recursive calls to *poly in order to multiply the coefficients. If the coefficients of the coefficients were themselves polynomials (as might be used to represent polynomials in three variables), the data direction would ensure that the system would follow through another level of recursive calls, and so on through as many levels as the structure of the data dictates.[29]

Representing term lists

Finally, we must confront the job of implementing a good representation for term lists. A term list is, in effect, a set of coefficients keyed by the order of the term. Hence, any of the methods for representing sets, as discussed in section 2.2.5, can be applied to this task. On the other hand, our procedures +terms and *terms always access term lists sequentially from highest to lowest order. Thus, we will use some kind of ordered list representation.

How should we structure the list that represents a term list? One consideration is the "density" of the polynomials we intend to manipulate. A polynomial is said to be *dense* if it has nonzero coefficients in terms of most orders. If it has many zero terms it is said to be *sparse*. For example,

A: $x^5 + 2x^4 + 3x^2 - 2x - 5$

is a dense polynomial, whereas

B: $x^{100} + 2x^2 + 1$

is sparse.

The term lists of dense polynomials are most efficiently represented as lists of the coefficients. For example, A above would be nicely represented as (1 2 0 3 -2 -5). The order of a term in this representation is the length of the sublist beginning with that term's coefficient, decremented

---

29 To make this work completely smoothly, we should also add to our generic arithmetic system the ability to coerce a "number" to a polynomial by regarding it as a polynomial of degree zero whose coefficient is the number. This is necessary if we are going to perform operations such as

$$[x^2 + (y+1)x + 5] + (x^2 + 2x + 1),$$

which requires adding the coefficient $y+1$ to the coefficient 2.

by 1.[30]   This would be a terrible representation for a sparse polynomial
such as B. There would be a giant list of zeros punctuated by a few lonely
nonzero terms. A more reasonable representation of the term list of a sparse
polynomial is as a list of the nonzero terms. Each term is a list containing
the order of the term and the coefficient for that order. In such a scheme,
polynomial B is efficiently represented as `((100 1) (2 2) (0 1))`. As
most polynomial manipulations are performed on sparse polynomials, we
will use this method. We will assume that term lists are represented as lists
of terms, arranged from highest-order to lowest-order term. Once we have
made this decision, implementing the selectors and constructors for terms
and term lists is straightforward:

```
(define (adjoin-term term term-list)
  (if (=zero? (coeff term))
      term-list
      (cons term term-list)))

(define (the-empty-termlist) '())
(define (first-term term-list) (car term-list))
(define (rest-terms term-list) (cdr term-list))
(define (empty-termlist? term-list) (null? term-list))

(define (make-term order coeff) (list order coeff))
(define (order term) (car term))
(define (coeff term) (cadr term))
```

where =zero? is as defined in exercise 2.54.[31]   (See also exercise 2.59 below.)
   Now only a few minor procedures remain to be defined:

```
(define (make-polynomial variable term-list)
  (attach-type 'polynomial (cons variable term-list)))

(define (variable p) (car p))

(define (term-list p) (cdr p))
```

30 In these polynomial examples, we assume that we have implemented the generic arithmetic system using the type mechanism suggested in exercise 2.49. Thus, coefficients
that are ordinary numbers will be represented as the numbers themselves rather than as
pairs whose `car` is the symbol `number`.

31 Although we are assuming that term lists are ordered, we have implemented `adjoin-`
`term` to simply cons the new term onto the existing term list. We can get away with
this so long as we guarantee that the procedures (such as `+terms`) that use `adjoin-term`
always call it with a higher-order term than appears in the list. If we did not want to
make such a guarantee, we could have implemented `adjoin-term` to be similar to the
`adjoin-set` constructor for the ordered-list representation of sets (exercise 2.35).

Exercise 2.59

Install =zero? for polynomials in the generic arithmetic package. This will allow adjoin-term to work for polynomials with coefficients that are themselves polynomials.

Exercise 2.60

Extend the polynomial system to include subtraction of polynomials.

Exercise 2.61

Define procedures that implement the term-list representation described above as appropriate for dense polynomials.

Exercise 2.62

Suppose we want to have a polynomial system that is efficient for both sparse and dense polynomials. One way to do this is to allow both kinds of term-list representations in our system. The situation is analogous to the complex-number example with which we began this chapter, where we allowed both rectangular and polar representations. To do this we must distinguish different types of term lists and make the operators on term lists generic. Redesign the polynomial system to implement this generalization. This is a major effort, not a local change.

Exercise 2.63

A univariate polynomial can be divided by another one to produce a polynomial quotient and a polynomial remainder. For example,

$$\frac{x^5 - 1}{x^2 - 1} = x^3 + x, \text{ remainder } x - 1.$$

Division can be performed via long division, as taught in high school. That is, divide the highest-order term of the dividend by the highest-order term of the divisor. The result is the first term of the quotient. Next, multiply the result by the divisor, subtract that from the dividend, and produce the rest of the answer by recursively dividing the difference by the divisor. Stop when the order of the divisor exceeds the order of the dividend and declare the dividend to be the remainder. Also, if the dividend ever reaches zero, return zero as both quotient and remainder.

We can design a /poly procedure on the model of +poly and *poly. The procedure checks to see if the two polynomials have the same variable. If so, /poly strips off the variable and passes the problem to /terms, which performs the division operation on term lists. /Poly finally reattaches the variable and the type to the result supplied by /terms. It is convenient to design /terms to compute both the quotient and the remainder of a division. /Terms can take two term lists as arguments and return a list of the quotient term list and the remainder term list.

Fill in the missing expressions to complete the following definition of /terms. Use this to implement /poly, which takes two polynomials as arguments and returns a list of the quotient and remainder polynomials.

```
(define (/terms L1 L2)
  (if (empty-termlist? L1)
      (list (the-empty-termlist) (the-empty-termlist))
      (let ((t1 (first-term L1))
            (t2 (first-term L2)))
        (if (> (order t2) (order t1))
            (list (the-empty-termlist) L1)
            (let ((new-c (div (coeff t1) (coeff t2)))
                  (new-o (- (order t1) (order t2))))
              (let ((rest-of-result
                     ⟨compute rest of result recursively⟩
                     ))
                ⟨form complete result⟩
                ))))))
```

Hierarchies of types in symbolic algebra

Our polynomial system illustrates how objects of one type (polynomials) may in fact be complex objects that have objects of many different types as parts. This poses no real difficulty in defining generic operators. We need only install appropriate generic operators for performing the necessary manipulations of the parts of the compound types. In fact, we saw that polynomials form a kind of "recursive data abstraction," in that parts of a polynomial may themselves be polynomials. Our generic operators and our data-directed programming style can handle this complication without much trouble.

On the other hand, polynomial algebra is a system for which the data types cannot be naturally arranged in a tower. For instance, it is possible to have polynomials in x whose coefficients are polynomials in y. It is also possible to have polynomials in y whose coefficients are polynomials in x. Neither of these types is "above" the other in any natural way, yet it is often necessary to add together elements from each set. There are several ways to do this. One possibility is to convert one polynomial to the type of the other by expanding and rearranging terms so that both polynomials have the same principal variable. One can impose a towerlike structure on this by ordering the variables and thus always converting any polynomial to a "canonical form" with the highest-priority variable dominant and the lower-priority variables buried in the coefficients. This strategy works fairly well, except that the conversion may expand a polynomial unnecessarily, making it hard to read and perhaps less efficient to work with. The tower strategy is certainly not natural for this domain or for any domain where the user can invent new types dynamically using old types in various combining forms, such as trigonometric functions, power series, and integrals.

It should not be surprising that controlling coercion is a serious problem in the design of large-scale algebraic-manipulation systems. Much of the complexity of such systems is concerned with relationships among diverse types. Indeed, it is fair to say that we do not yet completely understand coercion. In fact, we do not yet completely understand the concept of a data type. Nevertheless, what we know provides us with powerful structuring and modularity principles to support the design of large systems.

Exercise 2.64

By imposing an ordering on variables, extend the polynomial package so that addition and multiplication of polynomials works for polynomials in different variables. (This is not easy!)

Extended exercise: Rational functions

We can extend our generic arithmetic system to include *rational functions*. These are "fractions" whose numerator and denominator are polynomials, such as

$$\frac{x+1}{x^3-1}.$$

The system should be able to add, subtract, multiply, and divide rational functions, and to perform such computations as

$$\frac{x+1}{x^3-1} + \frac{x}{x^2-1} = \frac{x^3+2x^2+3x+1}{x^4+x^3-x-1}.$$

(Here the sum has been simplified by removing common factors. Straightforward "cross multiplication" would have produced a fourth-degree polynomial over a fifth-degree polynomial.)

If we modify our rational-arithmetic package so that it uses generic operators, then it will do what we want, except for the problem of reducing fractions to lowest terms.

Exercise 2.65

Modify the rational-arithmetic package to use generic operators, but change make-rat so that it does not attempt to reduce fractions to lowest terms. Also define the following constructor for creating rational numbers with manifest types:

```
(define (make-rational n d)
  (attach-type 'rational (make-rat n d)))
```

Test your system by calling make-rational on two polynomials to produce a rational function

```
(define p1 (make-polynomial 'x '((2 1)(0 1))))
(define p2 (make-polynomial 'x '((3 1)(0 1))))
(define rf (make-rational p2 p1))
```

Now add rf to itself, using add. (We assume here that rational-number arithmetic has been interfaced with the generic operators, as in exercise 2.52.) You will observe that this addition procedure does not reduce fractions to lowest terms.

We can reduce polynomial fractions to lowest terms using the same idea we used with integers: modifying make-rat to divide both the numerator and the denominator by their greatest common divisor. The notion of "greatest common divisor" makes sense for polynomials. In fact, we can compute the GCD of two polynomials using essentially the same Euclid's Algorithm that works for integers.[32] The integer version is

```
(define (gcd a b)
  (if (= b 0)
      a
      (gcd b (remainder a b)))))
```

Using this, we could make the obvious modification to define a GCD operation that works on term lists:

```
(define (gcd-terms a b)
  (if (empty-termlist? b)
      a
      (gcd-terms b (remainder-terms a b)))))
```

---

[32] The fact that Euclid's Algorithm works for polynomials is formalized in algebra by saying that polynomials form a kind of algebraic domain called a *Euclidean ring*. A Euclidean ring is a domain that admits addition, subtraction, and commutative multiplication, together with a way of assigning to each element x of the ring a positive integer "measure" $m(x)$ with the properties that $m(xy) \geq m(x)m(y)$ for any nonzero x and y and that, given any x and y, there exists a q such that $y = qx + r$ and either $r = 0$ or $m(r) < m(x)$. From an abstract point of view, this is what is needed to prove that Euclid's Algorithm works. For the domain of integers, the measure m of an integer is the absolute value of the integer itself. For the domain of polynomials, the measure of a polynomial is its degree.

where `remainder-terms` picks out the remainder component of the list
returned by the term-list division operation `/terms` that was implemented
in exercise 2.63.

Exercise 2.66

Using `/terms`, implement the procedure `remainder-terms` and use this to define
`gcd-terms` as above. Now write a procedure `gcd-poly` that computes the polynomial GCD of two polynomials. (The procedure should signal an error if the
two polynomials are not in the same variable.) Install in the system a generic
operator `greatest-common-divisor` that reduces to ordinary gcd for numbers
and to `gcd-poly` for polynomials. As a test, try

```
(define p1 (make-polynomial 'x '((4 1) (3 -1) (2 -2) (1 2))))
(define p2 (make-polynomial 'x '((3 1) (1 -1))))
(greatest-common-divisor p1 p2)
```

and check your result by hand.

Exercise 2.67

Define P_1, P_2, and P_3 to be the polynomials

P_1: $x^2 - 2x + 1$,

P_2: $11x^2 + 7$,

P_3: $13x + 5$.

Now define Q_1 to be the product of P_1 and P_2 and Q_2 to be the product of P_1
and P_3. Using the method outlined above, compute the GCD of Q_1 and Q_2.
The program will very likely give the wrong answer. Explain how this example
introduces noninteger operations into the computation, causing difficulties with
the GCD algorithm. Try tracing `gcd-terms` while computing the example in
exercise 2.66. Try performing the division by hand. What difficulty is the program encountering?

We can solve the problem exhibited in exercise 2.67 if we use the following
modification of the GCD algorithm (which really works only in the case of
polynomials with integer coefficients). Before performing any polynomial
division in the GCD computation, we multiply the dividend by an integer
constant factor, chosen to guarantee that no fractions will arise during the
division process. Our answer will thus differ from the actual GCD by an
integer constant factor, but this does not matter in the case of reducing
rational functions to lowest terms; the GCD will be used to divide both the
numerator and denominator, so the integer constant factor will cancel out.

More precisely, if P and Q are polynomials, let O_1 be the order of P (i.e., the order of the largest term of P) and let O_2 be the order of Q. Let c be the leading coefficient of Q. Then it can be shown that, if we multiply P by the *integerizing factor* $c^{1+O_1-O_2}$, the resulting polynomial can be divided by Q by using the /terms algorithm without introducing any fractions. The operation of multiplying the dividend by this constant and then dividing is sometimes called the *pseudodivision* of P by Q. The remainder of the division is called the *pseudoremainder*.

Thus, here is how to reduce a rational function to lowest terms:

- Compute the GCD of the numerator and denominator by following Euclid's Algorithm, but use pseudo-remainder rather than remainder.

- When you obtain the GCD, multiply both numerator and denominator by the same integerizing factor before dividing through by the GCD, so that division by the GCD will not introduce any noninteger coefficients. As the factor you can use the leading coefficient of the GCD raised to the power $1 + O_1 - O_2$, where O_2 is the order of the GCD and O_1 is the maximum of the orders of the numerator and denominator. This will ensure that dividing numerator and denominator by the GCD will not introduce any fractions.

- The result of this operation will be a rational function with integer coefficients. The coefficients will normally be very large because of all of the integerizing factors, so the last step is to remove the redundant factors by computing the (integer) greatest common divisor of all the coefficients of the numerator and the denominator and dividing through by this factor.

Exercise 2.68

Implement this algorithm as a procedure reduce that takes two term lists n and d as arguments and returns a pair nn, dd, which are n and d reduced to lowest terms via the algorithm given above. You should, of course, isolate different parts of the computation in different procedures, such as pseudo-remainder and gcd procedures for term lists.

Exercise 2.69

Write a make-rat-poly procedure that is analogous to the original make-rat for integers except that it uses the reduce procedure from exercise 2.68 to reduce the numerator and the denominator to lowest terms. You can now easily obtain a system that handles rational expressions in either integers or polynomials by renaming make-rat as make-rat-number and defining a new make-rat as a generic operation that calls `operate-2` to dispatch to either `make-rat-poly` or `make-rat-number`. To test your program, try the example at the beginning of this section:

```
(define p1 (make-polynomial 'x '((1 1)(0 1))))
(define p2 (make-polynomial 'x '((3 1)(0 -1))))
(define p3 (make-polynomial 'x '((1 1))))
(define p4 (make-polynomial 'x '((2 1)(0 -1))))

(define rf1 (make-rational p1 p2))
(define rf2 (make-rational p3 p4))

(add rf1 rf2)
```

See if you get the correct answer, correctly reduced to lowest terms. (`Make-rational` was defined in exercise 2.65.)

The GCD computation is at the heart of any system that does operations on rational functions. The algorithm used above, although mathematically straightforward, is extremely slow. The slowness is due partly to the large number of division operations and partly to the enormous size of the intermediate coefficients generated by the pseudodivisions. One of the active areas in the development of algebraic-manipulation systems is the design of better algorithms for computing polynomial GCDs.[33]

---

[33] One extremely efficient and elegant method for computing polynomial GCDs was discovered by Richard Zippel (1979). Zippel's method is a probabilistic algorithm, as is the fast test for primality that we discussed in chapter 1.

3

MODULARITY, OBJECTS, AND STATE

Μεταβάλλον ἀναπαύεται
(Even while it changes, it stands still.)
Heraclitus

Plus ça change, plus c'est la même chose.
Alphonse Karr

The preceding chapters introduced the basic elements from which programs are made. We saw how primitive procedures and primitive data are combined to construct compound entities, and we learned that abstraction is vital in helping us to cope with the complexity of large systems. But these tools are not sufficient for designing programs. Effective program synthesis also requires organizational principles that can guide us in formulating the overall design of a program. In particular, we need strategies to help us structure large systems so that they will be *modular*, that is, so that they can be divided "naturally" into coherent parts that can be separately developed and maintained.

One powerful design strategy, which is particularly appropriate to the construction of programs for modeling physical systems, is to base the structure of our programs on the structure of the system being modeled. For each object in the system, we construct a corresponding computational object. For each system action, we define a symbolic operation in our computational model. Our hope in using this strategy is that extending the model to accommodate new objects or new actions will require no strategic changes to the program, only the addition of the new symbolic analogs of those objects or actions. If we have been successful in our system organization, then to add a new feature or debug an old one we will have to work on only a localized part of the system.

To a large extent, then, the way we organize a large program is dictated by our perception of the system to be modeled. In this chapter we will investigate two prominent organizational strategies arising from two rather different "world views" of the structure of systems. The first organizational strategy concentrates on *objects*, viewing a large system as a collection of distinct objects whose behaviors may change over time. An alternative organizational strategy concentrates on the *streams* of information that flow in the system, much as an electrical engineer views a signal-processing system.

Both the object-oriented approach and the stream-processing approach force us to deal with a collection of linguistic issues in programming. With objects, we must be concerned with how a computational object can change and yet maintain its identity. This raises thorny issues, and it will force us to abandon our old substitution model of computation (section 1.1.5) in favor of a more mechanistic but less theoretically tractable *environment model* of computation. The stream approach can be most fully exploited when we decouple simulated time in our model from the order of the events that take place in the computer during evaluation. We will accomplish this using a technique known as *delayed evaluation*.

3.1 Assignment and Local State

We ordinarily view the world as populated by independent objects, each of which has a state that changes over time. An object is said to "have state" if its behavior is influenced by its history. We can characterize an object's state by one or more *state variables*, which among them maintain enough information about history to determine the object's current behavior. A bank account, for example, has state in that the answer to the question "Can I withdraw $100?" depends upon the history of deposit and withdrawal transactions. In a simple banking system, we could characterize the state of an account by a current balance rather than by remembering the entire history of account transactions.

In a system composed of many objects, the objects are rarely completely independent. Each may influence the states of others through interactions, which serve to couple the state variables of one object to those of other objects. Indeed, the view that a system is composed of separate objects is most useful when the state variables of the system can be grouped into closely coupled subsystems that are only loosely coupled to other subsystems.

The *object-oriented* view of a system can be a powerful framework for organizing computational models of the system. For such a model to be modular, it should be decomposed into computational objects that model the actual objects in the system. Each computational object must have its own *local state variables* describing the actual object's state. Since the states of objects in the system being modeled change over time, the state variables of the corresponding computational objects must also change. If we choose to model the flow of time in the system by the elapsed time in the computer, then we must have a way to construct computational objects whose behaviors change as our programs run. In particular, if we wish to model state variables by ordinary symbolic names in the programming language, then the language must provide an *assignment operator* to enable us to change the value associated with a name.

3.1.1 Local State Variables

To illustrate what we mean by having a computational object with time-varying state, let us model the situation of withdrawing money from a bank account. We will do this using a procedure withdraw, which takes as argument an amount to be withdrawn. If there is enough money in the account to accommodate the withdrawal, then withdraw should return the balance remaining after the withdrawal. Otherwise, withdraw should return the message *Insufficient funds*. For example, if we begin with $100 in the account, we should obtain the following sequence of responses using withdraw:

```
==> (withdraw 25)
75

==> (withdraw 25)
50

==> (withdraw 60)
Insufficient funds

==> (withdraw 15)
35
```

Notice that the same expression (withdraw 25), evaluated twice, yields different values. This is a new kind of behavior for a procedure. Until now, all our procedures could be viewed as specifications for computing mathematical functions. A call to a procedure computed the value of the function applied to the given arguments, and two consecutive calls to the same procedure with the same arguments always produced the same result.[1]

To implement withdraw, we can use a variable balance to indicate the balance of money in the account and define withdraw as a procedure that

---

1 Actually, this is not quite true. One exception was the random-number generator in section 1.2.6. Another exception was the put procedure, which we introduced in section 2.3.3 for inserting entries into operator/type tables. On the other hand, until we introduce assignment, we have no way to create such procedures ourselves.

accesses balance. The withdraw procedure checks to see if balance is at least as large as the requested amount. If so, withdraw decrements balance by amount and returns the new value of balance. Otherwise, withdraw returns the *Insufficient funds* message. Here are the definitions of balance and withdraw:

```
(define balance 100)
```

```
(define (withdraw amount)
  (if (>= balance amount)
      (sequence (set! balance (- balance amount))
                balance)
      "Insufficient funds"))
```

Decrementing balance is accomplished by the expression

```
(set! balance (- balance amount))
```

This uses the set! special form, whose syntax is

```
(set! ⟨name⟩ ⟨new-value⟩)
```

Here ⟨name⟩ is a symbol and ⟨new-value⟩ is any expression. Set! changes ⟨name⟩ so that its value is the result of evaluating ⟨new-value⟩. In the case at hand, we are changing balance so that its new value will be the result of subtracting amount from the previous value of balance.[2]

Withdraw also uses the sequence special form to specify that the action performed in the case where the if test is true should result in evaluating two expressions: first decrementing balance and then returning the value of balance. In general, evaluating the expression

```
(sequence ⟨exp₁⟩ ⟨exp₂⟩...⟨expₖ⟩)
```

causes the expressions ⟨exp₁⟩ through ⟨expₖ⟩ to be evaluated in sequence and the value of the final expression ⟨expₖ⟩ to be returned as the value of the entire sequence form.[3]

Although the withdraw procedure works as desired, the variable balance presents a problem. As specified above, balance is a name defined in the

---

2 The name set! reflects a naming convention used in Scheme: Operations that change the values of variables (or that change data structures, as we will see in section 3.3) are given names that end with an exclamation point. This is similar to the convention of designating predicates by names that end with a question mark.

3 We have already used sequence implicitly in our programs, because in Scheme the body of a procedure can be a sequence of expressions. Also, the ⟨consequent⟩ part of each clause in a cond expression can be a sequence of expressions rather than a single expression.

global environment and is freely accessible to be examined or modified by any procedure. It would be much better if we could somehow make balance internal to withdraw, so that withdraw would be the only procedure that could access balance directly and any other procedure could access balance only indirectly (through calls to withdraw). This would more accurately model the notion that balance is a local state variable used by withdraw to keep track of the state of the account.

We can make balance internal to withdraw by rewriting the definition as follows:

```
(define new-withdraw
  (let ((balance 100))
    (lambda (amount)
      (if (>= balance amount)
          (sequence (set! balance (- balance amount))
                    balance)
          "Insufficient funds"))))
```

What we have done here is use let to establish an environment with a local variable balance, bound to the initial value 100. Within this local environment, we use lambda to create a procedure that takes amount as an argument and behaves like our previous withdraw procedure. This procedure—returned as the result of evaluating the let expression—is new-withdraw, which behaves in precisely the same way as withdraw but whose variable balance is not accessible by any other procedure.[4]

Combining set! with local variables is the general programming technique that we will use for constructing computational objects with local state. Unfortunately, using this technique raises a serious problem: When we first introduced procedures, we also introduced the substitution model of evaluation (section 1.1.5) to provide an interpretation of what procedure application means. We said that applying a procedure should be interpreted as evaluating the body of the procedure with the formal parameters replaced by their values. The trouble is that, as soon as we introduce assignment into our language, substitution is no longer an adequate model of procedure application. (We will see why this is so in section 3.1.2.) As a consequence, we technically have at this point no way to understand why the new-withdraw procedure behaves as claimed above. In order to

4 In programming-language jargon, the variable balance is said to be *encapsulated* within the new-withdraw procedure. Encapsulation reflects the general system-design principle known as the *hiding principle*: One can make a system more modular and robust by protecting parts of the system from each other; that is, by providing information access only to those parts of the system that have a "need to know."

really understand a procedure such as `new-withdraw`, we will need to develop a new model of procedure application. In section 3.2 we will introduce such a model, together with an explanation of `set!` and local variables. First, however, we examine some variations on the theme established by `new-withdraw`.

The following procedure, `make-withdraw`, creates "withdrawal processors." The formal parameter `balance` in `make-withdraw` specifies the initial amount of money in the account.[5]

```
(define (make-withdraw balance)
  (lambda (amount)
    (if (>= balance amount)
        (sequence (set! balance (- balance amount))
                  balance)
        "Insufficient funds")))
```

`Make-withdraw` can be used as follows to create two objects W1 and W2:

```
(define W1 (make-withdraw 100))
(define W2 (make-withdraw 100))
```

```
==> (W1 50)
50
```

```
==> (W2 70)
30
```

```
==> (W2 40)
Insufficient funds
```

```
==> (W1 40)
10
```

Observe that W1 and W2 are completely independent objects, each with its own local state variable `balance`. Withdrawals from one do not affect the other.

We can also create objects that handle deposits as well as withdrawals, and thus we can represent simple bank accounts. Here is the resulting procedure, which returns a "bank account object" with a specified initial balance.

---

5 In contrast with `new-withdraw` above, we do not have to use `let` to make `balance` a local variable, since formal parameters are already local. This will be clearer after the discussion of the environment model of evaluation in section 3.2. (See also exercise 3.10.)

```
(define (make-account balance)
  (define (withdraw amount)
    (if (>= balance amount)
        (sequence (set! balance (- balance amount))
                  balance)
        "Insufficient funds"))
  (define (deposit amount)
    (set! balance (+ balance amount))
    balance)
  (define (dispatch m)
    (cond ((eq? m 'withdraw) withdraw)
          ((eq? m 'deposit) deposit)
          (else (error "Unknown request -- MAKE-ACCOUNT"
                       m))))
  dispatch)
```

Each call to make-account sets up an environment with a local state variable balance. Within this environment, make-account defines two procedures deposit and withdraw that access balance and an additional procedure dispatch that takes a "message" as input and returns one of the two local procedures. The dispatch procedure itself is returned as the value that represents the object. This is precisely the *message passing* style of programming that we saw in section 2.3.3, although here we are using it in conjunction with the ability to modify local variables.

Make-account can be used as follows:

```
(define acc (make-account 100))
```

```
==> ((acc 'withdraw) 50)
```
50

```
==> ((acc 'withdraw) 60)
```
Insufficient funds

```
==> ((acc 'deposit) 40)
```
90

```
==> ((acc 'withdraw) 60)
```
30

Each call to acc returns the locally defined deposit or withdraw procedure, which is then applied to the specified amount. As with make-withdraw, another call to `make-account`

```
(define acc2 (make-account 100))
```

will produce a completely separate account object, which maintains its own local balance.

Exercise 3.1

An *accumulator* is a procedure that is called repeatedly with a single numeric argument and accumulates its arguments into a sum. Each time it is called, it returns the currently accumulated sum. Write a procedure `make-accumulator` that generates accumulators. The input to `make-accumulator` should specify the initial value of the sum; for example

```
(define A (make-accumulator 5))

==> (A 10)
15

==> (A 10)
25
```

Exercise 3.2

In software-testing applications, it is useful to be able to count the number of times a given procedure is called during the course of a computation. Write a procedure `make-monitored` that takes as input a procedure, `f`, that itself takes one input. The result returned by `make-monitored` is a third procedure, say `mf`, that keeps track of the number of times it has been called by maintaining an internal counter. If the input to `mf` is the special symbol `how-many-calls?`, then `mf` returns the value of the counter. If the input is the special symbol `reset-count`, then `mf` resets the counter to zero. For any other input, `mf` returns the result of calling `f` on that input and increments the counter. For instance, we could make a monitored version of the `sqrt` procedure:

```
(define s (make-monitored sqrt))

==> (s 100)
10

==> (s 'how-many-calls?)
1
```

Exercise 3.3

Modify the `make-account` procedure so that it creates password-protected accounts. That is, `make-account` should take a symbol as an additional argument, as in

```
(define acc (make-account 100 'secret-password))
```

The resulting account object should process a request only if it is accompanied by the password with which the account was created, and should otherwise print a complaint:

```
==> ((acc 'secret-password 'withdraw) 40)
60

==> ((acc 'some-other-password 'deposit) 50)
incorrect password
```

Exercise 3.4

Modify the make-account procedure of exercise 3.3 by adding another local state variable so that, if an account is accessed more than seven consecutive times with an incorrect password, it invokes the procedure call-the-cops.

3.1.2 The Costs of Introducing Assignment

As we have seen, the set! operation enables us to model objects that have local state. However, this advantage comes at a price: Our programming language can no longer be interpreted in terms of the substitution model of procedure application that we introduced in section 1.1.5. Moreover, no simple model with "nice" mathematical properties can be an adequate framework for dealing with objects and assignment in programming languages.

To understand why this is true, consider a simplified version of the make-withdraw procedure of section 3.1.1 that does not bother to check for an insufficient amount:

```
(define (make-simplified-withdraw balance)
    (lambda (amount)
        (set! balance (- balance amount))
        balance))

(define W (make-simplified-withdraw 25))

==> (W 20)
5

==> (W 10)
-5
```

Compare this procedure with the following make-decrementer procedure, which does not use set!:

```
(define (make-decrementer balance)
  (lambda (amount)
    (- balance amount)))
```

Make-decrementer returns a procedure that subtracts its input from a designated amount balance, but there is no accumulated effect over successive calls, as with make-simplified-withdraw:

```
(define D (make-decrementer 25))
```

```
==> (D 20)
5
```

```
==> (D 10)
15
```

We can use the substitution model to explain how make-decrementer works. For instance, let us analyze the evaluation of the expression

```
((make-decrementer 25) 20)
```

We first simplify the operator of the combination by substituting 25 for balance in the body of make-decrementer. This reduces the expression to

```
((lambda (amount) (- 25 amount)) 20)
```

Now we apply the operator by substituting 20 for amount in the body of the lambda expression:

```
(- 25 20)
```

The final answer is 5.

Observe, however, what happens if we attempt a similar substitution analysis with make-simplified-withdraw:

```
((make-simplified-withdraw 25) 20)
```

We first simplify the operator by substituting 25 for balance in the body of make-simplified-withdraw. This reduces the expression to

```
((lambda (amount) (set! 25 (- 25 amount)) 25) 20)
```

Now we apply the operator by substituting 20 for amount in the body of the lambda expression:

```
(set! 25 (- 25 20)) 25
```

If we adhered to the substitution model, we would have to say that the meaning of the procedure application is to first set 25 to 5 and then return 25 as the value of the expression. This makes no sense at all.

The trouble here is that substitution is based ultimately on the notion that the symbols in our language are essentially names for values. But as soon as we introduce set! and the idea that the value of a variable can change, a variable can no longer be simply a name. Now a variable somehow refers to a place where a value can be stored, and the value stored at this place can change. In section 3.2 we will see how environments play this role of "place" in our computational model.

Sameness and change

The issue surfacing here is more profound than the mere breakdown of a particular model of computation. As soon as we introduce change into our computational models, many notions that were previously straightforward become problematical. Consider the concept of two things being "the same."

Suppose we create two procedures by calling the above make-decrementer procedure twice with the same argument:

```
(define D1 (make-decrementer 25))
```

```
(define D2 (make-decrementer 25))
```

Are D1 and D2 the same? An acceptable answer is yes, because D1 and D2 have the same computational behavior—each is a procedure that subtracts its input from 25. In fact, D1 could be substituted for D2 in any computation without changing the result. Another way to justify considering D1 and D2 the same is to observe that in the substitution view of computation D1 and D2 are both names for the same expression, (make-decrementer 25).

Contrast this with making two calls to make-simplified-withdraw:

```
(define W1 (make-simplified-withdraw 25))
```

```
(define W2 (make-simplified-withdraw 25))
```

Are W1 and W2 the same? Surely not, because calls to W1 and W2 have distinct effects, as shown by the following sequence of interactions:

```
==> (W1 20)
5
```

```
==> (W1 20)
-15
```

```
==>  (W2 20)
```

5

Even though W1 and W2 are "equal" in the sense that they are both created by evaluating the same expression, (make-simplified-withdraw 25), it is not true that W1 could be substituted for W2 in any expression without changing the result of evaluating the expression.

A language that supports the concept that "equals can be substituted for equals" without changing the values of expressions is said to be *referentially transparent*. Referential transparency is violated when we include set! in our computer language. This makes it tricky to determine when we can simplify expressions by substituting equivalent expressions. Consequently, reasoning about programs that use assignment becomes drastically more difficult, and programs with assignment are susceptible to bugs that cannot occur in the types of programs we have been dealing with until now.

Once we forgo referential transparency, the notion of what it means for computational objects to be "the same" becomes difficult to capture in a formal way. Indeed, the meaning of "same" in the real world that our programs model is hardly clear in itself. In general, we can determine that two apparently identical objects are indeed "the same one" only by modifying one object and then observing whether the other object has changed in the same way. But how can we tell if an object has "changed" other than by observing the "same" object twice and seeing whether some property of the object differs from one observation to the next? Thus, we cannot determine "change" without some *a priori* notion of "sameness," and we cannot determine sameness without observing the effects of change.

As an example of how this issue arises in programming, consider the situation where Peter and Paul have a bank account with $100 in it. There is a substantial difference between modeling this as

```
(define peter-acc (make-account 100))
(define paul-acc (make-account 100))
```

and modeling it as

```
(define peter-acc (make-account 100))
(define paul-acc peter-acc)
```

In the first situation, the two bank accounts are distinct. Transactions made by Peter will not affect Paul's account, and vice versa. In the second situation, however, we have defined paul-acc to be *the same thing* as peter-acc. In effect, Peter and Paul now have a joint bank account, and if Peter makes a withdrawal from peter-acc Paul will observe less money in `paul-acc`. These two similar but distinct situations can cause confusion in building computational models. With the shared account, in particular, it can be especially confusing that there is one object (the bank account) that has two different names (`peter-acc` and `paul-acc`); if we are searching for all the places in our program where `paul-acc` can be changed, we must remember to look also at things that change `peter-acc`.[6]

With reference to the above remarks on "sameness" and "change," observe that if Peter and Paul could only examine their bank balances, and could not perform operations that changed the balance, then the issue of whether the two accounts are distinct would be moot. In general, so long as we never modify data objects, we can regard a compound data object to be precisely the totality of its pieces. For example, a rational number is determined by giving its numerator and its denominator. But this view is no longer valid in the presence of change, where a compound data object has an "identity" that is something different from the pieces of which it is composed. A bank account is still "the same" bank account even if we change the balance by making a withdrawal; conversely, we could have two different bank accounts with the same state information. This complication is a consequence, not of our programming language, but of our perception of a bank account as an object. We do not, for example, ordinarily regard a rational number as a changeable object with identity, such that we could change the numerator and still have "the same" rational number.

Exercise 3.5

Consider the bank account objects created by `make-account`, with the password modification described in exercise 3.3. Suppose that our banking system requires the ability to make joint accounts. Define a procedure `make-joint` that accomplishes this. `Make-joint` should take three arguments. The first is a password-protected account. The second argument must match the password with which the account was defined in order for the `make-joint` operation to proceed. The third argument is a new password. `Make-joint` is to create an additional access to the original account using the new password. For example, if `peter-acc` is a bank account with password `open-sesame`, then

```
(define paul-acc
  (make-joint peter-acc 'open-sesame 'rosebud))
```

[6] The phenomenon of a single computational object being accessed by more than one name is known as *aliasing*. The joint bank account situation illustrates a very simple example of an alias. In section 3.3 we will see much more complex examples, such as "distinct" compound data structures that share parts. Bugs can occur in our programs if we forget that a change to an object may also, as a "side effect," change a "different" object because the two "different" objects are actually a single object appearing under different aliases. These so-called *side-effect bugs* are so difficult to locate and to analyze that some people have proposed that programming languages be designed in such a way as to not allow side effects or aliasing (Lampson et al. 1981; Morris et al. 1980).

will allow one to make transactions on `peter-acc` using the name `paul-acc` and the password `rosebud`. You may wish to modify your solution to exercise 3.3 to accommodate this new feature.

Exercise 3.6

When we defined the evaluation model in section 1.1.3, we said that the first step in evaluating an expression is to evaluate the subexpressions. But we never specified the order in which the subexpressions should be evaluated (e.g., left to right or right to left). When we introduce assignment, the order in which the arguments to a procedure are evaluated can make a difference to the result. Define a simple procedure `f` such that evaluating `(+ (f 0) (f 1))` will return 0 if the arguments to `+` are evaluated from left to right but will return 1 if the arguments are evaluated from right to left.

3.1.3 The Benefits of Introducing Assignment

Introducing assignment into our programming language leads us into a thicket of difficult conceptual issues. Nevertheless, viewing systems as collections of objects with local state is a powerful technique for maintaining a modular design. As a simple example, consider the design of a procedure `rand` that, whenever it is called, returns an integer chosen at random.

It is not at all clear what is meant by "chosen at random." What we presumably want is for successive calls to `rand` to produce a sequence of numbers that has statistical properties of uniform distribution. We will not discuss methods for generating suitable sequences here. Rather, let us assume that we have a procedure `rand-update` that has the property that if we start with a given number x_1 and form

$$x_2 = (\text{rand-update } x_1)$$
$$x_3 = (\text{rand-update } x_2)$$

then the sequence $x_1, x_2, x_3, \ldots$, will have the desired statistical properties.[7]

7 One common way to implement `rand-update` is to use the rule that x is updated to $ax + b$ modulo m, where a, b, and m are appropriately chosen integers. Chapter 3 of Knuth 1969 includes an extensive discussion of techniques for generating sequences of random numbers and establishing their statistical properties. Notice that the rand-update procedure computes a mathematical function: Given the same input twice, it produces the same output. Therefore, the number sequence produced by `rand-update` certainly is not "random," if by "random" we insist that each number in the sequence is unrelated to the preceding number. The relation between "real randomness" and so-called *pseudo-random* sequences, which are produced by well-determined computations and yet have suitable statistical properties, is a complex question involving difficult issues in mathematics and philosophy. Kolmogorov, Solomonoff, and Chaitin have made great progress in clarifying these issues; a discussion can be found in Chaitin 1975.

We can implement `rand` as a procedure with a local state variable `x` that is initialized to some fixed value `random-init`. Each call to `rand` computes `rand-update` of the current value of `x`, returns this as the random number, and also stores this as the new value of `x`.

```
(define rand
  (let ((x random-init))
    (lambda ()
      (set! x (rand-update x))
      x)))
```

Of course, we could generate the same sequence of random numbers without using assignment by simply calling `rand-update` directly. However, this would mean that any part of our program that used random numbers would have to explicitly remember the current value of `x` to be passed as an argument to `rand-update`. To realize what an annoyance this would be, consider using random numbers to implement a technique called *Monte Carlo simulation*.

The Monte Carlo method consists of choosing sample experiments at random from a large set and then making deductions on the basis of the probabilities estimated from tabulating the results of those experiments. For example, we can approximate π using the fact that $6/\pi^2$ is the probability that two integers chosen at random will have no factors in common; that is, that their greatest common divisor will be 1.[8] To obtain the approximation to π, we perform a large number of experiments. In each experiment we choose two integers at random and perform a test to see if their GCD is 1. The fraction of times that the test is passed gives us our estimate of $6/\pi^2$, and from this we obtain our approximation to π.

The heart of our program is a procedure `monte-carlo`, which takes as arguments the number of times to try an experiment, together with the experiment, represented as a no-argument procedure that will return either true or false each time it is run. `Monte-carlo` runs the experiment for the designated number of trials and returns a number telling the fraction of the trials in which the experiment was found to be true.

```
(define (estimate-pi trials)
  (sqrt (/ 6 (monte-carlo trials cesaro-test))))
```

```
(define (cesaro-test)
  (= (gcd (rand) (rand)) 1))
```

---

8 This theorem is due to E. Cesaro. See section 4.5.2 of Knuth 1969 for a discussion and a proof.

```
(define (monte-carlo trials experiment)
  (define (iter trials-remaining trials-passed)
    (cond ((= trials-remaining 0)
           (/ trials-passed trials))
          ((experiment)
           (iter (-1+ trials-remaining) (1+ trials-passed)))
          (else
           (iter (-1+ trials-remaining) trials-passed))))
  (iter trials 0))
```

Now let us try the same computation using rand-update directly rather than rand, the way we would be forced to proceed if we did not use assignment to model local state:

```
(define (estimate-pi trials)
  (sqrt (/ 6 (random-gcd-test trials random-init))))

(define (random-gcd-test trials initial-x)
  (define (iter trials-remaining trials-passed x)
    (let ((x1 (rand-update x)))
      (let ((x2 (rand-update x1)))
        (cond ((= trials-remaining 0)
               (/ trials-passed trials))
              ((= (gcd x1 x2) 1)
               (iter (-1+ trials-remaining)
                     (1+ trials-passed)
                     x2))
              (else
               (iter (-1+ trials-remaining)
                     trials-passed
                     x2))))))
  (iter trials 0 initial-x))
```

Although this is still a simple program, it betrays some painful breaches of modularity. In our first version of the program, using rand, we are able to express the Monte Carlo method directly as a general monte-carlo procedure that takes as an argument an arbitrary experiment procedure. In our second version of the program, with no local state for the random-number generator, random-gcd-test must explicitly manipulate the random numbers x1 and x2 and recycle x2 through the iterative loop as the new input to rand-update. This explicit handling of the random numbers intertwines the structure of accumulating test results with the fact that our particular experiment uses two random numbers, whereas other Monte Carlo experiments might use one random number or three. Even the top-level procedure estimate-pi has to be concerned with supplying an initial random number. The fact that the random-number generator's insides are leaking out into other parts of the program makes it difficult for us to isolate the Monte Carlo idea so that it can be applied to other tasks. In the first version of the program, assignment encapsulates the state of the random-number generator within the rand procedure, so that the details of random-number generation remain independent of the rest of the program.

It is tempting to conclude this discussion by saying that, by introducing assignment and the technique of hiding state in local variables, we are able to structure systems in a more modular fashion than if all state had to be manipulated explicitly, by passing additional parameters. Unfortunately, the story is not so simple. As we will see in section 3.4, the programming technique of *stream processing* enables us to gain a great deal of modularity without introducing assignment and its concomitant difficulties as indicated in section 3.1.2. However, to take advantage of stream processing we must adopt a very different perspective on objects and, most strikingly, a different perspective on time in our computer programs. We will return to this discussion in section 3.4. First, however, we will address the issue of providing a computational model for expressions that involve assignment, and explore the uses of objects in designing simulations.

Exercise 3.7

Monte Carlo integration is a method of estimating definite integrals by means of Monte Carlo simulation. Consider computing the area of a region of space described by a predicate $P(x, y)$ that is true for points (x, y) in the region and false for points not in the region. For example, the region contained within a circle of radius 3 centered at $(5, 7)$ is described by the predicate that tests whether $(x - 5)^2 + (y - 7)^2 \leq 3^2$. To estimate the area of the region described by such a predicate, begin by choosing a rectangle that contains the region. For example, a rectangle with diagonally opposite corners at $(2, 4)$ and $(8, 10)$ contains the circle above. The desired integral is the area of that portion of the rectangle that lies in the region. We can estimate the integral by picking, at random, points (x, y) that lie in the rectangle, and testing $P(x, y)$ for each point to determine whether the point lies in the region. If we try this with many points, then the fraction of points that fall in the region should give an estimate of the proportion of the rectangle that lies in the region. Hence, multiplying this fraction by the area of the entire rectangle should produce an estimate of the integral.

Implement Monte Carlo integration as a procedure estimate-integral that takes as arguments a predicate P, upper and lower bounds x1, x2, y1, and y2 for the rectangle, and the number of trials to perform in order to produce the estimate. Estimate-integral should use the same monte-carlo procedure that was used above to estimate π. Use your `estimate-integral` to produce an estimate of π by measuring the area of a unit circle.

You will find it useful to have a procedure that returns a real number chosen at random from a given range. The following `real-random` procedure implements this in terms of the integer-valued `random` procedure used in section 1.2.6. `Real-random` returns a randomly selected integer multiple of .0001 between the given bounds.

```
(define (real-random low high)
  (let ((range (- high low)))
    (+ low
       (/ (random (round (* 10000 range)))
          10000))))
```

(`Round` is a primitive that rounds a number to the nearest integer.)

Exercise 3.8

It is useful to be able to reset a random-number generator to produce a sequence starting from a given value. Design a new `rand` procedure that is called with an argument that is either the symbol `generate` or the symbol `reset` as follows: `(rand 'generate)` produces a new random number; `((rand 'reset) ⟨new-value⟩)` resets the internal state variable to the designated ⟨new-value⟩. Thus, by resetting the state, one can generate repeatable sequences. These are very handy to have when testing and debugging programs that use random numbers.

3.2 The Environment Model of Evaluation

When we introduced compound procedures in chapter 1, we used the substitution model of evaluation (section 1.1.5) to define what is meant by applying a procedure to arguments:

To apply a compound procedure to arguments, evaluate the body of the procedure with each formal parameter replaced by the corresponding argument.

Once we admit assignment into our programming language, such a definition is no longer adequate. In particular, section 3.1.2 argued that, in the presence of assignment, a variable can no longer be considered to be merely a name for a value. Rather, a variable must somehow designate a "place" in which values can be stored. In our new model of evaluation, these places will be maintained in structures called *environments*.

An environment is a sequence of *frames*. Each frame is a table (possibly empty) of *bindings*, which associate variables with their corresponding values. (A single frame may contain at most one binding for any variable.)

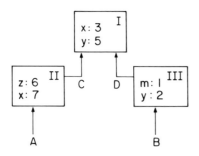

Figure 3.1
A simple environment structure.

Each frame also has a pointer to its *enclosing environment*, unless, for the purposes of discussion, the frame is considered to be *global*. The *value of a variable* with respect to an environment is the value given by the binding of the variable in the first frame in the environment that contains a binding for that variable. If no frame in the sequence specifies a binding for the variable, then the variable is said to be *unbound* in the environment.

Figure 3.1 shows a simple environment structure consisting of three frames, labeled I, II, and III. In the diagram, A, B, C, and D are pointers to environments. C and D point to the same environment. The variables z and x are bound in frame II, while y and x are bound in frame I. The value of x in environment D is 3. The value of x with respect to environment B is also 3. This is determined as follows: We examine the first frame in the sequence (frame III) and do not find a binding for x, so we proceed to the enclosing environment D and find the binding in frame I. On the other hand, the value of x in environment A is 7, because the first frame in the sequence (frame II) contains a binding of x to 7. With respect to environment A, the binding of x to 7 in frame II is said to *shadow* the binding of x to 3 in frame I.

The environment plays a crucial part in the evaluation process, because it determines the context in which an expression should be evaluated. Indeed, one could say that expressions in a programming language do not, in themselves, have any meaning. Rather, an expression acquires a meaning only with respect to some environment in which it is evaluated. Even the interpretation of an expression as straightforward as (+ 1 1) depends on an understanding that one is operating in a context in which + is the symbol for addition. Thus, in our model of evaluation we will always speak of evaluating an expression with respect to some environment. To describe interactions with the interpreter, we will suppose that there is a global environment, consisting of a single frame (with no enclosing environment) that includes values for the symbols associated with the primitive procedures. For example, the idea that + is the symbol for addition is captured by saying that the symbol + is bound in the global environment to the primitive addition procedure.

3.2.1 The Rules for Evaluation

The overall specification of how the interpreter evaluates a combination remains the same as when we first introduced it in section 1.1.3:

To evaluate a combination (other than a special form),

1. Evaluate the subexpressions of the combination.[9]

2. Apply the value of the operator subexpression to the values of the operand subexpressions.

The environment model of evaluation replaces the substitution model in specifying what it means to apply a compound procedure to arguments.

   In the environment model of evaluation, a procedure is always a pair consisting of some code and a pointer to an environment. Procedures are created in one way only: by evaluating a lambda expression. This produces a procedure whose code is obtained from the text of the lambda expression and whose environment is the environment in which the lambda expression was evaluated to produce the procedure. For example, consider the procedure definition

```
(define (square x)
  (* x x))
```

evaluated in the global environment. The procedure definition syntax is just syntactic sugar for an underlying implicit lambda expression. It would have been equivalent to have used

```
(define square
  (lambda (x) (* x x)))
```

which evaluates (lambda (x) (* x x)) and binds the variable square to the resulting value, all in the global environment.

   Figure 3.2 shows the result of evaluating this define expression. The procedure object is a pair whose code specifies that the procedure has

---

9 Assignment introduces a subtlety into step 1 of the evaluation rule. As shown in exercise 3.6, the presence of assignment allows us to write expressions that will produce different values depending on the order in which the subexpressions in a combination are evaluated. Thus, to be precise, we should specify an evaluation order in step 1 (e.g., left to right or right to left). However, this order should always be considered to be an implementation detail, and one should never write programs that depend on some particular order. For instance, a sophisticated compiler might optimize a program by varying the order in which subexpressions are evaluated.

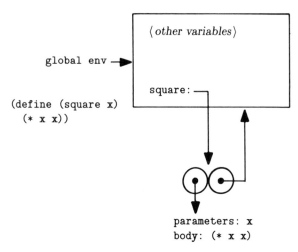

Figure 3.2
Result of evaluating (define (square x) (* x x)) in the global environment.

one formal parameter, namely x, and a procedure body (* x x). The environment part of the procedure is a pointer to the global environment, since that is the environment in which the lambda expression was evaluated to produce the procedure. A new binding, which associates the procedure object with the symbol square, has been added to the global frame. In general, define creates definitions by adding bindings to frames.

Now that we have seen how procedures are created, we can describe how procedures are applied. The environment model specifies: To apply a procedure to arguments, create a new environment containing a frame that binds the parameters to the actual values of the arguments. The enclosing environment of this frame is the environment specified by the procedure. Now, within this new environment, evaluate the procedure body.

To show how this rule is followed, figure 3.3 illustrates the environment structure created by evaluating the expression (square 5) in the global environment, where square is the procedure generated in figure 3.2. Applying the procedure results in the creation of a new environment, labeled E1 in the figure, that begins with a frame in which x, the formal parameter for the procedure, is bound to the argument 5. The pointer leading upward from this frame shows that the frame's enclosing environment is the global environment. The global environment is chosen here, because this is the environment that is indicated as part of the square procedure object. Within E1, we evaluate the body of the procedure (* x x). Since the value of x in E1 is 5, the result is (* 5 5), or 25.

The environment model of procedure application can be summarized by two rules:

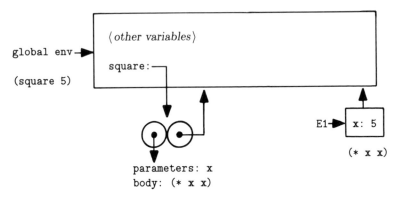

Figure 3.3
Environment created by evaluating (square 5) in the global environment.

• A procedure object is applied to a set of arguments by constructing a frame, binding the formal parameters of the procedure to the actual arguments of the call, and then evaluating the body of the procedure in the context of the new environment constructed. The new frame has as its enclosing environment the environment part of the procedure object being applied.

• A procedure is created by evaluating a lambda expression relative to a given environment. The resulting procedure object is a pair consisting of the text of the lambda expression and a pointer to the environment in which the procedure was created.

We also specify that defining a symbol using define creates a binding in the current environment frame and assigns to the symbol the indicated value.[10] Finally, we specify the behavior of set!, the operation that forced us to introduce the environment model in the first place. Evaluating the form (set! ⟨variable⟩ ⟨value⟩) in some environment locates the binding of the variable in the environment and changes that binding to indicate the new value. That is, one finds the first frame in the environment that contains a binding for the variable and modifies that frame. If the variable is unbound in the environment, then set! signals an error.

These evaluation rules, though considerably more complex than the substitution model, are still reasonably straightforward. Moreover, the evaluation model, though abstract, provides a correct description of how the interpreter evaluates expressions. In chapter 4 we shall see how this model can

---

10 If there is already a binding for the variable in the current frame, then the binding is changed. This is convenient because it allows redefinition of symbols; however, it also means that define can be used to change values, and this brings up the issues of assignment without explicitly using set!. Because of this, some people prefer redefinitions of existing symbols to signal errors or warnings.

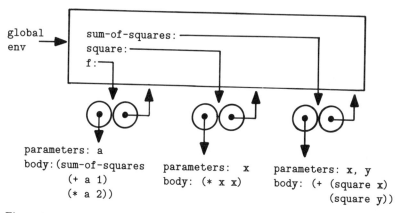

Figure 3.4
Procedure objects in the global frame.

serve as a blueprint for implementing a working interpreter. The following sections elaborate the details of the model by analyzing some illustrative programs.

3.2.2 Evaluating Simple Procedures

When we introduced the substitution model in section 1.1.5 we showed how the combination (f 5) evaluates to 136, given the following procedure definitions:

```
(define (square x)
  (* x x))

(define (sum-of-squares x y)
  (+ (square x) (square y)))

(define (f a)
  (sum-of-squares (+ a 1) (* a 2)))
```

We can analyze the same example using the environment model. Figure 3.4 shows the three procedure objects created by evaluating the definitions of f, square, and sum-of-squares in the global environment. Each procedure object consists of some code, together with a pointer to the global environment.

In figure 3.5 we see the environment structure created by evaluating the expression (f 5). The call to f creates a new environment E1 beginning with a frame in which a, the formal parameter of f, is bound to the argument 5. In E1, we evaluate the body of f:

```
(sum-of-squares (+ a 1) (* a 2))
```

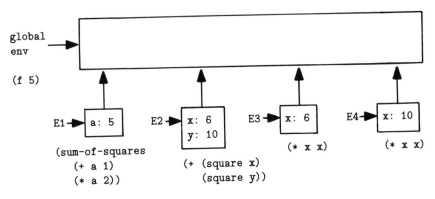

Figure 3.5
Environments created by evaluating (f 5) using the procedures in figure 3.4.

To evaluate this combination, we first evaluate the subexpressions. The first subexpression, sum-of-squares, has a value that is a procedure object. (Notice how this value is found: We first look in the first frame of E1, which contains no binding for sum-of-squares. Then we proceed to the containing environment, i.e. the global environment, and find the binding shown in figure 3.4.) The other two subexpressions are evaluated by applying the primitive operations + and * to evaluate the two combinations (+ a 1) and (* a 2) to obtain 6 and 10, respectively.

Now we apply the procedure object sum-of-squares to the arguments 6 and 10. This results in a new environment E2 in which the formal parameters x and y are bound to the arguments. Within E2 we evaluate the combination (+ (square x) (square y)). This leads us to evaluate (square x), where square is found in the global frame and x is 6. Once again, we set up a new environment, E3, in which x is bound to 6, and within this we evaluate the body of square, which is (* x x). Also as part of evaluating sum-of-squares, we must evaluate the subexpression (square y), where y is 10. This second call to square creates another environment, E4, in which x, the formal parameter of square, is bound to 10. And within E4 we must evaluate (* x x).

The important point to observe is that each call to square creates a new environment containing a binding for x. We can see here how the different frames serve to keep separate the different local variables all named x. Notice that each frame created by square points to the global environment, since this is the environment indicated by the square procedure object.

Once all the subexpressions have been evaluated, the results are returned. The two calls to square generate values, which are added by sum-of-squares. This result is returned by f. Since our focus here is on the environment structures, we will not dwell on how these returned values are passed from call to call; however, this is also an important aspect of the evaluation process, and we will return to it in detail in chapter 5.

Exercise 3.9

In section 1.2.1 we used the substitution model to analyze two procedures for computing factorials, a recursive version

```
(define (factorial n)
  (if (= n 1)
      1
      (* n (factorial (- n 1)))))
```

and an iterative version

```
(define (factorial n)
  (fact-iter 1 1 n))

(define (fact-iter product counter max-count)
  (if (> counter max-count)
      product
      (fact-iter (* counter product)
                 (+ counter 1)
                 max-count)))
```

Show the environment structures created during the computation of (factorial 6) by each of these procedures.[11]

3.2.3 Frames as the Repository of Local State

We can turn to the environment model to see how procedures and assignment can be used to represent objects with local state. As an example, consider the "withdrawal processor" from section 3.1.1, created by calling the procedure

```
(define (make-withdraw balance)
  (lambda (amount)
    (if (>= balance amount)
        (sequence (set! balance (- balance amount))
                  balance)
        "Insufficient funds")))
```

Let us describe the evaluation of

```
(define W1 (make-withdraw 100))
```

---

11 The environment model will not clarify our claim in section 1.2.1 that the interpreter can execute a procedure such as fact-iter in a constant amount of space using tail recursion. We will discuss tail recursion when we deal with the control structure of the interpreter in section 5.2.

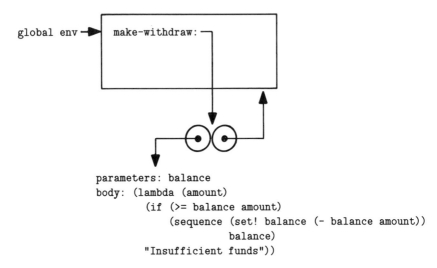

```
parameters: balance
body: (lambda (amount)
        (if (>= balance amount)
            (sequence (set! balance (- balance amount))
                      balance)
            "Insufficient funds"))
```

Figure 3.6
Result of defining make-withdraw in the global environment.

followed by

==> (W1 50)
50

Figure 3.6 shows the result of defining the make-withdraw procedure in the global environment. This produces a procedure object that contains a pointer to the global environment. So far, this is no different from the examples we have already seen, except that the body of the procedure code is itself a lambda expression. .

The interesting part of the computation happens when make-withdraw is applied to an argument:

(define W1 (make-withdraw 100))

We begin, as usual, by setting up an environment E1 in which the formal parameter balance is bound to the argument 100. Within this environment, we evaluate the body of make-withdraw, namely the lambda expression. This constructs a new procedure object, whose code is as specified by the lambda and whose environment is E1, the environment in which the lambda was evaluated to produce the procedure. The resulting procedure object is the value returned by the call to make-withdraw. This is bound to W1 in the global environment, since the define itself is being evaluated in the global environment. Figure 3.7 shows the resulting environment structure.

Now we can analyze what happens when W1 is applied to an argument:

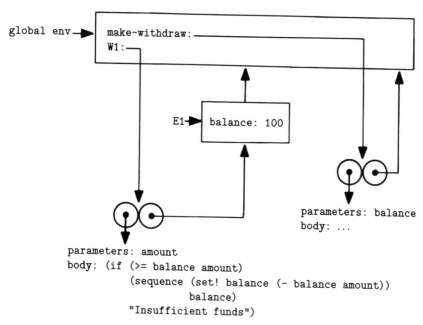

Figure 3.7
Result of (define W1 (make-withdraw 100)).

```
==> (W1 50)
50
```

We begin by constructing a frame in which amount, the formal parameter of W1, is bound to the argument 50. The crucial point to observe is that this frame has as its containing frame not the global environment, but rather the environment E1, because this is the environment that is specified by the W1 procedure object. Within this new environment, we evaluate the body of the procedure

```
(if (>= balance amount)
    (sequence (set! balance (- balance amount))
              balance)
    "Insufficient funds")
```

The resulting environment structure is shown in figure 3.8. The expression being evaluated references both amount and balance. Amount will be found in the first frame in the environment, while balance will be found by following the containing pointer to E1.

When the set! instruction is executed, the binding of balance in E1 is changed. At the completion of the call to W1, balance is 50, and the frame that contains balance is still pointed to by the procedure object W1. The local frame in which we executed the code that changed balance is no

Modularity, Objects, and State

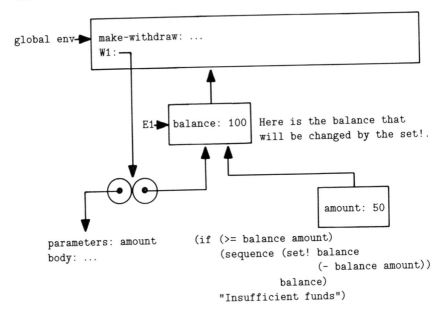

Figure 3.8
Environments created by applying the procedure object W1.

longer relevant, since the procedure call that constructed it has terminated, and there are no pointers to that frame from other parts of the environment. The next time W1 is called, this will build a new frame that binds amount and whose containing environment is E1. We see that E1 serves as the "place" that holds the local state variable for the procedure object W1. Figure 3.9 shows the situation after the call to W1.

Observe what happens when we create a second "withdraw" object by making another call to make-withdraw:

```
(define W2 (make-withdraw 100))
```

This produces the environment structure of figure 3.10, which shows that W2 is a procedure object, that is, a pair with some code and an environment. The environment E2 for W2 was created by the call to make-withdraw. It contains a frame with its own local binding for balance. On the other hand, W1 and W2 have the same code: the code specified by the lambda expression in the body of make-withdraw.[12] We see here why W1 and W2 behave as independent objects. Calls to W1 reference the state variable balance stored in E1, whereas calls to W2 reference the balance stored in E2. Thus, changes to the local state of one object do not affect the other object.

---

12 Whether or not W1 and W2 share the same physical code stored in the computer, or whether they each keep a copy of the code, is a detail of the implementation. For the interpreter we implement in chapter 4, the code is in fact shared.

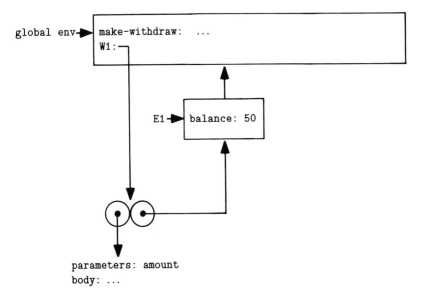

Figure 3.9
Result of calling W1 in figure 3.8.

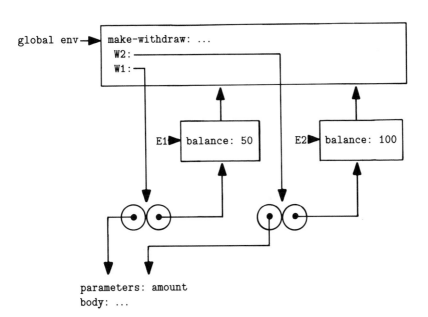

Figure 3.10
Using (define W2 (make-withdraw 100)) to create a second object.

Exercise 3.10

In the make-withdraw procedure, the local variable balance is created as a parameter of make-withdraw. We could also create the local state variable explicitly, using let, as follows:

```
(define (make-withdraw initial-amount)
  (let ((balance initial-amount))
    (lambda (amount)
      (if (>= balance amount)
          (sequence (set! balance (- balance amount))
                    balance)
          "Insufficient funds"))))
```

Recall from section 1.3.2 that let is simply syntactic sugar for a procedure call:

```
(let (((var) (exp))) (body))
```

is interpreted as an alternate syntax for

```
((lambda ((var)) (body)) (exp))
```

Use the environment model to analyze the behavior of this alternate version of make-withdraw, drawing figures like the ones above to illustrate the interactions

```
(define W1 (make-withdraw 100))
```

```
(W1 50)
```

```
(define W2 (make-withdraw 100))
```

Show that the two versions of make-withdraw create objects with the same behavior. How do the environment structures for the two versions of make-withdraw differ?

3.2.4 Internal Definitions

Section 1.1.8 introduced the idea that procedures can have internal definitions, thus leading to a block structure as in the following procedure to compute square roots:

```
(define (sqrt x)
  (define (good-enough? guess)
    (< (abs (- (square guess) x)) .001))
  (define (improve guess)
    (average guess (/ x guess)))
  (define (sqrt-iter guess)
    (if (good-enough? guess)
        guess
        (sqrt-iter (improve guess))))
  (sqrt-iter 1))
```

Now we can use the environment model to see why these internal definitions behave as desired. Figure 3.11 shows the point in the evaluation of the ex-

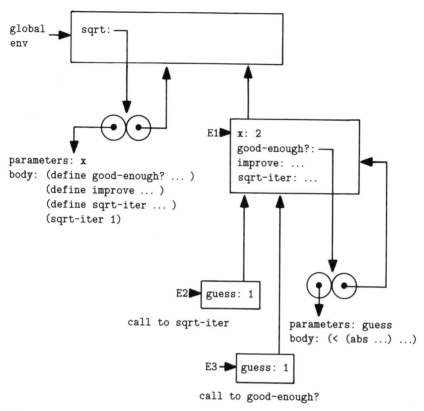

Figure 3.11
Sqrt procedure with internal definitions.

pression (sqrt 2) where the internal procedure good-enough? has been called for the first time with guess equal to 1.

Observe the structure of the environment. Sqrt is a symbol in the global environment that is bound to a procedure object whose associated environment is the global environment. When sqrt was called, it formed a new environment E1, subordinate to the global environment, in which the parameter x is bound to 2. The body of sqrt was then evaluated in E1. Since the first expression in the body of sqrt is

```
(define (good-enough? guess)
  (< (abs (- (square guess) x)) .001))
```

evaluating this expression defined the procedure good-enough? in the environment E1. To be more precise, the symbol good-enough? was added to the first frame of E1, bound to a procedure object whose associated environment is E1. Similarly, improve and sqrt-iter were defined as procedures in E1. For conciseness, figure 3.11 shows only the procedure object for good-enough? .

After the local procedures were defined, sqrt evaluated the expression (sqrt-iter 1), still in environment E1. So the procedure object bound to sqrt-iter in E1 was called with 1 as an argument. This created a new environment E2 in which guess, the parameter of sqrt-iter, is bound to 1. Sqrt-iter in turn called good-enough? with the value of guess (from E2) as the argument for good-enough?. This set up another environment E3 in which guess (the parameter of good-enough?) is bound to 1. Although sqrt-iter and good-enough? both have a parameter named guess, these are two distinct local variables located in different frames. Also, E2 and E3 both have E1 as their enclosing environment, because the sqrt-iter and good-enough? procedures both have E1 as their environment part. One consequence of this is that the symbol x that appears in the body of good-enough? will reference the binding of x that appears in E1, namely the value of x with which the original sqrt procedure was called.

The environment model thus explains the two key properties that make local procedure definitions a useful technique for modularizing programs:

• The names of the local procedures do not interfere with names external to the enclosing procedure, because the local procedure names will be bound in the frame that the procedure creates when it is run, rather than being bound in the global environment.

• The local procedures can access the arguments of the enclosing procedure, simply by using parameter names as free variables. This is because the body of the local procedure is evaluated in an environment that is subordinate to the evaluation environment for the enclosing procedure.

Exercise 3.11

In section 3.2.3 we saw how the environment model described the evaluation of procedures with local state. Now we have seen how internal definitions work. A typical message-passing procedure contains both of these aspects. Consider the bank account procedure of section 3.1.1:

```
(define (make-account balance)
  (define (withdraw amount)
    (if (>= balance amount)
        (sequence (set! balance (- balance amount))
                  balance)
        "Insufficient funds"))
  (define (deposit amount)
    (set! balance (+ balance amount))
    balance)
  (define (dispatch m)
    (cond ((eq? m 'withdraw) withdraw)
          ((eq? m 'deposit) deposit)
          (else (error "Unknown request -- MAKE-ACCOUNT" m))))
  dispatch)
```

Show the environment structure generated by the sequence of interactions

```
(define acc (make-account 50))
```

```
==> ((acc 'deposit) 40)
```
90

```
==> ((acc 'withdraw) 60)
```
30

Where is the local state for acc kept? Suppose we define another account

```
(define acc2 (make-account 100))
```

How are the local states for the two accounts kept distinct? Which parts of the environment structure are shared between acc and acc2?

3.3 Modeling with Mutable Data

Chapter 2 dealt with compound data as a means for constructing computational objects that have several parts, in order to model real-world objects that have several aspects. In that chapter we introduced the discipline of data abstraction, according to which data structures are specified in terms of constructors, which create data objects, and selectors, which access the parts of compound data objects. But we now know that there is another aspect of data that chapter 2 did not address. The desire to model systems composed of objects that have changing state leads us to the need to modify compound data objects, as well as to construct and select from them. In order to model compound objects with changing state, we will design data abstractions to include, in addition to selectors and constructors, operations called *mutators*, which modify data objects. For instance, modeling a banking system requires us to change account balances. Thus, a data structure for representing bank accounts might admit an operation

```
(set-balance! ⟨account⟩ ⟨new-value⟩)
```

that changes the balance of the designated account to the designated new value. Data objects for which mutators are defined are known as *mutable data objects*.

Chapter 2 showed that Lisp provides pairs as a general-purpose "glue" for synthesizing compound data. We begin this section by defining basic mutators for pairs, so that pairs can serve as building blocks for constructing mutable data objects. These mutators greatly enhance the representational power of pairs, enabling us to build data structures other than the sequences and trees that we worked with in section 2.2. We also present some examples of simulations in which complex systems are modeled as collections of objects with local state.

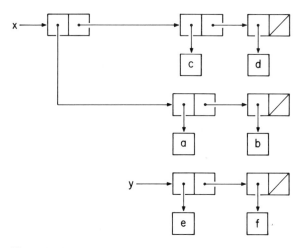

Figure 3.12
Lists **x**: ((a b) c d) and **y**: (e f).

3.3.1 Mutable List Structure

The basic operations on pairs—cons, car, and cdr—can be used to construct list structure and to select parts from list structure, but they are incapable of modifying list structure. The same is true of the list operations we have used so far, such as append and list, since these can be defined in terms of cons, car, and cdr. To modify list structures we need new operations.

The primitive mutators for list structure are set-car! and set-cdr!. Set-car! takes two arguments, the first of which must be a pair. It modifies this pair, replacing the car pointer by a pointer to the second argument of set-car!. As an example, suppose that x is bound to the list ((a b) c d) and y to the list (e f) as illustrated in figure 3.12. Evaluating the expression (set-car! x y) modifies the pair to which x is bound, replacing its car by the value of y. The result of the operation is shown in figure 3.13. The structure x has been modified and would now be printed by the interpreter as ((e f) c d). The pairs representing the list (a b), identified by the pointer that was replaced, are now detached from the original structure.[13]

Compare figure 3.13 with figure 3.14, which illustrates the result of executing (define z (cons y (cdr x))) with x and y bound to the original

13 We see from this that mutation operations on lists can create "garbage" that is not part of any accessible structure. We will see in section 5.4 that Lisp memory-management systems include a *garbage collector*, which identifies and recycles the memory space used by unneeded pairs.

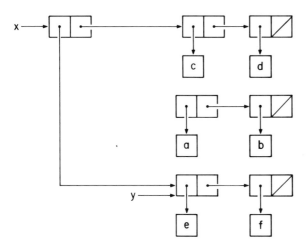

Figure 3.13
Effect of (set-car! x y) on the lists in figure 3.12.

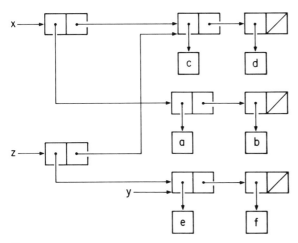

Figure 3.14
Effect of (define z (cons y (cdr x))) on the lists in figure 3.12.

lists of figure 3.12. The variable z is now bound to a new pair created by
the cons operation; the list to which x is bound is unchanged.

The set-cdr! operation is similar to set-car!. The only difference is
that the cdr pointer of the pair, rather than the car pointer, is replaced.
The effect of executing (set-cdr! x y) on the lists of figure 3.12 is shown
in figure 3.15. Here the cdr pointer of x has been replaced by the pointer to
(e f). Also, the list (c d), which used to be the cdr of x, is now detached
from the structure.

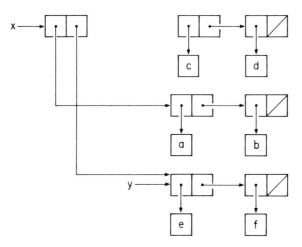

Figure 3.15
Effect of (set-cdr! x y) on the lists in figure 3.12.

Cons builds new list structure by creating new pairs, whereas set-car! and set-cdr! modify existing pairs. Indeed, we could implement cons in terms of the two mutators, together with a procedure get-new-pair, which returns a new pair that is not part of any existing list structure. We obtain the new pair, set its car and cdr pointers to the designated objects, and return the new pair as the result of the cons.[14]

```
(define (cons x y)
  (let ((new (get-new-pair)))
    (set-car! new x)
    (set-cdr! new y)
    new))
```

Exercise 3.12

The following procedure for appending two lists was introduced in section 2.2.1:

```
(define (append x y)
  (if (null? x)
      y
      (cons (car x) (append (cdr x) y))))
```

Append forms a new list by successively consing the elements of x onto y. The procedure append! is similar to append, but it is a mutator rather than a constructor. It appends the lists by actually splicing them together, modifying the final pair of x so that its cdr is now y. (Append! produces an error if x is empty.)

14 Get-new-pair is one of the operations that must be implemented as part of the memory management required by a Lisp implementation. We will discuss this in section 5.4.

```
(define (append! x y)
  (set-cdr! (last x) y)
  x)
```

Here `last` is a procedure that returns the last pair in its argument:

```
(define (last x)
  (if (null? (cdr x))
      x
      (last (cdr x))))
```

Consider the interaction

```
==> (define x '(a b))
x

==> (define y '(c d))
y

==> (define z (append  x y))
z

==> z
(a b c d)

==> (cdr x)
⟨exp₁⟩

==> (define w (append! x y))
w

==> w
(a b c d)

==> (cdr x)
⟨exp₂⟩
```

What are the expressions $\langle exp_1 \rangle$ and $\langle exp_2 \rangle$ printed by the interpreter? Draw box-and-pointer diagrams to explain your answer.

Exercise 3.13

Consider the following `make-cycle` procedure, which uses the `last` procedure defined in exercise 3.12:

```
(define (make-cycle x)
  (set-cdr! (last x) x)
  x)
```

Draw a box-and-pointer diagram that shows the structure z created by

```
(define z (make-cycle '(a b c)))
```

What happens if we try to compute (last z)?

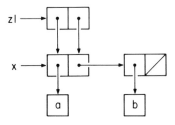

Figure 3.16
The list z1 formed by (cons x x).

Exercise 3.14

The following procedure is quite useful, although obscure:

```
(define (mystery x)
  (define (loop x y)
    (if (null? x)
        y
        (let ((temp (cdr x)))
          (set-cdr! x y)
          (loop temp x))))
  (loop x '()))
```

Notice that loop uses the temporary variable temp to hold the old value of the cdr of x, since the set-cdr! on the next line destroys the cdr. Explain what mystery does in general. Suppose v is defined by (define v '(a b c d)). Draw the box-and-pointer diagram that represents the list to which v is bound. Suppose that we now evaluate (define w (mystery v)). Draw box-and-pointer diagrams that show the structures v and w after evaluating this expression. What would the interpreter print as the values of v and w?

Sharing and identity

We mentioned in section 3.1.2 the theoretical issues of "sameness" and "change" raised by the introduction of assignment. These issues arise in practice when individual pairs are *shared* among different data objects. For example, consider the structure formed by

```
(define x (list 'a 'b))
(define z1 (cons x x))
```

As shown in figure 3.16, z1 is a pair whose car and cdr both point to the same pair x. This sharing of x by the car and cdr of z is a consequence of the straightforward way in which cons is implemented. In general, using cons to construct lists will result in an interlinked structure of pairs in which many individual pairs are shared by many different structures.

In contrast to figure 3.16, figure 3.17 shows the structure created by

```
(define z2 (cons (list 'a 'b) (list 'a 'b)))
```

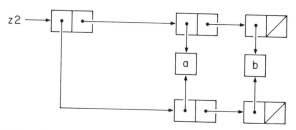

Figure 3.17
The list z2 formed by (cons (list 'a 'b) (list 'a 'b)).

In this structure, the pairs in the two (a b) lists are distinct, although the actual atoms are shared.[15]

When thought of as a list, z1 and z2 both represent "the same" list, ((a b) a b). In general, sharing is completely undetectable if we operate on lists using only cons, car, and cdr. However, if we allow mutators on list structure, sharing becomes significant. As an example of the difference that sharing can make, consider the following procedure, which modifies the car of the structure to which it is applied:

```
(define (set-to-wow! x)
  (set-car! (car x) 'wow)
  x)
```

Even though z1 and z2 are "the same" tree structure, applying set-to-wow! to them yields different results. With z1, altering the car also changes the cdr, because in z1 the car and the cdr are the same pair. With z2, whose car and cdr are distinct, only the car is modified by set-to-wow!:

```
==> z1
((a b) a b)

==> (set-to-wow! z1)
((wow b) wow b)

==> z2
((a b) a b)

==> (set-to-wow! z2)
((wow b) a b)
```

[15] The two pairs are distinct because each call to cons returns a new pair. The atoms are shared; in Scheme there is a unique symbol with any given name. Since Scheme provides no way to mutate an atom, this sharing is undetectable. Note also that the sharing is what enables us to compare symbols using eq?, which simply checks equality of pointers.

One way to detect sharing in list structures is to use the predicate eq?, which we introduced in section 2.2.3 as a way to test whether two symbols are equal. More generally, (eq? x y) tests whether x and y are the same object (that is, whether x and y are equal as pointers). Thus, with z1 and z2 as defined in figures 3.16 and 3.17, (eq? (car z1) (cdr z1)) is true and (eq? (car z2) (cdr z2)) is false.

As will be seen in the following sections, we can exploit sharing to greatly extend the repertoire of data structures that can be represented by pairs. On the other hand, sharing can also be dangerous, since modifications made to structures will also affect other structures that happen to share the modified parts. The mutation operations set-car! and set-cdr! should be used with care; unless we have a good understanding of how our data objects are shared, mutation can have unanticipated results.[16]

Exercise 3.15

Draw box-and-pointer diagrams to explain the effect of set-to-wow! on the structures z1 and z2 above.

Exercise 3.16

Ben Bitdiddle decides to write a procedure to count the number of pairs in any list structure. "It's easy," he reasons. "The number of pairs in any structure is the number in the car plus the number in the cdr plus one more to count the current pair. And the number of pairs for an atom (including the empty list) is zero." So Ben writes the following procedure:

```
(define (count-pairs x)
  (if (atom? x)
      0
      (+ (count-pairs (car x))
         (count-pairs (cdr x))
         1)))
```

Show that this procedure is not correct. In particular, draw box-and-pointer diagrams representing list structures made up of exactly three pairs for which Ben's procedure would return 3; return 4; return 7; never return at all.

---

16 The subtleties of dealing with sharing of mutable data objects reflect the underlying issues of "sameness" and "change" that were raised in section 3.1.2. We mentioned there that admitting change to our language requires that a compound object must have an "identity" that is something different from the pieces from which it is composed. In Lisp, we consider this "identity" to be the quality that is tested by eq?, i.e., by equality of pointers. Since in most Lisp implementations, a pointer is essentially a memory address, we are "solving the problem" of defining the identity of objects by stipulating that a data object "itself" is the information stored in some particular set of memory locations in the computer. This suffices for simple Lisp programs, but is hardly a general way to resolve the issue of "sameness" in computational models.

Exercise 3.17

Devise a correct version of the count-pairs procedure of exercise 3.16 that will
return the number of distinct pairs in any structure. (Hint: Traverse the structure,
maintaining an auxiliary data structure that is used to keep track of which pairs
have already been counted.)

Exercise 3.18

Write a procedure that examines a list and determines whether it contains a
cycle, that is, whether a program that tried to find the end of the list by taking
successive cdrs would go into an infinite loop. Exercise 3.13 constructed such
lists.

Exercise 3.19

Redo exercise 3.18 using an algorithm that takes only a constant amount of space.
(This requires a very clever idea.)

Mutation is just assignment

When we introduced compound data, we observed in section 2.1.3 that
pairs can be represented purely in terms of procedures:

```
(define (cons x y)
  (define (dispatch m)
    (cond ((eq? m 'car) x)
          ((eq? m 'cdr) y)
          (else (error "Undefined operation -- CONS" m))))
  dispatch)

(define (car z) (z 'car))

(define (cdr z) (z 'cdr))
```

The same observation is true for mutable data. We can implement mutable
data objects as procedures using assignment and local state. For instance,
we can extend the above pair implementation to handle set-car! and set-
cdr! in a manner analogous to the way we implemented bank accounts
using make-account in section 3.1.1:

```
(define (cons x y)
  (define (set-x! v) (set! x v))
  (define (set-y! v) (set! y v))
  ;; continued on next page
```

```
(define (dispatch m)
  (cond ((eq? m 'car) x)
        ((eq? m 'cdr) y)
        ((eq? m 'set-car!) set-x!)
        ((eq? m 'set-cdr!) set-y!)
        (else (error "Undefined operation -- CONS" m))))
  dispatch)

(define (car z) (z 'car))

(define (cdr z) (z 'cdr))

(define (set-car! z new-value)
  ((z 'set-car!) new-value)
  z)

(define (set-cdr! z new-value)
  ((z 'set-cdr!) new-value)
  z)
```

Assignment is all that is needed, theoretically, to account for the behavior of mutable data. As soon as we admit set! to our language, we raise all the issues, not only of assignment, but of mutable data in general.[17]

Exercise 3.20

Draw environment diagrams to illustrate the evaluation of the sequence

```
(define x (cons 1 2))
(define z (cons x x))
(set-car! (cdr z) 17)

==> (car x)
17
```

using the procedural implementation of pairs given above. (Compare exercise 3.11.)

3.3.2 Representing Queues

The mutators set-car! and set-cdr! enable us to use pairs to construct data structures that cannot be built with cons, car, and cdr alone. This

---

17 On the other hand, from the viewpoint of implementation, assignment requires us to modify the environment, which is itself a mutable data structure. Thus, assignment and mutation are equipotent: Each can be implemented in terms of the other.

Operation	Resulting queue
(define q (make-queue))	
(insert-queue! q 'a)	a
(insert-queue! q 'b)	a b
(delete-queue! q)	b
(insert-queue! q 'c)	b c
(insert-queue! q 'd)	b c d
(delete-queue! q)	c d

Figure 3.18
Queue operations.

section shows how to use pairs to represent a data structure called a queue. Section 3.3.3 will show how to represent data structures called tables.

A *queue* is a sequence in which items are inserted at one end (called the *rear* of the queue) and deleted from the other end (the *front*). Figure 3.18 shows an initially empty queue in which the items a and b are inserted. Then a is removed, c and d are inserted, and b is removed. Because items are always removed in the order in which they are inserted, a queue is sometimes called a *FIFO* (first in, first out) buffer.

In terms of data abstraction, we can regard a queue as defined by the following set of operations:

• a constructor:

(make-queue) returns an empty queue (a queue containing no items).

• two selectors:

(empty-queue? ⟨*queue*⟩) is true if the queue is empty, false otherwise.

(front ⟨*queue*⟩) returns the object at the front of the queue, signaling an error if the queue is empty; it does not modify the queue.

• two mutators:

(insert-queue! ⟨*queue*⟩ ⟨*item*⟩) inserts the item at the rear of the queue and returns the modified queue as its value.

(delete-queue! ⟨*queue*⟩) removes the item at the front of the queue and returns the modified queue as its value.

Because a queue is a sequence of items, we could certainly represent it as an ordinary list; the front of the queue would be the car of the list, inserting an item in the queue would amount to appending a new element

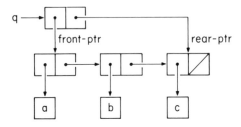

Figure 3.19
Implementation of a queue as a list with front and rear pointers.

at the end of the list, and deleting an item from the queue would just be taking the cdr of the list. However, this representation is inefficient, because in order to insert an item we must scan the list until we reach the end. Since the only method we have for scanning a list is by successive cdr operations, this scanning requires $O(n)$ time for a list of n items. A simple modification to the list representation overcomes this disadvantage by allowing the queue operations to be implemented so that they require $O(1)$ time; that is, so that the time needed is independent of the length of the queue.

The difficulty with the list representation arises from the need to scan to find the end of the list. The reason we need to scan is that, although the standard way of representing a list as a chain of pairs readily provides us with a pointer to the beginning of the list, it gives us no easily accessible pointer to the end. The modification that avoids the drawback is to represent the queue as a list, together with an additional pointer that indicates the final pair in the list. That way, when we go to insert an item, we can consult the rear pointer and so avoid scanning the list.

A queue is represented, then, as a pair of pointers, front-ptr and rear-ptr, which indicate, respectively, the first and last pairs in an ordinary list. Since we would like the queue to be an identifiable object, we can use cons to combine the two pointers. Thus, the queue itself will be the cons of the two pointers. Figure 3.19 illustrates this representation.

To define the queue operations we use the following procedures, which enable us to select and to modify the front and rear pointers of a queue:

```
(define (front-ptr queue) (car queue))

(define (rear-ptr queue) (cdr queue))

(define (set-front-ptr! queue item) (set-car! queue item))

(define (set-rear-ptr! queue item) (set-cdr! queue item))
```

Now we can implement the actual queue operations. We will consider a queue to be empty if its front pointer is the empty list:

```
(define (empty-queue? queue) (null? (front-ptr queue)))
```

The make-queue constructor returns, as an initially empty queue, a cons of two empty lists:

```
(define (make-queue) (cons '() '()))
```

To select the item at the front of the queue, we return the car of the pair indicated by the front pointer:

```
(define (front queue)
  (if (empty-queue? queue)
      (error "FRONT called with an empty queue" queue)
      (car (front-ptr queue))))
```

To insert an item in a queue, we follow the method whose result is indicated in figure 3.20. We first create a new pair whose car is the item to be inserted and whose cdr is nil. If the queue was initially empty, we set the front and rear pointers of the queue to this new pair. Otherwise, we modify the final pair in the queue to point to the new pair, and also set the rear pointer to the new pair.

```
(define (insert-queue! queue item)
  (let ((new-pair (cons item nil)))
    (cond ((empty-queue? queue)
           (set-front-ptr! queue new-pair)
           (set-rear-ptr! queue new-pair)
           queue)
          (else
           (set-cdr! (rear-ptr queue) new-pair)
           (set-rear-ptr! queue new-pair)
           queue))))
```

To delete the item at the front of the queue, we merely modify the front pointer so that it now points at the second item in the queue, which can be found by following the cdr pointer of the first item (see figure 3.21):[18]

[18] If the first item is the final item in the queue, the front pointer will be nil after the deletion, which will mark the queue as empty; we needn't worry about updating the rear pointer, which will still point to the deleted item, because empty-queue? looks only at the front pointer. If the queue is empty before the deletion, the procedure signals an error.

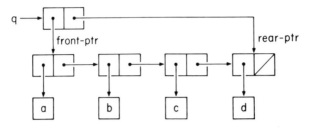

Figure 3.20
Result of using (insert-queue! q 'd) on the queue of figure 3.19.

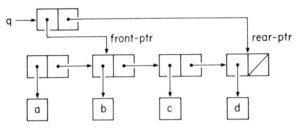

Figure 3.21
Result of using (delete-queue! q) on the queue of figure 3.20.

```
(define (delete-queue! queue)
  (cond ((empty-queue? queue)
         (error "Delete called with an empty queue" queue))
        (else
         (set-front-ptr! queue (cdr (front-ptr queue)))
         queue)))
```

Exercise 3.21

Ben Bitdiddle decides to test the queue implementation described above. He types in the procedures to the Lisp interpreter and proceeds to try them out:

```
==> (define q1 (make-queue))
q1
==> (insert-queue! q1 'a)
((a) a)
==> (insert-queue! q1 'b)
((a b) b)
==> (delete-queue! q1)
((b) b)
==> (delete-queue! q1)
(() b)
```

"It's all wrong!" he complains. "The interpreter's response shows that the last item is inserted into the queue twice. And when I delete both items, the second b is still there, so the queue isn't empty, even though it's supposed to be." Eva Lu Ator suggests that Ben has misunderstood what is happening. "It's not that the items are going into the queue twice," she explains. "It's just that the standard Lisp printer doesn't know how to make sense of the queue representation. If you want to see the queue printed correctly, you'll have to define your own print procedure for queues." Explain what Eva Lu is talking about. In particular, show why Ben's examples produce the printed results that they do. Define a procedure print-queue that takes a queue as input and prints the sequence of items in the queue.

Exercise 3.22

Instead of representing a queue as a pair of pointers, we can build a queue as a procedure with local state. The local state will consist of pointers to the beginning and the end of an ordinary list. Thus, the make-queue procedure will have the form

```
(define (make-queue)
  (let ((front-ptr ... )
        (rear-ptr ... ))
    ⟨ definitions of internal procedures⟩
    (define (dispatch m) ...)
    dispatch))
```

Complete the definition of make-queue and provide implementations of the queue operations using this representation.

Exercise 3.23

A *deque* ("double-ended queue") is a sequence in which items can be inserted and deleted at either the front or the rear. The data-access operations are make-deque, empty-deque?, front-deque, rear-deque, front-insert-deque!, rear-insert-deque!, front-delete-deque!, and rear-delete-deque!. Show how to represent deques using pairs, and give implementations of the operations. All operations should be accomplished in $O(1)$ time.

3.3.3 Representing Tables

When we studied various ways of representing sets in chapter 2, we mentioned in section 2.2.5 the task of maintaining a table of records indexed by identifying keys. In the implementation of data-directed programming in section 2.3.3, we made extensive use of two-dimensional tables, in which information is stored and retrieved using two keys. Here we see how to build tables as mutable list structures.

We first consider one-dimensional tables, in which each value is stored under a single key. We implement the table as a list of records, each of which is implemented as a pair consisting of a key and the associated value.

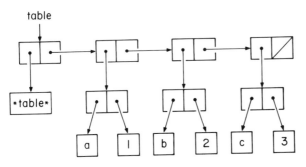

Figure 3.22
A table represented as a headed list.

The records are glued together to form a list by pairs whose cars point to successive records. These gluing pairs are called the *backbone* of the table. In order to have a place that we can change when we add a new record to the table, we build the table as a *headed list*. A headed list has a special backbone pair at the beginning, which holds a dummy "record"—in this case the arbitrarily chosen symbol *table* . Figure 3.22 shows the box-and-pointer diagram for the table

a: 1

b: 2

c: 3

To extract information from a table we use the lookup procedure, which takes a key as argument and returns the associated value (or nil if there is no value stored under that key). Lookup is defined in terms of the assq operation, which expects a key and a list of records as arguments. Note that assq never sees the dummy record. Assq returns the record that has the given key as its car. Lookup then checks to see that the record is not null, and returns the value (the cdr) of the record.

```
(define (lookup key table)
  (let ((record (assq key (cdr table))))
    (if (null? record)
        nil
        (cdr record))))

(define (assq key records)
  (cond ((null? records) nil)
        ((eq? key (caar records)) (car records))
        (else (assq key (cdr records)))))
```

To insert a value in a table under a specified key, we first use assq to see if there is already a record in the table with this key. If not, we form a new record by consing the key with the value, and insert this at the head of the table's list of records, after the dummy record. If there already is a record with this key, we set the cdr of this record to the designated new value. The header of the table provides us with a fixed location to modify in order to insert the new record.[19]

```
(define (insert! key value table)
  (let ((record (assq key (cdr table))))
    (if (null? record)
        (set-cdr! table
                  (cons (cons key value) (cdr table)))
        (set-cdr! record value)))
  'ok)
```

To construct a new table, we simply create a list containing the symbol *table* :

```
(define (make-table)
  (list '*table*))
```

Two-dimensional tables

In a two-dimensional table, each value is indexed by two keys. We can construct such a table as a one-dimensional table in which each key identifies a subtable. When we look up an item, we use the first key to identify the correct subtable. Then we use the second key to identify the record within the subtable. (The subtable doesn't need a special header symbol, since the first key serves this purpose.)

```
(define (lookup key-1 key-2 table)
  (let ((subtable (assq key-1 (cdr table))))
    (if (null? subtable)
        nil
        (let ((record (assq key-2 (cdr subtable))))
          (if (null? record)
              nil
              (cdr record))))))
```

---

[19] Thus, the first backbone pair is the object that represents the table "itself"; that is, a pointer to the table is a pointer to this pair. This same backbone pair always starts the table. If we did not arrange things in this way, insert! would have to return a new value for the start of the table when it added a new record.

To insert a new item under a pair of keys, we use assq to see if there is a subtable stored under the first key. If not, we build a new subtable containing the single record (key-2, value) and insert it into the table under the first key. If a subtable already exists for the first key, we insert the new record into this subtable, using the insertion method for one-dimensional tables described above:

```
(define (insert! key-1 key-2 value table)
  (let ((subtable (assq key-1 (cdr table))))
    (if (null? subtable)
        (set-cdr! table
                  (cons (list key-1
                              (cons key-2 value))
                        (cdr table)))
        (let ((record (assq key-2 (cdr subtable))))
          (if (null? record)
              (set-cdr! subtable
                        (cons (cons key-2 value)
                              (cdr subtable)))
              (set-cdr! record value)))))
  'ok)
```

Creating local tables

The lookup and insert! operations defined above take the table as an argument. This enables us to use programs that access more than one table. Another way to deal with multiple tables is to have separate lookup and insert! procedures for each table. We can do this by representing a table procedurally, as an object that maintains an internal table as part of its local state. When sent an appropriate message, this "table object" supplies the procedure with which to operate on the internal table. Here is a generator for two-dimensional tables represented in this fashion:

```
(define (make-table)
  (let ((local-table (list '*table*)))
    (define (lookup key-1 key-2)
      (let ((subtable (assq key-1 (cdr local-table))))
        (if (null? subtable)
            nil
            (let ((record (assq key-2 (cdr subtable))))
              (if (null? record)
                  nil
                  (cdr record))))))
```

;; *continued on next page*

```
(define (insert! key-1 key-2 value)
  (let ((subtable (assq key-1 (cdr local-table))))
    (if (null? subtable)
        (set-cdr! local-table
                  (cons (list key-1
                              (cons key-2 value))
                        (cdr local-table)))
        (let ((record (assq key-2 (cdr subtable))))
          (if (null? record)
              (set-cdr! subtable
                        (cons (cons key-2 value)
                              (cdr subtable)))
              (set-cdr! record value)))))
  'ok)
(define (dispatch m)
  (cond ((eq? m 'lookup-proc) lookup)
        ((eq? m 'insert-proc!) insert!)
        (else (error "Unknown operation -- TABLE" m))))

dispatch))
```

Using make-table, we could implement the get and put operations used in section 2.3.3 for data-directed programming, as follows:

```
(define operation-table (make-table))
(define get (operation-table 'lookup-proc))
(define put (operation-table 'insert-proc!))
```

Get takes as arguments two keys, and put takes as arguments two keys and a value. Both operations access the same local table, which is encapsulated within the object created by the call to make-table.

Exercise 3.24

In the table implementations above, the keys are tested for equality using eq?. This is not always the appropriate test. For instance, with numerical keys, we should test equality using =. (Whether or not two instances of the same number are eq?, that is, represented by equal pointers, is highly implementation-dependent.) Design a table constructor make-table that takes as an argument a same-key? procedure that will be used to test equality of keys. Make-table should return a dispatch procedure that can be used to access appropriate lookup and insert! procedures for a local table.

Exercise 3.25

Generalizing one- and two-dimensional tables, show how to implement a table in which values are stored under an arbitrary number of keys and different values may be stored under different numbers of keys. The lookup and insert! procedures should take as input a list of keys used to access the table.

Exercise 3.26

To search a table as implemented above, one needs to scan through the list of keys. This is basically the unordered list representation of section 2.2.5. For large tables, it may be more efficient to structure the table in a different manner. Describe a table implementation where the (key, value) records are organized using a binary tree, assuming that keys can be ordered in some way (e.g., numerically or alphabetically). (Compare exercise 2.38 of chapter 2.)

Exercise 3.27

Memoization (also called *tabulation*) is a technique that enables a procedure to record, in a local table, values that have previously been computed. This technique can make a vast difference in the performance of a program. A memoized procedure maintains a one-dimensional table in which values of previous calls are stored using as keys the arguments that produced the values. When the memoized procedure is asked to compute a value, it first checks the table to see if the value is already there and, if so, just returns that value. Otherwise, it computes the new value in the ordinary way and stores this in the table. As an example of memoization, recall from section 1.2.2 the exponential process for computing Fibonacci numbers:

```
(define (fib n)
  (cond ((= n 0) 0)
        ((= n 1) 1)
        (else (+ (fib (- n 1))
                 (fib (- n 2))))))
```

The memoized version of the same procedure is

```
(define memo-fib
  (memoize (lambda (n)
             (cond ((= n 0) 0)
                   ((= n 1) 1)
                   (else (+ (memo-fib (- n 1))
                            (memo-fib (- n 2))))))))
```

where the memoizer is defined as

```
(define (memoize f)
  (let ((table (make-table)))
    (lambda (x)
      (let ((previously-computed-result (lookup x table)))
        (if (not (null? previously-computed-result))
            previously-computed-result
            (let ((result (f x)))
              (insert! x result table)
              result))))))
```

Draw an environment diagram to analyze the computation of (memo-fib 3).
Explain why memo-fib computes the nth Fibonacci number in time proportional
to n. Would the scheme still work if we had simply defined memo-fib to be
(memoize fib)? (To run memo-fib, we should be sure that the table operations
are constructed so as to test keys for numeric equality. See exercise 3.24 above.)

3.3.4 A Simulator for Digital Circuits

Designing complex digital systems, such as computers, is an important
engineering activity. Digital systems are constructed by interconnecting
simple elements. Although the behavior of these individual elements is
simple, networks of them can have very complex behavior. Computer
simulation of proposed circuit designs is an important tool used by digital
systems engineers. In this section we design a system for performing digital
logic simulations.

Our computational model of a circuit will be composed of objects that
correspond to the elementary components from which the circuit is constructed. There are *wires*, which carry digital signals. A digital signal may
at any moment have only one of two possible values, 0 and 1. There are
also various types of digital *function boxes*, which connect wires carrying
input signals to other output wires. Such boxes produce output signals
computed from their input signals. The output signal is delayed by a time
that depends on the type of the function box. For example, an *inverter* is
a primitive function box that inverts the sense of its input. If the input
signal to an inverter changes to 0, then one inverter-delay later the inverter
will change its output signal to 1. If the input signal to an inverter changes
to 1, then one inverter-delay later the inverter will change its output signal
to 0. We draw an inverter symbolically as in figure 3.23. An *and-gate*, also
shown in figure 3.23, is a primitive function box with two inputs and one
output. It drives its output signal to a value that is the *logical and* of the
inputs. That is, if both of its input signals are 1, then one and-gate-delay
time later the and-gate will force its output signal to be 1; otherwise the
output will be 0. An *or-gate* is a similar two-input primitive function box
that drives its output signal to a value that is the *logical or* of the inputs.
That is, the output will become 1 if at least one of the input signals is 1;
otherwise the output will become 0.

We can connect primitive functions together to construct more complex
functions. This is accomplished by wiring the outputs of some function
boxes to the inputs of other function boxes. For example, the *half-adder*
circuit shown in figure 3.24 consists of an or-gate, two and-gates, and an
inverter. It takes two input signals, A and B, and has two output signals, S

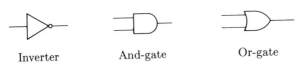

| Inverter | And-gate | Or-gate |

Figure 3.23
Primitive functions in the digital logic simulator.

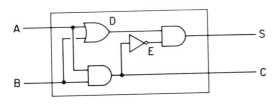

Figure 3.24
A half-adder circuit.

and C. S will become 1 whenever precisely one of A and B is 1, and C will become 1 whenever A and B are both 1. We can see from the figure that, because of the delays involved, the outputs may be generated at different times. Many of the difficulties in the design of digital circuits arise from this fact.

We will now build a program for modeling the digital logic circuits we wish to study. The program will construct computational objects modeling the wires, which will "hold" the signals. Function boxes will be modeled by procedures that enforce the correct relationships among the signals.

One basic element of our simulation will be a procedure `make-wire`, which constructs wires. For example, we can construct six wires as follows:

```
(define a (make-wire))
(define b (make-wire))
(define c (make-wire))
(define d (make-wire))
(define e (make-wire))
(define s (make-wire))
```

We attach a function box to a set of wires by calling a procedure that constructs that kind of box. The arguments to the constructor procedure are the wires to be attached to the box. For example, given that we can construct and-gates, or-gates, and inverters, we can wire together the half-adder shown in figure 3.24:

```
(or-gate a b d)
(and-gate a b c)
(inverter c e)
(and-gate d e s)
```

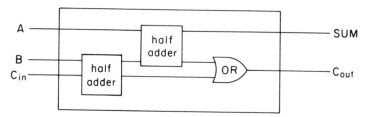

Figure 3.25
A full-adder circuit.

Better yet, we can explicitly name this operation by defining a half-adder procedure that constructs this circuit, given the four external wires to be attached to the half-adder:

```
(define (half-adder a b s c)
  (let ((d (make-wire)) (e (make-wire)))
    (or-gate a b d)
    (and-gate a b c)
    (inverter c e)
    (and-gate d e s)))
```

The importance of this way of proceeding is that we can now use half-adder itself as a building block in creating more complex circuits. Figure 3.25, for example, shows a *full-adder* composed of two half-adders and an or-gate.[20] We can construct a full-adder as follows:

```
(define (full-adder a b c-in sum c-out)
  (let ((s (make-wire))
        (c1 (make-wire))
        (c2 (make-wire)))
    (half-adder b c-in s c1)
    (half-adder a s sum c2)
    (or-gate c1 c2 c-out)))
```

Having defined `full-adder` as a procedure, we can now use it as a building block for creating still more complex circuits. (For example, see exercise 3.30.)

In essence, our simulator provides us with the tools to construct a language of circuits. If we adopt the general perspective on languages with

---

20 A full-adder is a basic circuit element used in adding two binary numbers. Here A and B are the bits at corresponding positions in the two numbers to be added, and C_{in} is the carry bit from the addition one place to the right. The circuit generates SUM, which is the sum bit in the corresponding position, and C_{out}, which is the carry bit to be propagated to the left.

which we approached the study of Lisp in section 1.1, we can say that the primitive function boxes form the primitive elements of the language, that wiring boxes together provides a means of combination, and that specifying wiring patterns as procedures serves as a means of abstraction.

Primitive function boxes

The primitive function boxes implement the "forces" by which a change in the signal on one wire influences the signals on other wires. To build function boxes, we use the following operations on wires:

(get-signal ⟨*wire*⟩) returns the current value of the signal on the wire.

(set-signal! ⟨*wire*⟩ ⟨*new value*⟩) changes the value of the signal on the wire to the new value.

(add-action! ⟨*wire*⟩ ⟨*procedure of no arguments*⟩) specifies that the designated procedure should be run whenever the signal on the wire changes value. Such procedures are the vehicles by which changes in the signal value on the wire are communicated to other wires.

In addition, we will make use of a procedure after-delay that takes a time delay and a procedure to be run and executes the given procedure after the given delay.

Using these procedures, we can define the primitive digital logic functions. To connect an input to an output through an inverter, we use add-action! to associate with the input wire a procedure that will be run whenever the signal on the input wire changes value. The procedure computes the logical-not of the input signal, and then, after one inverter-delay, sets the output signal to be this new value:

```
(define (inverter input output)
  (define (invert-input)
    (let ((new-value (logical-not (get-signal input))))
      (after-delay inverter-delay
                   (lambda ()
                     (set-signal! output
                                  new-value)))))
  (add-action! input invert-input))

(define (logical-not s)
  (cond ((= s 0) 1)
        ((= s 1) 0)
        (else (error "Invalid signal" s))))
```

An and-gate is more complex. The action procedure must be run if either of the inputs to the gate changes. It computes the `logical-and` (using a procedure analogous to `logical-not`) of the values of the signals on the input wires and sets up a change to the new value to occur on the output wire after one `and-gate-delay`.

```
(define (and-gate a1 a2 output)
  (define (and-action-procedure)
    (let ((new-value
           (logical-and (get-signal a1) (get-signal a2))))
      (after-delay and-gate-delay
                   (lambda ()
                     (set-signal! output new-value)))))
  (add-action! a1 and-action-procedure)
  (add-action! a2 and-action-procedure))
```

Exercise 3.28

Define an or-gate as a primitive function box. Your `or-gate` constructor should be similar to `and-gate`.

Exercise 3.29

Another way to construct an or-gate is as a compound digital logic device, built from and-gates and inverters. Define a procedure `or-gate` that accomplishes this. What is the delay time of the or-gate in terms of `and-gate-delay` and `inverter-delay`?

Exercise 3.30

Figure 3.26 shows a *ripple-carry adder* formed by stringing together n full-adders. This is the simplest form of parallel adder for adding two n-bit binary numbers. The inputs A_1, A_2, A_3, ..., A_n and B_1, B_2, B_3, ..., B_n are the two binary numbers to be added (each A_k and B_k is a 0 or a 1). The circuit generates S_1, S_2, S_3, ..., S_n, the n bits of the sum, and C, the carry from the addition. Write a procedure `ripple-carry-adder` that generates this circuit. The procedure should take as arguments three lists of n wires each—the A_k, the B_k, and the S_k—and also another wire C. The major drawback of the ripple-carry adder is the need to wait for the carry signals to propagate. What is the delay needed to obtain the complete output from an n-bit ripple-carry adder, expressed in terms of the delays for and-gates, or-gates, and inverters?

Representing wires

A wire in our simulation will be a computational object with two local state variables: a `signal-value` (initially taken to be 0) and a collection

Modularity, Objects, and State

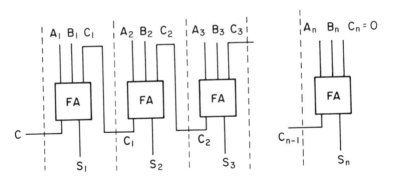

Figure 3.26
A ripple-carry adder for n-bit numbers.

of action-procedures to be run when the signal changes value. We implement the wire, using message-passing style, as a collection of local procedures together with a dispatch procedure that selects the appropriate local operation, just as we did with the simple bank-account object in section 3.1.1:

```
(define (make-wire)
  (let ((signal-value 0) (action-procedures '()))
    (define (set-my-signal! new-value)
      (if (not (= signal-value new-value))
          (sequence (set! signal-value new-value)
                    (call-each action-procedures))
          'done))

    (define (accept-action-procedure proc)
      (set! action-procedures (cons proc action-procedures))
      (proc))

    (define (dispatch m)
      (cond ((eq? m 'get-signal) signal-value)
            ((eq? m 'set-signal!) set-my-signal!)
            ((eq? m 'add-action!) accept-action-procedure)
            (else (error "Unknown operation -- WIRE" m))))

    dispatch))
```

The local procedure set-my-signal! tests whether the new signal value changes the signal on the wire. If so, it runs each of the action procedures, using the following procedure call-each, which calls each of the items in a list of no-argument procedures:

```
(define (call-each procedures)
  (if (null? procedures)
      'done
      (sequence
       ((car procedures))
       (call-each (cdr procedures)))))
```

The local procedure `accept-action-procedure` adds the given procedure to the list of procedures to be run, and then runs the new procedure once. (See exercise 3.31.)

With the local `dispatch` procedure set up as specified, we can provide the following procedures to access the local operations on wires:[21]

```
(define (get-signal wire)
  (wire 'get-signal))
```

```
(define (set-signal! wire new-value)
  ((wire 'set-signal!) new-value))
```

```
(define (add-action! wire action-procedure)
  ((wire 'add-action!) action-procedure))
```

Wires, which have time-varying signals and may be incrementally attached to devices, are typical of mutable objects. We have modeled them as procedures with local state variables that are modified by assignment. When a new wire is created, a new set of state variables is allocated (by the `let` expression in `make-wire`) and a new `dispatch` procedure is constructed and returned, capturing the environment with the new state variables.

The wires are shared among the various devices that have been connected to them. Thus, a change made by an interaction with one device will affect all the other devices attached to the wire. The wire communicates the change to its neighbors by calling the action procedures provided to it when the connections were established.

---

21 These procedures are simply syntactic sugar that allow us to use ordinary procedural syntax to access the local procedures of objects. It is striking that we can interchange the role of "procedures" and "data" in such a simple way. For example, if we write (`wire 'get-signal`) we think of `wire` as a procedure that is called with the message `get-signal` as input. Alternatively, writing (`get-signal wire`) encourages us to think of `wire` as a data object that is the input to a procedure `get-signal`. The truth of the matter is that, in a language in which we can deal with procedures as objects, there is no fundamental difference between "procedures" and "data," and we can choose our syntactic sugar to allow us to program in whatever style we choose.

The agenda

The only thing needed to complete the simulator is `after-delay`. The idea here is that we maintain a data structure, called an *agenda*, that contains a schedule of things to do. The following operations are defined for agendas:

(`empty-agenda?` ⟨*agenda*⟩) is true if the specified agenda is empty.

(`first-agenda-item` ⟨*agenda*⟩) returns the first item on the agenda.

(`remove-first-agenda-item!` ⟨*agenda*⟩) modifies the agenda by removing the first item.

(`add-to-agenda!` ⟨*time*⟩ ⟨*action*⟩ ⟨*agenda*⟩) modifies the agenda by adding the given action procedure to be run at the specified time.

(`current-time` ⟨*agenda*⟩) returns the current simulation time.

The particular agenda that we use is denoted by the global variable `the-agenda`. `After-delay` is a procedure that adds new elements to `the-agenda`:

```
(define (after-delay delay action)
  (add-to-agenda! (+ delay (current-time the-agenda))
                  action
                  the-agenda))
```

The simulation is driven by the procedure `propagate`, which operates on `the-agenda`, executing each procedure on the agenda in sequence. In general, as the simulation runs, new items will be added to the agenda, and `propagate` will continue the simulation as long as there are items on the agenda:

```
(define (propagate)
  (if (empty-agenda? the-agenda)
      'done
      (let ((first-item (first-agenda-item the-agenda)))
        (first-item)
        (remove-first-agenda-item! the-agenda)
        (propagate))))
```

A sample simulation

The following procedure, which places a "probe" on a wire, shows the simulator in action. The probe tells the wire that, whenever its signal changes value, it should print the new signal value, together with the current time and a name that identifies the wire:

```
(define (probe name wire)
  (add-action! wire
              (lambda ()
                (print name)
                (princ (current-time the-agenda))
                (princ "  New-value = ")
                (princ (get-signal wire))))))
```

We begin by initializing the agenda and specifying delays for the primitive function boxes:

```
(define the-agenda (make-agenda))
(define inverter-delay 2)
(define and-gate-delay 3)
(define or-gate-delay 5)
```

Now we define four wires, placing probes on two of them:

```
(define input-1 (make-wire))
(define input-2 (make-wire))
(define sum (make-wire))
(define carry (make-wire))
```

```
==> (probe 'sum sum)
```
sum 0 New-value = 0

```
==> (probe 'carry carry)
```
carry 0 New-value = 0

Next we connect the wires in a half-adder circuit (as shown in figure 3.24), set the signal on input-1 to 1, and run the simulation:

```
(half-adder input-1 input-2 sum carry)
(set-signal! input-1 1)
```

```
==> (propagate)
```
sum 8 New-value = 1
done

The sum signal changes to 1 at time 8. We are now eight time units from the beginning of the simulation. At this point, we can set the signal on input-2 to 1 and allow the values to propagate:

```
(set-signal! input-2 1)
```

```
==> (propagate)
```
carry 11 New-value = 1
sum 16 New-value = 0
done

The carry changes to 1 at time 11 and the sum changes to 0 at time 16.

Exercise 3.31
The internal procedure `accept-action-procedure` used by `make-wire` specifies that, whenever a new action procedure is added to a wire, the procedure is first run. Explain why this initialization is necessary. In particular, trace through the half-adder example in the paragraphs above and say how the system's response would differ if we had defined `accept-action-procedure` as

```
(define (accept-action-procedure proc)
  (set! action-procedures (cons proc action-procedures)))
```

Implementing the agenda
Finally, we give details of the agenda data structure, which holds the procedures that are scheduled for future execution.

The agenda is made up of *time segments*. Each time segment is a pair consisting of a number (the time) and a queue (see exercise 3.32) that holds the procedures that are scheduled to be run during that time segment.

```
(define (make-time-segment time queue)
  (cons time queue))
```

```
(define (segment-time s) (car s))
```

```
(define (segment-queue s) (cdr s))
```

We will operate on the time-segment queues using the queue operations described in section 3.3.2.

The agenda itself is a one-dimensional table of time segments. It differs from the tables described in section 3.3.3 in that the segments will be sorted in order of increasing time. The current time will always be the time associated with the first time segment on the agenda. We construct a new agenda as a headed list with an initial empty time segment that represents time 0, the current time:

```
(define (make-agenda)
  (list '*agenda*
        (make-time-segment 0 (make-queue))))
```

```
(define (segments agenda) (cdr agenda))

(define (first-segment agenda) (car (segments agenda)))

(define (rest-segments agenda) (cdr (segments agenda)))

(define (set-segments! agenda segments)
  (set-cdr! agenda segments))

(define (current-time agenda)
  (segment-time (first-segment agenda)))
```

An agenda is empty when the first segment has an empty queue and there are no more segments to be executed:

```
(define (empty-agenda? agenda)
  (and (empty-queue? (segment-queue (first-segment agenda)))
       (null? (rest-segments agenda))))
```

To add an action to the agenda, we scan the agenda, examining the time of each segment. If we find a segment for our appointed time, we add our action to the associated queue. If we reach a time later than the one to which we are appointed, we must insert a new time segment into the agenda just before it. Otherwise we continue scanning. If we hit the end of the agenda, we must create a new time segment at the end. Note that the appointed time can never be earlier than the time of the first agenda segment (the current time).

```
(define (add-to-agenda! time action agenda)
  (define (add-to-segments! segments)
    (if (= (segment-time (car segments)) time)
        (insert-queue! (segment-queue (car segments))
                       action)
        (let ((rest (cdr segments)))
          (cond ((null? rest)
                 (insert-new-time! time action segments))
                ((> (segment-time (car rest)) time)
                 (insert-new-time! time action segments))
                (else (add-to-segments! rest))))))
  (add-to-segments! (segments agenda)))
```

A new time segment is inserted by modifying the top-level structure of the agenda:

```
(define (insert-new-time! time action segments)
  (let ((q (make-queue)))
    (insert-queue! q action)
    (set-cdr! segments
              (cons (make-time-segment time q)
                    (cdr segments)))))
```

The procedure that removes the first item from the agenda assumes that the first item will always be at the front of the queue in the first segment of the agenda:

```
(define (remove-first-agenda-item! agenda)
  (delete-queue! (segment-queue (first-segment agenda))))
```

That the first agenda item is always in the first segment of the agenda is ensured by the procedure that returns a new first item. If this procedure discovers that the first time segment is empty, it removes it from the agenda. Our implementation assumes that this procedure will not be called if the agenda is empty:

```
(define (first-agenda-item agenda)
  (let ((q (segment-queue (first-segment agenda))))
    (if (empty-queue? q)
        (sequence (set-segments! agenda
                                 (rest-segments agenda))
                  (first-agenda-item agenda))
        (front q))))
```

Exercise 3.32

The procedures to be run during each time segment of the agenda are kept in a queue. Thus, the procedures for each segment are called in the order in which they were added to the agenda (first in, first out). Explain why this order must be used. In particular, trace the behavior of an and-gate whose inputs change from 0,1 to 1,0 in the same segment and say how the behavior would differ if we stored a segment's procedures in an ordinary list, adding and removing procedures only at the front (last in, first out).

3.3.5 Propagation of Constraints

Computer programs are traditionally organized in terms of one-directional computations, which perform operations on prespecified arguments to produce desired outputs. On the other hand, we often model systems in terms of relations among quantities. For example, a mathematical model of a mechanical structure might include the information that the deflection d of a metal rod is related to the force F on the rod, the length L of the rod, the cross-sectional area A, and the elastic modulus E via the equation

$$dAE = FL.$$

Such an equation is not one-directional. Given any four of the quantities, we can use it to compute the fifth. Yet translating the equation into a traditional computer language would force us to choose one of the quantities to be computed in terms of the other four. Thus, a procedure for computing the area A could not be used to compute the deflection d, even though the computations of A and d arise from the same equation.[22]

In this section, we sketch the design of a language that enables us to work in terms of relations themselves. The primitive elements of the language are *primitive constraints*, which state that certain relations hold between quantities. For example, (adder a b c) specifies that the quantities a, b, and c must be related by the equation $a + b = c$, (multiplier x y z) expresses the constraint $xy = z$, and (constant 3.14 x) says that the value of x must be 3.14.

Our language provides a means of combining primitive constraints in order to express more complex relations. We combine constraints by constructing *constraint networks*, in which constraints are joined by *connectors*. A connector is an object that "holds" a value that may participate in one or more constraints. For example, we know that the relationship between Fahrenheit and centigrade temperatures is

$$9C = 5(F - 32).$$

Such a constraint can be thought of as a network consisting of primitive adder, multiplier, and constant constraints (figure 3.27). In the figure, we see on the left a multiplier box with three terminals, labeled $m1$, $m2$, and p. These connect the multiplier to the rest of the network as follows: The $m1$ terminal is linked to a connector C, which will hold the centigrade temperature. The $m2$ terminal is linked to a connector w, which is also linked to a constant box that holds 9. The p terminal, which the multiplier box constrains to be the product of $m1$ and $m2$, is linked to the p terminal

---

[22] This idea first appeared in the incredibly forward-looking SKETCHPAD system of Ivan Sutherland (1963). A beautiful constraint-propagation system based on the Smalltalk language was developed by Alan Borning (1977) at Xerox Palo Alto Research Center. Sussman, Stallman, and Steele applied this idea to electrical circuit analysis (Sussman and Stallman 1975; Sussman and Steele 1980). TK!Solver™ (Software Arts 1982), an excellent commercial system of this sort, became available for use on personal computers in 1983.

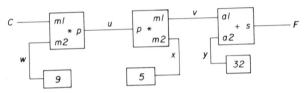

Figure 3.27
The relation $9C = 5(F - 32)$ expressed as a constraint network.

of another multiplier box, whose $m2$ is connected to a constant 5 and whose $m1$ is connected to one of the terms in a sum.

Computation by such a network proceeds as follows: When a connector is given a value (by the user or by a constraint box to which it is linked), it awakens all of its associated constraints (except for the constraint that just awakened it) to inform them that it has a value. Each awakened constraint box then polls its connectors to see if there is enough information to determine a value for a connector. If so, the box sets that connector, which then awakens all of its associated constraints, and so on. For instance, in conversion between centigrade and Fahrenheit, w, x, and y are immediately set by the constant boxes to 9, 5, and 32, respectively. The connectors awaken the multipliers and the adder, which determine that there is not enough information to proceed. If the user (or some other part of the network) sets C to a value (say 25), the leftmost multiplier will be awakened, and it will set u to $25 \cdot 9 = 225$. Then u awakens the second multiplier, which sets v to 45, and v awakens the adder, which sets F to 77.

Using the constraint system
To use the constraint system to carry out the temperature computation outlined above, we first create two connectors, C and F, by calling the constructor make-connector, and link C and F in an appropriate network:

```
(define C (make-connector))
(define F (make-connector))
(centigrade-fahrenheit-converter C F)
```

The procedure that creates the network is defined as follows:

```
(define (centigrade-fahrenheit-converter c f)
  (let ((u (make-connector))
        (v (make-connector))
        (w (make-connector))
        (x (make-connector))
        (y (make-connector)))
    ;; continued on next page
```

```
(multiplier c w u)
(multiplier v x u)
(adder v y f)
(constant 9 w)
(constant 5 x)
(constant 32 y)))
```

This procedure creates the internal connectors u, v, w, x, and y, and links them as shown in figure 3.27, using the primitive constraint constructors adder, multiplier, and constant. Just as with the digital-circuit simulator of section 3.3.4, expressing these combinations of primitive elements in terms of procedures automatically provides our language with a means of abstraction for compound objects.

To watch the network in action, we can place probes on the connectors C and F, using a probe procedure similar to the one we used to monitor wires in section 3.3.4. Placing a probe on a connector will cause a message to be printed whenever the connector is given a value:

```
(probe "centigrade temp" C)
(probe "Fahrenheit temp" F)
```

Next we set the value of C to 25. (The third argument to set-value! tells C that this directive comes from the user.)

```
==> (set-value! C 25 'user)
```
Probe: centigrade temp = 25
Probe: Fahrenheit temp = 77
done

The probe on C awakens and reports the value. C also propagates its value through the network as described above. This sets F to 77, which is reported by the probe on F.

Now we can try to set F to a new value, say 212:

```
==> (set-value! F 212 'user)
```
Error! Contradiction (77 212)

The connector complains that it has sensed a contradiction: Its value is 77, and someone is trying to set it to 212. If we really want to reuse the network with new values, we can tell C to forget its old value:

```
==> (forget-value! C 'user)
```
Probe: centigrade temp = ?
Probe: Fahrenheit temp = ?
done

C finds that the user, who set its value originally, is now retracting that value, so C agrees to lose its value, as shown by the probe, and informs the rest of the network of this fact. This information eventually propagates to F, which now finds that it has no reason for continuing to believe that its own value is 77. Thus, F also gives up its value, as shown by the probe.

Now that F has no value, we are free to set it to 212:

```
==> (set-value! F 212 'user)
```
Probe: Fahrenheit temp = 212
Probe: centigrade temp = 100
done

This new value, when propagated through the network, forces C to have a value of 100, and this is registered by the probe on C. Notice that the very same network is being used to compute C given F and to compute F given C. This nondirectionality of computation is the distinguishing feature of constraint-based systems.

Implementing the constraint system

The constraint system is implemented via procedural objects with local state, in a manner very similar to the digital-circuit simulator of section 3.3.4. Although the primitive objects of the constraint system are somewhat more complex, the overall system is simpler, since there is no concern about agendas and logic delays.

The basic operations on connectors are the following:

(has-value? ⟨connector⟩) tells whether the connector has a value.

(get-value ⟨connector⟩) returns the connector's current value.

(set-value! ⟨connector⟩ ⟨new-value⟩ ⟨informant⟩) tells the connector that some informant is requesting it to set its value to a new value.

(forget-value! ⟨connector⟩ ⟨retractor⟩) tells the connector that some retractor is requesting it to forget its value.

(connect ⟨connector⟩ ⟨new-constraint⟩) tells the connector that it should participate in a new constraint.

The connectors communicate with the constraints by means of the procedures inform-about-value, which tells the designated constraint that the connector has a value, and inform-about-no-value, which tells the constraint that the connector has lost its value.

Adder constructs an adder constraint among summand connectors a1 and a2 and a sum connector. An adder is implemented as a procedure with local state (the procedure me below):

```
(define (adder a1 a2 sum)
  (define (process-new-value)
    (cond ((and (has-value? a1) (has-value? a2))
           (set-value! sum
                       (+ (get-value a1) (get-value a2))
                       me))
          ((and (has-value? a1) (has-value? sum))
           (set-value! a2
                       (- (get-value sum) (get-value a1))
                       me))
          ((and (has-value? a2) (has-value? sum))
           (set-value! a1
                       (- (get-value sum) (get-value a2))
                       me))))

  (define (process-forget-value)
    (forget-value! sum me)
    (forget-value! a1 me)
    (forget-value! a2 me)
    (process-new-value))

  (define (me request)
    (cond ((eq? request 'I-have-a-value)
           process-new-value)
          ((eq? request 'I-lost-my-value)
           process-forget-value)
          (else
           (error "Unknown request -- ADDER" request))))

  (connect a1 me)
  (connect a2 me)
  (connect sum me)
  me)
```

Adder connects the new adder to the designated connectors and returns it as its value. The procedure me, which represents the adder, acts as a dispatch to the local procedures. The following "syntax interfaces" (see footnote 21 in section 3.3.4) are used in conjunction with the dispatch:

```
(define (inform-about-value constraint)
  ((constraint 'I-have-a-value)))
```

```
(define (inform-about-no-value constraint)
  ((constraint 'I-lost-my-value)))
```

The adder's local procedure process-new-value is called when the adder is informed that one of its connectors has a value. The adder first checks to see if both a1 and a2 have values. If so, it tells sum to set its value to the sum of the two addends. The informant argument to set-value! is me, which is the adder object itself. If a1 and a2 do not both have values, then the adder checks to see if perhaps a1 and sum have values. If so, it sets a2 to the difference of these two. Finally, if a2 and sum have values, this gives the adder enough information to set a1. If the adder is told that one of its connectors has lost a value, it requests that all of its connectors now lose their values. (Only those values that were set by this adder are actually lost.) Then it runs process-new-value. The reason for this last step is that one or more connectors may still have a value (that is, a connector may have had a value that was not originally set by the adder), and these values may need to be propagated back through the adder.

A multiplier is very similar to an adder. It will set its product to 0 if either of the factors is 0, even if the other factor is not known.

```
(define (multiplier m1 m2 product)
  (define (process-new-value)
    (cond ((or (if (has-value? m1) (= (get-value m1) 0) nil)
               (if (has-value? m2) (= (get-value m2) 0) nil))
           (set-value! product 0 me))
          ((and (has-value? m1) (has-value? m2))
           (set-value! product
                       (* (get-value m1) (get-value m2))
                       me))
          ((and (has-value? product) (has-value? m1))
           (set-value! m2
                       (/ (get-value product) (get-value m1))
                       me))
          ((and (has-value? product) (has-value? m2))
           (set-value! m1
                       (/ (get-value product) (get-value m2))
                       me)))))
```

;; continued on next page

```
(define (process-forget-value)
  (forget-value! product me)
  (forget-value! m1 me)
  (forget-value! m2 me)
  (process-new-value))

(define (me request)
  (cond ((eq? request 'I-have-a-value)
         process-new-value)
        ((eq? request 'I-lost-my-value)
         process-forget-value)
        (else
         (error "Unknown request -- MULTIPLIER" request)))))

(connect m1 me)
(connect m2 me)
(connect product me)
me)
```

A constant constructor simply sets the value of the designated connector.
Any I-have-a-value or I-lost-my-value message sent to the constant
box will produce an error.

```
(define (constant value connector)
  (define (me request)
    (error "Unknown request -- CONSTANT" request))
  (connect connector me)
  (set-value! connector value me)
  me)
```

Finally, a probe prints a message about the setting or unsetting of the
designated connector:

```
(define (probe name connector)
  (define (process-new-value)
    (newline)
    (princ "Probe: ")
    (princ name)
    (princ " = ")
    (princ (get-value connector)))
  ;; continued on next page
```

```
(define (process-forget-value)
  (newline)
  (princ "Probe: ")
  (princ name)
  (princ " = ")
  (princ "?"))

(define (me request)
  (cond ((eq? request 'I-have-a-value)
         process-new-value)
        ((eq? request 'I-lost-my-value)
         process-forget-value)
        (else
         (error "Unknown request -- PROBE" request))))

(connect connector me)
me)
```

Representing connectors

A connector is represented as a procedural object with local state variables value, the current value of the connector; informant, the object that set the connector's value; and constraints, a list of the constraints in which the connector participates.[23]

```
(define (make-connector)
  (let ((value nil) (informant nil) (constraints '()))
    (define (set-my-value newval setter)
      (cond ((not (has-value? me))
             (set! value newval)
             (set! informant setter)
             (for-each-except setter
                              inform-about-value
                              constraints))
            ((not (= value newval))
             (error "Contradiction" (list value newval)))))
    ;; continued on next page
```

---

[23] In this program there are several ifs without ⟨alternative⟩ expressions. When an if is being used to decide whether to do something rather than to select between two actions, the ⟨alternative⟩ expression can be omitted. (An if expression returns false if the predicate is false and there is no ⟨alternative⟩.)

```
(define (forget-my-value retractor)
  (if (eq? retractor informant)
      (sequence (set! informant nil)
                (for-each-except retractor
                                 inform-about-no-value
                                 constraints))))

(define (connect new-constraint)
  (if (not (memq new-constraint constraints))
      (set! constraints
            (cons new-constraint constraints)))
  (if (has-value? me)
      (inform-about-value new-constraint)))

(define (me request)
  (cond ((eq? request 'has-value?)
         (not (null? informant)))
        ((eq? request 'value) value)
        ((eq? request 'set-value!) set-my-value)
        ((eq? request 'forget) forget-my-value)
        ((eq? request 'connect) connect)
        (else (error "Unknown operation -- CONNECTOR"
                     request))))
  me))
```

The connector's local procedure set-my-value is called when there is a
request to set the connector's value. If the connector does not currently
have a value, it will set its value and remember as informant the constraint
that requested the value to be set.[24] Then the connector will notify all of
its participating constraints except the constraint that requested the value
to be set. This is accomplished using the following iterator, which applies
a designated procedure to all items in a list except a given one:

```
(define (for-each-except exception procedure list)
  (define (loop items)
    (cond ((null? items) 'done)
          ((eq? (car items) exception) (loop (cdr items)))
          (else (procedure (car items))
                (loop (cdr items)))))
  (loop list))
```

---

24 The setter might not be a constraint. In our temperature example, we used user as
the setter.

If a connector is asked to forget its value, it runs the local procedure forget-my-value, which first checks to make sure that the request is coming from the same object that set the value originally. If so, the connector informs its associated constraints about the loss of the value.

The local procedure connect adds the designated new constraint to the list of constraints if it is not already in that list. Then, if the connector has a value, it informs the new constraint of this fact.

The connector's procedure me serves as a dispatch to the other internal procedures and also represents the connector as an object. The following procedures provide a syntax interface for the dispatch:

```
(define (has-value? connector)
  (connector 'has-value?))

(define (get-value connector)
  (connector 'value))

(define (forget-value! connector retractor)
  ((connector 'forget) retractor))

(define (set-value! connector new-value informant)
  ((connector 'set-value!) new-value informant))

(define (connect connector new-constraint)
  ((connector 'connect) new-constraint))
```

Exercise 3.33

Using primitive multiplier, adder, and constant constraints, define a procedure averager that takes three connectors a, b, and c as inputs and establishes the constraint that the value of c is the average of the values of a and b.

Exercise 3.34

Louis Reasoner wants to build a squarer, a constraint device with two terminals such that the value of connector b on the second terminal will always be the square of the value a on the first terminal. He proposes the following simple device made from a multiplier:

```
(define (squarer a b)
  (multiplier a a b))
```

There is a serious flaw in this idea. Explain.

Exercise 3.35

Ben Bitdiddle tells Louis that one way to avoid the trouble in exercise 3.34 is to define a squarer as a new primitive constraint. Fill in the missing portions in Ben's outline for a procedure to implement such a constraint:

```
(define (squarer a b)
  (define (process-new-value)
    (if (has-value? b)
        (if (< (get-value b) 0)
            (error "square less than 0 -- SQUARER" (get-value b))
            ⟨ alternative1 ⟩)
          ⟨ alternative2 ⟩)))
  (define (process-forget-value) ⟨ body1 ⟩)
  (define (me request) ⟨ body2 ⟩)
  ⟨ rest of definition ⟩
  me)
```

Exercise 3.36

Suppose we evaluate the following sequence of expressions in the global environment:

```
(define a (make-connector))
(define b (make-connector))
(set-value! a 10 'user)
```

At some time during evaluation of the set-value!, the following expression from the connector's local procedure is evaluated:

```
(for-each-except setter inform-about-value constraints)
```

Draw an environment diagram showing the environment in which the above expression is evaluated.

Exercise 3.37

The centigrade-fahrenheit-converter procedure is cumbersome when compared with a more expression-oriented style of definition, such as

```
(define (centigrade-fahrenheit-converter x)
  (c+ (c* (c/ (cv 9) (cv 5))
          x)
      (cv 32)))
(define C (make-connector))
(define F (centigrade-fahrenheit-converter C))
```

Here c+, c*, etc. are the "constraint" versions of the arithmetic operations. For example, c+ takes two connectors as arguments and returns a connector that is related to these by an adder constraint:

```
(define (c+ x y)
  (let ((z (make-connector)))
    (adder x y z)
    z))
```

Define analogous procedures c-, c*, c/, and cv (constant value) that enable us to define compound constraints as in the converter example above.[25]

3.4 Streams

This section introduces new compound data structures called *streams*. We use streams to organize computations on collections of data in a way that corresponds in spirit to an electrical engineer's concept of a signal-processing system. Organizing computations in this way greatly enhances our ability to formulate abstractions that capture common patterns of data manipulation. Indeed, we will see how a few elegant stream operations can succinctly express the structural similarity of a wide range of programs. From an abstract point of view, a stream is simply a sequence of data objects. However, we will find that the straightforward implementation of streams as lists does not allow us to fully exploit the power of stream processing. To solve this problem, we introduce the technique of *delayed evaluation*, which enables us to represent very large (even infinite) data structures as streams.

In the previous sections of this chapter we used assignment and local state to model objects and change. In this section we will see how streams form the basis for a very different approach to modeling. Instead of using

[25] The expression-oriented format is convenient because it avoids the need to name the intermediate expressions in a computation. Our original formulation of the constraint language is cumbersome in the same way that many languages are cumbersome when dealing with operations on compound data. For example, if we wanted to compute $(a + b) \cdot (c + d)$, where the variables represent vectors, we could work in "imperative style," using procedures that set the values of designated vector arguments but do not themselves return vectors as values:

```
(v-sum a b temp1)
(v-sum c d temp2)
(v-prod temp1 temp2 answer)
```

Alternatively, we could deal with expressions, using procedures that return vectors as values, and thus avoid explicitly mentioning temp1 and temp2:

```
(define answer (v-prod (v-sum a b) (v-sum c d)))
```

Since Lisp allows us to return compound objects as values of procedures, we can transform our imperative-style constraint language into an expression-oriented style as shown in this exercise. In languages that are impoverished in handling compound objects, such as Algol, Basic, and Pascal (unless one explicitly uses Pascal pointer variables), one is usually stuck with the imperative style when manipulating compound objects. Given the advantage of the expression-oriented format, one might ask if there is any reason to have implemented the system in imperative style, as we did in this section. One reason is that the non-expression-oriented constraint language provides a handle on constraint objects (e.g., the value of the adder procedure) as well as on connector objects. This is useful if we wish to extend the system with new operations that communicate with constraints directly rather than only indirectly via operations on connectors. Although it is easy to implement the expression-oriented style in terms of the imperative implementation, it is very difficult to do the converse.

objects with changing local state, we construct a stream that represents the time history of the system being modeled. A consequence of this strategy is that it allows us to model systems that have state without ever using assignment or mutable data. This has important implications, both theoretical and practical, for it enables us to build models that avoid the drawbacks inherent in introducing assignment that we discussed in section 3.1.2. On the other hand, the stream framework raises difficulties of its own, and the question of which modeling technique leads to more modular and more easily maintained systems remains open.

3.4.1 Streams as Standard Interfaces

In section 1.3 we saw how program abstractions, implemented as higher-order procedures, can capture common patterns of usage in programs that deal with numerical data. We would now like to formulate analogous operations for working with compound data. Unfortunately, the style in which we have been writing procedures often masks the commonality that underlies many typical computations. Consider, for example, a procedure that takes as an argument a binary tree, all of whose leaves are integers, and computes the sum of the squares of the leaves that are odd:

```
(define (sum-odd-squares tree)
  (if (leaf-node? tree)
      (if (odd? tree)
          (square tree)
          0)
      (+ (sum-odd-squares (left-branch tree))
         (sum-odd-squares (right-branch tree)))))
```

On the surface, this procedure is very different from the following one, which constructs a list of all the odd Fibonacci numbers Fib(k), where k is less than or equal to a given integer n:

```
(define (odd-fibs n)
  (define (next k)
    (if (> k n)
        '()
        (let ((f (fib k)))
          (if (odd? f)
              (cons f (next (1+ k)))
              (next (1+ k))))))
  (next 1))
```

Despite the fact that these two procedures are structurally very different, a more abstract description of the two computations reveals a great deal of similarity. The first program

- enumerates the leaves of a tree;
- filters them, selecting the odd ones;
- squares each of the selected ones; and
- accumulates the results by adding, using +, starting with 0.

The second program

- enumerates the integers from 1 to n;
- computes the Fibonacci number for each integer;
- filters them, selecting the odd ones; and
- accumulates the results into a list, using cons, starting with the empty list.

An electrical engineer would find it easy to conceptualize these processes in terms of signals flowing through a cascade of stages, each of which implements part of the program plan. The first program realizes the following signal-flow plan:

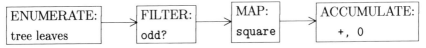

We begin with an *enumerator*, which generates a "signal" consisting of the leaves of a given tree. This signal is passed through a *filter*, which eliminates all but the odd elements. The resulting signal is in turn passed through a *map*, which is a "transducer" that applies the square procedure to each element. The output of the map is then fed to an *accumulator*, which combines the elements using +, starting from an initial 0. Here is an analogous signal-flow plan for the second program:

Unfortunately, the two procedures above fail to exhibit this signal-flow structure. For instance, if we examine the sum-odd-squares procedure, we find that the enumeration is implemented partly by the leaf-node? test and partly by the tree-recursive structure of the procedure. Similarly, the accumulation is found partly in the test and partly in the addition used in the recursion. In general, there are no distinct parts of either procedure that correspond to the elements in our signal-flow description.

The procedures decompose the computations in a different way, spreading the enumeration over the program and mingling it with the map, the filter, and the accumulation. If we could organize our programs to make the signal-flow structure manifest in the procedures we write, this would increase the conceptual clarity of the resulting code. It would also provide identifiable enumerator, filter, map, and accumulator program elements that we could mix and match to construct programs from standard, well-understood pieces.

Stream operations

Our traditional program organization concentrates on the order of events in a computation, rather than on the flow of data. Thus, the key to organizing programs so as to more clearly reflect the signal-flow structure is to concentrate on the signals that flow from one stage in the process to the next. We will implement these signals as data structures called streams, and we observe from our signal-flow diagrams that a stream is simply a sequence of elements. We can define streams abstractly, in terms of a constructor cons-stream and two selectors head and tail. These are related by the following condition: For any objects a and b, if x is (cons-stream a b) then (head x) is a and (tail x) is b. We will also assume that there is an object called the-empty-stream, which contains no elements, and a predicate empty-stream?, which tests whether a given stream is empty.

As far as this data abstraction is concerned, ordinary Lisp pairs provide a perfectly adequate implementation for streams; cons-stream, head, and tail can be implemented as cons, car, and cdr, respectively, the-empty-stream can be the empty list, and empty-stream? can be the predicate null?. Indeed, the above condition that defines the relationship among the three stream operations is identical to the condition that we used to define cons, car, and cdr in section 2.1.3. For the moment, in fact, we will consider streams to be ordinary lists, and cons-stream, head, and tail to be simply alternative names for cons, car, and cdr. This view of streams will be adequate until section 3.4.3, where we will concern ourselves with the efficiency of using streams to represent large aggregates of data.

Computing with streams

Now we can reformulate the two procedures above to match the signal-flow diagrams. For sum-odd-squares, we need to construct a stream that enumerates the leaves of the tree, filter a stream for oddness, square the elements of a stream, and sum the elements of a stream. We can enumerate the leaves of a tree as follows:

```
(define (enumerate-tree tree)
  (if (leaf-node? tree)
      (cons-stream tree the-empty-stream)
      (append-streams (enumerate-tree (left-branch tree))
                      (enumerate-tree (right-branch tree)))))
```

Append-streams is a procedure that takes two streams as arguments and produces a stream that contains all the elements of its first argument followed by all the elements of its second argument, as follows:[26]

```
(define (append-streams s1 s2)
  (if (empty-stream? s1)
      s2
      (cons-stream (head s1)
                   (append-streams (tail s1) s2))))
```

To filter a stream for oddness, we proceed as follows:

```
(define (filter-odd s)
  (cond ((empty-stream? s) the-empty-stream)
        ((odd? (head s))
         (cons-stream (head s) (filter-odd (tail s))))
        (else (filter-odd (tail s)))))
```

To square every element of a stream we can use

```
(define (map-square s)
  (if (empty-stream? s)
      the-empty-stream
      (cons-stream (square (head s))
                   (map-square (tail s)))))
```

And we can sum the elements of a stream with the following procedure:

```
(define (accumulate-+ s)
  (if (empty-stream? s)
      0
      (+ (head s) (accumulate-+ (tail s)))))
```

Now that we have these pieces, we can use them to reorganize the sum-odd-squares computation to correspond to the signal-flow diagram:

---

26 If we consider streams to be ordinary lists, writing cons for cons-stream, car for head, and so on, then append-streams is precisely the append procedure that we saw in section 2.2.1 and in exercise 3.12.

```
(define (sum-odd-squares tree)
  (accumulate-+
    (map-square
      (filter-odd
        (enumerate-tree tree)))))
```

With a few more building blocks, we can reformulate the odd-fibs procedure in the same way. We need to enumerate an interval of the integers to form a stream. We do this using the following procedure, which returns a stream of consecutive integers from low through high:

```
(define (enumerate-interval low high)
  (if (> low high)
      the-empty-stream
      (cons-stream low (enumerate-interval (1+ low) high))))
```

The following procedure applies fib to each element of a stream to obtain the stream of corresponding Fibonacci numbers:

```
(define (map-fib s)
  (if (empty-stream? s)
      the-empty-stream
      (cons-stream (fib (head s))
                   (map-fib (tail s)))))
```

The next procedure accumulates the items in a stream to form a list, by successively applying cons:

```
(define (accumulate-cons s)
  (if (empty-stream? s)
      '()
      (cons (head s) (accumulate-cons (tail s)))))
```

Now we can rewrite odd-fibs as follows:

```
(define (odd-fibs n)
  (accumulate-cons
    (filter-odd
      (map-fib
        (enumerate-interval 1 n)))))
```

This may seem to be a lot of work merely to write two simple procedures, but now that the two programs have similar structures we can mix and match the various pieces of our programs to construct other programs. For example, we can construct a list of the squares of the first n Fibonacci numbers as follows:

```
(define (list-square-fibs n)
  (accumulate-cons
    (map-square
      (map-fib
        (enumerate-interval 1 n)))))
```

3.4.2 Higher-Order Procedures for Streams

We have seen how to capture the commonality in two simple procedures by rewriting them in terms of stream operations. However, the two procedures have even more in common than we have yet shown. For example, the two accumulation procedures accumulate-+ and accumulate-cons differ only in the method used to accumulate the results and the initial value for beginning accumulation. Thus, we can express both of these procedures in terms of a general accumulator abstraction. In section 1.3 we saw how to formulate such abstractions as higher-order procedures. Applying this technique, we can write a general accumulate procedure that takes as arguments a method used to combine items, an initial value, and a stream to be accumulated:

```
(define (accumulate combiner initial-value stream)
  (if (empty-stream? stream)
      initial-value
      (combiner (head stream)
                (accumulate combiner
                            initial-value
                            (tail stream)))))
```

Many operations can be expressed in terms of accumulations. For example, we can find the sum of the elements in a stream with

```
(define (sum-stream stream)
  (accumulate + 0 stream))
```

or we can find the product of the elements in a stream with

```
(define (product-stream stream)
  (accumulate * 1 stream))
```

The accumulate-cons operation can be accomplished by

```
(define (accumulate-cons stream)
  (accumulate cons '() stream))
```

Another useful stream operation easily defined as an accumulation is
flatten, which takes as its argument a stream of streams and combines
all the elements of these streams to form a single stream:

```
(define (flatten stream)
  (accumulate append-streams the-empty-stream stream))
```

Evaluating a polynomial in x at a given value of x can also be formulated
as an accumulation. We evaluate the polynomial

$$a_n x^n + a_{n-1} x^{n-1} + \cdots + a_1 x + a_0$$

using a well-known algorithm called *Horner's rule*, which structures the
computation as

$$[\cdots (a_n x + a_{n-1}) x + \cdots + a_1] x + a_0.$$

In other words, we start with a_n, multiply by x, add a_{n-1}, multiply by x,
and so on, until we reach a_0.[27] If we assume that the coefficients of the
polynomial are arranged in a stream, from a_0 through a_n, then we can
express Horner's rule as an accumulation along the coefficient stream:

```
(define (horner-eval x coefficient-stream)
  (define (add-term coeff higher-terms)
    (+ coeff (* x higher-terms)))
  (accumulate add-term
              0
              coefficient-stream))
```

The idea of this procedure is that, for each coefficient in the stream, we
multiply the (already accumulated) higher terms by x and add in the new
coefficient.

Maps and filters

The examples above show how a single abstraction, accumulate, can capture many different operations on streams. We can define other abstractions in a similar manner. The map procedure generalizes the map-square

[27] According to Knuth (1969), this rule was formulated by W. G. Horner early in the
nineteenth century, but the method was actually used by Newton over a hundred years
earlier. Horner's rule evaluates the polynomial using fewer additions and multiplications
than does the straightforward method of first computing $a_n x^n$, then adding $a_{n-1} x^{n-1}$,
and so on. In fact, it is possible to prove that any algorithm for evaluating arbitrary
polynomials must use at least as many additions and multiplications as does Horner's
rule, and thus Horner's rule is an optimal algorithm for polynomial evaluation. This
was proved (for the number of additions) by A. M. Ostrowski in a 1954 paper that
essentially founded the modern study of optimal algorithms. The analogous statement
for multiplications was proved by V. Y. Pan in 1966. The book by Borodin and Munro
(1975) provides an overview of these and other results about optimal algorithms.

and `map-fib` procedures used in section 3.4.1. Map takes a procedure and a stream as arguments and generates the stream formed by applying the procedure to each item in the input stream:

```
(define (map proc stream)
  (if (empty-stream? stream)
      the-empty-stream
      (cons-stream (proc (head stream))
                   (map proc (tail stream)))))
```

The other general operation we used was to filter a stream, extracting those elements that satisfy a given predicate:

```
(define (filter pred stream)
  (cond ((empty-stream? stream) the-empty-stream)
        ((pred (head stream))
         (cons-stream (head stream)
                      (filter pred (tail stream))))
        (else (filter pred (tail stream)))))
```

By combining filters, maps, and accumulators, we can express new operations such as

```
(define (product-of-squares-of-odd-elements stream)
  (accumulate *
              1
              (map square
                   (filter odd? stream))))
```

We can also formulate conventional "data processing" applications in terms of streams. For example, suppose we have a stream of personnel records and we want to find the salary of the highest-paid programmer. Assume that we have a selector `salary` that returns the salary of a record, and a predicate `programmer?` that tests if a record is for a programmer. Then we can write

```
(define (salary-of-highest-paid-programmer record-stream)
  (accumulate max
              0
              (map salary
                   (filter programmer?
                           record-stream))))
```

These two examples give just a hint of the vast range of operations that can be expressed in this way.[28]

Another abstraction, similar to map, is for-each, which applies a procedure to every item in a stream but does not accumulate the results to form an output stream:

```
(define (for-each proc stream)
  (if (empty-stream? stream)
      'done
      (sequence (proc (head stream))
                (for-each proc (tail stream)))))
```

For example, to print a stream, we can use[29]

```
(define (print-stream s)
  (for-each print s))
```

Exercise 3.38

Consider the following alternate version of the accumulate procedure:

```
(define (left-accumulate combiner initial-value stream)
  (if (empty-stream? stream)
      initial-value
      (left-accumulate combiner
                       (combiner initial-value (head stream))
                       (tail stream))))
```

Does (left-accumulate + 0 x) return the same result as (accumulate + 0 x) for any stream of numbers x? Does (left-accumulate cons '() x) return the same result as (accumulate cons '() x) for any stream x? In general, for which combiner procedures will accumulate and left-accumulate give the same result?

Exercise 3.39

The procedure accumulate-n is similar to accumulate except that it takes as its third argument a stream of streams, which are all assumed to have the

---

28 Richard Waters (1979) developed a program that automatically analyzes traditional Fortran programs, viewing them in terms of maps, filters, and accumulations. He found that fully 60 percent of the code in the Fortran Scientific Subroutine Package fits neatly into this paradigm. One of the reasons for the success of Lisp as a programming language is that lists provide a standard medium for expressing ordered collections so that they can be manipulated using higher-order operations. The programming language APL owes much of its power and appeal to a similar choice. In APL all data are represented as arrays. There is a universal and convenient set of generic operators for all sorts of array operations.

29 If streams are represented as lists, the interpreter will automatically print them in standard list notation. If we use other representations for streams, as we will in section 3.4.3, then a procedure such as print-stream becomes necessary unless we build some conventional way for printing streams into the print primitive.

same number of elements. It applies the designated accumulation procedure
to combine all the first elements of the streams, all the second elements of the
streams, and so on, and returns a stream of the results. For instance, if S is a
stream containing four streams, ((1 2 3) (4 5 6) (7 8 9) (10 11 12)), then
the value of (accumulate-n + 0 S) should be the stream (22 26 30). Fill in the
expressions ⟨ exp_1 ⟩ and ⟨ exp_2 ⟩ in the following definition of accumulate-n:

```
(define (accumulate-n op init streams)
  (if (empty-stream? (head streams))
      the-empty-stream
      (cons-stream
        (accumulate op init ⟨exp₁⟩)
        (accumulate-n op init ⟨exp₂⟩))))
```

Exercise 3.40

Suppose we represent vectors $v = (v_i)$ as streams of numbers, and matrices $m = (m_{ij})$ as streams of vectors (the rows of the matrix). For example, the matrix

$$\begin{bmatrix} 1 & 2 & 3 & 4 \\ 4 & 5 & 6 & 6 \\ 6 & 7 & 8 & 9 \end{bmatrix}$$

is represented as the stream ((1 2 3 4) (4 5 6 6) (6 7 8 9)). With this
representation, we can use stream operations to concisely express the basic matrix
and vector operations. These operations (which are described in any book on
matrix algebra) are the following:

(dot-product v w)	returns the sum $\sum_i v_i w_i$;
(matrix-times-vector m v)	returns the vector t, where $t_i = \sum_j m_{ij} v_j$;
(matrix-times-matrix m n)	returns the matrix p, where $p_{ij} = \sum_k m_{ik} n_{kj}$;
(transpose m)	returns the matrix n, where $n_{ij} = m_{ji}$.

Fill in the missing expressions in the following procedures for computing these
operations. (The procedure accumulate-n is defined in exercise 3.39.)

```
(define (dot-product v w)
  (accumulate + 0 ⟨???⟩))

(define (matrix-times-vector m v)
  (map ⟨???⟩ m))

(define (transpose mat)
  (accumulate-n ⟨???⟩ ⟨???⟩ mat))
```

```
(define (matrix-times-matrix m n)
  (let ((cols (transpose n)))
    (map ⟨???⟩ m)))
```

Nested mappings

Consider this problem: Given a positive integer n, find all ordered pairs of distinct positive integers i and j, where $1 \le j < i \le n$, such that $i + j$ is prime. For example, if n is 6, then the pairs are the following:

i	j	$i + j$
2	1	3
3	2	5
4	1	5
4	3	7
5	2	7
6	1	7
6	5	11

A natural way to organize this computation is to generate the stream of all ordered pairs of integers (i, j) less than or equal to n, filter this stream of pairs to select those whose sum is prime, and then, for each pair that passes through the filter, produce the triple $(i, j, i + j)$.

Here is a way to generate the stream of pairs: For each integer i that is less than or equal to n, enumerate the integers j that are less than i. For each such i and j, create the pair (i, j). Specifically, map down the stream (enumerate-interval 1 n). For each i in this stream, map down the stream (enumerate-interval 1 (-1+ i)). For each j in this latter stream, generate the item (list i j). The inner map produces a stream of pairs for each i from the outer map. Appending together all of these streams (using flatten) produces the required stream of pairs for all i:

```
(flatten (map (lambda (i)
                (map (lambda (j) (list i j))
                     (enumerate-interval 1 (-1+ i))))
              (enumerate-interval 1 n)))
```

The composition of flatten and map is so common in this sort of program that we will isolate it as a separate procedure:

```
(define (flatmap f s) (flatten (map f s)))
```

Now filter this stream of pairs to find those whose sum is prime. The filter predicate is called for each element of the stream; its argument is a pair and it must extract the integers from the pair. Thus, the predicate to apply to each element in the stream is

```
(lambda (pair) (prime? (+ (car pair) (cadr pair))))
```

Finally, generate the stream of results by mapping over the stream of filtered pairs using the following procedure, which constructs a triple consisting of the two elements of the pair, along with their sum:

```
(lambda (pair)
  (list (car pair) (cadr pair) (+ (car pair) (cadr pair))))
```

Combining all these steps yields the complete procedure:

```
(define (prime-sum-pairs n)
  (map (lambda (pair) (list (car pair)
                            (cadr pair)
                            (+ (car pair) (cadr pair))))
       (filter (lambda (pair) (prime? (+ (car pair)
                                         (cadr pair))))
               (flatmap
                (lambda (i)
                  (map (lambda (j) (list i j))
                       (enumerate-interval 1 (-1+ i))))
                (enumerate-interval 1 n)))))
```

Another problem that can be handled in the same way is to find all triples of distinct positive integers i, j, and k less than or equal to a given integer n that sum to a given integer s. For example, with n equal to 9 and s equal to 15 the triples are[30]

(6 5 4) (7 5 3) (7 6 2) (8 4 3)
(8 5 2) (8 6 1) (9 4 2) (9 5 1)

This computation can be organized just as in prime-sum-pairs. Map along the interval from 1 to n, generating a stream for each i in the interval, and then combine these streams using flatten. The stream for each i is obtained by mapping along the interval from 1 to $i-1$, generating a stream for each j in the interval, and flattening the result. The stream for each j is obtained by mapping along the interval from 1 to $j-1$ and generating the triple (list i j k) for each k in the interval. The entire stream of triples is then filtered by the predicate

---

30 These triples represent all the wins in tic-tac-toe if we number the nine positions on a tic-tac-toe board as in the following "magic square":

4	9	2
3	5	7
8	1	6

```
(lambda (triple)
  (= (+ (car triple) (cadr triple) (caddr triple))
     s))
```

Here is the complete procedure:

```
(define (triples n s)
  (filter (lambda (triple)
            (= (+ (car triple) (cadr triple) (caddr triple))
               s))
          (flatmap
           (lambda (i)
             (flatmap
              (lambda (j)
                (map (lambda (k) (list i j k))
                     (enumerate-interval 1 (-1+ j))))
              (enumerate-interval 1 (-1+ i))))
           (enumerate-interval 1 n))))
```

In general, expressions that compute nested mappings have the form

```
(map (lambda (tuple)
       (let (((v₁) (car tuple))... ((vₙ) (ca...dr tuple)))
         (result)))
     (filter (lambda (tuple)
               (let (((v₁) (car tuple))
                       ⋮
                     ((vₙ) (ca...dr tuple)))
                 (restriction)))
             (flatmap
              (lambda ((v₁))
                (flatmap
                 (lambda ((v₂))
                   ⋮
                   (map (lambda ((vₙ))
                          (list (v₁)...(vₙ)))
                        (setₙ)))
                 ⋮
                 (set₂)))
              (set₁))))
```

We can make such expressions easier to deal with by creating some appropriate syntactic sugar, namely, a special form called collect. Collect is defined so that the above expression can be written in the following equivalent form:

(collect ⟨result⟩
        (((⟨v₁⟩ ⟨set₁⟩))

         ⋮

         ((⟨vₙ⟩ ⟨setₙ⟩)))
        ⟨restriction⟩))

Using collect, we can rewrite prime-sum-pairs as

(define (prime-sum-pairs n)
  (collect (list i j (+ i j))
           ((i (enumerate-interval 1 n))
            (j (enumerate-interval 1 (-1+ i))))
           (prime? (+ i j))))

and we can rewrite triples as[31]

(define (triples n s)
  (collect (list i j k)
           ((i (enumerate-interval 1 n))
            (j (enumerate-interval 1 (-1+ i)))
            (k (enumerate-interval 1 (-1+ j))))
           (= (+ i j k) s)))

We can think of the meaning of the collect as follows: For each ⟨v₁⟩ in ⟨set₁⟩ and for each ⟨v₂⟩ in ⟨set₂⟩ and ... for each ⟨vₙ⟩ in ⟨setₙ⟩, if all the ⟨vᵢ⟩ satisfy the ⟨restriction⟩ then accumulate the ⟨result⟩. These nested maps are similar to the "nested loops over index variables" found in many programming languages.[32]

Nested mappings are also useful for streams other than those that enumerate intervals. Suppose we wish to generate all the permutations of a set S

---

31 The use of collect causes extra computation in this case, because the triples (i, j, k), already available after the filter, are regenerated by the outer map.

32 The stream approach to nested mappings was shown to us by David Turner, whose language KRC provides an elegant formalism for dealing with these constructs. The examples in this section (see also exercise 3.41) are adapted from Turner 1981. One striking property of the stream approach is that with a small modification the same method works for very long or even infinite streams. We will show how to accomplish this in section 3.4.5.

of items; that is, all the ways of ordering the items in the set. For instance, the permutations of $\{a, b, c\}$ are $\{a, b, c\}$, $\{a, c, b\}$, $\{b, a, c\}$, $\{b, c, a\}$, $\{c, a, b\}$, and $\{c, b, a\}$. Here is a plan for generating the permutations of S: For each item x in S, recursively generate the stream of all permutations p of $S - x$. (The set $S - x$ is the set of all elements of S, excluding x.) Then, for each such permutation p adjoin x to the front of p. This yields for each x in S the stream of permutations of S that begin with x, and combining these streams gives all the permutations of S. Thus, we can reduce the problem of generating permutations of sets of n items to the problem of generating the permutations of sets of $n - 1$ items. If S itself is represented as a stream of elements, we can reduce the problem of generating the permutations of S to the problem of generating the permutations of shorter and shorter streams. This leads to the following procedure:

```
(define (permutations S)
  (if (empty-stream? S)
      (singleton the-empty-stream)
      (flatmap (lambda (x)
                 (map (lambda (p)
                        (cons-stream x p))
                      (permutations (remove x S))))
               S)))
```

In the terminal case, when we have worked our way down to the-empty-stream, which represents a set of no elements, we generate as the permutations a stream with one item, namely the set with no elements. The singleton procedure generates a stream that contains a single designated item:

```
(define (singleton s)
  (cons-stream s the-empty-stream))
```

We can rewrite the permutations procedure using collect:[33]

```
(define (permutations S)
  (if (empty-stream? S)
      (singleton the-empty-stream)
      (collect (cons-stream x p)
               ((x S)
                (p (permutations (remove x S)))))))
```

----

33 This collect form has no ⟨restriction⟩ clause. We assume that collect is defined so as to not impose a restriction if none is specified.

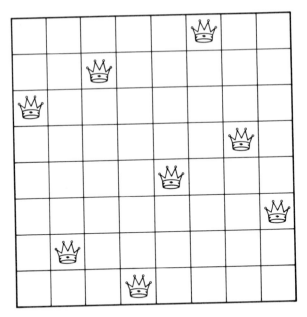

Figure 3.28
A solution to the eight-queens puzzle.

The remove procedure used in permutations returns all the items in a given stream except for a given item. This can be expressed as a simple filter:

```
(define (remove item stream)
  (filter (lambda (x) (not (equal? x item)))
          stream))
```

Exercise 3.41

The "eight-queens puzzle" asks how to place eight queens on a chess board so that no queen is in check from any other (i.e., no two queens are in the same row, column, or diagonal). One possible solution is shown in figure 3.28. One way to solve the puzzle is to work across the board, placing a queen in each column. Once we have placed $k-1$ queens, we must place the kth queen in a position where it does not check any of the queens already on the board. We can formulate this approach recursively: Assume that we have already generated the stream of all possible ways to place $k-1$ queens in the first $k-1$ columns of the board. For each of these ways, find all the rows r for which it is safe to place a queen in the rth row and the kth column, and generate the extended set of positions. This produces the stream of all ways to place k queens in the first k columns. By continuing this process, we will produce not only one solution but the stream of all solutions to the puzzle.

We implement this solution as a procedure **queens**, which returns a stream of all solutions to the problem of placing n queens on an $n \times n$ chess board. This calls a procedure **queen-cols**, which returns the stream of all ways to place queens in the first k columns of a board of specified size.

```
(define (queens board-size)
  (define (queen-cols k)
    (if (= k 0)
        (singleton empty-board)
        (collect (adjoin-position new-row k rest-of-queens)
                 ((rest-of-queens (queen-cols (-1+ k)))
                  (new-row (enumerate-interval 1 board-size)))
                 (safe? new-row k rest-of-queens))))
  (queen-cols board-size))
```

In the collect used by queen-cols, rest-of-queens is a way to place $k - 1$ queens in the first $k - 1$ columns and new-row is a proposed row in the kth column in which to place the next queen. Complete the program by implementing the representation for sets of board positions, including the procedure adjoin-position, which adjoins a new row and column to a set of positions, and empty-board, which represents an empty set of positions. You must also implement the procedure safe?, which determines whether it is safe to place a queen at a proposed row and column, so that it does not attack any of the queens at a given set of positions. Also, rewrite the queen-cols procedure without using collect.

Exercise 3.42

Louis Reasoner is having a terrible time doing exercise 3.41. His queens procedure seems to work, but it runs extremely slowly. (Louis never does manage to wait long enough for it to solve even the 6×6 case.) When Louis asks Eva Lu Ator for help, she points out that he has interchanged two lines in the queen-cols procedure, writing the collect form as

```
(collect (adjoin-position new-row k rest-of-queens)
         ((new-row (enumerate-interval 1 board-size))
          (rest-of-queens (queen-cols (-1+ k))))
         (safe? new-row k rest-of-queens))
```

Explain why this interchange makes the program run slowly. Estimate how long it will take Louis's program to solve the eight-queens puzzle, assuming that the program in exercise 3.41 solves the puzzle in time T.

3.4.3 Implementing Streams

As we have seen, streams can serve as standard interfaces for combining program modules. By using streams, we can formulate powerful abstractions that capture a wide variety of operations in a manner that is both succinct and elegant. Unfortunately, this elegance is bought at the price of severe inefficiency with respect to both the time and space required by our computations—at least this will be the case if we represent streams as ordinary lists, with cons-stream, head, and tail defined, respectively, as cons, car, and cdr.

If we represent streams as lists, our programs must construct and copy data structures (which may be huge) at every step of a stream process. To see why this is true, let us compare two programs for computing the sum of all the prime numbers in an interval. The first program is written in standard iterative style:

```
(define (sum-primes a b)
  (define (iter count accum)
    (cond ((> count b) accum)
          ((prime? count) (iter (1+ count) (+ count accum)))
          (else (iter (1+ count) accum))))
  (iter a 0))
```

The second program performs the same computation using streams:

```
(define (sum-primes a b)
  (accumulate +
              0
              (filter prime?
                      (enumerate-interval a b))))
```

In carrying out the computation, the first program needs to store only the sum being accumulated. In contrast, with streams represented as lists, the filter in the second program cannot do any testing until enumerate-interval has constructed a complete list of the numbers in the interval. The filter generates another list, which in turn is passed to accumulate before being collapsed to form a sum. Such large intermediate storage is not needed by the first program, which we can think of as enumerating the interval incrementally, adding each prime to the sum as it is generated.

Even more inefficiency arises if we try to compute the second prime in the interval from 10,000 to 1,000,000 by evaluating the expression

```
(head (tail (filter prime?
                    (enumerate-interval 10000 1000000))))
```

This expression does find the second prime, but the computational overhead seems outrageous. We construct a list of almost a million integers, filter this list by testing each element for primality, and then ignore almost all of the result. In a more traditional programming style, we would interleave the enumeration and the filtering and stop when we reached the second prime.

By changing the representation of streams, we can achieve the best of both worlds: We can use the elegant stream formulation while preserving the efficiency of incremental computation. The basic idea is to arrange for cons-stream to construct a stream only partially and to pass the partial construction to the program that consumes the stream. If the consumer attempts to access a part of the stream that has not yet been constructed, the stream will automatically construct just enough more of itself to enable the consumer to access the required part, thus preserving the illusion that the entire stream exists. In other words, although we will write programs as if we were processing complete streams, we design our stream implementation to automatically and transparently interleave the construction of the stream with its use.

To make streams behave in this way, we will arrange for the tail of a stream to be evaluated when it is accessed by the tail procedure rather than when the stream is constructed by cons-stream. This implementation choice is reminiscent of our discussion of rational numbers in section 2.1.2, where we saw that we can implement rational numbers so that the reduction of numerator and denominator to lowest terms is performed either at construction time or at selection time. The two rational-number implementations produce the same data abstraction, but the choice has an effect on efficiency. There is a similar relationship between streams and ordinary lists. As a data abstraction, streams are the same as lists. The difference is the time at which the elements are evaluated. With ordinary lists, both the car and the cdr are evaluated at construction time. With streams, the tail is evaluated at selection time.

Our implementation of streams will be based on a special form called delay. Evaluating the form (delay ⟨exp⟩) does not evaluate the expression ⟨exp⟩, but rather returns a so-called *delayed object*, which we can think of as a "promise" to evaluate ⟨exp⟩ at some future time. As a companion to delay we have an operator called force that takes a delayed object as argument and performs the evaluation—in effect, forcing the delay to fulfill its promise. We will see below how delay and force can be implemented, but first let us use these to construct streams.

Cons-stream is a special form defined so that (cons-stream ⟨a⟩ ⟨b⟩) is equivalent to (cons ⟨a⟩ (delay ⟨b⟩)). What this means is that we will construct streams using pairs, but rather than placing the value of the tail into the cdr of the pair we will put there a promise to compute the tail if it is ever requested. Head and tail can now be defined as procedures:

```
(define (head stream) (car stream))
```

```
(define (tail stream) (force (cdr stream)))
```

Head selects the car of the pair that was constructed by cons-stream; tail selects the cdr of the pair and evaluates the delayed expression found there to obtain the tail.[34]

The stream implementation in action

To see how this implementation behaves, let us analyze the "outrageous" prime computation.

```
(head (tail (filter prime?
                    (enumerate-interval 10000 1000000))))
```

We will see that, in fact, it works efficiently. The evaluation begins by calling enumerate-interval with the arguments 10,000 and 1,000,000. Recall that enumerate-interval is defined as

```
(define (enumerate-interval low high)
  (if (> low high)
      the-empty-stream
      (cons-stream low (enumerate-interval (1+ low) high))))
```

and thus the result, formed by the cons-stream, is[35]

```
(cons 10000 (delay (enumerate-interval 10001 1000000)))
```

That is, the result is a stream represented as a pair whose car is 10,000 and whose cdr is a promise to enumerate more of the interval if so requested. This stream is now filtered for primes, using the filter procedure:

```
(define (filter pred stream)
  (cond ((empty-stream? stream) the-empty-stream)
        ((pred (head stream))
         (cons-stream (head stream)
                      (filter pred (tail stream))))
        (else (filter pred (tail stream)))))
```

Filter tests the head of the stream (the car of the pair, which is 10,000) and finds that this is not prime, so filter examines the tail of its input stream. The call to tail forces evaluation of the delayed enumerate-interval, which now returns

---

34 Although head and tail can be defined as procedures, cons-stream must be a special form. If cons-stream were a procedure, then, according to our model of evaluation, evaluating (cons-stream ⟨a⟩ ⟨b⟩) would automatically cause ⟨b⟩ to be evaluated, which is precisely what we do not want to happen. For the same reason, delay must be a special form.

35 Of course, the numbers shown here do not really appear in the delayed expression. What actually appears is the original expression, in an environment in which the variables are bound to the appropriate numbers. For example, (1+ low) with low bound to 10,000 actually appears where 10,001 is shown.

```
(cons 10001 (delay (enumerate-interval 10002 1000000)))
```

Filter now looks at the head of this stream, 10,001, sees that this is not prime either, forces another `tail`, and so on, until `enumerate-interval` yields the prime 10,007, whereupon `filter`, according to its definition, returns

```
(cons-stream (head stream)
             (filter pred (tail stream)))
```

which in this case is

```
(cons 10007
      (delay
       (filter prime?
               (cons 10008
                     (delay (enumerate-interval 10009
                                                1000000))))))
```

This result is now passed to `tail` in our original expression. `Tail` forces the delayed `filter`, which keeps forcing the delayed `enumerate-interval` until it finds the next prime, which is 10,009. Finally, the result passed to `head` in our original expression is

```
(cons 10009
      (delay
       (filter prime?
               (cons 10010
                     (delay (enumerate-interval 10011
                                                1000000))))))
```

Head returns 10,009, and the computation is complete. Only as many integers were tested for primality as were necessary to find the second prime, and the interval was enumerated only as far as was necessary to feed the prime filter.

   In general, we can think of delayed evaluation as "demand-driven" programming, whereby each stage in the stream process is activated only enough to satisfy the next stage. What we have done is to decouple the actual order of events in the computation from the apparent structure of our procedures. We write procedures as if the streams existed "all at once" when, in reality, the computation is performed incrementally, as in traditional programming styles.

Implementing delay **and** force

Although delay and force may seem like powerful and complex operations, their implementation is really quite straightforward. Delay must package an expression so that it can be evaluated later on demand, and we can accomplish this simply by treating the expression as the body of a procedure. Delay can be a special form such that (delay ⟨exp⟩) is syntactic sugar for (lambda () ⟨exp⟩). Force simply calls the procedure (of no arguments) produced by delay, so we can implement force as a procedure:

```
(define (force delayed-object)
  (delayed-object))
```

This implementation suffices for delay and force to work as advertised, but there is an important optimization that we can make. In many applications, we end up forcing the same delayed object many times. This can lead to serious inefficiency in recursive programs involving streams. (See exercise 3.47.) The solution is to build a delayed object so that the first time it is forced, it stores the value that is computed. Subsequent forcings will simply return the stored value without repeating the computation. In other words, we implement delay as a special-purpose memoized procedure similar to the one described in exercise 3.27. One way to accomplish this is to use the following procedure, which takes as argument a procedure (of no arguments) and returns a memoized version of the procedure. The first time the memoized procedure is run, it saves the computed result. On subsequent evaluations, it simply returns the result.

```
(define (memo-proc proc)
  (let ((already-run? nil) (result nil))
    (lambda ()
      (if (not already-run?)
          (sequence (set! result (proc))
                    (set! already-run? (not nil))
                    result)
          result))))
```

Delay is then defined so that (delay ⟨exp⟩) is equivalent to

(memo-proc (lambda () ⟨exp⟩))

and force is as defined previously.[36]

---

[36] There are many possible implementations of streams other than the one described in this section. Delayed evaluation, which is the key to making streams practical, was inherent in Algol 60's *call-by-name* parameter-passing method. The use of this mechanism to implement streams was first described by Landin (1965). Delayed evaluation for

Exercise 3.43

In order to take a closer look at delayed evaluation, we will use the following procedure, which simply returns its argument after printing it:

```
(define (show x)
  (print x)
  x)
```

The next procedure, which is similar to the nth procedure of section 2.2.1, extracts a given item from a stream:

```
(define (nth-stream n s)
  (if (= n 0)
      (head s)
      (nth-stream (-1+ n) (tail s)))))
```

What does the interpreter print in response to evaluating each expression in the following sequence?[37]

```
(define x (map show (enumerate-interval 0 10)))

==> (nth-stream 5 x)
⟨printed response⟩
==> (nth-stream 7 x)
⟨printed response⟩
```

Exercise 3.44

Consider the sequence of expressions

```
(define sum 0)

(define (accum x)
  (set! sum (+ x sum))
  sum)

(define seq (map accum (enumerate-interval 1 20)))

(define y (filter even? seq))
```

---

streams was introduced into Lisp by Friedman and Wise (1976). In their implementation, cons always delays evaluating its arguments, so that lists automatically behave as streams. The memoizing optimization is also known as *call-by-need*. The Algol community would refer to our original delayed objects as *call-by-name* thunks and to the optimized versions as *call-by-need thunks*.

[37] Exercises such as 3.43, 3.44, and 3.45 are valuable for testing our understanding of how **delay** works. On the other hand, intermixing delayed evaluation with printing—and, even worse, with assignment—is extremely confusing, and instructors of courses on computer languages have traditionally tormented their students with examination questions such as the ones in this section. Needless to say, writing programs that depend on such subtleties is odious programming style. Part of the power of stream processing is that it lets us ignore the order in which events actually happen in our programs. Unfortunately, this is precisely what we cannot afford to do in the presence of assignment, which forces us to be concerned with time and change.

```
(define z (filter (lambda (x) (= (remainder x 5) 0))
                  seq))
```

==> (nth-stream 7 y)
⟨*printed response*⟩

==> (print-stream z)
⟨*printed response*⟩

What is the value of sum after each of the above expressions is evaluated? What is the printed response to evaluating the nth-stream and print-stream expressions? Would these responses be different if we had implemented (delay ⟨*exp*⟩) simply as (lambda () ⟨*exp*⟩) without using the optimization provided by memo-proc? Explain.

Exercise 3.45

Ben Bitdiddle has become severely annoyed while doing exercise 3.40, because he has realized that he cannot use cons-stream as an argument to a higher-order procedure. (Supplementary exercise: Why does Ben want to do this in exercise 3.40?) To make the best of a bad situation, he has decided to use cons instead. To explore the effect this will have on his programs, he uses the show procedure of exercise 3.43 to compare two procedures for copying streams. The first accumulates with cons-stream, but, since Ben can't use accumulate explicitly, he writes out the accumulation pattern

```
(define (copy-stream s)
  (if (empty-stream? s)
      the-empty-stream
      (cons-stream (head s) (copy-stream (tail s)))))
```

The second program is the accumulation that Ben would rather have written, except that he writes cons in place of cons-stream:

```
(define (*copy-stream s)
  (accumulate cons the-empty-stream s))
```

What does Ben see printed in response to each of the following expressions?

==> (sequence (copy-stream (map show (enumerate-interval 1 10)))
              'done)
⟨*printed response*⟩

==> (sequence (*copy-stream (map show (enumerate-interval 1 10)))
              'done)
⟨*printed response*⟩

3.4.4 Infinitely Long Streams

We have seen how to support the illusion of manipulating streams as complete entities even though, in actuality, we compute only as much of the stream as we need to access. We can exploit this technique to efficiently represent sequences as streams, even if the sequences are very long. What is more striking, we can use streams to represent sequences that are infinitely long. For instance, consider the following definition of the stream of positive integers:

```
(define (integers-starting-from n)
  (cons-stream n (integers-starting-from (1+ n))))
```

```
(define integers (integers-starting-from 1))
```

This makes sense because `integers` will be a pair whose `car` is 1 and whose `cdr` is a promise to produce the integers beginning with 2. This is an infinitely long stream, but in any given time we can examine only a finite portion of it. Thus, our programs will never know that the entire infinite stream is not there.

Using `integers` we can define other infinite streams, such as the stream of integers that are not divisible by 7:

```
(define (divisible? x y) (= (remainder x y) 0))
```

```
(define no-sevens
  (filter (lambda (x) (not (divisible? x 7)))
          integers))
```

Then we can find integers not divisible by 7 simply by accessing elements of this stream:[38]

```
==> (nth-stream 100 no-sevens)
117
```

In analogy with `integers`, we can define the infinite stream of Fibonacci numbers:

```
(define (fibgen a b)
  (cons-stream a (fibgen b (+ a b))))
```

```
(define fibs (fibgen 0 1))
```

Fibs is a pair whose `car` is 0 and whose `cdr` is a promise to evaluate (`fibgen 1 1`), which, when we evaluate it, will produce a pair whose `car` is 1 and whose `cdr` is a promise to evaluate (`fibgen 1 2`), and so on.

For a look at a more exciting infinite stream, we can generalize the no-sevens example to construct the infinite stream of prime numbers, using a

38 The `nth-stream` procedure was defined in exercise 3.43.

method known as the *sieve of Eratosthenes*.[39]   We start with the integers
beginning with 2, which is the first prime. To get the rest of the primes,
we start by filtering the multiples of 2 from the rest of the integers. This
leaves a stream beginning with 3, which is the next prime. Now we filter the
multiples of 3 from the rest of this stream. This leaves a stream beginning
with 5, which is the next prime, and so on. In other words, we construct
the primes by a sieving process, described as follows: To sieve a stream S,
form a stream whose head is the head of S and whose tail is obtained by
filtering all multiples of the head of S out of the tail of S and sieving the
result. This process is readily described in terms of stream operations:

```
(define (sieve stream)
  (cons-stream
    (head stream)
    (sieve (filter
             (lambda (x) (not (divisible? x (head stream))))
             (tail stream)))))
```

```
(define primes (sieve (integers-starting-from 2)))
```

Now to find a particular prime we need only ask for it:

```
==> (nth-stream 50 primes)
233
```

It is interesting to contemplate the signal-processing system set up by
sieve, shown in the "Henderson diagram" in figure 3.29.[40] The input
stream feeds into an "unconser" that separates the head of the stream
from the tail. The head is used to construct a divisibility filter, through
which the tail is passed, and the output of the filter is fed to another sieve
box. Then the original head is consed onto the output of the internal sieve
to give the output stream. Thus, not only is the stream infinite, but the
signal processor is also infinite, because the sieve contains a sieve within it.

---

39 Eratosthenes, a third century B.C. Alexandrian Greek philosopher, is famous for giving the first accurate estimate of the circumference of the Earth, which he computed by
observing shadows cast at noon on the day of the summer solstice. Eratosthenes's sieve
method, although ancient, has formed the basis for special-purpose hardware "sieves"
that, until very recently, were the most powerful tools in existence for locating large
primes. Over the past few years, these methods have been superseded by outgrowths of
the probabilistic techniques discussed in section 1.2.6.

40 We have named these figures after Peter Henderson, who was the first person to show
us diagrams of this sort as a way of thinking about stream processing. Each solid line
represents a stream of values being transmitted. The dashed line from the head to the
cons and the filter indicates that this is a single value rather than a stream.

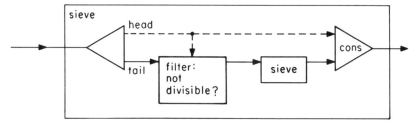

Figure 3.29
The prime sieve viewed as a signal-processing system.

Defining streams implicitly

The integers and fibs streams above were defined by specifying "generating" procedures that explicitly compute the stream elements one by one. An alternative way to specify streams is to take advantage of delayed evaluation to define streams implicitly. For example, the following expression defines the stream ones to be an infinite stream of ones:

```
(define ones (cons-stream 1 ones))
```

This works much like the definition of a recursive procedure: ones is a pair whose car is 1 and whose cdr is a promise to evaluate ones. Evaluating the cdr gives us again a 1 and a promise to evaluate ones, and so on.

We can do more interesting things by using procedures such as add-streams, which produces the elementwise sum of two given streams:

```
(define (add-streams s1 s2)
  (cond ((empty-stream? s1) s2)
        ((empty-stream? s2) s1)
        (else
         (cons-stream (+ (head s1) (head s2))
                      (add-streams (tail s1) (tail s2))))))
```

Now we can define the integers as follows:

```
(define integers (cons-stream 1 (add-streams ones integers)))
```

This works by defining integers to be a stream whose head is 1 and whose tail is the sum of integers and ones. Thus, the head of the tail is the head of integers plus 1, or 2; the third element of integers is 1 plus the second element of integers, or 3; and so on. This definition works because, at any point, enough of the integers stream has been generated so that we can feed it back into the definition to produce the next integer.

We can define the Fibonacci numbers in the same style:

```
(define fibs
  (cons-stream 0
               (cons-stream 1
                            (add-streams (tail fibs) fibs))))
```

This definition says that fibs is a stream beginning with 0 and 1, such that the stream can be generated by adding it to itself shifted by one place:

0	1	1	2	3	5	8	13	21 ...
	0	1	1	2	3	5	8	13 ...
1	2	3	5	8	13	21	34 ...	

Another useful procedure in formulating such stream definitions is scale-stream, which multiplies each item in a stream by a given constant:

```
(define (scale-stream c stream)
  (map (lambda (x) (* x c)) stream))
```

For example,

```
(define double (cons-stream 1 (scale-stream 2 double)))
```

produces the stream of powers of 2: 1, 2, 4, 8, 16, 32,....

An alternate definition of the stream of primes can be given by starting with the integers and filtering them by testing for primality. We will need the first prime, 2, to get started:

```
(define primes
  (cons-stream 2 (filter prime? (integers-starting-from 3))))
```

This definition is not so straightforward as it appears, because we will test whether a number n is prime by checking whether n is divisible by a prime (not by just any integer) less than or equal to $\sqrt{n}$:

```
(define (prime? n)
  (define (iter ps)
    (cond ((> (square (head ps)) n) t)
          ((divisible? n (head ps)) nil)
          (else (iter (tail ps)))))
  (iter primes))
```

This is a recursive definition, since primes is defined in terms of the prime? predicate, which itself uses the primes stream. The reason this procedure works is that, at any point, enough of the primes stream has been generated to test the primality of the numbers we need to check next. That is, for every n we test for primality, either n is not prime (in which case there is a prime already generated that divides it) or n is prime (in which case there is a prime already generated—i.e., a prime less than n—that is greater than $\sqrt{n}$).[41]

Exercise 3.46

A famous problem, first raised by R. Hamming, is to enumerate, in ascending order with no repetitions, all positive integers with no prime factors other than 2, 3, or 5. One obvious way to do this is to simply test each integer in turn to see whether it has any factors other than 2, 3, and 5. But this is very inefficient, since, as the integers get larger, fewer and fewer of them fit the requirement. As an alternative, let us call the required stream of numbers S and notice the following facts about it.

- S begins with 1.
- The elements of (scale-stream 2 S) are also elements of S.
- The same is true for (scale-stream 3 S) and (scale-stream 5 S).
- These are all the elements of S.

Now all we have to do is combine elements from these four sources. For this we define a procedure merge that combines two ordered streams into one ordered result stream, eliminating repetitions:

```
(define (merge s1 s2)
  (cond ((empty-stream? s1) s2)
        ((empty-stream? s2) s1)
        (else
         (let ((h1 (head s1))
               (h2 (head s2)))
           (cond ((< h1 h2) (cons-stream h1 (merge (tail s1) s2)))
                 ((> h1 h2) (cons-stream h2 (merge s1 (tail s2))))
                 (else
                  (cons-stream h1
                               (merge (tail s1) (tail s2)))))))))
```

Then the required stream may be constructed with merge, as follows:

```
(define S (cons-stream 1 (merge ⟨???⟩ ⟨???⟩)))
```

Fill in the missing expressions in the places marked ⟨???⟩ above.

Exercise 3.47

How many additions are performed when we compute the nth Fibonacci number using the definition of fibs based on the add-streams procedure? Show that the number of additions would be exponentially greater if we had implemented

---

[41] This last point is very subtle and relies on the fact that $p_{n+1} \leq p_n^2$. (Here, p_k denotes the kth prime.) Estimates such as these are very difficult to establish. The ancient proof by Euclid that there are an infinite number of primes shows that $p_{n+1} \leq p_1 p_2 \cdots p_n + 1$, and no substantially better result was proved until 1851, when the Russian mathematician P. L. Chebyshev established that $p_{n+1} \leq 2p_n$ for all n. This result, originally conjectured in 1845, is known as *Bertrand's hypothesis*. A proof can be found in section 22.3 of Hardy and Wright 1960.

(delay ⟨exp⟩) simply as (lambda () ⟨exp⟩), without using the optimization provided by the memo-proc procedure as described in section 3.4.3.[42]

Exercise 3.48

Give an interpretation of the stream computed by the following procedure:

```
(define (expand num den radix)
  (cons-stream (quotient (* num radix) den)
               (expand (remainder (* num radix) den) den radix)))
```

(Quotient is a primitive that returns the integer quotient of two integers.) What are the successive elements produced by (expand 1 7 10)? (expand 3 8 10)?

Exercise 3.49

In section 2.4.3 we saw how to implement a polynomial arithmetic system representing polynomials as lists of terms. In a similar way, we can work with *power series*, such as

$$e^x = 1 + x + \frac{x^2}{2} + \frac{x^3}{3 \cdot 2} + \frac{x^4}{4 \cdot 3 \cdot 2} + \cdots,$$

$$\cos x = 1 - \frac{x^2}{2} + \frac{x^4}{4 \cdot 3 \cdot 2} - \cdots,$$

$$\sin x = x - \frac{x^3}{3 \cdot 2} + \frac{x^5}{5 \cdot 4 \cdot 3 \cdot 2} - \cdots,$$

represented as streams of infinitely many terms. We can integrate power series termwise using the operation

```
(define (integrate-term t)
  (let ((new-order (1+ (order t))))
    (make-term new-order
               (rat/int (coeff t) new-order))))
(define (integrate-series series)
  (map integrate-term series))
```

This uses the basic constructors and selectors for terms defined in section 2.4.3. It also assumes that all coefficients are rational numbers and uses a special-purpose arithmetic operator for dividing rational numbers by integers:

```
(define (rat/int r i) (/rat r (make-rat i 1)))
```

We can use these operations to generate the power series for e^x, starting from the

---

42 This exercise shows how call-by-need is closely related to ordinary memoization as described in exercise 3.27. In that exercise, we used assignment to explicitly construct a local table. Our call-by-need stream optimization effectively constructs such a table automatically, storing values in the previously forced tails of the stream.

fact that the function $x \mapsto e^x$ is its own derivative. This implies that e^x and the integral of e^x are the same series, except for the constant term, which is $e^0 = 1$. Accordingly, the series for e^x can be defined as the series whose zero-order term is 1 and whose higher-order terms are given (recursively) by the integral of the series for e^x. We can express this definition by the following expressions, which generate the series for e^x, starting from a unit-term, which represents 1.

```
(define unit-term (make-term 0 (make-rat 1 1)))

(define exp-series
  (cons-stream unit-term (integrate-series exp-series)))
```

In a similar way we can generate the series for sine and cosine, starting from the facts that the derivative of sine is cosine and the derivative of cosine is the negative of sine. Show how to do this by filling in the missing parts of the following definitions:

```
(define cosine-series
  (cons-stream unit-term ⟨???⟩))

(define sine-series
  ⟨???⟩)
```

Streams as signals

We began our discussion of streams by describing them as computational analogs of the "signals" in signal-processing systems. In fact, we can use streams to model signal-processing systems in a very direct way, representing the values of a signal at successive time intervals as consecutive elements of a stream. For instance, we can implement an *integrator* or *summer* that, for an input stream $x = (x_i)$, an initial value C, and a small increment dt, accumulates the sum

$$S_i = C + \sum_{j=1}^{i} x_j \, dt$$

and returns the stream of values $S = (S_i)$. The `integral` procedure is reminiscent of the "implicit style" definition of the stream of integers given above.

```
(define (integral integrand initial-value dt)
  (define int
    (cons-stream initial-value
                 (add-streams (scale-stream dt integrand)
                              int)))
  int)
```

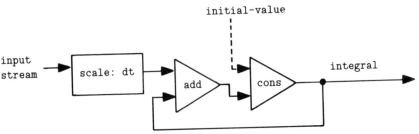

Figure 3.30
The integral procedure viewed as a signal-processing system.

Figure 3.30 is a picture of a signal-processing system that corresponds to the integral procedure. The input stream is scaled by dt and passed through an adder, whose output is passed back through the same adder. The self-reference in the definition of int is reflected in the figure by the feedback loop that connects the output of the adder to one of the inputs.

Exercise 3.50

We can model electrical systems using streams to represent the values of currents or voltages at a sequence of times. For instance, suppose we have an RC *circuit* consisting of a resistor of resistance R and a capacitor of capacitance C in series. The voltage response v of the system to an injected current i is determined by the formula in figure 3.31, whose structure is shown by the accompanying signal-flow diagram.

Write a procedure RC that models this system. RC should take as inputs the values of R, C, and dt and should return a procedure that takes as inputs a stream representing the current i and an initial value for the capacitor voltage v_0 and produces as output the stream of voltages v. For example, you should be able to use RC to model an RC circuit with $R = 5$ ohms, $C = 1$ farad, and a 0.5-second time step by evaluating (define RC1 (RC 5 1 0.5)) to define RC1 as a procedure that takes a stream representing the time sequence of currents and an initial capacitor voltage and produces the output stream of voltages.

Exercise 3.51

Alyssa P. Hacker is designing a system to process signals coming from physical sensors. One important feature she wishes to produce is a signal that describes the *zero crossings* of the input signal. That is, the resulting signal should be $+1$ whenever the input signal changes from negative to positive, -1 whenever the input signal changes from positive to negative, and 0 otherwise. (Assume that the sign of a 0 input is positive.) For example, a typical input signal with its associated zero-crossing signal would be

```
... 1  2  1.5  1  0.5  -0.1  -2  -3  -2  -0.5  0.2  3  4 ...
... 0  0   0   0   0    -1    0   0   0    0    1   0  0 ...
```

In Alyssa's system, the signal from the sensor is represented as a stream sense-data and the stream zero-crossings is to be the corresponding stream of zero

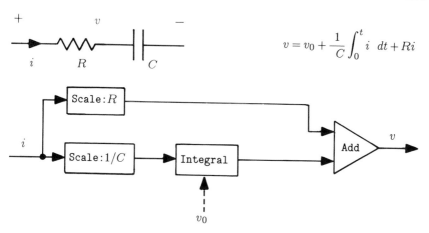

$$v = v_0 + \frac{1}{C} \int_0^t i\ dt + Ri$$

Figure 3.31
An RC circuit and the associated signal-flow diagram.

crossings. Alyssa first writes a procedure sign-change-detector that takes two values as arguments and compares the signs of the values to produce an appropriate 0, 1, or −1. She then constructs her zero-crossing stream as follows:

```
(define (make-zero-crossings input-stream last-value)
  (cons-stream (sign-change-detector (head input-stream) last-value)
               (make-zero-crossings (tail input-stream)
                                    (head input-stream))))

(define zero-crossings (make-zero-crossings sense-data 0))
```

Alyssa's boss, Eva Lu Ator, walks by and suggests that this program is approximately equivalent to the following one, which uses a higher-order procedure:

```
(define (map-2 proc s1 s2)
  (cons-stream (proc (head s1) (head s2))
               (map-2 proc (tail s1) (tail s2))))

(define zero-crossings
  (map-2 sign-change-detector sense-data ⟨expression⟩))
```

Complete the program by supplying the indicated ⟨expression⟩.

Exercise 3.52

Unfortunately, Alyssa's zero-crossing detector in exercise 3.51 proves to be insufficient, because the noisy signal from the sensor leads to spurious zero crossings. Lem E. Tweakit, a hardware specialist, suggests that Alyssa smooth the signal to filter out the noise before extracting the zero crossings. Alyssa takes his advice and decides to extract the zero crossings from the signal constructed by averaging each value of the sense data with the previous value. She explains the problem to her assistant, Louis Reasoner, who implements the idea, altering Alyssa's program from exercise 3.51 as follows:

```
(define (make-zero-crossings input-stream last-value)
  (let ((avpt (/ (+ (head input-stream) last-value) 2)))
    (cons-stream (sign-change-detector avpt last-value)
                 (make-zero-crossings (tail input-stream) avpt))))
```

This seems to work, but a close look at the output shows that the signals are in fact too smooth. Find the bug that Louis has installed and fix it without changing the structure of the program. (Hint: You will need to increase the number of arguments to `make-zero-crossings`.)

Exercise 3.53

Eva Lu Ator has a criticism of Louis's approach in exercise 3.52. The program he wrote is not modular, because it intermixes the operation of smoothing with the zero-crossing extraction. For example, the extractor should not have to be changed if Alyssa finds a better way to condition her input signal. Help Louis by writing a procedure `smooth` that takes a stream as input and produces a stream, each element of which is the average of two successive input stream elements. Then use `smooth` as a component to implement the zero-crossing detector in a more modular style.

3.4.5 Streams and Delayed Evaluation

The `integral` procedure at the end of the preceding section shows how we can use streams to model signal-processing systems that contain feedback loops. The feedback loop for the adder shown in figure 3.30 is modeled by the fact that `integral`'s internal stream `int` is defined in terms of itself:

```
(define int
  (cons-stream initial-value
               (add-streams (scale-stream dt integrand)
                            int)))
```

The interpreter's ability to deal with such an implicit definition depends on the `delay` that is incorporated into `cons-stream`. Without this `delay`, the interpreter could not construct `int` before evaluating both arguments to `cons-stream`, which would require that `int` already be defined. In general, `delay` is crucial for using streams to model signal-processing systems that contain loops. Without `delay`, our models would have to be formulated so that the inputs to any signal-processing component would be fully evaluated before the output could be produced. This would outlaw loops.

Unfortunately, stream models of signal-processing systems with loops may require uses of `delay` beyond the "hidden delay" supplied automatically by `cons-stream`. For instance, figure 3.32 shows a signal-processing system for solving the differential equation $dy/dt = f(y)$ where f is a given mathematical function. The figure shows a `map` component, which applies

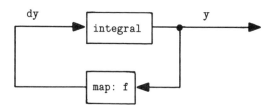

Figure 3.32
An "analog computer circuit" that solves the equation $dy/dt = f(y)$.

f to its input signal, linked in a feedback loop to an integrator in a manner very similar to that of the analog computer circuits that are actually used to solve such equations.

Assuming we are given an initial value y-init for y, we could try to model this system using the procedure

```
(define (solve f y-init dt)
  (define y (integral dy y-init dt))
  (define dy (map f y))
  y)
```

This procedure does not work, because in the first line of solve the call to integral requires that the input dy be defined, which does not happen until the second line of solve.

Exercise 3.54

Why can't we fix the problem by simply interchanging the first two lines of solve to define dy before y?

On the other hand, the intent of our definition does make sense, because we can, in principle, begin to generate the y stream without knowing dy. Indeed, integral and many other stream operations have properties similar to those of cons-stream, in that we can generate part of the answer given only partial information about the arguments. For integral, the head of the output stream is the specified initial-value. Thus, we can generate the head of the output stream without evaluating the integrand dy. Once we know the head of y, the map in the second line of solve can begin working to generate the first element of dy, which will produce the next element of y, and so on.

To take advantage of this idea, we will redefine integral to expect the integrand stream to be a *delayed argument*. Integral will force the integrand to be evaluated only when it is required to generate more than the head of the output stream:

```
(define (integral delayed-integrand initial-value dt)
  (define int
    (cons-stream initial-value
                 (let ((integrand (force delayed-integrand)))
                   (add-streams (scale-stream dt integrand)
                                int))))
  int)
```

Now we can implement our solve procedure by delaying the evaluation of dy in the definition of y:

```
(define (solve f y-init dt)
  (define y (integral (delay dy) y-init dt))
  (define dy (map f y))
  y)
```

In general, every caller of integral must now delay the integrand argument.

Exercise 3.55

The integral procedure used above was analogous to the "implicit" definition of the infinite stream of integers in section 3.4.4. Alternatively, we can give a definition of integral that is more like the "generating function" procedure that used integers-starting-from:

```
(define (integral integrand initial-value dt)
  (cons-stream initial-value
               (if (empty-stream? integrand)
                   the-empty-stream
                   (integral (tail integrand)
                             (+ (* dt (head integrand))
                                initial-value)
                             dt))))
```

When used in systems with loops, this procedure has the same problem as does our original version of integral. Modify the procedure so that it expects the integrand as a delayed argument and hence can be used in the solve procedure shown above.

Exercise 3.56

Consider the problem of designing a signal-processing system to study the homogeneous second-order linear differential equation

$$\frac{d^2y}{dt^2} - a\frac{dy}{dt} - by = 0.$$

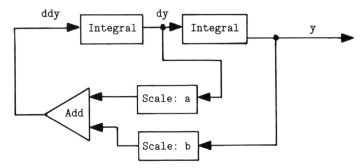

Figure 3.33
Signal-flow diagram for the solution to a second-order linear differential equation.

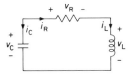

Figure 3.34
A series RLC circuit.

The output stream, modeling y, is generated by a network that contains a loop. This is because the value of d^2y/dt^2 depends upon the values of y and dy/dt and both of these are determined by integrating d^2y/dt^2. The diagram we would like to encode is shown in figure 3.33. Write a procedure 2nd that takes as arguments the constants a, b, and dt and the initial values y_0 and dy_0 for y and dy/dt and generates the stream of successive values of y.

Exercise 3.57

Generalize the 2nd procedure of exercise 3.56 so that it can be used to solve general second-order differential equations $d^2y/dt^2 = f(dy/dt, y)$.

Exercise 3.58

A *series RLC circuit* consists of a resistor, a capacitor, and an inductor connected in series, as shown in figure 3.34. If R, L, and C are the resistance, inductance, and capacitance, v_C is the voltage across the capacitor, and i_L is the current in the inductor, then relations between voltage and current for the three components are described by the equations

$$v_R = i_R R,$$

$$v_L = L\frac{di_L}{dt},$$

$$i_C = C\frac{dv_C}{dt},$$

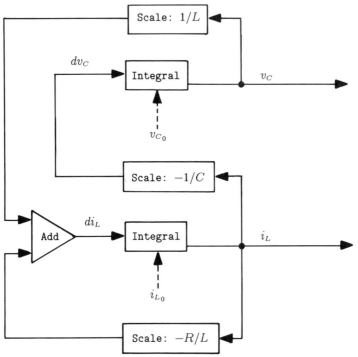

Figure 3.35
A signal-flow diagram for the solution to a series RLC circuit.

and the connections dictate the relations

$$i_R = i_L = -i_C,$$

$$v_C = v_L + v_R.$$

Combining these equations shows that the state of the circuit is described by the pair of differential equations

$$\frac{dv_C}{dt} = -\frac{i_L}{C},$$

$$\frac{di_L}{dt} = \frac{1}{L}v_C - \frac{R}{L}i_L.$$

The signal-flow diagram representing this system of differential equations is shown in figure 3.35.

Write a procedure RLC that takes as arguments the parameters R, L, and C of the circuit and the time increment dt. In a manner similar to that of the RC procedure of exercise 3.50, RLC should produce a procedure that takes the initial values of the state variables, v_{C_0} and i_{L_0}, and produces a pair (using cons) of the streams of states v_C and i_L. Using RLC, generate the pair of streams that models the behavior of a series RLC circuit with $R = 1$ ohm, $C = 0.2$ farad, $L = 1$ henry, $dt = 0.1$ second, and initial values $i_{L_0} = 0$ amps and $v_{C_0} = 10$ volts.

Nested mappings over infinite streams
In section 3.4.2 we developed programs that perform nested mappings over streams. Some changes are necessary to make these programs work for infinite streams. To see why this is so, consider the following program, which generates all pairs of elements (i, j), where i runs through a stream S_1 and j runs through a stream S_2:

```
(define (pairs S1 S2)
  (collect (list i j)
           ((i S1)
            (j S2))))
```

The collect form, as we saw, is syntactic sugar, and the pair-generation procedure is essentially equivalent to

```
(define (pairs S1 S2)
  (flatmap (lambda (i)
             (map (lambda (j) (list i j))
                  S2))
           S1))
```

This program is not satisfactory for very long streams (much less for infinite streams). The difficulty lies in the flatten procedure, which is used by flatmap to combine the streams of pairs:

```
(define (flatmap f s) (flatten (map f s)))
```

```
(define (flatten stream)
  (accumulate append-streams the-empty-stream stream))
```

This definition of flatten causes trouble for two reasons: the order in which flatten collects elements to form the output stream, and the fact that our use of accumulate in this context requires additional delayed evaluation in order to work properly.

The order-of-collection trouble arises because flatten simply appends the streams generated for successive values of the index variables, and therefore it will try to process the entire stream for the first value of an index variable before proceeding to the second value. This is unsuitable for infinite streams, for if we try to generate all pairs of positive integers using

```
(pairs integers integers)
```

our stream of results will first try to run through all pairs of integers with i equal to 1, and hence will never proceed to any other values of i. Consequently, if we tried to use this stream in the expression

```
(filter (lambda (pair) (> (car pair) 1))
        (pairs integers integers))
```

the computation would never produce anything, because the filter would have to discard an infinite number of elements before reaching a pair whose first element is greater than 1.

To handle infinite streams, we need to devise an order of collection that ensures that all elements will eventually be reached if we let our program run long enough.[43]   An elegant way to accomplish this is to modify the definition of flatten to use the following interleave procedure in place of append-streams:

```
(define (interleave s1 s2)
  (if (empty-stream? s1)
      s2
      (cons-stream (head s1)
                   (interleave s2
                               (tail s1)))))
```

The only difference between interleave and append-streams is that the arguments in the recursive call are interchanged. Append-streams takes all the elements from the first stream before starting on the second stream, whereas interleave takes elements alternately from the two streams. Thus, even if the first stream is infinite, every element of the second stream will eventually find its way into the resulting interleaved stream.[44]

Substituting interleave for append-streams fixes the trouble with order of collection, but there is another problem with the flatten procedure. This arises from the fact that we propose to define flatten in terms of accumulate:

```
(define (flatten stream)
  (accumulate interleave the-empty-stream stream))
```

where accumulate (from section 3.4.2) is

43 The precise statement of the required property is as follows: If we are collecting over n streams, then there should be a function f of n variables such that the element of the result corresponding to element i_1 of the first stream, element i_2 of the second stream, ..., element i_n of the nth stream will appear as element number $f(i_1, i_2, \ldots, i_n)$ of the output stream.

44 This technique was shown to us by David Turner, who uses it to implement collections in the KRC language (Turner 1981). In KRC, which uses normal-order evaluation, this modification is all that is necessary to handle infinite streams. In Lisp, there is an additional complication of delayed evaluation, as we discuss next.

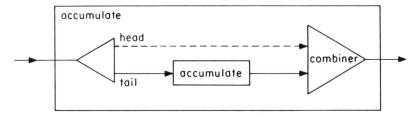

Figure 3.36
Accumulate for an infinite stream.

```
(define (accumulate combiner initial-value stream)
  (if (empty-stream? stream)
      initial-value
      (combiner (head stream)
                (accumulate combiner
                            initial-value
                            (tail stream)))))
```

Unfortunately, accumulate (and therefore flatten) will always go into an infinite loop when given an infinite stream as argument. The reason for this is that when accumulate calls the combiner (in this case, interleave) the arguments to combiner are evaluated, which causes a recursive call to accumulate. If the input stream is infinite, this cycle continues forever, because no (tail stream) will ever produce an empty stream, and the combiner is never called at all.

Compare accumulate with the prime-number sieve procedure of section 3.4.4:

```
(define (sieve stream)
  (cons-stream (head stream)
               (sieve (filter
                       (lambda (x)
                         (not (divisible? x (head stream))))
                       (tail stream)))))
```

Figure 3.36 shows the structure of accumulate (ignoring the empty-stream? case, which can't arise for an infinite stream). This process has the same structure as the sieve shown in figure 3.29; however, the sieve procedure works when given an infinite stream, whereas accumulate does not. The difference is that sieve uses cons-stream to construct the output stream. The hidden delay in cons-stream allows the output stream to be constructed without evaluating the tail of the stream (i.e., without recursively calling sieve).

We can thus overcome the difficulty with the accumulation by using a new version of accumulate that delays the recursive call. We use an explicit delay, since we cannot take advantage of the hidden delay in cons-stream:

```
(define (accumulate-delayed combiner initial-value stream)
  (if (empty-stream? stream)
      initial-value
      (combiner (head stream)
                (delay
                  (accumulate-delayed combiner
                                      initial-value
                                      (tail stream))))))
```

In order for this method of accumulation to work, it must be used in conjunction with a combiner procedure that expects to be called with a second argument that is delayed and forces this argument when needed. We modify interleave to have this structure:

```
(define (interleave-delayed s1 delayed-s2)
  (if (empty-stream? s1)
      (force delayed-s2)
      (cons-stream (head s1)
                   (interleave-delayed (force delayed-s2)
                                       (delay (tail s1))))))
```

Now we redefine flatten using these new versions of accumulate and interleave:

```
(define (flatten stream)
  (accumulate-delayed interleave-delayed
                      the-empty-stream
                      stream))
```

With this modification, flatmap and collect work with infinite streams.

Including the delay inside accumulate does not enable us to accumulate an arbitrary combiner over an infinite stream. If the combiner must always force its second argument in order to begin producing an answer, there will still be an infinite recursion. Our ability to process infinitely long streams depends on the fact that for many stream operations we can generate the initial part of an answer before examining all of the inputs. Interleave can work with infinite streams because it produces the first element of its output stream without examining its second argument. The same is true of append-streams, integral, and of course cons-stream, whose hidden

delay is the basis of the stream implementation. Indeed, this observation—
that in many cases one can make progress in computing the result of an
operation without having fully evaluated all of the arguments—points out
the essential reason for the additional computing power provided by delayed
evaluation.

Exercise 3.59

Generate the stream of all pairs of positive integers i, j, as suggested above.
What are the first few pairs produced? In this order of evaluation, j grows much
faster than i. How large has j become by the time i reaches 10?

Exercise 3.60

Generate the stream of triples of positive integers i, j, k such that $i+j > k$. (Hint:
If you do this in the most straightforward way, with i, j, and k each running
through all the positive integers, your program will be extremely inefficient. Why?
A better method makes use of the fact that k must lie in the interval between 1
and $i + j$.)

Exercise 3.61

Generate the stream of all Pythagorean triples of positive integers i, j, k such
that $i > j$ and $i^2 + j^2 = k^2$. (See the hint in exercise 3.60.)

Exercise 3.62

Generate the stream of all positive integers that can be expressed as the sum
of two cubes in two different ways. The first such number, 1,729, is called
Ramanujan's number, in honor of the mathematician Srinavasa Ramanujan.[45]
What is the second such number?

Normal-order evaluation

The examples in this section illustrate how the explicit use of delay and
force provides great programming flexibility, but the same examples also
show how this can make our programs more complex. Our new integral
procedure, for instance, gives us the power to model systems with loops,
but we must now remember that integral should be called with a delayed
integrand, and every procedure that uses integral must be aware of this.
In effect, we have created two classes of procedures: ordinary procedures and
procedures that take delayed arguments. To see the trouble this can cause,

---

45 To quote from G. H. Hardy's obituary of Ramanujan: "It was Mr. Littlewood (I
believe) who remarked that 'every positive integer was one of his friends.' I remember
once going to see him when he was lying ill at Putney. I had ridden in taxi-cab No.
1729, and remarked that the number seemed to me a rather dull one, and that I hoped
it was not an unfavorable omen. 'No,' he replied, 'it is a very interesting number; it is
the smallest number expressible as the sum of two cubes in two different ways.'" (Hardy
1921)

note that in the flatten example the new interleave procedure, with its delayed argument, requires a special version of accumulate that takes this delay into account. In general, creating separate classes of procedures forces us to create separate classes of higher-order procedures as well.[46]

One way to avoid the need for two different classes of procedures is to make all procedures take delayed arguments. We could adopt a model of evaluation in which all arguments to procedures are automatically delayed and arguments are forced only when they are actually needed (for example, when they are required by a primitive operation). This would transform our language to use normal-order evaluation, which we first described when we introduced the substitution model for evaluation in section 1.1.5. Converting to normal-order evaluation provides a uniform and elegant way to simplify the use of delayed evaluation, and this would be a natural strategy to adopt if we were concerned only with stream processing. In section 4.2.1, after we have studied the evaluator, we will see how to transform our language in just this way. Unfortunately, including delays in procedure calls wreaks havoc with our ability to design programs that depend on the order of events, such as programs that use assignment, mutate data, or perform input or output. Even the single delay in cons-stream can cause great confusion, as illustrated by the exercises at the end of section 3.4.3. As far as anyone knows, mutability and delayed evaluation do not mix well in programming languages, and devising ways to deal with both of these at once is an active area of research.

3.4.6 Using Streams to Model Local State

Let us now return to the issues of objects and state that were raised at the beginning of this chapter and examine them in a new light. We introduced assignment statements and mutable objects in an attempt to improve the modularity of programs that model systems with local state. We constructed computational objects with local state variables and used assign-

---

46 This is a small reflection, in Lisp, of the difficulties that conventional strongly typed languages such as Pascal have in coping with higher-order procedures. In such languages, the programmer must specify the data types of the arguments and the result of each procedure: number, logical value, sequence, and so on. Consequently, we could not express an abstraction such as "accumulate all the elements in a sequence using a given combiner operation" by a single higher-order procedure such as accumulate. Rather, we would need a different accumulation procedure for each different combination of argument and result data types that might be specified for a combiner. Maintaining a practical notion of "data type" in the presence of higher-order procedures raises many difficult issues. One promising approach is illustrated by the language ML (Gordon 1979), whose "polymorphic data types" include templates for higher-order transformations between data types. Moreover, data types for most procedures in ML are never explicitly declared by the programmer. Instead, ML includes a *type-inferencing* mechanism that uses information in the environment to deduce the data types for newly defined procedures.

ment to modify these variables. We modeled the temporal behavior of the objects in the world by the temporal behavior of the corresponding computational objects. Now we have seen that streams provide an alternative way to model objects with local state. We can model a changing quantity, such as the local state of some object, using a stream that represents the time history of successive states. In essence, we represent time explicitly, using streams, so that we decouple time in our simulated world from the sequence of events that take place during evaluation. Indeed, because of the presence of delay there may be little relation between simulated time in the model and the order of events during the evaluation.

In order to contrast these two approaches to modeling, let us reconsider the implementation of a "withdrawal processor" that monitors the balance in a bank account. In section 3.1.2 we implemented a simplified version of such a processor:

```
(define (make-simplified-withdraw balance)
  (lambda (amount)
    (set! balance (- balance amount))
    balance))
```

Calls to make-simplified-withdraw produce computational objects, each with a local state variable balance that is decremented by each successive call to the object. The object takes an amount as an argument and returns the new balance. We can imagine the user of a bank account typing successive inputs to such an object and watching the sequence of returned values shown on a display screen.

Alternatively, we can model a withdrawal processor as a procedure that takes as input a balance and a stream of amounts to withdraw and produces the stream of successive balances in the account:

```
(define (stream-withdraw balance amount-stream)
  (cons-stream balance
               (stream-withdraw (- balance
                                   (head amount-stream))
                                (tail amount-stream))))
```

Stream-withdraw is a well-defined mathematical function whose output is fully determined by its input. Suppose, however, that the input amount-stream is the stream of successive values typed by the user and that the resulting stream of balances is displayed. Then, from the perspective of the user who is typing values and watching results, the stream process has the same behavior as the object created by make-simplified-withdraw. However, with the stream version, there is no assignment, no local state variable, and consequently none of the theoretical difficulties that we encountered in section 3.1.2. Yet the system has state![47]

Exercise 3.63

Extend the `stream-withdraw` procedure to a more complete model for bank accounts, thus producing a stream analog of the `make-account` procedure of section 3.1.1.

Monte Carlo simulation revisited

As we saw in section 3.1.3, one of the major benefits of introducing assignment is that we can increase the modularity of our systems by encapsulating, or "hiding," parts of the state of a large system within local variables. Stream models can provide an equivalent modularity without the use of assignment. As an illustration, we can reimplement the Monte Carlo estimation of π, which we examined in section 3.1.3, from a stream-processing point of view.

The key modularity issue was that we wished to hide the internal state of a random-number generator from programs that used random numbers. We began with a function `rand-update`, whose successive values furnished our supply of random numbers, and used this to produce a random-number generator:

```
(define rand
  (let ((x random-init))
    (lambda ()
      (set! x (rand-update x))
      x)))
```

In the stream formulation there is no random-number generator *per se,* just a stream of random numbers produced by successive calls to `rand-update`:

```
(define random-numbers
  (cons-stream random-init
               (map rand-update random-numbers)))
```

---

47 This is really remarkable. Even though `stream-withdraw` is a well-defined mathematical function whose behavior does not change, the user's perception here is that he is interacting with a system that has a changing state. One way to resolve this paradox is to realize that it is the user's temporal existence that imposes state on the system. For example, when we observe a moving particle, we say that the position (state) of the particle is changing. However, from the perspective of the particle's worldline in space-time there is no change involved. Similarly, if the user could step back from the interaction and think in terms of streams of balances rather than individual transactions, he could regard the system as stateless.

We use this to construct the stream of outcomes of the Cesaro experiment performed on consecutive pairs in the `random-numbers` stream:

```
(define cesaro-stream
  (map-successive-pairs (lambda (r1 r2) (= (gcd r1 r2) 1))
                        random-numbers))

(define (map-successive-pairs f s)
  (cons-stream (f (head s) (head (tail s)))
               (map-successive-pairs f (tail (tail s)))))
```

The `cesaro-stream` is now fed to a `monte-carlo` procedure, which produces a stream of estimates of probabilities. The results are then converted into a stream of estimates of π. This version of the program doesn't need a parameter telling how many trials to perform. Better estimates of π (from performing more experiments) are obtained by looking farther into the `pi` stream:

```
(define (monte-carlo experiment-stream nt nf)
  (define (next nt nf)
    (cons-stream (/ nt (+ nt nf))
                 (monte-carlo (tail experiment-stream)
                              nt
                              nf)))
  (if (head experiment-stream)
      (next (+ nt 1) nf)
      (next nt (+ nf 1))))

(define pi
  (map (lambda (p) (sqrt (/ 6 p)))
       (monte-carlo cesaro-stream 0 0)))
```

There is considerable modularity in this approach, because we still can formulate a general `monte-carlo` procedure that can deal with arbitrary experiments. Yet there is no assignment or local state.

Exercise 3.64

Exercise 3.8 discussed generalizing the random-number generator to allow one to reset the random-number sequence so as to produce repeatable sequences of "random" numbers. Produce a stream formulation of this same generator that operates on an input stream of requests to generate a new random number or to reset the sequence to a specified value and that produces the desired stream of random numbers.

Exercise 3.65

Redo exercise 3.7 on Monte Carlo integration in terms of streams. The stream version of `estimate-integral` will not have an argument telling how many trials to perform. Instead, it will produce a stream of estimates based on successively more trials.

Streams versus objects

Streams with delayed evaluation can be a powerful modeling tool, providing many of the benefits of local state and assignment. Moreover, they avoid the theoretical tangles that, as we saw in section 3.1.2, must accompany the introduction of assignment into a programming language. In essence, assignment complicates reasoning about programs because it introduces time boundaries into processes. The value of a variable is changed by an assignment at the moment of the assignment, which makes uses of that variable before the assignment different from uses of that variable after the assignment.

The possibility of avoiding these problems has led many current researchers to propose so-called *functional programming languages*, which do not include any provision for assignment or mutable data. In such a language, all procedures are well-defined mathematical functions of their arguments, whose behavior does not change. The functional approach is extremely attractive when we turn to the design of programming languages for multiprocessing computers, in which many computations are carried out in parallel. The absence of assignment means that the programmer need not be concerned with synchronization errors caused by values being updated in the wrong order; the possibility of such errors poses a serious problem in the implementation of traditional programs on multiprocessing systems. Because future computers are likely to be highly parallel, it seems certain that functional methods will play an increasingly important role in the future development of programming languages and techniques.[48]

On the other hand, it is an open question whether all need for assignment can be reasonably bypassed using delayed evaluation. One particularly troublesome area arises when we wish to design interactive systems, especially ones that model interactions between independent entities. For instance, consider implementing a banking system that permits joint bank accounts. In a conventional system using assignment and objects, we would model the fact that Peter and Paul share an account by having both Peter

---

[48] John Backus, the inventor of Fortran, gave high visibility to the functional programming movement when he was awarded the ACM Turing award in 1978. His acceptance speech (Backus 1978) strongly advocated the functional approach. A good overview of functional programming is given in Henderson 1980 and in Darlington, Henderson, and Turner 1982.

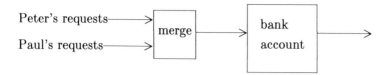

Figure 3.37
A joint bank account, modeled by merging two streams of transaction requests.

and Paul send their transaction requests to the same bank-account object, as we saw in section 3.1.2. From the stream point of view, where there are no "objects" *per se*, we have already indicated (exercise 3.63) that a bank account can be modeled as a process that operates on a stream of transaction requests to produce a stream of responses. Accordingly, we could model the fact that Peter and Paul have a joint bank account by merging Peter's stream of transaction requests with Paul's stream of requests and feeding the result to the bank-account stream process, as shown in figure 3.37.

The trouble with this formulation is in the notion of *merge*. It will not do to merge the two streams by simply taking alternately one request from Peter and one request from Paul. Suppose Paul accesses the account only very rarely. We could hardly force Peter to wait for Paul to access the account before he could issue a second transaction. In order to deal with this problem, most researchers agree that it is necessary to supplement the purely functional basis of the language with some new constructs. However, we must be careful not to add a construct powerful enough to enable us to implement assignment, thus reintroducing the same problems that the functional style was meant to eliminate. One proposed construct is known as *fair merge* (or *nondeterministic merge*). Roughly, the fair merge of two streams will wait for an input to appear on either stream and produce the received value, alternating between the two streams in some fair way whenever both of them produce inputs. Even this informal description of fair merge centrally involves the notion of time (through waiting), which is precisely what we wish to avoid by adopting the functional approach.[49]

49 A more formal description of fair merge requires that we consider it to be a relation rather than a function. That is to say, if we consider only the elements of the input streams typed by Peter and Paul (with no regard for timing) then there are many possible output streams that could be the fair merge of the two input streams. Thus, to formalize the idea of fair merge requires that we either introduce time or deal with "functions" whose outputs are not fully determined by their inputs. Moreover, even fair merge does not solve all our problems. Although fair merge can model shared bank accounts, it is awkward to use in more complex resource-allocation situations. Consequently, researchers on functional programming have proposed more powerful constructs to deal with these situations. One example is the *resource manager* introduced by Arvind and Brock (1983).

Another difficulty with the stream formulation is that it is inherently biased toward models whose components have "inputs" and "outputs." For example, one could use streams as the basis for an elegant reformulation of the digital-circuit simulator of section 3.3.4, in which the elementary gates are viewed as processes on streams of zeros and ones. On the other hand, it is unclear how to give a natural stream formulation of the constraint-propagation system of section 3.3.5, where in maintaining a constraint such as $A + B = C$ there is no fixed element that can be viewed as the output determined by the other two values; $A + B = C$ is a relation, not a function. Systems that are naturally described in terms of clusters of communicating entities are often inherently relational rather than functional, and forcing these into a signal-flow mold can lead to distortion in the model.[50] Perhaps the best that one can say at present is that time-varying objects and time-invariant streams both lead to powerful modeling disciplines. The choice between them is far from clear, and the search for a uniform approach that combines the benefits of both of these perspectives is a central concern of research in programming methodology.

50 Exercise 3.58 gives an example of such a distortion. If we compare the RLC circuit shown in figure 3.34 with the signal-flow diagram shown in figure 3.35, we see that by moving to the state-equation formulation we have lost the physical structure of the system as a series combination of three devices. The device parameters have been spread over a number of signal-processing modules, each with its own modular organization, and this does not reflect the physical interconnection.

4

METALINGUISTIC ABSTRACTION

...It's in words that the magic is—Abracadabra,
Open Sesame, and the rest—but the magic words in
one story aren't magical in the next. The real magic
is to understand which words work, and when, and
for what; the trick is to learn the trick.
...And those words are made from the letters of our
alphabet: a couple-dozen squiggles we can draw with
the pen. This is the key! And the treasure, too, if we
can only get our hands on it! It's as if—as if the key
to the treasure *is* the treasure!

John Barth, *Chimera*

In our study of program design, we have seen that expert programmers
control the complexity of their designs by using the same general techniques
used by designers of all complex systems. They combine primitive elements
to form compound objects, they abstract compound objects to form higher-
level building blocks, and they preserve modularity by adopting appropriate
large-scale views of system structure. In illustrating these techniques, we
have used Lisp as a language for describing processes and for constructing
computational data objects and processes to model complex phenomena in
the real world. However, as we confront increasingly complex problems,
we will find that Lisp, or indeed any fixed programming language, is not
sufficient for our needs. We must constantly turn to new languages in
order to express our ideas more effectively. Establishing new languages is a
powerful strategy for controlling complexity in engineering design; we can
often enhance our ability to deal with a complex problem by adopting a
new language that enables us to describe (and hence to think about) the
problem in a different way, using primitives, means of combination, and
means of abstraction that are particularly well suited to the problem at
hand.

For example, electrical engineers use many different languages for describing circuits. Two of these are the language of electrical *networks* and the
language of electrical *systems*. The network language emphasizes the physical modeling of devices in terms of discrete electrical elements. The primitive objects of the network language are primitive electrical components

such as resistors, capacitors, inductors, and transistors, which are characterized in terms of physical variables called voltage and current. When describing circuits in the network language, the engineer is concerned with the physical characteristics of a design. In contrast, the primitive objects of the system language are signal-processing modules such as filters and amplifiers. Only the functional behavior of the modules is relevant, and signals are manipulated without concern for their physical realization as voltages and currents. The system language is erected on the network language, in the sense that the elements of signal-processing systems are constructed from electrical networks. Here, however, the concerns are with the large-scale organization of electrical devices to solve a given application problem; the physical feasibility of the parts is assumed.

Programming is similarly endowed with a multitude of languages. There are physical languages, such as the machine languages for particular computers. These languages are concerned with the representation of data and control in terms of individual bits of storage and primitive machine instructions. The machine-language programmer is concerned with using the given hardware to erect systems and utilities for the efficient implementation of resource-limited computations. High-level languages are erected on a machine-language substrate in much the same way as the electrical-systems language is erected on a substrate of electrical networks. High-level languages hide concerns about the representation of data as collections of bits and the representation of programs as sequences of primitive instructions. These languages have means of combination and abstraction, such as procedure definition, that are appropriate to the larger-scale organization of systems.

Metalinguistic abstraction—the establishment of new descriptive languages—plays an important role in all branches of engineering design. It is particularly important to computer programming, because in programming not only can we formulate new languages but we can also implement these languages by constructing evaluators. An *evaluator* (or interpreter) for a programming language is a procedure that, when applied to an expression of the language, performs the actions required to evaluate that expression. Thus, given a language that a computer knows how to evaluate, if we can implement in that language an evaluator for a second language, then our computer will also be able to evaluate expressions of the latter language. This method of implementing a language is known as constructing an *embedded language.*

It is not too much of a distortion to regard almost any program as the evaluator for some language. For instance, the polynomial manipulation system of section 2.4.3 embodies the rules of polynomial arithmetic and implements them in terms of operations on list-structured data. If we augment this system with procedures to read and print polynomial expressions, we have the core of a special-purpose language for dealing with problems in symbolic mathematics. The digital logic simulator of section 3.3.4 and the constraint propagator of section 3.3.5 are legitimate languages in their own right, each with its own primitives, means of combination, and means of abstraction. Seen from this perspective, the technology for coping with large-scale computer systems merges with the technology for building new computer languages, and computer science itself becomes no more (and no less) than the discipline of constructing appropriate descriptive languages.

We now embark on a tour of the technology by which languages are established in terms of other languages. In this chapter we shall use Lisp as a base, implementing evaluators as Lisp procedures. Lisp is particularly well suited to this task, because of its ability to represent and manipulate symbolic expressions. We will take the first step in understanding how languages are implemented by building an evaluator for Lisp itself. The language implemented by our evaluator will be a subset of the Scheme dialect of Lisp that we use in this book. Although the evaluator described in this chapter is written for a particular dialect of Lisp, it contains the essential structure of an evaluator for any expression-oriented language designed for writing programs for a sequential machine. (In fact, most language processors contain, deep within them, a little "Lisp" evaluator.) The evaluator has been simplified for the purposes of illustration and discussion, and a number of features have been left out that would be important to include in a production-quality Lisp system.[1] Nevertheless, this simple evaluator is adequate to execute most of the programs in this book.

Our evaluator for Lisp will be implemented as a Lisp program. It may seem circular to think about evaluating Lisp programs using an evaluator that is itself implemented in Lisp. However, evaluation is a process, so it is appropriate to describe the evaluation process using Lisp, which, after all, is our tool for describing processes.[2] An evaluator that is written in the same language that it evaluates is said to be *metacircular*.

An important advantage of formulating the evaluator as a Lisp program is that we can consider alternative evaluation rules by describing these as

[1] The most important of these are mechanisms for handling errors and supporting debugging.

[2] Even so, there will remain important aspects of the evaluation process that are not elucidated by our evaluator. The most important of these are the detailed mechanisms by which procedures call other procedures and return values to their callers. We will address these issues in chapter 5, where we take a closer look at the evaluation process by implementing the metacircular evaluator as a very simple machine.

modifications to the evaluator program. We will use this technique in section 4.2 to explore variations of Lisp, including a language in which variables are dynamically bound rather than lexically scoped and a language that uses normal-order rather than applicative-order evaluation. Both of these can be implemented by making modest changes to the original Scheme evaluator. In section 4.3 we show how to use explicit evaluation to organize large programs into separate packages. The final sections of this chapter present an extended example of metalinguistic abstraction. We implement a logic programming language, which allows a programmer to retrieve information from data bases by formulating queries and rules of inference. Even though the query language is strikingly different from Lisp (or any other procedural language), the evaluator for the query language contains many of the central elements found in a Lisp evaluator.

4.1 The Metacircular Evaluator

Our evaluator will embody the environment model of evaluation described in section 3.2. Recall that the model has two basic parts:

1. To evaluate a compound expression (other than a special form), evaluate the subexpressions and then apply the value of the operator subexpression to the values of the operand subexpressions.

2. To apply a compound procedure to a set of arguments, evaluate the body of the procedure in a new environment. To construct this environment, extend the environment part of the procedure object by a frame in which the formal parameters of the procedure are bound to the actual arguments to which the procedure is to be applied.

These two rules describe the essence of the evaluation process, a basic cycle in which expressions to be evaluated in environments are reduced to procedures to be applied to arguments, which in turn are reduced to new expressions to be evaluated in new environments, and so on, until expressions are reduced to symbols, whose values are looked up in the environment, and to primitive procedures, which are applied directly. This evaluation cycle will be embodied by the interplay between the two critical procedures in the evaluator, `eval` and `apply`, which are described in section 4.1.1.

To handle primitive procedures, we assume that we have available the following procedures:

(`apply-primitive-procedure` ⟨*procedure*⟩ ⟨*args*⟩) returns the result of applying the given primitive procedure to the argument values in the list ⟨*args*⟩.

(`primitive-procedure?` ⟨*procedure*⟩) returns true or false, telling whether the procedure is a primitive procedure.

These mechanisms for handling primitives are described in section 4.1.4.[3]

The evaluator also needs operations for manipulating environments. In adherence to the discipline of data abstraction, our evaluator will operate on environments without making any commitment to how environments are represented. As explained in section 3.2, an environment is a sequence of frames, where each frame is a table of bindings that associate variables with their corresponding values. We assume that we have available the following operations for manipulating environments:

(`lookup-variable-value` ⟨*variable*⟩ ⟨*env*⟩) returns the value bound to the symbol ⟨*variable*⟩ in the environment ⟨*env*⟩, or signals an error if the variable is unbound.

(`extend-environment` ⟨*variables*⟩ ⟨*values*⟩ ⟨*base-env*⟩) returns a new environment, consisting of a frame in which the symbols in the list ⟨*variables*⟩ are bound to the corresponding elements in the list ⟨*values*⟩, where the enclosing environment is the specified environment ⟨*base-env*⟩.

(`define-variable!` ⟨*variable*⟩ ⟨*value*⟩ ⟨*env*⟩) adds to the first frame in the environment ⟨*env*⟩ a new binding that associates the specified variable with the specified value.

(`set-variable-value!` ⟨*variable*⟩ ⟨*value*⟩ ⟨*env*⟩) changes the binding of the given variable in the environment ⟨*env*⟩ so that the variable is now bound to the specified value, or signals an error if the variable is unbound.

The implementation of these procedures is given in section 4.1.3.

---

3 If we grant ourselves the ability to apply primitives, then what remains for us to implement in the evaluator? The job of the evaluator is not so much to specify the primitives of the language as to provide the connective tissue—the means of combination and the means of abstraction—that binds a collection of primitives to form a language. Specifically:

• The evaluator enables us to deal with nested expressions. For example, although the simple mechanism of `apply-primitive-procedure` would suffice for evaluating the expression (+ 1 6), it is not able to handle (+ 1 (* 2 3)), because, as far as the primitive procedure + is concerned, its arguments must be numbers, and it would choke if we passed it the expression (* 2 3) as an argument. One important role of the evaluator is to choreograph the composition of functions so that (* 2 3) is reduced to 6 before being passed as an argument to +.

• The evaluator allows us to use variables. For example, the primitive procedure + has no way to deal with expressions such as (+ x 1). We need an evaluator to keep track of variables and replace them with their values before invoking the primitive procedures.

• The evaluator allows us to define compound procedures. This involves keeping track of procedure definitions, knowing how to use these definitions in evaluating expressions, and providing a mechanism that enables procedures to accept arguments.

• The evaluator provides the special forms, which must be evaluated differently from procedure calls.

Finally, we need a representation for the expressions being evaluated. Again, we will use data abstraction to make the evaluator independent of the representation. Implementation of expressions will be described in section 4.1.2.

4.1.1 The Core of the Evaluator

The evaluation process can be described as the interplay between two procedures: `eval` and `apply`.

Eval

`Eval` takes as arguments an expression and an environment. It classifies the expression and directs its evaluation. `Eval` is structured as a case analysis of the syntactic type of the expression to be evaluated. In order to keep the procedure general, we express the determination of the type of an expression abstractly, making no commitment to any particular representation for the various types of expressions. Each type of expression has a predicate that tests for it and an abstract means for selecting its parts. This *abstract syntax* makes it easy to see how we might use a similar evaluator to interpret another language.

`Eval` handles the various types of expressions as follows.

Primitive expressions:

For self-evaluating expressions, such as numbers, `eval` returns the expression itself.

`Eval` must look up variables in the environment to find their values.

Special forms:

For quoted expressions, `eval` returns the expression that was quoted.

An assignment to (or a definition of) a variable must recursively call `eval` to compute the new value to be associated with the variable. The environment must be modified to change (or create) the binding of the variable.

A `lambda` expression must be transformed into an applicable procedure by attaching an environment to the specified procedure text.

A conditional expression requires special processing of its clauses to evaluate the consequent associated with the first predicate that evaluates to true.

Other combinations:

For an ordinary procedure application, `eval` must recursively evaluate the operator part and the operands of the application. The resulting procedure and arguments are passed to `apply`, which handles the actual procedure application.

Here is the definition of eval:

```
(define (eval exp env)
  (cond ((self-evaluating? exp) exp)
        ((quoted? exp) (text-of-quotation exp))
        ((variable? exp) (lookup-variable-value exp env))
        ((definition? exp) (eval-definition exp env))
        ((assignment? exp) (eval-assignment exp env))
        ((lambda? exp) (make-procedure exp env))
        ((conditional? exp) (eval-cond (clauses exp) env))
        ((application? exp)
         (apply (eval (operator exp) env)
                (list-of-values (operands exp) env)))
        (else (error "Unknown expression type -- EVAL" exp))))
```

For clarity, eval has been implemented as a case analysis using cond. The disadvantage of this is that our procedure handles only a few distinguishable types of expressions, and no new ones can be defined without editing the definition of eval. In most Lisp implementations, dispatching on the type of an expression is done in a data-directed style. This allows a user to add new types of expressions that eval can distinguish, without modifying the definition of eval itself.

Exercise 4.1

Rewrite eval so that the dispatch is done in data-directed style. You will have to initialize an appropriate table to hold the dispatch procedures. Compare this with the data-directed differentiation procedure of exercise 2.45.

Apply

Apply takes two inputs, a procedure and a list of arguments to which the procedure is to be applied. Apply classifies procedures into two kinds and directs their application. Primitive procedures are applied directly by apply-primitive-procedure. Compound procedures are applied by sequentially evaluating the expressions that make up the body of the procedure (using an auxiliary procedure eval-sequence, which calls eval) in an environment constructed by extending the base environment carried by the procedure to include a frame that binds the parameters of the procedure to the arguments to which the procedure is to be applied. Here is the definition of apply:

```
(define (apply procedure arguments)
  (cond ((primitive-procedure? procedure)
         (apply-primitive-procedure procedure arguments))
        ((compound-procedure? procedure)
         (eval-sequence (procedure-body procedure)
                        (extend-environment
                         (parameters procedure)
                         arguments
                         (procedure-environment procedure))))
        (else
         (error "Unknown procedure type -- APPLY" procedure))))
```

Arguments to procedures

When eval processes a procedure application, it uses list-of-values to produce the list of arguments to which the procedure is to be applied. List-of-values takes as an argument the operands of the combination. It evaluates each operand and returns the list of corresponding values:

```
(define (list-of-values exps env)
  (cond ((no-operands? exps) '())
        (else (cons (eval (first-operand exps) env)
                    (list-of-values (rest-operands exps)
                                    env)))))
```

Conditionals

Eval-cond scans the list of clauses of a conditional expression, evaluating the predicate part of each clause to see if it is true. If the predicate part is true, or if an else clause is found, the consequent part of that clause (extracted by the syntax procedure actions) is evaluated. Otherwise, the scan continues. Running out of clauses causes the cond to return nil.

```
(define (eval-cond clist env)
  (cond ((no-clauses? clist) nil)
        ((else-clause? (first-clause clist))
         (eval-sequence (actions (first-clause clist)) env))
        ((true? (eval (predicate (first-clause clist)) env))
         (eval-sequence (actions (first-clause clist)) env))
        (else (eval-cond (rest-clauses clist) env))))
```

Sequences

Eval-sequence is used by apply to evaluate the sequence of expressions in a procedure body and by eval-cond to evaluate the sequence of consequent expressions in a cond clause. It takes as arguments a sequence of expressions and an environment, and evaluates the expressions in the order in which they occur. The value returned is the value of the final expression.

```
(define (eval-sequence exps env)
  (cond ((last-exp? exps) (eval (first-exp exps) env))
        (else (eval (first-exp exps) env)
              (eval-sequence (rest-exps exps) env))))
```

Assignments and definitions

The following procedure handles assignments to variables. It calls eval to find the value to be assigned and transmits the variable and the resulting value to set-variable-value! to be installed in the designated environment.[4]

```
(define (eval-assignment exp env)
  (let ((new-value (eval (assignment-value exp) env)))
    (set-variable-value! (assignment-variable exp)
                         new-value
                         env)
    new-value))
```

Definitions of variables are handled in a similar manner.[5] The specification of define requires that the procedure return as its value the symbol being defined.

```
(define (eval-definition exp env)
  (define-variable! (definition-variable exp)
                    (eval (definition-value exp) env)
                    env)
  (definition-variable exp))
```

4.1.2 Representing Expressions

The evaluator is reminiscent of the symbolic differentiation program discussed in section 2.2.4. Both programs operate on symbolic expressions.

---

4 We have chosen here to make the assignment operator return as its value the new value being assigned, even though this is not stipulated by the Scheme dialect of Lisp, which considers the result of a set! operation to be unspecified.

5 This implementation of define ignores a subtle issue in the handling of internal definitions, although it works correctly in most cases. We will see what the problem is and how to solve it in section 5.2.5.

In both programs, the result of operating on a compound expression is determined by operating recursively on the pieces of the expression and combining the results in a way that depends on the type of the expression. In both programs we used data abstraction to decouple the general rules of operation from the details of how expressions are represented. In the differentiation program this meant that the same differentiation procedure could deal with algebraic expressions in prefix form, in infix form, or in some other form. For the evaluator, this means that the syntax of the language being evaluated is determined solely by the procedures that classify and extract pieces of expressions.

- The only self-evaluating items are numbers:[6]

```
(define (self-evaluating? exp) (number? exp))
```

- Quotations are expressions of the form (quote ⟨text-of-quotation⟩):[7]

```
(define (quoted? exp)
  (if (atom? exp)
      nil
      (eq? (car exp) 'quote)))
```

```
(define (text-of-quotation exp) (cadr exp))
```

- Variables are represented by symbols:

```
(define (variable? exp) (symbol? exp))
```

- Assignments are expressions of the form (set! ⟨variable⟩ ⟨value⟩):

```
(define (assignment? exp)
  (if (atom? exp)
      nil
      (eq? (car exp) 'set!)))
```

```
(define (assignment-variable exp) (cadr exp))
```

```
(define (assignment-value exp) (caddr exp))
```

6 Many Lisp implementations also treat the symbols nil and t as self-evaluating. In Scheme, nil and t are ordinary symbols that are initially bound in the global environment to appropriate values.

7 As mentioned in section 2.2.3, this expanded quote form is the form in which the evaluator sees quoted expressions, even if these expressions are typed with the quotation mark. For example, the expression 'a would be seen by the evaluator as (quote a). See exercise 2.30.

- Definitions are expressions of the form

(define ⟨*variable*⟩ ⟨*value*⟩)

or of the form

(define (⟨*variable*⟩ ⟨*parameter*₁⟩ ... ⟨*parameter*ₙ⟩)
  ⟨*body*⟩)

The latter form (standard procedure definition) is syntactic sugar for

(define ⟨*variable*⟩
  (lambda (⟨*parameter*₁⟩ ... ⟨*parameter*ₙ⟩)
    ⟨*body*⟩)))

The corresponding syntax procedures are the following:

```
(define (definition? exp)
  (if (atom? exp)
      nil
      (eq? (car exp) 'define)))

(define (definition-variable exp)
  (if (variable? (cadr exp))
      (cadr exp)
      (caadr exp)))

(define (definition-value exp)
  (if (variable? (cadr exp))
      (caddr exp)
      (cons 'lambda
            (cons (cdadr exp)        ;formal parameters
                  (cddr exp)))))     ;body
```

- Lambda expressions are lists that begin with the symbol lambda:

```
(define (lambda? exp)
  (if (atom? exp)
      nil
      (eq? (car exp) 'lambda)))
```

- Conditionals begin with cond and have a list of predicate-action clauses. A predicate is considered to be true if it is non-nil. A clause is an else clause if its predicate is the symbol else.

```
(define (conditional? exp)
  (if (atom? exp)
      nil
      (eq? (car exp) 'cond)))

(define (clauses exp) (cdr exp))

(define (no-clauses? clauses) (null? clauses))

(define (first-clause clauses) (car clauses))

(define (rest-clauses clauses) (cdr clauses))

(define (predicate clause) (car clause))

(define (actions clause) (cdr clause))

(define (true? x) (not (null? x)))

(define (else-clause? clause)
  (eq? (predicate clause) 'else))
```

• A sequence of expressions is a list of expressions, given in the order in which they are to be evaluated:

```
(define (last-exp? seq) (null? (cdr seq)))

(define (first-exp seq) (car seq))

(define (rest-exps seq) (cdr seq))
```

• A procedure application is any nonatomic expression that is not one of the above expression types. The car of the expression is the operator, and the cdr is the list of operands:

```
(define (application? exp) (not (atom? exp)))

(define (operator app) (car app))

(define (operands app) (cdr app))
```

```
(define (no-operands? args) (null? args))

(define (first-operand args) (car args))

(define (rest-operands args) (cdr args))
```

• Applicable procedures are constructed from lambda expressions and environments with the constructor make-procedure :

```
(define (make-procedure lambda-exp env)
  (list 'procedure lambda-exp env))

(define (compound-procedure? proc)
  (if (atom? proc)
      nil
      (eq? (car proc) 'procedure)))
```

Since a lambda expression has the syntax

(lambda $\langle parameters \rangle$ $\langle exp_1 \rangle \ldots \langle exp_n \rangle$)

the result of make-procedure is

(procedure (lambda $\langle parameters \rangle$ $\langle exp_1 \rangle \ldots \langle exp_n \rangle$) $\langle env \rangle$)

Thus, the selectors for the parts of a procedure are

```
(define (parameters proc) (cadr (cadr proc)))

(define (procedure-body proc) (cddr (cadr proc)))

(define (procedure-environment proc) (caddr proc))
```

Exercise 4.2

The interpreter described above supports cond but not if. Modify the interpreter to add if to the language. Following the style used in the rest of the implementation, you should define selectors that return the various parts of an if expression, and a procedure eval-if that is analogous to eval-cond.

Exercise 4.3

The let expression is simply syntactic sugar, because

(let $((\langle var_1 \rangle \ \langle exp_1 \rangle) \ldots (\langle var_n \rangle \ \langle exp_n \rangle))$
  $\langle body \rangle$)

is equivalent to

```
((lambda (⟨var₁⟩ ... ⟨varₙ⟩)
   ⟨body⟩)
 ⟨exp₁⟩
   ⋮
 ⟨expₙ⟩)
```

Modify the evaluator to recognize and correctly handle let expressions.

Exercise 4.4

By using data abstraction, we were able to write an eval procedure that is independent of the particular syntax of the language to be evaluated. To illustrate this, design and implement a new syntax by modifying the procedures in this section.

4.1.3 Operations on Environments

An environment is a sequence of frames, each of which is a table of bindings that associate variables with values. The operations on environments that are required by the evaluator can be implemented in terms of operations on frames and bindings. We first present these operations abstractly, assuming that there are chosen representations for environments, frames, and bindings.

A variable in an environment is looked up by finding the binding for the variable in the environment and returning the value part of the binding. An error is signaled if no binding is found.

```
(define (lookup-variable-value var env)
  (let ((b (binding-in-env var env)))
    (if (found-binding? b)
        (binding-value b)
        (error "Unbound variable" var))))
```

The following procedure returns the binding of a variable in a specified environment. It searches each frame in succession until it finds a frame in which the variable has a binding.

```
(define (binding-in-env var env)
  (if (no-more-frames? env)
      no-binding
      (let ((b (binding-in-frame var (first-frame env))))
        (if (found-binding? b)
            b
            (binding-in-env var (rest-frames env))))))
```

To extend an environment by a new frame that associates variables with values, we construct a new frame of bindings and adjoin this frame to the environment:

```
(define (extend-environment variables values base-env)
  (adjoin-frame (make-frame variables values) base-env))
```

To set a variable to a new value in a specified environment, we alter the value part of the binding, or else signal an error if the variable is unbound:

```
(define (set-variable-value! var val env)
  (let ((b (binding-in-env var env)))
    (if (found-binding? b)
        (set-binding-value! b val)
        (error "Unbound variable" var))))
```

To define a variable, we adjoin a new binding to the head of the first frame in the environment; if the variable is already bound in that frame, we assign it the new value:

```
(define (define-variable! var val env)
  (let ((b (binding-in-frame var (first-frame env))))
    (if (found-binding? b)
        (set-binding-value! b val)
        (set-first-frame!
         env
         (adjoin-binding (make-binding var val)
                         (first-frame env))))))
```

Representing environments

An environment can be represented as a list of frames. We have the following operations for selecting the first frame in a given environment, selecting all but the first frame, deciding when we have run out of frames, adjoining a frame to an environment, and changing the first frame of an environment:

```
(define (first-frame env) (car env))

(define (rest-frames env) (cdr env))

(define (no-more-frames? env) (null? env))

(define (adjoin-frame frame env) (cons frame env))

(define (set-first-frame! env new-frame)
  (set-car! env new-frame))
```

Representing frames

We can implement a frame as a list of bindings in which each binding associates a variable with a value. The following procedure takes a list of variables and a list of values as arguments and constructs the corresponding frame. It signals an error if the number of variables is not equal to the number of values.

```
(define (make-frame variables values)
  (cond ((and (null? variables) (null? values)) '())
        ((null? variables)
         (error "Too many values supplied" values))
        ((null? values)
         (error "Too few values supplied" variables))
        (else
         (cons (make-binding (car variables) (car values))
               (make-frame (cdr variables) (cdr values))))))
```

The following procedure adjoins a binding to an existing frame:

```
(define (adjoin-binding binding frame)
  (cons binding frame))
```

Since a frame is a list of bindings each containing a variable and a value, we can get the binding of a variable in a given frame by using the assq operation, which was described in section 3.3.3. We have modified it slightly to use our data abstraction.

```
(define (assq key bindings)
  (cond ((null? bindings) no-binding)
        ((eq? key (binding-variable (car bindings)))
         (car bindings))
        (else (assq key (cdr bindings)))))
```

```
(define (binding-in-frame var frame)
  (assq var frame))
```

Binding-in-frame returns nil if it doesn't find the binding.

```
(define (found-binding? b)
  (not (eq? b no-binding)))
```

```
(define no-binding nil)
```

Representing bindings

If we represent bindings as pairs, then we have the following procedures for constructing bindings, selecting the variable and value parts of a binding, and changing the value part of a binding:

```
(define (make-binding variable value)
  (cons variable value))

(define (binding-variable binding)
  (car binding))

(define (binding-value binding)
  (cdr binding))

(define (set-binding-value! binding value)
  (set-cdr! binding value))
```

Summary

We have represented an environment as a list of frames, a frame as a list of bindings, and a binding as a pair consisting of a variable and a value. This is only one of many plausible ways to represent environments. Since we used data abstraction to isolate the rest of the evaluator from the detailed choice of representation, we could change the environment representation if we wanted to. (See exercise 4.5.) In a production Lisp system, the speed of the evaluator's environment operations—especially that of variable lookup—has a major impact on the performance of the system. The representation described here, although conceptually simple, is not efficient and would not ordinarily be used in a production system.[8]

Exercise 4.5

Instead of representing a frame as a list of pairs, we can represent a frame as a pair of lists: a list of names and a list of corresponding values. This speeds up procedure application, since make-frame is now implemented simply as cons (if we ignore error checking). Rewrite the other environment operations to use this new representation.

Exercise 4.6

Lisp allows us to define new symbols by means of define, but provides no way to get rid of symbols. Implement for the interpreter an operation make-unbound that takes a symbol as argument and removes its binding from the environment given

[8] The representation described above is called *deep binding*. Its drawback is that the evaluator may have to search through many frames in order to find the binding for a given variable. One way to avoid this inefficiency is to make use of a strategy called *lexical addressing*, which will be discussed in section 5.3.

as an argument. This problem is not completely specified. (For example, should we remove only the binding in the first frame of the environment?) Complete the specification and justify any choices you make.

4.1.4 Running the Evaluator as a Lisp Program

We have used Lisp—our chosen language for describing processes—to describe the process by which Lisp expressions themselves are evaluated. We can, in fact, run the evaluator as a Lisp program. This will provide a working "Lisp within Lisp" that can serve as a framework for experimenting with alternative evaluation rules, as we shall do in section 4.2.

In order to run the evaluator, we need a mechanism for applying primitive procedures. There must be a binding for each primitive procedure name, so that when eval evaluates the operator of an application of a primitive it will find an object to pass to apply. We thus set up a global environment that associates unique objects with the names used to refer to the primitive procedures in the expressions we will be evaluating. The global environment also includes bindings for the symbols t and nil.

```
(define primitive-procedure-names
  '(car cdr cons ⟨names of more primitives⟩))

(define primitive-procedure-objects
  ⟨list of objects representing primitives⟩)

(define (setup-environment)
  (let ((initial-env
         (extend-environment primitive-procedure-names
                             primitive-procedure-objects
                             '())))
    (define-variable! 'nil nil initial-env)
    (define-variable! 't (not nil) initial-env)
    initial-env))

(define the-global-environment (setup-environment))
```

We must now decide what to use as the primitive-procedure-objects. It does not matter what these primitive objects are, so long as apply can identify and apply them by using the procedures primitive-procedure? and apply-primitive-procedure. In section 4.1.2 we represented compound procedures as lists beginning with the symbol procedure. Similarly, we can represent primitive procedures as lists beginning with the symbol primitive.

```
(define (primitive-procedure? proc)
  (if (atom? proc)
      nil
      (eq? (car proc) 'primitive)))
```

To apply a primitive procedure, we will check to see which primitive it is, then perform the operation using the underlying Lisp in which the evaluator is implemented. The list representing the primitive thus need contain only enough information to distinguish one primitive from another. The name of the primitive can serve this purpose.

```
(define (primitive-id proc) (cadr proc))
```

```
(define primitive-procedure-objects
  '((primitive car)
    (primitive cdr)
    (primitive cons)
    ⟨more primitives⟩))
```

```
(define (apply-primitive-procedure proc args)
  (let ((p (primitive-id proc)))
    (cond ((eq? p 'car) (car (car args)))
          ((eq? p 'cdr) (cdr (car args)))
          ((eq? p 'cons) (cons (car args) (cadr args)))
          ⟨more primitives⟩
          (else (error "Unknown primitive procedure" proc)))))
```

The args argument to this procedure is a list of arguments to which the primitive should be applied. Thus, to apply car we take the first item in the list—(car args)—and apply car.[9]

Exercise 4.7

The above implementation of apply-primitive-procedure and the construction of the initial global environment are very awkward, because they depend on coordinating the two lists primitive-procedure-objects and primitive-procedure-names and on keeping these consistent with the actual underlying operations used in apply-primitive-procedure. This will be a likely source of bugs if we begin to add new primitives to our language. Redesign the implementation so that all information is kept in a single, conveniently modified data

9 The interface shown here to the primitives of the underlying Lisp, although straightforward, is extremely cumbersome. Exercises 4.7 and 4.8 illustrate better ways to handle primitives.

structure, from which the global environment is constructed at system start-up time. Also, rewrite `apply-primitive-procedure` so that it will select the appropriate underlying operation by performing a data-directed dispatch based on information included in the data structure and thus will not have to be modified when new primitive procedures are added to the language.

Finally, we provide a driver loop that repeatedly prints a prompt, reads an input expression, evaluates this expression in the global environment, and prints the result.

```
(define (driver-loop)
  (newline)
  (princ "MC-EVAL==> ")
  (user-print (eval (read) the-global-environment))
  (driver-loop))
```

We have chosen the prompt `MC-EVAL==>` to be distinct from the ordinary system prompt, so that when we run the interpreter we can tell whether we are typing at our interpreter or typing at the underlying Lisp system. We use a special printing procedure here to avoid printing the environment part of a compound procedure, which may be a very long (or even circular) list.

```
(define (user-print object)
  (cond ((compound-procedure? object)
         (print (list 'compound-procedure
                      (parameters object)
                      (procedure-body object)
                      '[procedure-env])))
        (else (print object))))
```

Now we can run the evaluator:

```
==> (define the-global-environment (setup-environment))
the-global-environment

==> (driver-loop)

MC-EVAL==> (define (append x y)
             (cond ((null? x) y)
                   (else (cons (car x)
                               (append (cdr x) y)))))

append

MC-EVAL==> (append '(a b c) '(d e f))
(a b c d e f)
```

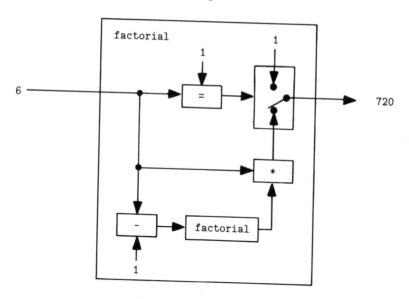

Figure 4.1
The factorial program, viewed as an abstract machine.

4.1.5 Treating Expressions as Programs

In thinking about a Lisp program that evaluates Lisp expressions, an analogy might be helpful. One operational view of the meaning of a program is that a program is a description of an abstract (perhaps infinitely large) machine. For example, consider the following program to compute factorials:

```
(define (factorial n)
  (if (= n 1)
      1
      (* (factorial (- n 1)) n)))
```

We may regard this program as the description of a machine containing parts that decrement, multiply, and test for equality, together with a two-position switch and another factorial machine. (The factorial machine is infinite because it contains another factorial machine within it.) Figure 4.1, a flow diagram for the factorial machine, shows how the parts are wired together.

In a similar way, we can regard the evaluator as a very special machine that takes as input a description of a machine. Given this input, the evaluator configures itself to emulate the machine described. For example, if we feed our evaluator the definition of factorial, as shown in figure 4.2, the evaluator will be able to compute factorials.

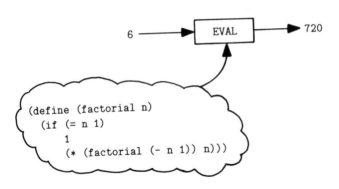

Figure 4.2
The evaluator emulating a factorial machine.

From this perspective, an evaluator is seen to be a universal machine. It mimics other machines when these are described as Lisp programs. This is quite striking. Try to imagine an evaluator for electrical circuits. This would be a circuit that takes as input a signal encoding a schematic diagram, that is, the plans for some other circuit, such as a filter. Given this input, the circuit evaluator would then behave like a filter with the same description. Such a universal electrical circuit mimic is almost unimaginably complex. It is remarkable that the program evaluator is a rather simple program.[10]

Another striking aspect of the evaluator is that it acts as a bridge between the data objects that are manipulated by our programming language and the programming language itself. Imagine that the evaluator program (implemented in Lisp) is running, and that a user is typing expressions to the evaluator and observing the results. From the perspective of the user, an input expression such as (* x x) is an expression in the programming language, which the evaluator is to execute. From the perspective of the evaluator, however, the expression is simply a list (in this case, a list of three symbols: *, x, and x) that is to be manipulated according to a well-defined set of rules.

That the user's programs are the evaluator's data need not be a source of confusion. In fact, it is sometimes convenient to ignore this distinction, and to give the user the ability to explicitly evaluate a data object as a Lisp expression, by making eval available for use in programs.

---

10 Some people find it counterintuitive that an evaluator, which is implemented by a relatively simple procedure, can emulate programs that are more complex than the evaluator itself. The existence of a universal evaluator machine is a deep and wonderful property of computation. *Recursion theory*, a branch of mathematical logic, is concerned with logical limits of computation. Douglas Hofstadter's beautiful book *Gödel, Escher, Bach* (1979) explores some of these ideas.

Lisp provides a primitive `eval` procedure that takes as arguments an expression and an environment and evaluates the expression relative to the environment. Thus,

```
(eval '(* 5 5) user-initial-environment)
```

and

```
(eval (cons '* (list 5 5)) user-initial-environment)
```

will both return 25.[11] In section 4.3 we will see how to use relative evaluation to divide large programs into packages that can be accessed separately.

In addition to `eval`, Lisp systems also provide `apply` as a user-accessible operation. For example,

```
(apply + (list 1 2 3 4))
```

would return 10. Apply is useful in implementing embedded languages, since it provides a uniform way to access the primitives of the underlying Lisp and to incorporate these into an embedded language, as illustrated in exercise 4.8.

Exercise 4.8

Redesign the interface between the metacircular evaluator and the underlying Lisp given in section 4.1.4 so that `apply-primitive-procedure` can simply apply the primitives directly, by calling `apply` from the underlying Lisp.[12] This can be done in such a way that arbitrary Lisp procedures can easily be installed as primitives in the embedded language. You should define a procedure called `install-primitive` that is used as follows:

```
(install-primitive 'square (lambda (x) (* x x)))
```

This installs a primitive called `square` in the embedded Lisp by binding `square` in the global environment to an object that consists of the procedure created (in the underlying Lisp) by the `lambda`, together with the tag that allows this

---

11 Warning: The `eval` primitive is not identical to the `eval` procedure we implemented in section 4.1, because it uses *actual* Scheme environments rather than the sample environment structures we built in section 4.1.3. These actual environments cannot be manipulated by the user as ordinary lists; they must be accessed via `eval` or other special operations. In the MIT implementation of Scheme, `user-initial-environment` is a symbol that is bound to the initial environment in which the user's input expressions are evaluated.

12 One technical problem you will encounter here is that the `apply` you must call is the primitive operator `apply`, while the metacircular evaluator defines its own procedure `apply` that will mask the definition of the primitive. One way around this is to rename the metacircular `apply` to avoid conflict with the name of the primitive operator. Another solution is to use

```
(define apply-in-underlying-scheme apply)
```

before defining the metacircular `apply`, to access the original version of `apply` under a different name.

to be recognized by `primitive-procedure?` as a primitive procedure. The real
primitives are installed in a similar way.

4.2 Variations on a Scheme

Now that we have an evaluator expressed as a Lisp program, we can
experiment with alternative choices in language design simply by modifying
the evaluator. Indeed, new languages are often invented by first writing
an evaluator that embeds the new language within an existing high-level
language. For example, if we wish to discuss some aspect of a proposed
modification to Lisp with another member of the Lisp community, we can
supply a metacircular interpreter that embodies the change. The recipient
can then experiment with the new interpreter and send back comments as
further modifications. Not only does the high-level implementation base
make it easier to test and debug the evaluator; in addition, the embedding
enables the designer to snarf[13]features from the underlying language, just
as our embedded Lisp interpreter uses primitives and control structure
from the underlying Lisp. Only later (if ever) need the designer go to the
trouble of building a complete implementation in a low-level language or
in hardware.

In this section we will explore some variations on Lisp. In the first
variation we will transform our language to use normal-order evaluation,
so that arguments to procedures are delayed automatically; in the second
variation we will look at a language in which variables are bound dynamically rather than statically. Both of these changes are accomplished with
minimal changes to our metacircular evaluator.

4.2.1 Normal-Order Evaluation

In ordinary Lisp, when a procedure is applied, all the arguments to the
procedure are evaluated. This discipline, as mentioned in section 1.1.5, is
known as *applicative-order evaluation*. We also described an alternative
evaluation rule, *normal-order evaluation*, that delays evaluation of procedure arguments until the last possible moment (e.g., until they are required
by a primitive operation). Consider the procedure

```
(define (try a b)
  (cond ((= a 0) 1)
        (else b)))
```

13 Snarf: "To grab, especially a large document or file for the purpose of using it either
with or without the owner's permission." Snarf down: "To snarf, sometimes with the
connotation of absorbing, processing, or understanding." (These definitions were snarfed
from Steele et al. 1983.)

Evaluating (try 0 (/ 1 0)) generates an error in Lisp. If Lisp used normal-order evaluation, there would be no error; (try 0 (/ 1 0)) would return 1, because the argument (/ 1 0) to try would never be evaluated.

In chapter 3 we introduced special constructs called force and delay. These provided a restricted kind of normal-order evaluation that was crucial to the implementation of streams described in section 3.4.3. If we were to transform our language to use normal-order evaluation, such constructs would be unnecessary; arguments to procedures would be delayed automatically and would be forced only when their values were actually needed. On the other hand, such widespread use of delayed evaluation would make it more difficult to deal with mutation and assignment, as illustrated by the exercises at the end of section 3.4.3.

Our explicit use of force and delay in chapter 3 was one way to obtain some of the benefits of normal-order evaluation within an overall applicative-order language. An alternative approach is to change the evaluator to include procedures with both kinds of argument evaluation. Procedure definitions will explicitly identify arguments that are to be delayed when the procedure is called; other arguments are to be evaluated as before.[14] For instance, we could define if in terms of cond as follows:

```
(define (if pred (delayed consequent) (delayed alternative))
  (cond (pred consequent)
        (else alternative)))
```

The consequent and alternative arguments are automatically delayed when passed to if and automatically forced when they are used.

It is not difficult to modify the interpreter so that the language admits such automatically delayed arguments. Here are the major steps:

• When eval evaluates an application, it must first determine which arguments must be evaluated and which must be delayed. Thus, the operator part of the application must be evaluated first, and the text of the resulting procedure must be consulted. (Note that the operator might itself have been delayed; if so, it must be forced to allow the text to be consulted.) The delayed arguments are not evaluated; instead, they are transformed into objects called *thunks*.[15] The thunk must contain the information required to produce the value of the argument when it is needed, as if it

14 This is somewhat like the approach taken in the language Algol 60, which includes both kinds of argument passing, known as *call-by-name* (corresponding to normal order) and *call-by-value* (corresponding to applicative order).

15 The word *thunk* derives from the implementation of call-by-name in Algol 60. We do not know the origin of this name, but we have heard that it refers to the sound made by data when pushed onto the stack in a running Algol system.

had been evaluated at the time of the application. Thus, the thunk must contain the argument expression and the environment in which the procedure application is being evaluated. A thunk is analogous to the procedure object produced by an explicit `delay`.

• A delayed argument is to be evaluated only when its value is really needed. For example, if x is delayed, then (+ x y) must determine the numerical value of x before trying to add it to the value of y. Most primitive procedures require that their arguments be fully evaluated. One way to do this is to modify `apply-primitive-procedure` so that it forces any thunks that were passed to it. Forcing a thunk is accomplished by evaluating the thunk expression in the thunk environment.

Exercise 4.9

Make the modifications outlined above to transform the evaluator to include procedures with delayed arguments. You should define a new data object, a thunk, together with appropriate selectors and constructors, and a predicate that tests whether an object is a thunk. Test your implementation by evaluating

```
(define (unless pred (delayed default-action) (delayed exception))
  (if (not pred)
      default-action
      exception))

(define (factorial n)
  (unless (= n 1)
          (* (factorial (- n 1)) n)
          1))

(factorial 4)
```

Exercise 4.10

Consider the following:

```
(define (foo (delayed x))
  (cond (x 0)
        (else 1)))

(foo nil)
```

If the interpreter you implemented in exercise 4.9 responds with a 0, you probably forgot a place where it is necessary to force thunks. Find it.

Exercise 4.11

In chapter 3 we said that streams are like lists, except that the second argument to `cons-stream` is delayed. However, with automatically delayed arguments, streams can be identical to lists. To make lists behave like streams, define cons as a (nonprimitive) procedure with delayed arguments. Cons will use a new primitive procedure `internal-cons` that does not force its arguments, as do the other primitive procedures. Modify `apply-primitive-procedure` to handle `internal-cons`. (If you prefer, you can do what Scheme `cons-stream` does and delay only the second argument to `cons`.)

Exercise 4.12

The delayed evaluation mechanism outlined above is very inefficient, because each thunk may be forced over and over again, each time it is used by a primitive operator. As mentioned in section 3.4.3, this can be rectified by memoizing the thunks. Explain in detail how you would modify your evaluator to perform this optimization.[16]

Exercise 4.13

In section 3.4.5 we had to use `delay` and `force` explicitly to solve a differential equation. Show how to use automatically delayed arguments to avoid the use of `delay` and `force` in the `integral` and `solve` procedures given in that section.

Exercise 4.14

In section 3.4.5 we used `delay` and `force` explicitly to make `flatten` work for infinite streams. Show how to use automatically delayed arguments to avoid the use of `delay` and `force` in `accumulate` and `interleave`. You should be able to use the original `accumulate` procedure to implement `flatten` as follows:

```
(define (flatten stream)
  (accumulate interleave the-empty-stream stream))
```

Exercise 4.15

Alyssa P. Hacker says that she greatly prefers the delayed-argument mechanism implemented in this section to the explicit use of `force` and `delay` as in chapter 3. Ben Bitdiddle disagrees. He complains that the issues raised by mutation and assignment are confusing enough when delayed objects are forced explicitly using `force`, and that implicit forcing only makes things worse. What are the major points on each side of this debate? Give examples to illustrate the comparative benefits and drawbacks of each approach. Which method do you prefer? (The phenomenon illustrated in exercise 4.14 is an important argument for Alyssa's position. Explain.)

4.2.2 Alternative Binding Disciplines

In Scheme, variables are bound *statically*. A free variable in a procedure gets its value from the environment in which the procedure is defined.

---

16 This kind of optimization is known as *call-by-need* argument passing. Call-by-name causes difficulties in understanding programs with assignments and in controlling the space complexity of programs, but this is innocence itself when compared with the theoretical problems created by call-by-need in the presence of assignments. The excellent article by Clinger (1982) attempts to clarify the multiple dimensions of confusion that arise here.

This means that the binding of a variable in a program is determined by the static structure of the program, not by its run-time behavior. In this discipline, an occurrence of a variable in an expression always refers to the innermost lexically apparent binding of that variable. For this reason, static binding is also called lexical scoping.

As an example, recall the sum procedure from section 1.3.1:

```
(define (sum term a next b)
  (if (> a b)
      0
      (+ (term a)
         (sum term (next a) next b))))
```

Sum is a simple instance of a procedure that takes a procedure as an argument. It provides a template, capturing the structure of a class of procedures. The procedural argument allows the programmer to fill in the template, tailoring it to his needs. Using sum, we can define a procedure sum-cubes as follows:

```
(define (cube x)
  (expt x 3))
```

```
(define (sum-cubes a b)
  (sum cube a 1+ b))
```

We could extend this idea to arbitrary powers by defining a procedure sum-powers that takes an argument n, specifying the power to which each summand should be raised:

```
(define (sum-powers a b n)
  (define (nth-power x)
    (expt x n))
  (sum nth-power a 1+ b))
```

The definition of nth-power is internal to sum-powers, so the n that is free in nth-power will be in the scope of the formal parameter n of sum-powers.

When we write a procedure, we have two ways to specify parametric control of the computation that will be performed in the body of the procedure: We can communicate with a procedure by passing arguments through formal parameters, and we can also bind the procedure's free variables. This extra degree of freedom is crucial in creating high-order procedural abstractions. This demonstrates the real power of internal definitions.

Dynamic binding

Traditionally, Lisp systems have been implemented so that variables are bound *dynamically* rather than statically.[17] In a language with dynamic binding, free variables in a procedure get their values from the environment from which the procedure is called rather than from the environment in which the procedure is defined. For example, the free variable n in nth-power would get whatever value n had when sum called it. In this example, since sum does not rebind n, the only definition of n is still the one from sum-powers; thus, the effect is the same. On the other hand, suppose we had used the name n instead of next in the definition of sum. In this case, when sum called nth-power, nth-power's free variable n would refer to sum's third argument, which is not what we intended. This would produce an error, since the value of n here is not a number, as required by nth-power.

As this example shows, dynamic binding violates the principle that a procedure should be regarded as a "black box," such that changing the name of a parameter throughout a procedure's definition will not change the procedure's behavior. In the above example, we saw that it makes a difference whether the third variable to sum is called next or n. In general, dynamic binding admits the constant potential for symbol conflicts, in which higher-order procedures *capture* free variables in procedures passed as arguments.[18] This is an important modularity issue, because the user of a higher-order procedure (say, a higher-order procedure written by someone else) must make assumptions about the names of the parameters of that procedure.

It may seem obvious from the above example that static binding is a better choice than dynamic binding. But there are also reasons to prefer dynamic binding. In a statically bound language, the sum-powers program above must contain the definition of nth-power as a local procedure. Thus, if nth-power represents a common pattern of usage, its definition must be repeated as an internal definition in many contexts. This is a problem of abstraction. It would be attractive to be able to move the definition of nth-power to a more global context, where it can be shared among many procedures. In a dynamically bound Lisp, if we have sum and product accumulator procedures, we can define sum-powers and product-powers to share the same nth-power procedure:

---

17 APL also uses dynamic binding of free variables. Most other languages, such as those descended from Algol 60, use static binding.

18 In the traditional Lisp literature, such capture of free variables is known as the *downward funarg problem*. There is also a complementary *upward funarg problem*, in which procedures that are returned as values can "lose" the bindings for their free variables. See exercise 4.17 for an example.

```
(define (sum-powers a b n)
  (sum nth-power a 1+ b))

(define (product-powers a b n)
  (product nth-power a 1+ b))

(define (nth-power x)
  (expt x n))
```

The attempt to make this work was what motivated the development
of dynamic binding disciplines. In general, dynamically bound variables
can be helpful in structuring large programs. They can simplify procedure
calls by acting as implicit parameters. For example, a low-level procedure
nprint called by the system print procedure for printing numbers might
reference a free variable called radix that specifies the base in which the
number is to be printed. Procedures that call nprint, such as the system
print operation, should not need to know about this feature. On the other
hand, a user might want to temporarily change the radix. In a statically
bound language, radix would have to be a global variable.[19] After setting
radix to a new value, the user would have to explicitly reset it. But the
dynamic binding mechanism could accomplish this setting and resetting
automatically, in a structured way. For example:

```
(define (print-in-new-radix number radix)
  (print number))

(define (print frob)
  ⟨expressions that involve nprint⟩)

(define (nprint number)
  . . .
  radix
  . . .)
```

Since there are sometimes advantages to dynamic binding, we might wish
to provide features for dynamic binding in our otherwise statically bound
language. Exercises 4.18 and 4.19 explore means of doing this.

Implementing dynamic binding

Remarkably enough, modifying our evaluator so that the language it interprets will use dynamic binding rather than static binding requires only a

19 In section 4.3 we will see how to use packages to avoid making such variables global.

tiny change. When `apply` builds the environment for evaluating the body of a compound procedure, it extends the evaluation environment of the combination that called for the procedure application rather than the environment of the procedure's definition. This environment must therefore be passed from `eval` to `apply` as an additional argument. The starred lines are the only ones that were altered to implement this change.

```
(define (eval exp env)
  (cond ((self-evaluating? exp) exp)
        ((quoted? exp) (text-of-quotation exp))
        ((variable? exp) (lookup-variable-value exp env))
        ((definition? exp) (eval-definition exp env))
        ((assignment? exp) (eval-assignment exp env))
        ((lambda? exp) (make-procedure exp env))
        ((conditional? exp) (eval-cond (clauses exp) env))
        ((application? exp)
         (apply (eval (operator exp) env)
                (list-of-values (operands exp) env)
                env))                           ;***
        (else (error "Unknown expression type -- EVAL" exp))))


(define (apply procedure arguments env)    ;***
  (cond ((primitive-procedure? procedure)
         (apply-primitive-procedure procedure arguments))
        ((compound-procedure? procedure)
         (eval-sequence (procedure-body procedure)
                        (extend-environment
                         (parameters procedure)
                         arguments
                         env)))                 ;***
        (else
         (error "Unknown procedure type -- APPLY"
                procedure))))
```

In a dynamically bound Lisp it is unnecessary for `make-procedure` to attach the definition environment to a procedure, since this is never used.

Exercise 4.16

Consider the following simple procedure:

```
(define (factorial n)
  (cond ((= n 1) 1)
        (else (* (factorial (- n 1)) n))))
```

Suppose that this definition is executed in the global environment. If variables are statically bound, how many frames with variable n must be searched before the value of * is found? What happens if variables are dynamically bound? Draw environment diagrams to illustrate your answer.

Exercise 4.17

Dynamically bound languages do not conveniently allow a procedure to constrain the values of free variables in a procedure that it returns as a value. Consider the following example:

```
(define (make-adder increment)
  (lambda (x) (+ x increment)))
```

What happens if we attempt to evaluate ((make-adder 3) 4) in a dynamically bound Lisp?

Exercise 4.18

Since there are advantages to both static and dynamic binding, we might wish to build a Lisp system that has both static and dynamic variables. The nprint example discussed above might then look as follows:

```
(define (print-in-new-radix number (dynamic radix))
  (print number))
```

```
(define (print frob)
  ⟨expressions that involve nprint⟩)
```

```
(define (nprint number)
  ...
  (dynamic-reference radix)
  ...)
```

We declared radix to be dynamic using a new syntax in the formal parameter list of print-in-new-radix, and we explicitly referenced it as a dynamic variable in nprint. Extend the evaluator of section 4.1 to include dynamic variables of this type by maintaining two separate environments, one for static and one for dynamic variables. This will require implementing the dynamic-reference special form and the dynamic declaration in parameter lists.

Exercise 4.19

Another way to achieve the desirable effects of dynamic binding is to use static variables only but to provide a structured means for temporarily changing the value of a variable. For example,

```
(define (with-new-radix new-radix proc)
  (let ((old-radix radix))
    (set! radix new-radix)
    (let ((value (proc)))
      (set! radix old-radix)
      value)))
```

Show how to use `with-new-radix` to define the `print-in-new-radix` procedure of exercise 4.18. Also, modify the evaluator of section 4.1 to include a new piece of syntactic sugar called `fluid-let`, so that `with-new-radix` could be defined as

```
(define (with-new-radix new-radix proc)
  (fluid-let ((radix new-radix))
    (proc)))
```

4.3 Packages

Throughout this book, we have been concerned with establishing techniques for decomposing large programs into pieces that can be worked on separately. Building abstraction barriers, using data-directed style, and decomposing programs into models of real-world objects are methods for enhancing the modularity of software systems. Another important modularity issue is the use of names in our programs. When we divide a large program into smaller pieces that are to be developed independent of each other, we must be able to combine the pieces without introducing name conflicts. If two pieces of the program each have a variable called x, or a procedure called add, then we cannot just combine these in the same global environment; we need some methods for structuring the *name space* of a program. One such method, which we have used extensively, is block structure. We construct procedures that have procedures defined within them, so that the internal procedures are accessible only from within the outer procedures. Block structure thus provides a way to decompose the name space of a program on a microscopic scale—that is, within an individual procedure.

There is, however, a more macroscopic version of the name-space problem. We would like to be able to decompose large programs into *packages* of related procedures and data. It should be possible to write each package independent of the others, except for prior agreement on the names of a restricted set of procedures and data in the interface. Within a package, the names used for the procedures that implement the package should be of concern only to the programmer who is in charge of that package. In addition, a user of the package need not even know all of the names in the package interface; he need know only those he explicitly wants to use. This leaves the package implementer free to add new features without the possibility of causing old programs to fail. In this section we will see how to implement such packages by using environments and explicit evaluation relative to an environment. As an application, we will see how to restructure the generic-arithmetic system of section 2.4 to use packages.

4.3.1 Using Environments to Create Packages

One way to decompose a program into packages is the message-passing style, discussed in section 3.1.1. We used block structure to define a set of internal action procedures and data for a bank account and return a dispatch procedure that gave access to those procedures and data, as follows:

```
(define (make-account balance)
  (define (withdraw amount)
    (if (= balance amount)
        (sequence (set! balance (- balance amount))
                  balance)
        "Insufficient funds"))
  (define (deposit amount)
    (set! balance (+ balance amount))
    balance)
  (define (dispatch m)
    (cond ((eq? m 'withdraw) withdraw)
          ((eq? m 'deposit) deposit)
          (else (error "Unknown request -- MAKE-ACCOUNT"
                       m))))
  dispatch)
```

In this scheme, a package is made by a procedure that has local variables naming the procedures and the data that are internal to the package. It returns a dispatch procedure, which serves as a gatekeeper, limiting access to precisely the intended material. The dispatcher also maps the external names of the *exported* data and procedures to the names they have internal to the package. (In the bank-account example, the internal and external names are the same and all the internal data and procedures are accessible; however, this need not be true in general, as is illustrated by the make-wire procedure of section 3.3.4.)

The message-passing style is just right for implementing objects such as bank accounts. There are to be many bank accounts, so we need a procedure that constructs individual accounts. Each account is a small package with a few exported capabilities, and these must be carefully controlled. For example, we must not let a depositor directly modify his own balance; we must check that he is withdrawing only as much money as he has deposited. In a real situation, we would want to provide him with a unique password to control transactions with the account (as illustrated in exercise 3.3). We also would provide the bank with a way to find out the balance in an account and to deposit interest (based on the balance). The bank would need its own special password for controlling these operations.

In most programming situations such careful access control is unnecessary, so writing a dispatch procedure would be counterproductive. Consider a large package of procedures, such as a scientific subroutine library. We have no reason to prevent a user from getting at one of the internal implementation procedures or data structures if he really wants to do so (though we may warn him that unadvertised features may not be supported in the next version of the library). The real purpose of packaging the library is to give the library implementer the freedom to choose implementation names without constraining the choice of names that the user may have. By providing environments and explicit evaluation, we can arrange for this kind of structure.

The dynamic binding evaluator of section 4.2.2 illustrates how we can experiment, by modifying the evaluator, with evaluating expressions in environments other than the ones dictated by the usual evaluation rules. Another way to cause expressions to be evaluated in alternate environments is to write programs that explicitly use the `eval` primitive (section 4.1.5), which evaluates a given expression in a given environment. This requires no change to the interpreter, because calls to `eval` can be included in ordinary programs.

For use in conjunction with `eval`, Scheme provides a special form called `make-environment` that constructs an environment, evaluates a designated sequence of expressions within this environment, and returns the environment as the value of the `make-environment` expression. The enclosing environment of the new environment is the environment in which the `make-environment` expression was evaluated.

With `make-environment`, we can construct environments that serve as packages containing local information. To access this information, we use `eval` to evaluate expressions relative to these environments. For example, a fragment of a scientific subroutine library might look as follows:

```
(define scientific-library
  (make-environment
    ...
    (define (iterative-improve good-enuf? improve first-guess)
      (define (try guess) ...)
      (try first-guess))
    (define (square-root x)
      (iterative-improve ...))
    ...
    ))
```

A user can access procedures in the package by explicitly using `eval` to perform evaluations relative to the `scientific-library` environment. For example, either of the following expressions could be used to compute the square root of 4:

```
((eval 'square-root scientific-library) 4)
```

```
(eval '(square-root 4) scientific-library)
```

Important procedures that we want to be more globally available can be given global names and then used directly:

```
(define sqrt (eval 'square-root scientific-library))
```

```
(sqrt 4)
```

There could be other packages with `square-root` procedures, and a user could even define his own `square-root`. These names would not conflict.

Exercise 4.20

Even though implementing bank accounts as environments presents security problems, it is instructive to understand how this could be done. Write a procedure `make-account-env`, analogous to `make-account`, that takes a balance as argument and produces an environment representation of a bank account. Your representation should have a balance and various procedures for accessing the account.

Draw an environment diagram (section 3.2.3) to illustrate the structure created by a call to `make-account-env`. Compare this with exercise 3.11.

Is it possible to implement a secure bank account using environment objects as the representation medium? If you believe you can do so, show how. If not, explain why.

Exercise 4.21

Rewrite the digital logic simulator of section 3.3.4 so that wires are represented as environments rather than as procedures. Show how to modify the interface procedures `get-signal`, `set-signal!`, and `add-action!` so that the rest of the simulator need not be modified to accommodate this new representation.

Exercise 4.22

Extend the metacircular evaluator of section 4.1 to include `make-environment` and user-accessible `eval`. To do this, you should include environments as a new kind of data object in the user-level language. (You can represent an environment as a pair whose car is the symbol `environment` and whose cdr is the actual environment data structure used by the evaluator. Compare the implementation of `make-procedure` in section 4.1.2.) Eval should check that its second argument is an environment. User-print (section 4.1.4) should also be modified so that it will not attempt to print the actual environment data structure.

4.3.2 Packages in a Generic Arithmetic System

In section 2.4 we saw how to use data-directed programming to combine packages for performing arithmetic operations on different types of numbers. The packages were not independent, however, in that procedures in different packages could not have the same names. We thus chose distinct names for the operators for each data type. (For example, `real-part-rectangular` and `real-part-polar` are both names for `real-part`, for different data types.) We can repair this defect in the generic arithmetic system by representing each package as an environment. Different packages can then contain procedures that have the same name, yet there will be no conflict.

Assume for simplicity that there are only two types of numbers: real numbers and complex numbers. The overall structure of the package environments will be as follows:[20]

```
(define real
  (let (...)
    (make-environment ⟨definitions of real operations⟩)))

(define complex
  (let (...)
    (define rectangular
      (let (...)
        (make-environment
         ⟨definitions of rectangular operations⟩)))
    (define polar
      (let (...)
        (make-environment
         ⟨definitions of polar operations⟩)))
    ...
    (let (...)
      (make-environment
       ⟨definitions of complex operations⟩))))
```

We have embedded the `rectangular` and `polar` packages in the `complex` package, on the grounds that these are not useful outside the context of complex numbers. This illustrates how a large system can be structured as a tree of packages.

20 We will see what the `let`s are for when we consider the package details below.

Generic operators

As in section 2.3, we work with typed data objects:

```
(define (attach-type type contents)
  (cons type contents))
```

```
(define (type datum) (car datum))
```

```
(define (contents datum) (cdr datum))
```

In our new implementation, the type of a data object will be represented by an environment—the package itself—rather than a simple symbol.

To apply a generic operator to an argument, we extract the type of the argument and use this as an environment in which to evaluate the symbol that is the operation name. This produces the actual procedure, which we apply to the (contents of the) argument. The following procedure, which we use to construct generic operators of one argument, embodies this strategy:

```
(define (make-generic-operator-1 operator)
  (lambda (arg)
    ((eval operator (type arg)) (contents arg))))
```

```
(define real-part (make-generic-operator-1 'real-part))
(define imag-part (make-generic-operator-1 'imag-part))
(define magnitude (make-generic-operator-1 'magnitude))
(define angle (make-generic-operator-1 'angle))
```

For generic operators of two arguments, we first check to see if the types are the same before applying the appropriate operator

```
(define (make-generic-operator-2 operator)
  (lambda (arg1 arg2)
    (let ((t1 (type arg1)))
      (if (eq? t1 (type arg2))
          ((eval operator t1) (contents arg1)
                              (contents arg2))
          (error "Operands not of same type"
                 (list operator arg1 arg2))))))
```

```
(define add (make-generic-operator-2 'add))
(define sub (make-generic-operator-2 'sub))
(define mul (make-generic-operator-2 'mul))
(define div (make-generic-operator-2 'div))
```

This implementation of generic operators behaves just like the implementation using `operate` and `operate-2` in section 2.4.1, except in the case where the operator is not defined for the argument type. `Operate` and `operate-2` recognize this explicitly and print a specific error message when they fail to find a procedure in the operation table. In the environment implementation, lack of an operation shows up as an "unbound variable" error when we evaluate the operator in the package.

In addition to packaging the operations on objects of various types, we would like to package the constructors for objects of various types. For example, we would like to avoid having to define `make-rectangular` globally. To do this, we will include in each package an operation called `maker` that is used to construct data objects of the appropriate type. For example, the operation that constructs a rectangular complex number from a real part and an imaginary part, to be included in the `rectangular` subpackage of the `complex` package, is

```
(define (maker x y) (cons x y))
```

To access these `maker` procedures in a uniform way, we supply a special generic operator called `make`, which takes as arguments a type and a list of parts, applies the `maker` operation for the given type, and then attaches the type itself onto the result. For instance, the expression

```
(make rectangular (list (make real (list 5))
                        (make real (list 6))))
```

returns a `rectangular` number whose real part is 5 and whose imaginary part is 6.[21] Here is the definition of `make`:

```
(define (make type object-parts)
  (attach-type type (apply (eval 'maker type) object-parts)))
```

In implementing `make`, we have to contend with the fact that the `maker` procedures for different data types may take different numbers of parts. Thus, `make`—the generic operator—may need to accept different numbers of arguments, given different types. We get around this by having `make` always take a list of the object parts as its second argument. We then use `apply` in the body of `make` to apply an operator to this list of arguments.

The need to combine the arguments to `make` in a list makes it somewhat awkward to use. We can avoid the awkwardness by taking advantage of an extended syntax for `define` that enables us to define procedures that accept a variable number of arguments. In the definition for `make` shown below, the dot before the `object-parts` parameter indicates that in evaluating

---

21 In chapter 2 we built complex numbers out of untyped numbers. Here we use numbers of type `real`.

an expression of the form

(make $\langle \text{arg}_1 \rangle$ $\langle \text{arg}_2 \rangle$ ... $\langle \text{arg}_n \rangle$)

the symbol type is to be bound to the evaluated $\langle \text{arg}_1 \rangle$ and object-parts is to be bound to the remaining part of the list of evaluated arguments ($\langle \text{arg}_2 \rangle$ ... $\langle \text{arg}_n \rangle$). In general, this *dot notation* in Lisp is used to indicate that the symbol following the dot is to be bound to the rest of the corresponding list. We can define make with dot notation

```
(define (make type . object-parts)
  (attach-type type (apply (eval 'maker type) object-parts)))
```

and use the procedure as follows:

```
(make rectangular (make real 5) (make real 6))
```

Package structure
There is still some work to be done before we can fill in the details of our packages. Generic arithmetic is one of the most difficult cases for any packaging scheme. The problem is that a package must deal with as many as three classes of names: names for procedures to be exported, names for procedures to be imported from other packages, and names for internal procedures. For example, adding complex numbers requires the ability to add the real components of the complex numbers. The adder for real numbers is not the add being defined, nor is it the generic add, because a complex number must have real components, not complex ones. Thus, the complex package must somehow be able to access the add from the real-number package.

On the other side of the coin, manipulations within a package should not need to know about the types of the things manipulated in that package. For example, within the complex package there should be no overhead on the use of complex addition. Thus, the complex addition operation should not have to strip off the complex type from its arguments, nor should it have to adjoin this type to the value it returns; these are jobs for the interface between the complex package and the rest of the system. As a consequence of this, we must distinguish between the exported complex addition procedure and the internal complex addition procedure.

The definitions of the arithmetic operators for complex numbers in the generic arithmetic system shown below are thus divided into three distinct sections: an import section, which defines the access to procedures that are used from other packages; a definition body, where the actual manipulations for data of type complex are defined; and an export text, which defines the procedures to be used by other packages. The rectangular package is structured similarly, except that it has no definition body, just imports and exports.

The procedures imported into our arithmetic packages are restrictions of the generic procedures. The restriction of a unary generic operator to a particular type is constructed by the procedure `restrict-1`, as follows:

```
(define (restrict-1 operator type-pack)
  (let ((proc (eval operator type-pack)))
    (lambda (arg)
      (if (eq? type-pack (type arg))
          (proc (contents arg))
          (error "Type mismatch -- restricted operator"
                 (list operator type-pack arg))))))
```

Binary restrictions are constructed in an analogous manner.

All the pieces are now in place for the construction of a complete generic arithmetic system that includes complex numbers in both rectangular and polar forms, such that the packages have independent name spaces.

```
(define (square x) (mul x x))          ;generic square operator

(define real ⟨definition of real package⟩)

(define complex
  ;; First we declare the imported procedures.
  (let ((+ (restrict-2 'add real))
        (- (restrict-2 'sub real))
        (* (restrict-2 'mul real))
        (/ (restrict-2 'div real)))

    ;; Next, we define the subpackages.
    (define rectangular
      (let ((sqrt (restrict-1 'sqrt real))
            (atan (restrict-2 'atan real)))
        (make-environment
         (define (real-part z) (car z))
         (define (imag-part z) (cdr z))
         (define (magnitude z)
           (sqrt (+ (square (car z)) (square (cdr z)))))
         (define (angle z)
           (atan (cdr z) (car z)))
         (define (maker x y) (cons x y))
         )))
    ;; complex package continued on next page
```

```
(define polar ⟨definition of polar package⟩)

;; Next we define the body of the complex manipulations.
(define (add z1 z2)
  (make rectangular
        (+ (real-part z1) (real-part z2))
        (+ (imag-part z1) (imag-part z2))))
(define (sub z1 z2)
  (make rectangular
        (- (real-part z1) (real-part z2))
        (- (imag-part z1) (imag-part z2))))
(define (mul z1 z2)
  (make polar
        (* (magnitude z1) (magnitude z2))
        (+ (angle z1) (angle z2))))
(define (div z1 z2)
  (make polar
        (/ (magnitude z1) (magnitude z2))
        (- (angle z1) (angle z2))))

;; Finally, we define the exports from the complex package.
(let ((+ add) (- sub) (* mul) (/ div))
  (make-environment
   (define (add z1 z2)
     (attach-type complex (+ z1 z2)))
   (define (sub z1 z2)
     (attach-type complex (- z1 z2)))
   (define (mul z1 z2)
     (attach-type complex (* z1 z2)))
   (define (div z1 z2)
     (attach-type complex (/ z1 z2)))

   ;; We choose (somewhat arbitrarily) to make complex numbers
   ;; initially in rectangular form.
   (define (maker real imag)
     (make rectangular real imag))
   ;; End of complex package
   ))))
```

Exercise 4.23

Complete the sketch of the generic arithmetic system by implementing the `real` and `polar` packages.

By analogy with section 2.4, show how to embed your real and complex number implementation within a generic arithmetic system that also includes packages to handle rational numbers and polynomials with arbitrary coefficients.

Exercise 4.24

The `complex` package does not export definitions of the `real-part`, `imag-part`, `magnitude`, and `angle` operators. What happens if you ask for the `magnitude` of a number of type `complex`?

Exercise 4.25

Show how to replace `make-generic-operator-1` and `make-generic-operator-2` by a single procedure `make-generic-operator` that constructs generic operators of any number of arguments. (Use dot notation, as in the definition of `make`.)

Exercise 4.26

Discuss various ways to extend the environment-based generic arithmetic implementation to handle coercion (section 2.4.2). How could you modify the procedure `make-generic-operator` of exercise 4.25 so that the resulting operators will attempt to deal with operands that are not all of the same type, in analogy with the `operate-2` procedure given in section 2.4.2? Can you implement, in this context, some of the more sophisticated coercion strategies, such as those discussed in exercises 2.55–2.57?

4.4 Logic Programming

In chapter 1 we stressed that computer science deals with imperative (how to) knowledge, whereas mathematics deals with declarative (what is) knowledge. Indeed, programming languages require that the programmer express knowledge in a form that indicates the step-by-step methods for solving particular problems. On the other hand, high-level languages provide, as part of the language implementation, a substantial amount of methodological knowledge that frees the user from concern with numerous details of how a specified computation will progress.

Most programming languages, including Lisp, are organized around computing the values of mathematical functions. Expression-oriented languages (such as Lisp, Fortran, and Algol) capitalize on the "pun" that an expression that describes the value of a function may also be interpreted as a means of computing that value. Because of this, most program-

ming languages are strongly biased toward unidirectional computations
(computations with well-defined inputs and outputs). Over the past few
years, however, people have begun to experiment with a radically different
class of programming languages that relax this bias. We saw one such example in section 3.3.5, where the objects of computation were arithmetic
constraints. In a constraint system the direction and the order of computation are not so well specified; in carrying out a computation the system must
therefore provide more detailed "how to" knowledge than would be the case
with an ordinary arithmetic computation. This does not mean, however,
that the user is released altogether from the responsibility of providing imperative knowledge. There are many constraint networks that implement
the same set of constraints, and the user must choose from the set of mathematically equivalent networks a suitable network to specify a particular
computation.

Logic programming moves even further from the view that programming
is about constructing algorithms for computing unidirectional functions.
This growing movement in computer science advocates considering the objects of programming to be mathematical relations, which have, in general,
multiple answers for any set of inputs.[22]

This approach, when it works, can be a very powerful way to write
programs. Part of the power comes from the fact that a single "what
is" fact can be used to solve a number of different problems that would
have different "how to" components. As an example, consider the append

---

[22] Logic programming has grown out of a long history of research in automatic theorem
proving. Early theorem-proving programs could accomplish very little, because they
exhaustively searched the space of possible proofs. The major breakthrough that made
such a search plausible was the discovery in the early 1960s of the *unification algorithm*
and the *resolution principle* (Robinson 1965). Resolution was used, for example, by
Green and Raphael (1968) (see also Green 1969) as the basis for a deductive question-
answering system. During most of this period, researchers concentrated on algorithms
that are guaranteed to find a proof if one exists. Such algorithms were difficult to
control and to direct toward a proof. Hewitt (1969), recognized the possibility of
merging the control structure of a programming language with the operations of a logic-
manipulation system. A restricted version of his idea was implemented by Sussman,
Winograd, and Charniak (1971), and was used as the basis of several significant problem-
solving programs (see, e.g., Winograd 1971). At the same time that this was being done,
Colmerauer, in Marseille, was developing rule-based systems for manipulating natural
language (see Colmerauer et al. 1973). He invented a programming language called
Prolog for representing those rules. Kowalski (1973; 1979), in Edinburgh, recognized
that execution of a Prolog program could be interpreted as proving theorems (using
a proof technique called linear Horn-clause resolution). The merging of the last two
strands led to the current logic-programming movement. Thus, in assigning credit for
the development of logic programming, the French can point to Prolog's genesis at the
University of Marseille, while the British can highlight the work at the University of
Edinburgh. According to people at MIT, logic programming was developed by these
groups in an attempt to figure out what Hewitt was talking about in his brilliant but
impenetrable Ph.D. thesis. For a history of logic programming, see Robinson 1983.

operation, which takes two lists as arguments and combines their elements to form a single list. In a procedural language such as Lisp, we could define append in terms of the basic list constructor cons, as we did in section 2.2.1:

```
(define (append x y)
  (if (null? x)
      y
      (cons (car x) (append (cdr x) y))))
```

This procedure can be regarded as a translation into Lisp of the following two rules, the first of which covers the case where the first list is empty and the second of which handles the case of a nonempty list, which is a cons of two parts:

- For any list y, the empty list and y append to form y.
- For any u, v, y, and z, (cons u v) and y append to form (cons u z) if v and y append to form z.[23]

Using the append procedure, we can answer questions such as

Find the append of (a b) and (c d).

But the same two rules are also sufficient for answering the following sorts of questions, which the procedure can't answer:

Find a list y that appends with (a b) to produce (a b c d).

Find all x and y that append to form (a b c d).

In a logic programming language, the programmer writes an append "procedure" by stating the two rules about append given above. "How to" knowledge is provided automatically by the interpreter to allow this single pair of rules to be used to answer all three types of questions about append.[24]

Logic programming is an extremely active field of research in computer science. Contemporary logic programming languages (including the one we implement here) have substantial deficiencies, in that their general "how to" methods can lead them into spurious infinite loops or other undesirable behavior. Most researchers believe that creating a satisfactory (yet not

23 To see the correspondence between the rules and the procedure, let x in the procedure (where x is nonempty) correspond to (cons u v) in the rule. Then z in the rule corresponds to the append of (cdr x) and y.

24 This certainly does not relieve the user of the entire problem of how to compute the answer. There are many different mathematically equivalent sets of rules for formulating the append relation, only some of which can be turned into effective devices for computing in any direction. In addition, sometimes "what is" information gives no clue "how to" compute an answer. For example, consider the problem of computing the y such that $y^2 = x$.

hopelessly inefficient) logic programming implementation will require the use of radically new, massively parallel computer architectures.[25]

Earlier in this chapter we explored the technology of implementing interpreters and described the elements that are basic to an interpreter for a Lisp-like language (indeed, to an interpreter for any conventional language). Now we will apply these ideas to discuss an interpreter for a logic programming language. We call this language the *query language*, because it is very useful for retrieving information from data bases by formulating *queries*, or questions, expressed in the language. Even though the query language is very different from Lisp, we will find it convenient to describe the language in terms of the same general framework we have been using all along: as a collection of primitive elements, together with means of combination that enable us to combine simple elements to create more complex elements and means of abstraction that enable us to regard complex elements as single conceptual units. An interpreter for a logic programming language is considerably more complex than an interpreter for a language such as Lisp. Nevertheless, we will see that our query-language interpreter contains many of the same elements found in the interpreter of section 4.1. In particular, there will be an "eval" part that classifies expressions according to type and an "apply" part that implements the language's abstraction mechanism (procedures in the case of Lisp, and *rules* in the case of logic programming). Also, a central role is played in the implementation by a frame data structure, which determines the correspondence between symbols and their associated values. One additional interesting aspect of our query-language implementation is that we make substantial use of streams, which were introduced in chapter 3.

4.4.1 Deductive Information Retrieval

Logic programming excels in providing interfaces to data bases for information retrieval. The query language we shall implement in this chapter is designed to be used in this way.

In order to illustrate what the query system does, we will show how it can be used to manage the data base of personnel records for the Itsey

---

25 Logic programming received a big impetus in 1981 when the Japanese government began an ambitious project aimed at building superfast computers optimized to run logic programming languages. The speed of such computers is to be measured in LIPS (Logical Inferences Per Second) rather than the usual FLOPS (FLoating-point Operations Per Second). The only languages the Japanese consider worth worrying about for computers of the future are Lisp and Prolog. This has proved rather disconcerting to the bulk of the U.S. computer industry and to the majority of U.S. computer scientists, who seem entrenched in the Pascal-PL/I-Ada camp.

Bitsey Machine Corporation, a thriving high-technology company in the Boston area. The language provides pattern-directed access to personnel information and can also take advantage of general rules in order to make logical deductions.

A sample data base

The personnel data base for the Itsey Bitsey Machine Corporation contains *assertions* about company personnel. Here is the information about Ben Bitdiddle, the resident computer wizard:

```
(address (Bitdiddle Ben) (Slumerville (Ridge Road) 10))
(job (Bitdiddle Ben) (computer wizard))
(salary (Bitdiddle Ben) 40000)
```

Each assertion is a list (in this case a triple) whose elements can themselves be lists.

As resident wizard, Ben is in charge of the company's computer division, and he supervises two programmers and one technician. Here is the information about them:

```
(address (Hacker Alyssa P) (Cambridge (Mass Ave) 78))
(job (Hacker Alyssa P) (computer programmer))
(salary (Hacker Alyssa P) 35000)
(supervisor (Hacker Alyssa P) (Bitdiddle Ben))

(address (Fect Cy D) (Cambridge (Ames Street) 3))
(job (Fect Cy D) (computer programmer))
(salary (Fect Cy D) 32000)
(supervisor (Fect Cy D) (Bitdiddle Ben))

(address (Tweakit Lem E) (Boston (Bay State Road) 22))
(job (Tweakit Lem E) (computer technician))
(salary (Tweakit Lem E) 15000)
(supervisor (Tweakit Lem E) (Bitdiddle Ben))
```

There is also a programmer trainee, who is supervised by Alyssa:

```
(address (Reasoner Louis) (Slumerville (Pine Tree Road) 80))
(job (Reasoner Louis) (computer programmer trainee))
(salary (Reasoner Louis) 20000)
(supervisor (Reasoner Louis) (Hacker Alyssa P))
```

All of these people are in the computer division, as indicated by the word computer as the first item in their job descriptions.

Ben is a high-level employee. His supervisor is the company's big wheel himself:

```
(supervisor (Bitdiddle Ben) (Warbucks Oliver))
```

```
(address (Warbucks Oliver) (Swellesley (Top Heap Road)))
(job (Warbucks Oliver) (administration big wheel))
(salary (Warbucks Oliver) 100000)
```

Besides the computer division supervised by Ben, the company has an accounting division, consisting of a chief accountant and his assistant:

```
(address (Scrooge Eben) (Weston (Shady Lane) 10))
(job (Scrooge Eben) (accounting chief accountant))
(salary (Scrooge Eben) 69000)
(supervisor (Scrooge Eben) (Warbucks Oliver))
```

```
(address (Cratchet Robert) (Allston (N Harvard Street) 16))
(job (Cratchet Robert) (accounting scrivener))
(salary (Cratchet Robert) 12000)
(supervisor (Cratchet Robert) (Scrooge Eben))
```

There is also a secretary for the big wheel:

```
(address (Forrest Rosemary) (Slumerville (Onion Square) 5))
(job (Forrest Rosemary) (administration secretary))
(salary (Forrest Rosemary) 15000)
(supervisor (Forrest Rosemary) (Warbucks Oliver))
```

The data base also contains assertions about which kinds of jobs can be done by people holding other kinds of jobs. For instance, a computer wizard can do the jobs of both a computer programmer and a computer technician:

```
(can-do-job (computer wizard) (computer programmer))
(can-do-job (computer wizard) (computer technician))
```

A computer programmer could fill in for a trainee:

```
(can-do-job (computer programmer)
            (computer programmer trainee))
```

Also, as is well known,

```
(can-do-job (administration secretary)
            (administration big wheel))
```

Simple queries

The query language allows users to retrieve information from the data base by posing queries in response to the system's `query==>` prompt. For example, to find all computer programmers one can say

```
query==> (job ?x (computer programmer))
```

The system will respond with the following items:

```
(job (Hacker Alyssa P) (computer programmer))
(job (Fect Cy D) (computer programmer))
```

The input query specifies that we are looking for entries in the data base that match a certain *pattern*. In this example, the pattern specifies entries consisting of three items, of which the first is the literal symbol job, the second can be anything, and the third is the literal list (computer programmer). The "anything" that can be the second item in the matching list is specified by a *pattern variable*, ?x. The general form of a pattern variable is a symbol, taken to be the name of the variable, preceded by a question mark. We will see below why it is useful to specify names for pattern variables rather than just putting ? into patterns to represent "anything." The system responds to a simple query by showing all entries in the data base that match the specified pattern.

A pattern can have more than one variable. For example, the query

```
query==> (address ?x ?y)
```

will list all the employees' addresses.

A pattern can have no variables, in which case the query simply determines whether that pattern is an entry in the data base. If so, there will be one match; if not, there will be no matches.

The same pattern variable can appear more than once in a query, specifying that the same "anything" must appear in each position. This is why variables have names. For example,

```
query==> (supervisor ?x ?x)
```

finds all people who supervise themselves (though there are no such assertions in our sample data base).

The query

```
query==> (job ?x (computer ?type))
```

matches all job entries whose third item is a two-element list whose first item is computer:

```
(job (Bitdiddle Ben) (computer wizard))
(job (Hacker Alyssa P) (computer programmer))
(job (Fect Cy D) (computer programmer))
(job (Tweakit Lem E) (computer technician))
```

This same pattern does *not* match

```
(job (Reasoner Louis) (computer programmer trainee))
```

because the third item in the entry is a list of three elements, and the pattern's third item specifies that there should be two elements. If we wanted to change the pattern so that the third item could be any list beginning with computer, we could specify

```
query==> (job ?x (computer . ?type))
```

The use of the period in this pattern is an example of *dot notation*, in which a period followed by a variable in a list expression is used to designate the rest of the list. Thus, the pattern

```
(computer . ?type)
```

matches the data

```
(computer programmer trainee)
```

with ?type as the list (programmer trainee). It also matches the data

```
(computer programmer)
```

with ?type as the list (programmer).

We can describe the query language's processing of simple queries as follows:

- The system finds all assignments to variables in the query pattern that *satisfy* the pattern – that is, all sets of values for the variables such that if the pattern variables are *instantiated with* (replaced by) the values, the result is in the data base.

- The system responds to the query by listing all instantiations of the query pattern with the variable assignments that satisfy it.

Note that if the pattern has no variables, the query reduces to a determination of whether that pattern is in the data base. If so, the empty assignment, which assigns no values to variables, satisfies that pattern for that data base.

Exercise 4.27

Give simple queries that retrieve the following information from the data base:
all people supervised by Ben Bitdiddle;
the names and jobs of all people in the accounting division;
the names and addresses of all people who live in Slumerville.

Compound queries

Simple queries form the primitive operations of the query language. In
order to form compound operations, the query language provides means
of combination. One thing that makes the query language a logic programming language is that the means of combination mirror the means of
combination used in forming logical expressions: and, or, and not. (Here
and, or, and not are not the Lisp primitives, but rather operations built
into the query language.)

We can use and as follows to find the addresses of all the computer
programmers:

```
query==> (and (job ?person (computer programmer))
              (address ?person ?where))
```

The resulting output is

```
(and (job (Hacker Alyssa P) (computer programmer))
     (address (Hacker Alyssa P) (Cambridge (Mass Ave) 78)))
```

```
(and (job (Fect Cy D) (computer programmer))
     (address (Fect Cy D) (Cambridge (Ames Street) 3)))
```

In general,

```
(and ⟨query₁⟩ ⟨query₂⟩ ... ⟨queryₙ⟩)
```

is satisfied by all sets of values for the pattern variables that simultaneously
satisfy $\langle query_1 \rangle \ldots \langle query_n \rangle$.

As for simple queries, the system processes a compound query by finding
all assignments to the pattern variables that satisfy the query, then displaying instantiations of the query with those values.

Another means of constructing compound queries is through or. For
example,

```
query==> (or (supervisor ?x (Bitdiddle Ben))
             (supervisor ?x (Hacker Alyssa P)))
```

will find all employees supervised by Ben Bitdiddle or Alyssa P. Hacker:

```
(or (supervisor (Hacker Alyssa P) (Bitdiddle Ben))
    (supervisor (Hacker Alyssa P) (Hacker Alyssa P)))

(or (supervisor (Fect Cy D) (Bitdiddle Ben))
    (supervisor (Fect Cy D) (Hacker Alyssa P)))

(or (supervisor (Tweakit Lem E) (Bitdiddle Ben))
    (supervisor (Tweakit Lem E) (Hacker Alyssa P)))

(or (supervisor (Reasoner Louis) (Bitdiddle Ben))
    (supervisor (Reasoner Louis) (Hacker Alyssa P)))
```

In general,

(or $\langle query_1 \rangle$ $\langle query_2 \rangle$ ... $\langle query_n \rangle$)

is satisfied by all sets of values for the pattern variables that satisfy at least one of $\langle query_1 \rangle$ ... $\langle query_n \rangle$.

Compound queries can also be formed with not. For example,

```
query==> (and (supervisor ?x (Bitdiddle Ben))
              (not (job ?x (computer programmer)))))
```

finds all people supervised by Ben Bitdiddle who are not computer programmers. In general,

(not $\langle query_1 \rangle$)

is satisfied by all assignments to the pattern variables that do not satisfy $\langle query_1 \rangle$.[26]

The final combining form is called lisp-value. When lisp-value is the first element of a pattern, it specifies that the next element is a Lisp predicate to be applied to the rest of the (instantiated) elements as arguments. In general,

(lisp-value $\langle predicate \rangle$ $\langle arg_1 \rangle$ ... $\langle arg_n \rangle$)

is satisfied by assignments to the pattern variables for which the $\langle predicate \rangle$ applied to the instantiated $\langle arg_1 \rangle$ ... $\langle arg_n \rangle$ is true. For example, to find all people whose salary is greater than $30,000 we could write

```
query==> (and (salary ?person ?amount)
              (lisp-value > ?amount 30000))
```

---

26 Actually, this description of not is valid only for simple cases. The real behavior of not is more complex. We will examine not's peculiarities in sections 4.4.2 and 4.4.3.

Exercise 4.28

Formulate compound queries that retrieve the following information:

the names of all people who are supervised by Ben Bitdiddle, together with their addresses;

all people whose salary is less than Ben Bitdiddle's, together with their salary and Ben Bitdiddle's salary;

all people who are supervised by someone who is not in the computer division, together with the supervisor's name and job.

Rules

In addition to primitive queries and compound queries, the query language provides means for abstracting queries. These are given by *rules*. The rule

```
(rule (lives-near ?person-1 ?person-2)
    (and (address ?person-1 (?town . ?rest-1))
        (address ?person-2 (?town . ?rest-2))
        (not (lisp-value equal? ?person-1 ?person-2))))
```

specifies that two people live near each other if they live in the same town. The final not clause prevents the rule from saying that all people live near themselves. The following rule declares that a person is a "wheel" in an organization if he supervises someone who is in turn a supervisor:

```
(rule (wheel ?person)
    (and (supervisor ?middle-manager ?person)
        (supervisor ?x ?middle-manager)))
```

The general form of a rule is

```
(rule ⟨conclusion⟩ ⟨body⟩)
```

where ⟨conclusion⟩ is a pattern and ⟨body⟩ is any query.[27] We can think of a rule as representing a large (even infinite) set of assertions, namely all instantiations of the rule conclusion with variable assignments that satisfy the rule body. When we described simple queries (patterns), we said that an assignment to variables satisfies a pattern if the instantiated pattern is in the data base. But the pattern needn't be explicitly in the data base as an assertion. It can be an implicit assertion implied by a rule. For example, the query

```
query==> (lives-near ?x (Bitdiddle Ben))
```

---

27 We will also allow rules without bodies, and we will interpret such a rule to mean that the rule conclusion is satisfied by any values of the variables.

results in

```
(lives-near (Reasoner Louis) (Bitdiddle Ben))
(lives-near (Forrest Rosemary) (Bitdiddle Ben))
```

To find all computer programmers who live near Ben Bitdiddle, we can ask

```
query==> (and (job ?x (computer programmer))
              (lives-near ?x (Bitdiddle Ben)))
```

As in the case of compound procedures, rules can be used as parts of other rules or even be defined recursively. For instance, the rule

```
(rule (outranked-by ?staff-person ?boss)
      (or (supervisor ?staff-person ?boss)
          (and (supervisor ?staff-person ?middle-manager)
               (outranked-by ?middle-manager ?boss))))
```

says that a staff person is outranked by a boss in the organization if the boss is the person's supervisor or (recursively) if the person's supervisor is outranked by the boss.

Exercise 4.29

Define a rule that says that person 1 can replace person 2 if either person 1 does the same job as person 2 or someone who does person 1's job can also do person 2's job, and if person 1 and person 2 are not the same person. Using your rule, give queries that find the following:

all persons who can replace Cy D. Fect;

all persons who can replace someone who is being paid more than they are, together with the two salaries.

Exercise 4.30

Define a rule that says that a person is a "big shot" in a division if the person works in the division but does not have a supervisor who works in the division.

Exercise 4.31

By giving the query

```
query==> (lives-near ?person (Hacker Alyssa P))
```

Alyssa P. Hacker is able to find people who live near her, with whom she can ride to work. On the other hand, when she tries to find all pairs of people who live near each other by querying

```
query==> (lives-near ?person-1 ?person-2)
```

she notices that each pair of people who live near each other is listed twice; for example,

```
(lives-near (Hacker Alyssa P) (Fect Cy D))
(lives-near (Fect Cy D) (Hacker Alyssa P))
```
⋮

Why does this happen? Suggest a way (such as by defining a new rule) to find a list of people who live near each other, in which each pair appears only once.

Logic as programs

We can regard a rule as a kind of logical implication: *If* an assignment of values to pattern variables satisfies the body, *then* it satisfies the conclusion. Consequently, we can regard the query language as having the ability to perform *logical deductions* based upon the rules. As an example, consider the append operation described at the beginning of section 4.4. As we said, append can be characterized by the following two rules:

- For any list y, the empty list and y append to form y.
- For any u, v, y, and z, (cons u v) and y append to form (cons u z) if v and y append to form z.

To express this in our query language, we define two rules for a relation

```
(append-to-form x y z)
```

which we can interpret to mean "x and y append to form z":

```
(rule (append-to-form () ?y ?y))
```

```
(rule (append-to-form (?u . ?v) ?y (?u . ?z))
      (append-to-form ?v ?y ?z))
```

The second rule makes use of the dot notation introduced above. The first rule has no body, which means that the conclusion holds for any value of ?y.

Given these two rules, we can formulate queries that compute the append of two lists:

```
query==> (append-to-form (a b) (c d) ?z)
(append-to-form (a b) (c d) (a b c d))
```

What is more striking, we can use the same rules to ask the question "Which list, when appended to (a b), yields (a b c d)?" This is done as follows:

```
query==> (append-to-form (a b) ?y (a b c d))
(append-to-form (a b) (c d) (a b c d))
```

We can also ask for all pairs of lists that append to form (a b c d):

```
query==> (append-to-form ?x ?y (a b c d))
(append-to-form () (a b c d) (a b c d))
(append-to-form (a) (b c d) (a b c d))
(append-to-form (a b) (c d) (a b c d))
(append-to-form (a b c) (d) (a b c d))
(append-to-form (a b c d) () (a b c d))
```

The query system may seem to exhibit quite a bit of intelligence in using the rules to deduce the answers to the queries above. Actually, as we will see in the next section, the system is following a well-determined algorithm in unraveling the rules. Unfortunately, although the system works impressively in the append case, the general methods may break down in more complex cases, as we will see in section 4.4.3.

Exercise 4.32

Define rules to implement the last operation of exercise 2.16, which returns a list containing the last element of a nonempty list. Check your rules on queries such as (last (3) ?x), (last (1 2 3) ?x), and (last (2 ?x) (3)). Can your rules work on queries such as (last ?x (3))?

Exercise 4.33

The following data base (see Genesis 4) traces the genealogy of the descendants of Ada back to Adam, by way of Cain:

```
(son Adam Cain)
(son Cain Enoch)
(son Enoch Irad)
(son Irad Mehujael)
(son Mehujael Methushael)
(son Methushael Lamech)
(wife Lamech Ada)
(son Ada Jabal)
(son Ada Jubal)
```

Formulate rules such as "If S is the son of F, and F is the son of G, then S is the grandson of G" and "If W is the wife of M, and S is the son of W, then S is the son of M" (which was supposedly more true in biblical times than today) that will enable the query system to find the grandson of Cain; the sons of Lamech; the grandsons of Methushael.

Exercise 4.34

Beginning with the data base and the rules you formulated in exercise 4.33, devise a new rule for adding "greats" to a grandson relationship. This should enable the system to deduce that Irad is the great-grandson of Adam, or that that Jabal and Jubal are the great-great-great-great-great-grandsons of Adam. (Hint: Represent

the fact about Irad, for example, as ((great grandson) Adam Irad). Write rules
that determine whether a list ends in the word grandson. Use this to express a
rule that allows one to derive the relationship ((great . ?rel) ?x ?y), where
?rel is a list ending in grandson.)

4.4.2 How the Query System Works

In section 4.5 we will present an implementation of the query interpreter as
a collection of procedures. In this section we give an overview that explains
the general structure of the system independent of low-level implementation
details. After describing the implementation of the interpreter, we will be in
a position to understand some of its limitations and some of the subtle ways
in which the query language's logical operations differ from the operations
of mathematical logic.

The query system is organized around two central operations called
pattern matching and *unification*. We begin by discussing pattern matching
and how this operation, together with the organization of information
in terms of streams of frames, enables us to implement both simple and
compound queries. We next discuss unification, a generalization of pattern
matching needed to implement rules. Finally, we show how the entire query
interpreter fits together through a procedure that classifies expressions in a
manner analogous to the way eval classifies expressions for the interpreter
described in section 4.1.

Pattern matching

A *pattern matcher* is a program that tests whether some datum fits a
specified pattern. For example, the data list ((a b) c (a b)) matches
the pattern (?x c ?x) with the pattern variable ?x bound to (a b). The
same data list matches the pattern (?x ?y ?z) with ?x and ?z both bound
to (a b) and ?y bound to c. It also matches ((?x ?y) c (?x ?y)) with
?x bound to a and ?y bound to b. However, it does not match the pattern
(?x a ?y), since that pattern specifies a list whose second element is the
symbol a.

The pattern matcher used by the query system takes as inputs a pattern,
a datum, and a *frame* that specifies bindings for various pattern variables.
It checks whether the datum matches the pattern in a way that is consistent
with the bindings already in the frame. If so, it returns the given frame
augmented by any bindings that may have been determined by the match.
Otherwise, it indicates that the match has failed.

For example, using the pattern (?x ?y ?x) to match (a b a) given an
empty frame will return a frame specifying that ?x is bound to a and ?y is
bound to b. Trying the match with the same pattern, the same datum, and
a frame specifying that ?y is bound to a will fail. Trying the match with the

same pattern, the same datum, and a frame in which ?y is bound to b and
?x is unbound will return the given frame augmented by a binding of ?x
to a.

The pattern matcher is all the mechanism that is needed to process
simple queries that don't involve rules. For instance, to process the query

```
(job ?x (computer programmer))
```

we scan through all assertions in the data base and select those that match
the pattern with respect to an initially empty frame. For each match we
find, we use the frame returned by the match to instantiate the pattern
with a value for ?x.

Streams of frames

The testing of patterns against frames is organized through the use of
streams. Given a single frame, the matching process runs through the data-
base entries one by one. For each data-base entry, the matcher generates
either a special symbol indicating that the match has failed or an extension
to the frame. The results for all the data-base entries are collected into a
stream, which is passed through a filter to weed out the failures. The result
is a stream of all the frames that extend the given frame via a match to
some assertion in the data base.[28]

In our system, a query takes an input stream of frames and performs the
above matching operation for every frame in the stream, as indicated in
figure 4.3. That is, for each frame in the input stream, the query generates
a new stream consisting of all extensions to that frame by matches to
assertions in the data base. All these streams are then appended to form
one huge stream, which contains all possible extensions of every frame in
the input stream. This stream is the output of the query.

To answer a simple query, we use the query with an input stream consisting of a single empty frame. The resulting output stream contains all
extensions to the empty frame (that is, all answers to our query). This
stream of frames is then used to generate a stream of copies of the original
query pattern with the variables instantiated by the values in each frame,
and this is the stream that is finally printed at the terminal.

---

[28] Because matching is generally very expensive, we would like to avoid applying the
full matcher to every element of the data base. This is usually arranged by breaking up
the process into a fast, coarse match and the final match. The coarse match filters the
data base to produce a small set of candidates for the final matcher. With care, we can
arrange our data base so that some of the work of coarse matching can be done when
the data base is constucted rather then when we want to select the candidates. This is
called *indexing* the data base. There is a vast technology built around data-base-indexing
schemes. Our implementation, described in section 4.5.5, contains a simple-minded form
of such an optimization.

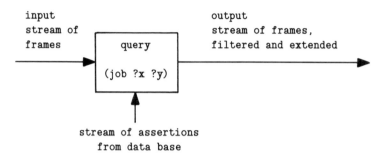

input
stream of
frames

query

(job ?x ?y)

output
stream of frames,
filtered and extended

stream of assertions
from data base

Figure 4.3
A query processes a stream of frames.

Compound queries

The real elegance of the stream-of-frames implementation is evident when we deal with compound queries. The processing of compound queries makes use of the ability of our matcher to demand that a match be consistent with a specified frame. For example, to handle the and of two queries, such as

```
(and (can-do-job ?x (computer programmer trainee))
     (job ?person ?x))
```

(informally, "Find all people who can do the job of a computer programmer trainee"), we first find all entries that match the pattern

```
(can-do-job ?x (computer programmer trainee))
```

This produces a stream of frames, each of which contains a binding for ?x. Then for each frame in the stream we find all entries that match

```
(job ?person ?x)
```

in a way that is consistent with the given binding for ?x. Each such match will produce a frame containing bindings for ?x and ?person. The and of two queries can be viewed as a series combination of the two component queries, as shown in figure 4.4. The frames that pass through the first query filter are filtered and further extended by the second query.

Figure 4.5 shows the analogous method for computing the or of two queries as a parallel combination of the two component queries. The input stream of frames is extended separately by each query. The two resulting streams are then merged (for example, by appending the streams) to produce the final output stream.

Even from this high-level description, it is apparent that the processing of compound queries can be slow. In general, if there are D items in the data base and n clauses in the compound query, we can expect to check

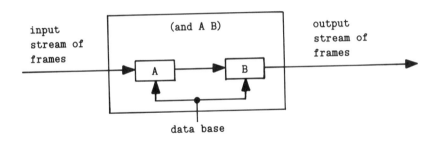

Figure 4.4
The **and** combination of two queries is produced by operating on the stream of frames
in series.

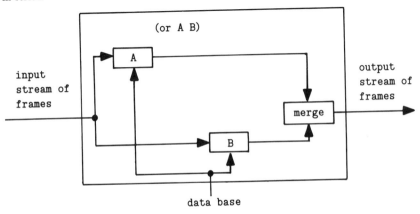

Figure 4.5
The **or** combination of two queries is produced by operating on the stream of frames in
parallel and merging the results.

on the order of Dn matches. This means that as we form more and more
complex queries the amount of computation required grows considerably.
Though systems for handling only simple queries are quite practical, it
is generally agreed that dealing with complex queries will require new
computer architectures that will make it possible to apply strategies based
on parallel processing.

From the stream-of-frames viewpoint, the **not** of some query acts as a
filter that removes all frames for which the query can be satisfied. For
instance, given the pattern

```
(not (job ?x (computer programmer)))
```

we attempt, for each frame in the input stream, to produce extension
frames that satisfy (job ?x (computer programmer)). We remove from
the input stream all frames for which such extensions exist. The result is

a stream consisting of only those frames in which the binding for ?x does not satisfy (job ?x (computer programmer)). For example, in processing the query

```
(and (supervisor ?x ?y)
     (not (job ?x (computer programmer)))))
```

the first clause will generate frames with bindings for ?x and ?y. Taking and with the not clause will filter these by removing all frames in which the binding for ?x satisfies the restriction that ?x is a computer programmer.[29]

The lisp-value special form is implemented as a similar filter on frame streams. We use each frame in the stream to instantiate any variables in the pattern, then apply the Lisp predicate. We remove from the input stream all frames for which the predicate fails.

Unification

In order to handle rules in the query language, we must be able to find the rules whose conclusions match a given query pattern. Rule conclusions are like assertions except that they can contain variables, so we will need a generalization of pattern matching—called *unification*—in which both the "pattern" and the "datum" may contain variables.

A unifier takes two patterns, each containing constants and variables, and determines whether it is possible to assign values to the variables that will make the two patterns equal. If so, it returns a frame containing these bindings. For example, unifying (?x a ?y) and (?y ?z a) will specify a frame in which ?x, ?y, and ?z must all be bound to a. On the other hand, unifying (?x ?y a) and (?x b ?y) will fail, because there is no value for ?y that can make the two patterns equal. (For the second elements of the patterns to be equal, ?y would have to be b; however, for the third elements to be equal, ?y would have to be a.) The unifier used in the query system, like the pattern matcher, takes a frame as input and performs unifications that are consistent with this frame.[30]

The unification algorithm is the most technically difficult part of the query system. With complex patterns, performing unification may seem to require deduction. To unify (?x ?x) and ((a ?y c) (a b ?z)), for example, the algorithm must infer that ?x should be (a b c), ?y should be b, and ?z should be c. We may think of this process as solving a

---

29 There is a subtle difference between this filter implementation of not and the usual meaning of not in mathematical logic. See section 4.4.3 below.

30 Another way to think of unification is that it generates the most general pattern that is a specialization of the two input patterns. That is, the unification of (?x a ?y) and (?y ?z a) is (a a a). For our implementation, it is more convenient to think of the result of unification as a frame rather than a pattern.

set of equations among the pattern components. In general, these are simultaneous equations, which may require substantial manipulation to solve.[31] For example, unifying (?x ?x) and ((a ?y c) (a b ?z)) may be thought of as specifying the simultaneous equations

```
?x = (a ?y c)
?x = (a b ?z)
```

These equations imply that

```
(a ?y c) = (a b ?z)
```

which in turn implies that

```
a = a,   ?y = b,   c = ?z,
```

and hence that

```
?x = (a b c)
```

In a successful pattern match, all pattern variables become bound, and the values to which they are bound contain only constants. This is also true of all the examples of unification we have seen so far. In general, however, a successful unification may not completely determine the variable values; some variables may remain unbound and others may be bound to values that contain variables.

Consider the unification of (?x a) and ((b ?y) ?z). We can deduce that ?x = (b ?y) and a = ?z, but we cannot further solve for ?x or ?y. The unification doesn't fail, since it is certainly possible to make the two patterns equal by assigning values to ?x and ?y. Since this match in no way restricts the values ?y can take on, no binding for ?y is put into the result frame. The match does, however, restrict the value of ?x. Whatever value ?y has, ?x must be (b ?y). A binding of ?x to the pattern (b ?y) is thus put into the frame. If a value for ?y is later determined and added to the frame (by a pattern match or unification that is required to be consistent with this frame), the previously bound ?x will refer to this value.

Applying rules
Unification is the key to the component of the query system that makes inferences from rules. To see how this is accomplished, consider processing a query that involves applying a rule, such as

```
(lives-near ?x (Hacker Alyssa P))
```

---

31 In one-sided pattern matching, all the equations that contain pattern variables are explicit and already solved for the unknown (the pattern variable).

To process this query, we first use the ordinary pattern-match procedure described above to see if there are any assertions in the data base that match this pattern. (There will not be any in this case, since our data base includes no direct assertions about who lives near whom.) The next step is to attempt to unify the query pattern with the conclusion of each rule. We find that the pattern unifies with the conclusion of the rule

```
(rule (lives-near ?person-1 ?person-2)
      (and (address ?person-1 (?town . ?rest-1))
           (address ?person-2 (?town . ?rest-2))
           (not (lisp-value equal? ?person-1 ?person-2))))
```

resulting in a frame specifying that ?person-2 should be bound to (Hacker Alyssa P) and that ?x should be bound to (have the same value as) ?person-1. Now, relative to this frame, we evaluate the compound query given by the body of the rule. Successful matches will extend this frame by providing a binding for ?person-1, and consequently a value for ?x, which we can use to instantiate the original query pattern.

In general, the query interpreter uses the following method to apply a rule in trying to establish a query pattern in a given frame that specifies bindings for some of the pattern variables:

• Unify the query with the conclusion of the rule to form, if successful, an extension of the original frame.

•.Relative to the extended frame, evaluate the query formed by the body of the rule.

Notice how similar this is to the method for applying a procedure in the eval/apply interpreter for Lisp:

• Bind the procedure's parameters to its arguments to form a frame that extends the original procedure frame.

• Relative to the extended frame, evaluate the expression formed by the body of the procedure.

Simple queries

We saw earlier in this section how to evaluate simple queries in the absence of rules. Now that we have seen how to apply rules, we can describe how to evaluate simple queries by using both rules and assertions.

Given the query pattern and a stream of frames, we produce, for each frame in the input stream, two streams:

• a stream of extended frames obtained by matching the pattern against all assertions in the data base (using the pattern matcher), and

- a stream of extended frames obtained by applying all possible rules (using the unifier).[32]

Appending these two streams produces a stream that consists of all the ways that the given pattern can be satisfied consistent with the original frame. These streams (one for each frame in the input stream) are now all combined to form one large stream, which therefore consists of all the ways that any of the frames in the original input stream can be extended to produce a match with the given pattern.

The query evaluator and the driver loop

Despite the complexity of the underlying matching operations, the system is organized much like an evaluator for any language. The procedure that coordinates the matching operations is called qeval, and it plays a role analogous to that of the eval procedure for Lisp. Qeval takes as inputs a query and a stream of frames. Its output is a stream of frames, corresponding to successful matches to the query pattern, that extend some frame in the input stream, as indicated in figure 4.3. Like eval, qeval classifies the different types of expressions (queries) and dispatches to an appropriate procedure for each. There is a procedure for each special form (and, or, not, and lisp-value) and one for simple queries.

The driver loop, which is analogous to the driver-loop procedure shown in section 4.1.4 for the Lisp interpreter, reads queries from the terminal. For each query, it calls qeval with the query and a stream that consists of a single empty frame. This will produce the stream of all possible matches (all possible extensions to the empty frame). For each frame in the resulting stream, it instantiates the original query using the values of the variables found in the frame. This stream of instantiated queries is then printed.

The driver also checks for the special command assert!, which signals that the input is not a query but rather an assertion or rule to be added to the data base. For instance,

```
query==> (assert! (job (Bitdiddle Ben) (computer wizard)))

query==> (assert!
            (rule (wheel ?person)
                  (and (supervisor ?middle-manager ?person)
                       (supervisor ?x ?middle-manager))))
```

---

32 Since unification is a generalization of matching, we could simplify the system by using the unifier to produce both streams. On the other hand, the full-blown unification algorithm requires much more work than the simple matcher, and our system will run more efficiently if we use simple matching wherever we can get away with it.

4.4.3 Is Logic Programming Mathematical Logic?

The means of combination used in the query language may at first seem identical to the operations and, or, and not of mathematical logic, and the application of query-language rules is in fact accomplished through a legitimate method of inference.[33] This identification of the query language with mathematical logic is not really valid, though, because the query language provides a *control structure* that interprets the logical statements procedurally. We can often take advantage of this control structure. For example, to find all of the supervisors of programmers we could formulate a query in either of two logically equivalent forms:

```
(and (job ?x (computer programmer))
     (supervisor ?x ?y))
```

or

```
(and (supervisor ?x ?y)
     (job ?x (computer programmer)))
```

If a company has many more supervisors than programmers (the usual case), it is better to use the first form rather than the second because the data base must be scanned for each intermediate result (frame) produced by the first clause of the and.

The aim of logic programming is to provide the programmer with techniques for decomposing a computational problem into two separate problems: "what" is to be computed, and "how" this should be computed. This is accomplished by selecting a subset of the statements of mathematical logic that is powerful enough to be able to describe anything one might want to compute, yet weak enough to have a controllable procedural interpretation. The intention here is that, on the one hand, a program specified in a logic programming language should be an effective program that can be carried out by a computer. Control ("how" to compute) is effected by using the order of evaluation of the language. We should be able to arrange the order of clauses and the order of subgoals within each clause so that the computation is done in an order deemed to be effective and efficient. At the same time, we should be able to view the result of the computation ("what" to compute) as a simple consequence of the laws of logic.

Our query language can be regarded as just such a procedurally interpretable subset of mathematical logic. An assertion represents a simple fact (an atomic proposition). A rule represents the implication that the

---

33 That a particular method of inference is legitimate is not a trivial assertion. One must prove that if one starts with true premises, only true conclusions can be derived. The method of inference represented by rule applications is *modus ponens*, the familiar method of inference that says that if A is true and A *implies* B is true, then we may conclude that B is true.

rule conclusion holds for those cases where the rule body holds. A rule
has a natural procedural interpretation: To establish the conclusion of the
rule, establish the body of the rule. Rules, therefore, specify computations.
However, because rules can also be regarded as statements of mathematical
logic, we can justify any "inference" accomplished by a logic program by
asserting that the same result could be obtained by working entirely within
mathematical logic.[34]

Infinite loops

A consequence of the ability to control the execution of a logic program by
imposing order on the clauses is that it is possible to construct hopelessly
inefficient programs for solving certain problems. An extreme case of
inefficiency occurs when the system falls into infinite loops in making
deductions. As a simple example, suppose we are setting up a data base of
famous marriages, including

```
query==> (assert! (married Minnie Mickey))
```

If we now ask

```
query==> (married Mickey ?who)
```

we will get no response, because the system doesn't know that if A is
married to B, then B is married to A. So we assert the rule

```
query==> (assert! (rule (married ?x ?y)
                        (married ?y ?x)))
```

and again query

```
query==> (married Mickey ?who)
```

Unfortunately, this will drive the system into an infinite loop, as follows:

• The system finds that the `married` rule is applicable; that is, the rule
conclusion (married ?x ?y) successfully unifies with the query pattern
(married Mickey ?who) to produce a frame in which ?x is bound to
Mickey and ?y is bound to ?who. So the interpreter proceeds to evaluate

---

34 We must qualify this statement by agreeing that, in speaking of the "inference"
accomplished by a logic program, we assume that the computation terminates. Unfortunately, even this qualified statement is false for our implementation of the query language (and also false for programs in Prolog and most other current logic programming
languages) because of our use of not and lisp-value. As we will describe below, the
not implemented in the query language is not always consistent with the not of mathematical logic, and lisp-value introduces additional complications. We could implement
a language consistent with mathematical logic by simply removing not and lisp-value
from the language and agreeing to write programs using only simple queries, and, and
or. However, this would greatly restrict the expressive power of the language. One of
the major concerns of research in logic programming is to find ways to achieve more
consistency with mathematical logic without unduly sacrificing expressive power.

the rule body (married ?y ?x) in this frame—in effect, to process the query (married ?who Mickey).

• One answer is found directly as an assertion in the data base: (married Minnie Mickey).

• The married rule is also applicable, though, so the interpreter again evaluates the rule body, which this time is equivalent to (married Mickey ?who).

The system is now in an infinite loop. Indeed, whether the system will find the simple answer (married Minnie Mickey) before it goes into the loop depends on implementation details concerning the order in which the system checks the items in the data base. This is a very simple example of the kinds of loops that can occur. Collections of interrelated rules can lead to loops that are much harder to anticipate, and the appearance of a loop can depend on low-level details concerning the order in which the system processes queries.[35]

Exercise 4.35

While Louis Reasoner is using the personnel data base, he mistakenly deletes the outranked-by rule introduced in section 4.4.1. When he realizes this, he quickly reinstalls it. Unfortunately, he makes a slight change in the rule, and types it in as

```
(rule (outranked-by ?staff-person ?boss)
      (or (supervisor ?staff-person ?boss)
          (and (outranked-by ?middle-manager ?boss)
               (supervisor ?staff-person ?middle-manager)))))
```

Just after Louis types this information into the system, Rosemary Forrest comes by to find out who outranks Ben Bitdiddle. She issues the query

query==> (outranked-by (Bitdiddle Ben) ?who)

Instead of answering, the system goes into an infinite loop. Explain why.

Exercise 4.36

Cy D. Fect, looking forward to the day when he will rise in the organization, adds to the personnel data base the following rule for determining who is a "wheel":

---

[35] This is not a problem of the logic but one of the procedural interpretation of the logic provided by our interpreter. We could write an interpreter that would not fall into a loop here. For example, we could enumerate all the proofs derivable from our assertions and our rules in a breadth-first rather than a depth-first order. However, such a system makes it more difficult to take advantage of the order of deductions in our programs. One attempt to build sophisticated control into such a program is described in deKleer et al. 1977. Another technique, which does not lead to such serious control problems, is to put in special knowledge, such as detectors for particular kinds of loops (exercise 4.38). However, there can be no general scheme for reliably preventing a system from going down infinite paths in performing deductions. Imagine a diabolical rule of the form "To show $P(x)$ is true, show that $P(f(x))$ is true," for some suitably chosen function f.

```
(rule (wheel ?person)
      (and (supervisor ?middle-manager ?person)
           (supervisor ?x ?middle-manager)))
```

To test the rule, he gives a query to find all the wheels:

query==> (wheel ?who)

To his surprise, the system responds

```
(wheel (Warbucks Oliver))
(wheel (Bitdiddle Ben))
(wheel (Warbucks Oliver))
(wheel (Warbucks Oliver))
(wheel (Warbucks Oliver))
```

Why is Oliver Warbucks listed four times?

Exercise 4.37

Ben has been generalizing the query system to provide statistics about the company. For example, to find the total salaries of all the computer programmers one will be able to type

```
(sum ?amount
     (and (job ?x (computer programmer))
          (salary ?x ?amount)))
```

In general, Ben's new system allows expressions of the form

```
(accumulation-function ⟨ variable⟩
                       ⟨ query pattern⟩)
```

where accumulation-function can be things like sum, average, or maximum. Ben reasons that it should be a cinch to implement this. He will simply feed the query pattern to qeval. This will produce a stream of frames. He will then pass this stream through a mapping function that extracts the value of the designated variable from each frame in the stream and feed the resulting stream of values to the accumulation function. Just as Ben completes the implementation and is about to try it out, Cy walks by, still puzzling over the wheel query result in exercise 4.36. When Cy shows Ben the system's response, Ben groans, "Oh, no, my simple accumulation scheme won't work!"

What has Ben just realized? Outline a method that he can use to salvage the situation.

Exercise 4.38

Devise a way to install a loop detector in the query system so as to avoid the kinds of simple loops illustrated in the text and in exercise 4.35. The general idea is that the system should maintain some sort of history of its current chain of deductions and should not begin processing a query that it is already working on. Describe what kind of information (patterns and frames) is included in this history, and how the check should be made. (After you study the details of the query-system implementation in section 4.5, you may want to modify the system to include your loop detector.)

Exercise 4.39

Define rules to implement the `reverse` operation of exercise 2.17, which returns a list containing the same elements as a given list in reverse order. Can your rules answer both `(reverse (1 2 3) ?x)` and `(reverse ?x (1 2 3))`?

Problems with not

Another quirk in the query system concerns not. Given the data base of section 4.4.1, consider the following two queries:

```
(and (supervisor ?x ?y)
     (not (job ?x (computer programmer)))))

(and (not (job ?x (computer programmer)))
     (supervisor ?x ?y))
```

These two queries do not produce the same result. The first query begins by finding all entries in the data base that match (supervisor ?x ?y), and then filters the resulting frames by removing the ones in which the value of ?x satisfies (job ?x (computer programmer)). The second query begins by filtering the incoming frames to remove those that can satisfy (job ?x (computer programmer)). Since the only incoming frame is empty, it checks the data base to see if there are any patterns that satisfy (job ?x (computer programmer)). Since there generally are entries of this form, the not clause filters out the empty frame and returns an empty stream of frames. Consequently, the entire compound query returns an empty stream.

The trouble is that our implementation of not really is meant to serve as a filter on values for the variables. If a not clause is processed with a frame in which some of the variables remain unbound (as does ?x in the example above), the system will produce unexpected results. Similar problems occur with the use of lisp-value—the Lisp predicate can't work if some of its arguments are unbound. See exercise 4.43.

There is also a much more serious way in which the not of the query language differs from the not of mathematical logic. In logic, we interpret the statement "not P" to mean that P is not true. In the query system, however, "not P" means that P is not deducible from the knowledge in the data base. For example, given the personnel data base of section 4.4.1, the system would happily deduce all sorts of not statements, such as that Ben Bitdiddle is not a baseball fan, that it is not raining outside, and that $2 + 2$ is not 4.[36] In other words, the not of logic programming languages

---

36 Consider the query (not (baseball-fan (Bitdiddle Ben))). The system finds that (baseball-fan (Bitdiddle Ben)) is not in the data base, so the empty frame does not satisfy the pattern and is not filtered out of the initial stream of frames. The result of the query is thus the empty frame, which is used to instantiate the input query to produce (not (baseball-fan (Bitdiddle Ben))).

reflects the so-called *closed world assumption* that all relevant information
has been included in the data base.[37]

4.5 Implementing the Query System

Section 4.4.2 described how the query system works. Now we fill in the
details by presenting a complete implementation of the system.

4.5.1 The Driver Loop and Instantiation

The driver loop for the query system reads expressions from the terminal,
using Lisp's `read` primitive. If the expression indicates that this is a rule
or assertion to be added to the data base, then the information is added.
Otherwise the expression is assumed to be a query. The driver passes
this query to the evaluator `qeval` together with an initial frame stream
consisting of a single empty frame. The result of the evaluation is a stream
of frames generated by satisfying the query with variable values found in
the data base. These frames are used to form a new stream consisting of
copies of the original query in which the variables are instantiated with
values supplied by the stream of frames, and this final stream is printed at
the terminal:

```
(define (query-driver-loop)
  (newline)
  (princ "query==> ")
  (let ((q (query-syntax-process (read))))
    (if (assertion-to-be-added? q)
        (sequence (add-rule-or-assertion!
                    (add-assertion-body q))
                  (print "assertion added to data base")
                  (query-driver-loop))
        (sequence
          (print-stream-elements-on-separate-lines
           (map (lambda (frame)
                  (instantiate q
                               frame
                               (lambda (v f)
                                 (contract-question-mark v))))
                (qeval q (singleton '()))))
          (query-driver-loop)))))
```

---

37 A discussion and justification of this treatment of *not* can be found in the article by
Clark (1978).

Here, as in the Lisp evaluator of section 4.1, we use an abstract syntax for the expressions of the query language. The implementation of the expression syntax, including the predicate `assertion-to-be-added?` and the selector `add-assertion-body`, is given in section 4.5.6. The printing procedure is also shown in that section. `Add-rule-or-assertion!` is defined in section 4.5.5.

Before doing any processing on an input expression, the driver loop transforms it syntactically into a form that makes the processing more efficient. This involves changing the representation of pattern variables. When the query is instantiated, any variables that remain unbound are transformed back before being printed. `Query-syntax-process` and `contract-question-mark` are implemented, along with the other procedures that deal with syntax, in section 4.5.6.

To instantiate an expression, we copy it, replacing any variables in the expression by their values in a given frame. The values are themselves instantiated, since they could contain variables (for example, if `?x` in `exp` is bound to `?y` as the result of unification and `?y` is in turn bound to 5). The action to take if a variable cannot be instantiated is given by a procedural argument to `instantiate`.

```
(define (instantiate exp frame unbound-var-handler)
  (define (copy exp)
    (cond ((constant? exp) exp)
          ((var? exp)
           (let ((vcell (binding-in-frame exp frame)))
             (if (null? vcell)
                 (unbound-var-handler exp frame)
                 (copy (binding-value vcell)))))
          (else (cons (copy (car exp))
                      (copy (cdr exp))))))
  (copy exp))
```

The procedures that manipulate bindings are defined in section 4.5.6.

4.5.2 The Evaluator

The `qeval` procedure, called by the `query-driver-loop`, is the basic evaluator of the query system. It takes as inputs a query and a stream of frames, and it returns a stream of extended frames. It identifies special forms by a data-directed dispatch using `get` and `put`, just as we did in implementing generic operations in chapter 2. Any query that is not identified as a special form is assumed to be a simple query, to be processed by `asserted?`.

```
(define (qeval query frame-stream)
  (let ((qproc (get (type query) 'qeval)))
    (if (not (null? qproc))
        (qproc (contents query) frame-stream)
        (asserted? query frame-stream))))
```

Type and contents, defined in section 4.5.6, implement the abstract syntax
of the special forms.

Simple queries

The asserted? procedure handles simple queries. It takes as arguments a
simple query (a pattern) together with a stream of frames, and it returns
the stream formed by extending each frame by all data-base matches of the
query. To accomplish this, it uses the procedure find-assertions (section
4.5.3), which generates for each frame a stream of extended frames. To
apply find-assertions to each frame in the input stream and consolidate
the output frames for each frame into one large output stream, we apply the
flatmap procedure, which was introduced in section 3.4.2 to perform just
this kind of mapping and accumulation. Similarly, apply-rules (section
4.5.4) is used to generate a stream of extensions found by applying rules
for each frame in the input stream; again the results are accumulated
using flatmap. Finally, the two streams—one generated by checking the
assertions and one generated by applying the rules—are appended to form
a single output stream.

```
(define (asserted? query-pattern frame-stream)
  (append-streams
   (flatmap (lambda (frame)
              (find-assertions query-pattern frame))
            frame-stream)
   (flatmap (lambda (frame)
              (apply-rules query-pattern frame))
            frame-stream)))
```

Compound queries

And queries are handled as illustrated in figure 4.4 by the conjoin procedure. Conjoin takes as inputs the conjuncts and the frame stream and
returns the stream of extended frames. First, conjoin filters the stream of
frames by finding the stream of all possible extensions to the first query in
the conjunction. Then, using this as the new frame stream, it recursively
applies conjoin to the rest of the queries.

```
(define (conjoin conjuncts frame-stream)
  (if (empty-conjunction? conjuncts)
      frame-stream
      (conjoin (rest-conjuncts conjuncts)
               (qeval (first-conjunct conjuncts)
                      frame-stream))))
```

The expression

```
(put 'and 'qeval conjoin)
```

sets up qeval to dispatch to conjoin when an and form is encountered.

Or forms are handled similarly, according to the diagram in figure 4.5. The output streams for the various disjuncts of the or are computed separately and then merged through use of interleave (section 3.4.5):

```
(define (disjoin disjuncts frame-stream)
  (if (empty-disjunction? disjuncts)
      the-empty-stream
      (interleave (qeval (first-disjunct disjuncts)
                         frame-stream)
                  (disjoin (rest-disjuncts disjuncts)
                           frame-stream))))
```

```
(put 'or 'qeval disjoin)
```

The predicates and selectors for the syntax of conjuncts and disjuncts are given in section 4.5.6.

Filters

Not is handled by the method outlined in section 4.4.2. We attempt to extend each frame in the input stream to satisfy the query being negated, and we include a given frame in the output stream only if it cannot be extended.

```
(define (negate a frame-stream)
  (flatmap
   (lambda (frame)
     (if (empty-stream? (qeval (negated-query a)
                               (singleton frame)))
         (singleton frame)
         the-empty-stream))
   frame-stream))
```

```
(put 'not 'qeval negate)
```

Lisp-value is a filter similar to not. Each frame in the stream is used to instantiate the variables in the pattern, the indicated predicate is applied, and the frames for which the predicate returns false are filtered out of the input stream. An error results if there are unbound pattern variables.

```
(define (lisp-value call frame-stream)
  (flatmap
   (lambda (frame)
     (if (execute
          (instantiate call
                       frame
                       (lambda (v f)
                         (error "Unknown pat var--LISP-VALUE"
                                v))))
         (singleton frame)
         the-empty-stream))
   frame-stream))
```

```
(put 'lisp-value 'qeval lisp-value)
```

```
(define (execute exp)
  (apply (eval (predicate exp) user-initial-environment)
         (args exp)))
```

Execute must eval the predicate expression to get the procedure to apply. However, it must not evaluate the arguments, since they are not Lisp expressions.[38]

The always-true special form provides for a query that is always satisfied. It ignores its contents (normally empty) and simply passes through all the frames in the input stream. Always-true is used by the rule-body selector (section 4.5.6) to provide bodies for rules that were defined without bodies (that is, rules whose conclusions are always satisfied).

```
(define (always-true ignore frame-stream)
  frame-stream)
```

```
(put 'always-true 'qeval always-true)
```

---

[38] For example, assume that we have a predicate middle-name? that decides whether a person has a middle name by looking at the length of the list representing the name. The evaluation of
(lisp-value middle-name? (Bitdiddle Ben))
must not try to evaluate (Bitdiddle Ben) as a Lisp expression before giving it to middle-name?.

The selectors that define the syntax of not and `lisp-value` are given in section 4.5.6.

4.5.3 Finding Assertions by Pattern Matching

Find-assertions, called by `asserted?` (section 4.5.2), takes as input a pattern and a frame. It returns a stream of frames, each extending the given one by a data-base match of the given pattern. It uses `fetch-assertions` (section 4.5.5) to get a stream of all the assertions in the data base that should be checked for a match against the pattern and the frame. The reason for `fetch-assertions` here is that we can often apply simple tests that will eliminate many of the entries in the data base from the pool of candidates for a successful match. The system would still work if we eliminated `fetch-assertions` and simply returned a stream of all assertions in the data base, but the computation would be less efficient because we would need to make many more calls to the matcher.

```
(define (find-assertions pattern frame)
  (flatmap (lambda (datum)
             (pattern-match pattern datum frame))
           (fetch-assertions pattern frame)))
```

The basic pattern matcher takes as arguments a pattern, a data object, and a frame and returns either a one-element stream containing the extended frame or the-empty-stream if the match fails.

```
(define (pattern-match pat dat frame)
  (let ((result (internal-match pat dat frame)))
    (if (eq? result 'failed)
        the-empty-stream
        (singleton result))))
```

The main pattern-match procedure calls `internal-match`, which returns either the symbol `failed` or an extension of the given frame. The basic idea of the matcher is to check the pattern against the data, element by element, accumulating bindings for the pattern variables. We first consider the cases where the pattern element is primitive (a constant or a variable). If it is a variable we extend the current frame by binding the variable to the data, so long as this is consistent with the bindings already in the frame. If the pattern element is a constant, then either it is equal to the data (in which case the match succeeds and we return the frame of bindings accumulated so far) or it is not equal to the data (in which case the match fails and we return the symbol `failed`). In the next case the pattern is not primitive but the data object is a constant, so the match must fail. Finally, if the pattern and the data are both nonprimitive, we (recursively) match the `car` of the pattern against the `car` of the data to produce a frame. In this frame we then match the `cdr` of the pattern against the `cdr` of the data.

```
(define (internal-match pat dat frame)
  (cond ((eq? frame 'failed) 'failed)
        ((var? pat) (extend-if-consistent pat dat frame))
        ((constant? pat)
         (if (constant? dat)
             (if (same-constant? pat dat) frame 'failed)
             'failed))
        ((constant? dat) 'failed)
        (else (internal-match (cdr pat)
                              (cdr dat)
                              (internal-match (car pat)
                                              (car dat)
                                              frame)))))
```

Here is the procedure that extends a frame by adding a new binding, if this is consistent with the bindings already in the frame:

```
(define (extend-if-consistent var dat frame)
  (let ((value (binding-in-frame var frame)))
    (if (null? value)
        (extend var dat frame)
        (internal-match (binding-value value) dat frame))))
```

If there is no binding for the variable in the frame, we simply add the binding of the variable to the data. Otherwise we match, in the frame, the data against the value of the variable in the frame. If the stored value contains only constants, as it must if it was stored by `extend-if-consistent` during pattern matching, then the match simply tests whether the stored and new values are the same. If so, it returns the unmodified frame; if not, it returns a failure indication. The stored value may, however, contain pattern variables if it was stored during unification (see section 4.5.4). The recursive match of the stored pattern against the new data will add or check bindings for the variables in this pattern. For example, suppose we have a frame in which `?x` is bound to `(f ?y)` and `?y` is unbound, and we wish to augment this frame by a binding of `?x` to `(f b)`. We look

up ?x and find that it is bound to (f ?y). This leads us to match (f ?y)
against the proposed new binding (f b) in the same frame. Eventually
this match extends the frame by adding a binding of ?y to b. ?X remains
bound to (f ?y). We never modify a stored binding and we never store
more than one binding for a given variable.

The procedures used by extend-if-consistent to manipulate frames
and bindings, and the procedures used by internal-match to deal with
constants and variables, are defined in section 4.5.6.

Dot notation

In section 4.4.1 we introduced dot notation for patterns. We said that if a
pattern contains a period followed by a pattern variable, the pattern variable matches the rest of the data list (rather than the next element of the
data list). Although the pattern matcher we have just implemented doesn't
look for periods, it does behave as we want for dot notation. This is because
the Lisp read primitive, which was used by query-driver-loop to read
the query and represent it as a list structure, treats periods in a special
way. When read sees a dot, instead of making the next item be the next
element of a list (the car of a cons whose cdr will be the rest of the list) it
makes the next item be the cdr of the list structure. For example, the list
structure produced by read for the pattern (computer ?type) could be
constructed by evaluating the expression (cons 'computer (cons '?type
nil)), and that for (computer . ?type) could be constructed by evaluating the expression (cons 'computer '?type). Thus, as internal-match
recursively compares cars and cdrs of a data list and a pattern that had
a dot, it eventually matches the variable after the dot (which is a cdr
of the pattern) against a sublist of the data list, binding the variable to
that list. For example, matching (computer . ?type) against (computer
programmer trainee) will match ?type against (programmer trainee).

4.5.4 Rules and Unification

Apply-rules is the rule analog of find-assertions (section 4.5.3). It
takes as input a pattern and a frame, and it forms a stream of extension
frames by applying rules from the data base. Flatmap maps apply-a-
rule down the stream of possibly applicable rules (selected by a procedure
fetch-rules, analogous to the fetch-assertions procedure defined in
section 4.5.5) and combines the resulting streams of frames.

```
(define (apply-rules pattern frame)
  (flatmap (lambda (rule)
             (apply-a-rule rule pattern frame))
           (fetch-rules pattern frame)))
```

Apply-a-rule applies rules by using the method outlined in section 4.4.2. It first augments its argument frame by unifying the rule conclusion with the pattern in the given frame. If this succeeds, it evaluates the rule body in this new frame. (The selectors rule-body and rule-condition that extract parts of a rule are defined in section 4.5.6.)

Before any of this happens, however, the program renames all the variables in the rule with unique new names. The reason for this is to prevent the variables for different rule applications from becoming confused with each other. For instance, if two rules both use a variable named ?x, then each one may add a binding for ?x to the frame when it is applied. These two ?x's have nothing to do with each other, and we should not be fooled into thinking that the two bindings must be consistent. Rather than rename variables, we could devise a more clever environment structure; however, the renaming approach we have chosen here is the most straightforward, even if not the most efficient. (See exercise 4.44.) Here is the apply-a-rule procedure:

```
(define (apply-a-rule rule query-pattern query-frame)
  (let ((clean-rule (rename-variables-in rule)))
    (let ((unify-result (unify-match query-pattern
                                     (conclusion clean-rule)
                                     query-frame)))
      (if (empty-stream? unify-result)
          the-empty-stream
          (qeval (rule-body clean-rule) unify-result)))))
```

We generate unique variable names by associating a unique identifier (such as a number) with each rule application and combining this identifier with the original variable names. For example, if the rule-application identifier is 7, we might change each ?x in the rule to ?x-7 and each ?y in the rule to ?y-7.

```
(define (rename-variables-in rule)
  (let ((rule-application-id (new-rule-application-id)))
    (define (tree-walk exp)
      (cond ((constant? exp) exp)
            ((var? exp)
             (make-new-variable exp rule-application-id))
            (else (cons (tree-walk (car exp))
                        (tree-walk (cdr exp))))))
    (tree-walk rule)))
```

Make-new-variable and new-rule-application-id are included with the
syntax procedures in section 4.5.6.

The unification algorithm is implemented as a procedure that takes as
inputs two patterns and a frame and returns either a stream containing
an extended frame or else the empty stream. The actual unification is
performed by internal-unify, which returns either the extended frame
or the symbol failed.

```
(define (unify-match p1 p2 frame)
  (let ((result (internal-unify p1 p2 frame)))
    (if (eq? result 'failed)
        the-empty-stream
        (singleton result))))
```

The unifier is just like the pattern matcher except that it is symmetrical—
variables are allowed on both sides of the match. The program is basically
the same, except that there is an extra line (marked "***" below) that
tests for the possibility that the object on the right side of the match is a
variable.

```
(define (internal-unify p1 p2 frame)
  (cond ((eq? frame 'failed) 'failed)
        ((var? p1) (extend-if-possible p1 p2 frame))
        ((var? p2) (extend-if-possible p2 p1 frame))    ;***
        ((constant? p1)
         (if (constant? p2)
             (if (same-constant? p1 p2) frame 'failed)
             'failed))
        ((constant? p2) 'failed)
        (else (internal-unify (cdr p1)
                              (cdr p2)
                              (internal-unify (car p1)
                                              (car p2)
                                              frame)))))
```

In unification, as in one-sided pattern matching, we want to accept
a proposed extension of the frame only if it is consistent. The procedure extend-if-possible used in unification is the same as the extend-
if-consistent used in pattern matching except for two special checks,
marked "***" in the program below. The checks deal with attempts to bind
a variable to a pattern that includes that variable. Such a situation can occur whenever a variable is repeated in both patterns. Consider, for example,
unifying the two patterns (?x ?x) and (?y ⟨expression involving ?y⟩) in
a frame where both ?x and ?y are unbound. First ?x is matched against

?y, making a binding of ?x to ?y. Next, the same ?x is matched against the given expression involving ?y. Since ?x is already bound to ?y, this results in matching ?y against the expression. If we think of the unifier as finding a set of values for the pattern variables that make the patterns the same, then these patterns imply instructions to find a ?y such that ?y is equal to the expression involving ?y. There is no general method for solving such equations, so we reject such bindings; these cases are recognized by the predicate freefor?.[39]   On the other hand, we do not want to reject attempts to bind a variable to itself. For example, consider unifying (?x ?x) and (?y ?y). The second attempt to bind ?x to ?y matches ?y (the stored value of ?x) against ?y (the new value of ?x). Binding something to itself is never inconsistent, so we explicitly admit this case by a special equality check at the beginning of the frame extender.

```
(define (extend-if-possible var val frame)
  (if (equal? var val)                               ;***
      frame
      (let ((value-cell (binding-in-frame var frame)))
        (if (null? value-cell)
            (if (freefor? var val frame)             ;***
                (extend var val frame)
                'failed)
            (internal-unify (binding-value value-cell)
                            val
                            frame)))))
```

[39] In general, unifying ?y with an expression involving ?y would require our being able to find a fixed point of the equation ?y = ⟨ expression involving ?y ⟩. It is sometimes possible to syntactically form an expression that appears to be the solution. For example, ?y = (f ?y) seems to have the fixed point (f (f (f ...))), which we can produce by beginning with the expression (f ?y) and repeatedly substituting (f ?y) for ?y. Unfortunately, not every such equation has a meaningful fixed point. The issues that arise here are similar to the issues of manipulating infinite series in mathematics. For example, we know that 2 is the solution to the equation $y = 1 + y/2$. Beginning with the expression $1 + y/2$ and repeatedly substituting $1 + y/2$ for y gives

$$2 = y = 1 + y/2 = 1 + (1 + y/2)/2 = 1 + 1/2 + y/4 = \cdots,$$

which leads to

$$2 = 1 + 1/2 + 1/4 + 1/8 + \cdots.$$

However, if we try the same manipulation beginning with the observation that -1 is the solution to the equation $y = 1 + 2y$, we obtain

$$-1 = y = 1 + 2y = 1 + 2(1 + 2y) = 1 + 2 + 4y = \cdots,$$

which leads to

$$-1 = 1 + 2 + 4 + 8 + \cdots.$$

Although the formal manipulations used in deriving these two equations are identical, the first result is a valid assertion about infinite series but the second is not. Similarly, for our unification results, reasoning with an arbitrary syntactically constructed expression may lead to errors.

Freefor? is a predicate that tests whether an expression proposed to be the value of a pattern variable contains the variable. This must be done relative to the current frame because the expression may contain occurrences of a variable that already has a value that contains our test variable. The structure of freefor? is a simple recursive tree walk in which we substitute for the values of variables whenever necessary.

```
(define (freefor? var exp frame)
  (define (freewalk e)
    (cond ((constant? e) t)
          ((var? e)
           (if (equal? var e)
               nil
               (freewalk (lookup-in-frame e frame))))
          ((freewalk (car e)) (freewalk (cdr e)))
          (else nil)))
  (freewalk exp))
```

4.5.5 Maintaining the Data Base

One important problem in designing logic programming languages is that of arranging things so that as few irrelevant data-base entries as possible will be examined in checking a given pattern. In the present system we store all assertions whose cars are constant symbols in separate streams, in a table indexed by the symbol. To fetch an assertion that may match a pattern, we first check to see if the car of the pattern is a constant symbol. If so, we return (to be tested using the matcher) all the stored assertions that have the same car. If the pattern's car is not a constant symbol, we return all the stored assertions. More clever methods could also take advantage of information in the frame, or try also to optimize the case where the car of the pattern is not a constant symbol. We avoid building our criteria for indexing (using the car, handling only the case of constant symbols) into the program; instead we call on predicates and selectors that embody our criteria.

```
(define THE-ASSERTIONS the-empty-stream)

(define (fetch-assertions pattern frame)
  (if (use-index? pattern)
      (get-indexed-assertions pattern)
      (get-all-assertions)))
```

```
(define (get-all-assertions) THE-ASSERTIONS)

(define (get-indexed-assertions pattern)
  (get-stream (index-key-of pattern) 'assertion-stream))
```

Get-stream looks up a stream in the table and returns an empty stream if nothing is stored there.

```
(define (get-stream key1 key2)
  (let ((s (get key1 key2)))
    (if (null? s) the-empty-stream s)))
```

Rules are stored similarly, using the car of the rule conclusion. Rule conclusions are arbitrary patterns, however, so they differ from assertions in that they can contain variables. A pattern whose car is a constant symbol can match rules whose conclusions start with a variable as well as rules whose conclusions have the same car. Thus, when fetching rules that might match a pattern whose car is a constant symbol we fetch all rules whose conclusions start with a variable as well as those whose conclusions have the same car as the pattern. For this purpose we store all rules whose conclusions start with a variable in a separate stream in our table, indexed by the symbol ? .

```
(define THE-RULES the-empty-stream)

(define (fetch-rules pattern frame)
  (if (use-index? pattern)
      (get-indexed-rules pattern)
      (get-all-rules)))

(define (get-all-rules) THE-RULES)

(define (get-indexed-rules pattern)
  (append-streams
   (get-stream (index-key-of pattern) 'rule-stream)
   (get-stream '? 'rule-stream)))
```

Add-rule-or-assertion! is used by query-driver-loop to add assertions and rules to the data base. Each item is stored in the index, if appropriate, and in a stream of all assertions or rules in the data base.

```
(define (add-rule-or-assertion! assertion)
  (if (rule? assertion)
      (add-rule! assertion)
      (add-assertion! assertion)))
```

```
(define (add-assertion! assertion)
  (store-assertion-in-index assertion)
  (let ((old-assertions THE-ASSERTIONS))
    (set! THE-ASSERTIONS
          (cons-stream assertion old-assertions))
    'ok))

(define (add-rule! rule)
  (store-rule-in-index rule)
  (let ((old-rules THE-RULES))
    (set! THE-RULES (cons-stream rule old-rules))
    'ok))
```

To actually store an assertion or a rule, we check to see if it can be indexed. If so, we store it in the appropriate stream.

```
(define (store-assertion-in-index assertion)
  (if (indexable? assertion)
      (let ((key (index-key-of assertion)))
        (let ((current-assertion-stream
               (get-stream key 'assertion-stream)))
          (put key
               'assertion-stream
               (cons-stream assertion
                            current-assertion-stream))))))

(define (store-rule-in-index rule)
  (let ((pattern (conclusion rule)))
    (if (indexable? pattern)
        (let ((key (index-key-of pattern)))
          (let ((current-rule-stream
                 (get-stream key 'rule-stream)))
            (put key
                 'rule-stream
                 (cons-stream rule
                              current-rule-stream)))))))
```

The following procedures define how the data-base index is used. A pattern (an assertion or a rule conclusion) will be stored in the table if it starts with a variable or a constant symbol.

```
(define (indexable? pat)
  (or (constant-symbol? (car pat))
      (var? (car pat))))
```

The key under which a pattern is stored in the table is either ? (if it starts with a variable) or the constant symbol with which it starts.

```
(define (index-key-of pat)
  (let ((key (car pat)))
    (if (var? key) '? key)))
```

The index will be used to retrieve items that might match a pattern if the pattern starts with a constant symbol.

```
(define (use-index? pat)
  (constant-symbol? (car pat)))
```

Exercise 4.40

What is the purpose of the let bindings in the procedures add-assertion! and add-rule! shown above? What would be wrong with the following implementation of add-assertion!?

```
(define (add-assertion! assertion)
  (store-assertion-in-index assertion)
  (set! THE-ASSERTIONS
        (cons-stream assertion THE-ASSERTIONS))
  'ok)
```

4.5.6 Utility Procedures

This section presents the procedures that implement the syntax of query expressions, frames, and printing.

Procedures that implement the abstract syntax of queries

Type and contents, used by qeval (section 4.5.2), specify that a special form is identified by the symbol in its car.

```
(define (type exp)
  (if (atom? exp)
      (error "Unknown expression TYPE" exp)
      (if (symbol? (car exp)) (car exp) nil)))
```

```
(define (contents exp)
  (if (atom? exp)
      (error "Unknown expression CONTENTS" exp)
      (cdr exp)))
```

The following procedures, used by query-driver-loop (section 4.5.1),
specify that rules and assertions are added to the data base by expressions
of the form (assert! ⟨ *rule-or-assertion* ⟩) :

```
(define (assertion-to-be-added? exp)
  (eq? (type exp) 'assert!))

(define (add-assertion-body exp)
  (car (contents exp)))
```

The following, used in section 4.5.2, define the syntax of the and, or,
not, and lisp-value special forms:

```
(define empty-conjunction? null?)
(define first-conjunct car)
(define rest-conjuncts cdr)

(define empty-disjunction? null?)
(define first-disjunct car)
(define rest-disjuncts cdr)

(define negated-query car)

(define predicate car)
(define args cdr)
```

The following three procedures define the syntax of rules:

```
(define (rule? statement)
  (if (atom? statement)
      nil
      (eq? (car statement) 'rule)))

(define conclusion cadr)

(define (rule-body rule)
  (if (null? (cddr rule))
      '(always-true)
      (caddr rule)))
```

Query-driver-loop (section 4.5.1) calls query-syntax-process in order to transform pattern variables in the expression, which have the form
?symbol, into the internal format (? symbol). That is to say, a pat-

tern such as (job ?x ?y) is actually represented internally by the system
as (job (? x) (? y)). This increases the efficiency of query processing,
since it means that the system can check to see if an expression is a pattern variable by checking whether the car of the expression is the symbol
?, rather than having to extract characters from the symbol. The syntax
transformation is accomplished by the following procedure:[40]

```
(define (query-syntax-process exp)
  (map-over-atoms expand-question-mark exp))

(define (map-over-atoms proc exp)
  (if (atom? exp)
      (proc exp)
      (cons (map-over-atoms proc (car exp))
            (map-over-atoms proc (cdr exp)))))

(define (expand-question-mark atom)
  (if (symbol? atom)
      (let ((characters (explode atom)))
        (if (eq? (car characters) '?)
            (list '? (implode (cdr characters)))
            atom))
      atom))
```

The program uses the primitives explode (which separates a symbol into
a list of characters) and implode (which assembles a list of characters to
form a new symbol). We have abstracted out the control structure map-
over-atoms, which applies a procedure to every atom in a list structure.

Once the variables are transformed in this way, the variables in a pattern
are lists starting with ?, the constants (nonvariables) are just the atoms,
and the constant symbols are just the symbols.

```
(define (var? exp)
  (if (atom? exp)
      nil
      (eq? (car exp) '?)))
```

```
(define constant? atom?)
(define constant-symbol? symbol?)
(define same-constant? equal?)
```

Unique variables are constructed during rule application (section 4.5.4) with the following procedures. The unique identifier for a rule application is a number, which is incremented each time a rule is applied.

```
(define rule-counter 0)

(define (new-rule-application-id)
  (set! rule-counter (1+ rule-counter))
  rule-counter)

(define (make-new-variable var rule-application-id)
  (cons '? (cons rule-application-id (cdr var))))
```

When query-driver-loop instantiates the query to print the answer, it converts any unbound pattern variables back to the right form for printing, using

```
(define (contract-question-mark variable)
  (implode (cons '? (explode (if (number? (cadr variable))
                                 (caddr variable)
                                 (cadr variable)))))))
```

Frame access operations
Frames are represented as lists of pairs, as they were in our Lisp evaluator of section 4.1.3.

```
(define (make-binding variable value)
  (cons variable value))

(define (binding-variable binding)
  (car binding))

(define (binding-value binding)
  (cdr binding))

(define (binding-in-frame variable frame)
  (assoc variable frame))

(define (extend variable value frame)
  (cons (make-binding variable value) frame))
```

```
(define (lookup-in-frame variable frame)
  (binding-value (binding-in-frame variable frame)))
```

Assoc, used instead of assq in binding-in-frame, is the same as assq except that it finds the list element whose car is equal? (rather than eq?) to the given key. This is necessary here because the variables are represented as lists.

Printing utility

The following procedure is used to print the stream of instantiated queries:

```
(define (print-stream-elements-on-separate-lines s)
  (if (empty-stream? s)
      (print "done")
      (sequence (print (head s))
                (print-stream-elements-on-separate-lines
                 (tail s)))))
```

Exercise 4.41

Implement for the query language a new special form called unique. Unique should succeed if there is precisely one item in the data base satisfying a specified query. For example,

query==> (unique (job ?x (computer wizard)))

should print the one-item stream

(unique (job (Bitdiddle Ben) (computer wizard)))

since Ben is the only computer wizard, and

query==> (unique (job ?x (computer programmer)))

should print the empty stream, since there is more than one computer programmer. Moreover,

query==> (and (job ?x ?j)
              (unique (job ?anyone ?j)))

should list all the jobs that are filled by only one person, and the persons who fill them.

There are two parts to implementing unique. The first is to write a procedure that handles this form, and the second is to make qeval dispatch to that procedure. The second part is trivial, since qeval does its dispatching in a data-directed way. If your procedure is called uniquely-asserted?, all you need to do is

(put 'unique 'qeval uniquely-asserted?)

and qeval will dispatch to this procedure for every query whose type (car) is the symbol unique.

The real problem is to write the procedure uniquely-asserted?. This should take as input the contents (cdr) of the unique query, together with a stream of frames. For each frame in the stream, it should use `qeval` to find the stream of all extensions to the frame that satisfy the given query. Any stream that does not have exactly one item in it should be eliminated. The remaining streams should be passed back to be accumulated into one big stream that is the result of the `unique` query. This is similar to the implementation of the `not` special form.

Test your implementation by forming a query that lists all persons who supervise precisely one person.

Exercise 4.42

Our implementation of `and` as a series combination of queries (section 4.4.2) is elegant, but it is inefficient because in processing the second query of the `and` we must scan the data base for each frame produced by the first query. If the data base has N elements, and a typical query produces a number of output frames proportional to N (say N/k), then scanning the data base for each frame produced by the first query will require N^2/k calls to the pattern matcher. Another approach would be to process the two clauses of the `and` separately, then look for all pairs of output frames that are compatible. If each query produces N/k output frames, then this means that we must perform N^2/k^2 compatibility checks—a factor of k fewer than the number of matches required in our current method.

Devise an implementation of `and` that uses this strategy. You must implement a procedure that takes two frames as inputs, checks whether the bindings in the frames are compatible, and, if so, produces a frame that merges the two sets of bindings. This operation is similar to unification.

Exercise 4.43

In section 4.4.3 we saw that `not` and `lisp-value` can cause the query language to give "wrong" answers if these filtering operations are applied to frames in which variables are unbound. Devise a way to fix this shortcoming. One idea is to perform the filtering in a "delayed" manner by appending to the frame a "promise" to filter that is fulfilled only when enough variables have been bound to make the operation possible. We could wait to perform filtering until all other operations have been performed. However, for efficiency's sake, we would like to perform filtering as soon as possible so as to cut down on the number of intermediate frames generated.

Exercise 4.44

When we implemented the Lisp evaluator in section 4.1, we saw how to use local environments to avoid name conflicts between the parameters of procedures. For example, in evaluating

```
(define (square x)
  (* x x))

(define (sum-of-squares x y)
  (+ (square x) (square y)))

==> (sum-of-squares 3 4)
```

there will be no confusion between the x in square and the x in sum-of-squares, because we evaluate the body of each procedure in an environment that is specially constructed to contain bindings for the local variables. In the query system, we used a different strategy to avoid name conflicts in applying rules. As explained in section 4.5.4, each time we apply a rule we rename the variables with new names that are guaranteed to be unique. The analogous strategy for the Lisp evaluator would be to do away with local environments and simply rename the variables in the body of a procedure each time we apply the procedure. On the other hand, we saw that the use of environments can lead to important tools for structuring programs, because environments furnish a context in which computations can take place. One example of this is block structure. Another is the packaging mechanism discussed in section 4.3.

Implement for the query language a rule-application method that uses environments rather than substitution. See if you can build on your environment structure to create constructs in the query language for dealing with large systems, such as the rule analog of block-structured procedures. Can you relate any of this to the problem of making deductions in a context (e.g., "If I supposed that P were true, then I would be able to deduce A and B") as a method of problem solving? (This problem is open-ended. A good answer is probably worth a Ph.D.)

5

COMPUTING WITH
REGISTER MACHINES

My aim is to show that the heavenly machine is not
a kind of divine, live being, but a kind of clockwork
(and he who believes that a clock has soul attributes
the maker's glory to the work), insofar as nearly all
the manifold motions are caused by a most simple
and material force, just as all motions of the clock
are caused by a single weight.

Johannes Kepler (letter to Herwart von Hohenburg,
1605)

We began this book by studying processes and by describing processes in
terms of procedures written in Lisp. To explain the meanings of these
procedures, we used a succession of models of evaluation: the substitution model of chapter 1, the environment model of chapter 3, and the
metacircular evaluator of chapter 4. Our examination of the metacircular
evaluator, in particular, dispelled much of the mystery of how Lisp-like
languages are interpreted. But even the metacircular evaluator leaves important questions unanswered, because it fails to elucidate the mechanisms
of control in a Lisp system. For instance, the evaluator does not explain
how the evaluation of a subexpression manages to return a value to the
expression that uses this value, nor does the evaluator explain how some
procedures generate iterative processes (that is, are evaluated using constant space) whereas other procedures generate recursive processes. These
questions remain unanswered because the metacircular evaluator is itself
a Lisp program and hence inherits the control structure of the underlying
Lisp system. In order to provide a more complete description of the control structure of the Lisp evaluator, we must work at a more primitive level
than Lisp itself.

In this chapter we describe processes in terms of the step-by-step operation of a traditional computer. Such a computer, or *register machine*,
sequentially executes *instructions* that manipulate the contents of a fixed
set of storage elements called *registers*. A typical register-machine instruction applies a primitive operation to the contents of some registers and assigns the result to another register. Our descriptions of processes executed

by register machines will look very much like so-called machine-language programs for traditional computers. However, instead of focusing on the machine language of any particular computer, we will examine several Lisp procedures and design a specific register machine to execute each procedure. Thus, we will approach our task from the perspective of a hardware architect rather than that of a machine-language computer programmer. In designing register machines, we will develop mechanisms for implementing important programming constructs such as recursion. We will also present a language for describing designs for register machines. In section 5.1.5 we will implement a Lisp program that uses these descriptions to simulate the machines we design.

In section 5.2, after we have accumulated experience formulating simple procedures as register machines, we will design a machine that carries out the algorithm described by the metacircular evaluator of section 4.1. This will fill in the gap in our understanding of how Lisp expressions are interpreted, by providing an explicit model for the mechanisms of control in the evaluator. In section 5.3 we will study a simple compiler that translates Lisp programs into sequences of instructions that can be executed directly with the registers and operations of the evaluator register machine.

Most of the primitive operations of our register machines are very simple. For example, an operation might increment the value of a number stored in a register. Such an operation can be performed by easily described hardware. In order to deal with list structure, however, we will also use the memory operations car, cdr, and cons, which require an elaborate storage-allocation mechanism. We will start by using these operations as if they were primitive. Later, in section 5.4, we will study their implementation in terms of more elementary operations.

5.1 Designing Register Machines

To design a register machine, we must design its *data paths* (registers and operations) and the *controller* that sequences these operations. To illustrate the design of a simple register machine, let us examine Euclid's Algorithm, which is used to compute the greatest common divisor (GCD) of two integers. As we saw in section 1.2.5, Euclid's Algorithm can be carried out by an iterative process, as specified by the following procedure:

```
(define (gcd a b)
  (if (= b 0)
      a
      (gcd b (remainder a b))))
```

A machine to carry out this algorithm must keep track of two numbers, a and b, so let us assume that these numbers are stored in two registers by those names. The basic operations required are testing whether the contents of register b is zero and computing the remainder of the contents of register a divided by the contents of register b. The remainder operation is a complex process, but assume for the moment that we have a primitive device that computes remainders. On each cycle of the GCD algorithm, the contents of register a must be replaced by the contents of register b, and the contents of b must be replaced by the remainder of the old contents of a divided by the old contents of b. It would be convenient if these replacements could be done simultaneously, but in our model of register machines we will assume that only one register can be assigned a new value at each step. To accomplish the replacements, our machine will use a third "temporary" register, which we call t. (First the remainder will be placed in t, then the contents of b will be placed in a, and finally the remainder stored in t will be placed in b.)

We can illustrate the registers and operations required for this machine by using the data-path diagram shown in figure 5.1. In this diagram, the registers (a, b, and t) are represented by rectangular boxes. Each way to assign a value to a register is indicated by an arrow with an X behind the head, pointing from the source of data to the register. We can think of the X as a button that, when pushed, allows the value at the source to "flow" into the designated register. The label next to each button is the name we will use to refer to the button. The names are arbitrary, and can be chosen to have mnemonic value (for example, a<-b denotes pushing the button that assigns the contents of register b to register a). The source of data for a register can be another register (as in the a<-b assignment), a function result (as in the t<-r assignment), or a constant (a built-in value that cannot be changed).[1] An operation that computes a function of constants and values stored in registers is represented in a data-path diagram by a trapezoid containing a name for the function. For example, the box marked rem in figure 5.1 represents the remainder operation, which computes the remainder of the contents of the registers a and b to which it is attached. Arrows (without buttons) point from the input registers and constants to the function box, and arrows connect the function's output value(s) to registers. An operation that computes a predicate is represented by a circle containing a name for the test. For example, our GCD machine has an operation that tests whether the contents of register b is zero. A test,

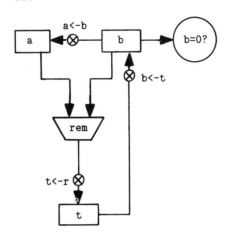

Figure 5.1
Data paths for a GCD machine.

like a function, has arrows from its input registers and constants. Unlike a function, it has no output arrows; its value is used by the controller rather than by the data paths. Overall, the data-path diagram shows the registers and operations that are required for the machine and how they must be connected. If we view the arrows as wires and the X buttons as switches, the data-path diagram is very like the wiring diagram for a machine that could be constructed from electrical components.

In order for the data paths to actually compute GCDs, the buttons must be pushed in the correct sequence. We will describe this sequence in terms of a controller diagram, as illustrated in figure 5.2. The elements of the controller diagram, unlike those of the data-path diagram, do not represent physical components of the machine. Rather, they indicate how the data-path components should be operated. The rectangular boxes in the controller diagram identify data-path buttons to be pushed, and the arrows describe the sequencing from one step to the next. The diamond in the diagram represents a decision. One of the two sequencing arrows will be followed, depending on the value of the data-path test identified in the diamond. We can interpret the controller in terms of a physical analogy: Think of the diagram as a maze in which a marble is rolling. When the marble rolls into a box, it pushes the data-path button that is named by the box. When the marble rolls into a decision node (such as the test for $b = 0$), it leaves the node on the path determined by the result of the indicated test. Taken together, the data paths and the controller completely describe a machine for computing GCDs. We start the controller (the rolling marble) at the place marked start, after placing numbers in registers a and b. When the controller reaches done, we will find the value of the GCD in register a.

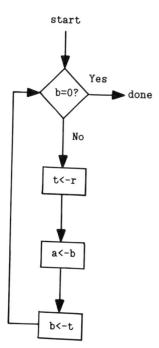

Figure 5.2
Controller for a GCD machine.

Exercise 5.1

Design a register machine to compute factorials using the iterative algorithm specified by the following procedure. Draw data-path and controller diagrams for this machine.

```
(define (factorial n)
  (define (iter product counter)
    (if (> counter n)
        product
        (iter (* counter product)
              (+ counter 1))))
  (iter 1 1))
```

5.1.1 A Language for Describing Register Machines

Data-path and controller diagrams are adequate for representing simple machines such as GCD, but they are unwieldy for describing large machines such as a Lisp interpreter. To make it possible to deal with complex machines, we will create a language that presents, in textual form, all the information given by the data-path and controller diagrams.

We define the data paths of a machine by describing the registers, the functions, and the tests. To describe a register, we give it a name and specify the buttons that control assignment to it. We give each of these buttons a name and specify the source of the data that enters the register under the button's control. (The source is a register, a constant, or a function.) To describe a function or a test, we give it a name and specify the inputs (registers or constants) and a Lisp procedure that has the same behavior as the function or test (that is, produces the same output value given the same input values). The purpose of the procedure is to describe what the function or test actually does. This information was not provided in the data-path diagram, which only gave names for the functions and tests. Although a name may be mnemonic, it is only a name—not a definition of behavior.

We define the controller of a machine as a sequence of *instructions* together with *labels* that identify *entry points* in the sequence.[2] An instruction is one of the following:

• The name of a data-path button to push to assign a value to a register. (This corresponds to a box in the controller diagram.)

• A conditional branch (`branch` instruction) naming a data-path test and a controller label. (This corresponds to a diamond in the controller diagram.) If the test is false, the controller should continue with the next instruction in the sequence. Otherwise, the controller should continue with the instruction after the label.

• An unconditional branch (`goto` instruction) naming a controller label at which to continue execution.

The machine starts at the beginning of the controller instruction sequence and stops when execution reaches the end of the sequence. Except when a branch changes the flow of control, instructions are executed in the order in which they are listed.

Figure 5.3 shows the GCD machine described in this way. This example only hints at the generality of these descriptions, since the GCD machine is a very simple case: Each register has only one button, and each button and test is used only once in the controller.

Unfortunately, it is difficult to read such a description. In order to understand the controller instructions we must constantly refer back to the definitions of the button names and the test names, and to understand what the buttons do we may have to refer to the definitions of the function names. In this chapter we will describe machines using a different notation that

---

2 In the context of machine design, controller instruction sequences are often called *microprograms*.

```
(data-paths
 (registers
  ((name a)
   (buttons ((name a<-b) (source (register b)))))
  ((name b)
   (buttons ((name b<-t) (source (register t)))))
  ((name t)
   (buttons ((name t<-r) (source (function rem)))))))

 (functions
  ((name rem)
   (inputs (register a) (register b))
   (lisp-definition remainder)))

 (tests
  ((name b=0?)
   (inputs (register b))
   (lisp-definition zero?))))

(controller
 test-b                          ;label
   (branch b=0? gcd-done)        ;conditional branch
   (t<-r)                        ;button push
   (a<-b)                        ;button push
   (b<-t)                        ;button push
   (goto test-b)                 ;unconditional branch
 gcd-done)                       ;label
```

Figure 5.3
A specification of the GCD machine.

combines the information from the data-path and controller descriptions so that we see it all together. To obtain this form of description, we will replace the arbitrary button, function, and test names by the definitions of their behavior. That is, instead of saying (in the controller) "Push button t<-r" and separately saying (in the data paths) "Button t<-r assigns the value of the rem function to register t" and "The rem function computes the remainder (as defined by Lisp's remainder procedure) of the contents of registers a and b," we will say (in the controller) "Push the button that assigns to register t the remainder of the contents of registers a and b." We will omit the button, function, and test definitions from the data-path description, leaving only register-name definitions there.

A machine description will thus consist of a list of register names followed by a list of controller instructions. We will use the syntax

```
(define-machine ⟨machine-name⟩
  (registers ⟨register names⟩)
  (controller ⟨controller instructions⟩))
```

Thus, the GCD machine is described as follows:

```
(define-machine gcd
  (registers a b t)
  (controller
   test-b
     (branch (zero? (fetch b)) gcd-done)
     (assign t (remainder (fetch a) (fetch b)))
     (assign a (fetch b))
     (assign b (fetch t))
     (goto test-b)
   gcd-done))
```

The define-machine form of description is easier to read than the kind of description illustrated in figure 5.3, but it also has disadvantages:

• Define-machine is more verbose for large machines, because complete descriptions of the data-path elements are repeated whenever the elements are mentioned in the controller instruction sequence. This is not a problem in the GCD example, because each test, function, and button is used only once. Moreover, repeating the data-path descriptions obscures the actual data-path structure of the machine; it is not obvious for a large machine how many functions, tests, and buttons there are and how they are interconnected.

• Because the controller instructions in a machine definition look a lot like Lisp expressions, it is easy to forget that they are not arbitrary Lisp expressions. They can only notate legal machine operations. (For example, tests and functions can operate only on constants and the contents of registers.)

In spite of these disadvantages, we will use define-machine throughout the rest of this chapter, because we will be more concerned with understanding controllers than with understanding the elements and connections in data paths. We should keep in mind, however, that data-path design is crucial in designing real machines.

Exercise 5.2

Use define-machine to describe the iterative factorial machine of exercise 5.1.[3]

Actions

Let us modify the gcd machine so that we can type in the numbers whose GCD we want and get the answer printed at our terminal. We will not

---

3 To denote use of a constant, just write the constant. For example, (assign t 0) denotes the instruction that stores 0 in register t.

discuss how to make a machine that can read and print, but will assume (as we do when we use `read` and `print` in Lisp) that they are available as primitive operations.[4]

Read is like the functions we have been using in that it produces a value that can be stored in a register. But `read` does not take inputs from any registers; its value depends on something that happens outside the parts of the machine we are designing. We will allow our machine's functions to have such behavior, and thus will draw and notate the use of `read` just as we do any other function.

Print, on the other hand, differs from the functions we have been using in a fundamental way: It does not produce an output value to be stored in a register. Though it has an effect, this effect is not on a part of the machine we are designing. We will refer to this kind of operation as an *action*. We will represent an action in a data-path diagram just as we represent a function: as a trapezoid that contains the name of the action. Arrows point to the action box from any inputs (registers or constants). We also associate a button with the action. Pushing the button makes the action happen. To make a controller push an action button we use a new kind of instruction called `perform`. Thus, the action of printing the contents of register a is represented in a controller sequence by the instruction

```
(perform (print (fetch a)))
```

Figure 5.4 shows the data paths and controller for the new gcd machine. Instead of having the machine stop after printing the answer, we have made it start over, so that it repeatedly reads a pair of numbers, computes their GCD, and prints the result. This structure is like the driver loops we used in the interpreters of chapter 4.

5.1.2 Abstraction in Machine Design

We will often define a machine to include "primitive" operations that are actually very complex. For example, in section 5.2 we will treat a Lisp interpreter's environment manipulations as primitive. Such abstraction is valuable because it allows us to ignore the details of parts of a machine so that we can concentrate on other aspects of the design. The fact that we have swept a lot of complexity under the rug, however, does not mean that a machine design is unrealistic. We can always replace the complex "primitives" by simpler primitive operations.

Consider the gcd machine of section 5.1.1. The machine has an instruction that computes the remainder of the contents of registers a and b and

---

4 This assumption glosses over a great deal of complexity. Usually a large portion of the implementation of a Lisp system is dedicated to making `read` and `print` work.

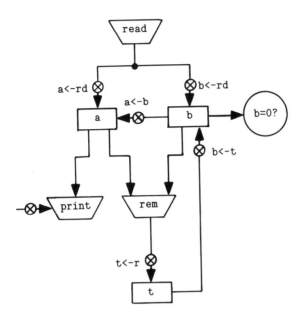

```
(define-machine gcd
  (registers a b t)
  (controller
   gcd-loop
     (assign a (read))
     (assign b (read))
   test-b
     (branch (zero? (fetch b)) gcd-done)
     (assign t (remainder (fetch a) (fetch b)))
     (assign a (fetch b))
     (assign b (fetch t))
     (goto test-b)
   gcd-done
     (perform (print (fetch a)))
     (goto gcd-loop)))
```

Figure 5.4
A GCD machine that reads inputs and prints results.

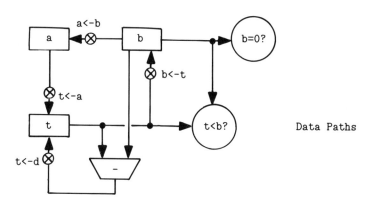

Data Paths

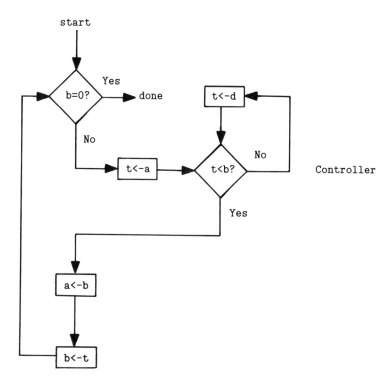

Controller

Figure 5.5
Data paths and controller for the elaborated GCD machine.

assigns the result to register t. If we want to construct the gcd machine without using a primitive `remainder` operation, we must specify how to compute remainders in terms of simpler operations, such as subtraction. Indeed, we can write a Lisp procedure that finds remainders in this way:

```
(define (remainder n d)
  (if (< n d)
      n
      (remainder (- n d) d)))
```

We can thus replace the `remainder` function in the gcd data paths with a subtraction function and a comparison test. Figure 5.5 shows the data paths and controller for the elaborated machine. The instruction

```
(assign t (remainder (fetch a) (fetch b)))
```

in the gcd controller definition is replaced by a sequence of instructions that contains a loop:

```
(define-machine gcd
  (registers a b t)
  (controller
   test-b
     (branch (zero? (fetch b)) gcd-done)
     (assign t (fetch a))
   rem-loop
     (branch (< (fetch t) (fetch b)) rem-done)
     (assign t (- (fetch t) (fetch b)))
     (goto rem-loop)
   rem-done
     (assign a (fetch b))
     (assign b (fetch t))
     (goto test-b)
   gcd-done))
```

Exercise 5.3

Design a machine to compute square roots using Newton's method, as described in section 1.1.7:

```
(define (sqrt x)
  (define (good-enough? guess)
    (< (abs (- (square guess) x)) .001))
  (define (improve guess)
    (average guess (/ x guess)))
  ;; continued on next page
```

```
(define (sqrt-iter guess)
  (if (good-enough? guess)
      guess
      (sqrt-iter (improve guess))))
(sqrt-iter 1))
```

Begin by assuming that good-enough? and improve operations are available as primitives. Then show how to expand these in terms of arithmetic operations. Describe each version of the sqrt machine design by drawing a data-path diagram and writing a controller definition in the register-machine language.

5.1.3 Subroutines

When designing a machine to perform a computation, we would often prefer to arrange for components to be shared by different parts of the computation rather than duplicate the components. Consider a machine that includes two GCD computations: one that finds the GCD of the contents of registers a and b and one that finds the GCD of the contents of registers c and d. We might start by assuming we have a primitive gcd operation, then expand the two instances of gcd in terms of more primitive operations. Figure 5.6 shows just the GCD portions of the resulting machine's data paths, without showing how they connect to the rest of the machine. The figure also shows the corresponding portions of the machine's controller sequence.

This machine has two remainder function boxes and two zero-testing boxes. If the duplicated components are complicated, as is the remainder box, this will not be an economical way to build the machine. We can avoid duplicating the data-path components by using the same components for both GCD computations, provided that doing so will not affect the rest of the larger machine's computation. If the values in registers a and b are not needed by the time the controller gets to gcd-2 (or if these values can be moved to other registers for safekeeping), we can change the machine so that it uses registers a and b, rather than registers c and d, in computing the second GCD as well as the first. If we do this, we obtain the controller sequence shown in figure 5.7.

We have removed the duplicate data-path components, but the controller now has two GCD sequences that differ only in their entry-point labels. It would be better to replace these two sequences by branches to a single sequence—a gcd *subroutine*—at the end of which we branch back to the correct place in the main instruction sequence. We can accomplish this as follows: Before branching to gcd, we place a distinguishing value (such as 0 or 1) into a special register, continue. At the end of the gcd subroutine

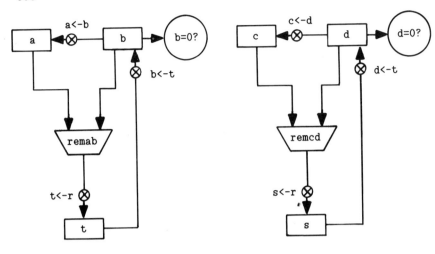

```
gcd-1
    (branch (zero? (fetch b)) after-gcd-1)
    (assign t (remainder (fetch a) (fetch b)))
    (assign a (fetch b))
    (assign b (fetch t))
    (goto gcd-1)
after-gcd-1
      .
      .
      .
gcd-2
    (branch (zero? (fetch d)) after-gcd-2)
    (assign s (remainder (fetch c) (fetch d)))
    (assign c (fetch d))
    (assign d (fetch s))
    (goto gcd-2)
after-gcd-2
```

Figure 5.6
Portions of the data paths and controller sequence for a machine with two GCD computations.

```
gcd-1
    (branch (zero? (fetch b)) after-gcd-1)
    (assign t (remainder (fetch a) (fetch b)))
    (assign a (fetch b))
    (assign b (fetch t))
    (goto gcd-1)
  after-gcd-1
    ⋮

gcd-2
    (branch (zero? (fetch b)) after-gcd-2)
    (assign t (remainder (fetch a) (fetch b)))
    (assign a (fetch b))
    (assign b (fetch t))
    (goto gcd-2)
  after-gcd-2
```

Figure 5.7
Portions of the controller sequence for a machine that uses the same data-path components for two different GCD computations.

```
gcd
    (branch (zero? (fetch b)) gcd-done)
    (assign t (remainder (fetch a) (fetch b)))
    (assign a (fetch b))
    (assign b (fetch t))
    (goto gcd)
  gcd-done
    (branch (zero? (fetch continue)) after-gcd-1)
    (goto after-gcd-2)
    ⋮

;; Before branching to gcd from the first place where
;; it is needed, we place 0 in the continue register
    (assign continue 0)
    (goto gcd)
  after-gcd-1
    ⋮

;; Before the second use of gcd, we place 1 in the continue register
    (assign continue 1)
    (goto gcd)
  after-gcd-2
```

Figure 5.8
Using a continue register to eliminate the duplicate controller sequence in figure 5.7.

we return either to after-gcd-1 or to after-gcd-2, depending on the value of the continue register. Figure 5.8 shows the relevant portion of the resulting controller program, which includes only a single copy of the gcd instructions.

This is a reasonable approach for handling small problems, but it would be awkward if there were many instances of GCD computations in the controller program. To decide where to continue executing after the gcd subroutine, we would need tests in the data paths and branch instructions in the controller for all the places that use gcd. A more powerful method for implementing subroutines is to have the continue register hold the label of the entry point in the controller program at which execution should continue when the subroutine is finished. Implementing this strategy requires a new kind of connection between the data paths and the controller of a register machine: There must be a way to assign to a register a label in the controller program in such a way that this value can be fetched from the register and used to continue execution at the designated entry point. To reflect this ability, we will extend the assign instruction of the register-machine language to allow a register to be assigned as value a label from the controller sequence (as a special kind of constant). We will also extend the goto instruction to allow execution to continue at the entry point described by the contents of a register rather than only at an entry point described by a constant label. Using these new constructs we can terminate the gcd subroutine with a branch to the location stored in the continue register. This leads to the program shown in figure 5.9.

If our machine has more than one subroutine, we could allocate a separate continuation register for each (e.g., gcd-continue, factorial-continue) or we could have them all share a single continue register. Sharing is more economical, but we must be careful if we have a subroutine (sub1) that calls another subroutine (sub2). Unless sub1 saves the contents of continue in some other register before setting up continue for the call to sub2, sub1 will not know where to go when it is finished. The mechanism developed in the next section to handle recursion also provides a better solution to this problem of nested subroutine calls.

5.1.4 Using a Stack to Implement Recursion

With the ideas illustrated so far, we can implement any iterative process by specifying a register machine that has a register corresponding to each state variable of the process. The machine repeatedly executes a controller program loop, changing the contents of the registers, until some termination condition is satisfied. At each point in the controller program, the state of the machine (representing the state of the iterative process) is

```
gcd
    (branch (zero? (fetch b)) gcd-done)
    (assign t (remainder (fetch a) (fetch b)))
    (assign a (fetch b))
    (assign b (fetch t))
    (goto gcd)
gcd-done
    (goto (fetch continue))
    ⋮

;; Before calling gcd, we assign to continue
;; the label to which gcd should return.
    (assign continue after-gcd-1)
    (goto gcd)
after-gcd-1

    ⋮

;; Here is the second call to gcd, with a
;; different continuation.
    (assign continue after-gcd-2)
    (goto gcd)
after-gcd-2
```

Figure 5.9
Assigning labels to the continue register simplifies and generalizes the strategy shown in figure 5.8.

completely determined by the contents of the registers (the values of the state variables).

Implementing recursive processes, however, requires an additional mechanism. Consider the following recursive method for computing factorials, which we first examined in section 1.2.1:

```
(define (factorial n)
  (if (= n 1)
      1
      (* (factorial (- n 1)) n)))
```

As we see from the procedure, computing $n!$ requires computing $(n-1)!$. Our gcd machine, modeled on the procedure

```
(define (gcd a b)
  (if (= b 0)
      a
      (gcd b (remainder a b)))))
```

similarly had to compute another GCD. But there is an important difference between the gcd procedure, which reduces the original computation to a new GCD computation, and `factorial`, which requires computing another factorial as a subproblem. In GCD, the answer to the new GCD computation is the answer to the original problem. To compute the next GCD, we simply place the new arguments in the input registers of the gcd machine and reuse the machine's data paths by executing the same controller sequence. When the machine is finished solving the final GCD problem, it has completed the entire computation.

In the case of factorial (or any recursive process) the answer to the new factorial subproblem is not the answer to the original problem. The value obtained for $(n - 1)!$ must be multiplied by n to get the final answer. If we try to imitate the gcd design, and solve the factorial subproblem by decrementing the n register and rerunning the factorial machine, we will no longer have available the old value of n by which to multiply the result. We thus need a second factorial machine to work on the subproblem. This second factorial computation itself has a factorial subproblem, which requires a third factorial machine, and so on. Since each factorial machine contains another factorial machine within it, the total machine contains an infinite nest of similar machines and hence cannot be constructed from a fixed, finite number of parts.

Nevertheless, we can implement the factorial process as a register machine if we can arrange to use the same components for each nested instance of the machine. Specifically, the machine that computes $n!$ should use the same components to work on the subproblem of computing $(n-1)!$, on the subproblem for $(n - 2)!$, and so on. This is plausible because, although the factorial process dictates that an unbounded number of copies of the same machine are needed to perform a computation, only one of these copies needs to be active at any given time. When the machine encounters a recursive subproblem, it can suspend work on the main problem, reuse the same physical parts to work on the subproblem, then continue the suspended computation.

In the subproblem, the contents of the registers will be different than they were in the main problem. (In this case the n register is decremented.) In order to be able to continue the suspended computation, the machine must save the contents of any registers that will be needed after the subproblem is solved so that these can be restored to continue the suspended computation. In the case of factorial, we will save the old value of n, to be restored when we are finished computing the factorial of the decremented n register.[5]

---

5 One might argue that we don't need to save the old n; after we decrement it and solve the subproblem, we could simply increment it to recover the old value. Although this strategy works for factorial, it cannot work in general, since the old value of a register cannot always be computed from the new one.

Since there is no *a priori* limit on the depth of nested recursive calls, we may need to save an arbitrary number of register values. These values must be restored in the reverse of the order in which they were saved, since in a nest of recursions the last subproblem to be entered is the first to be finished. This dictates the use of a *stack*, or "last in, first out" data structure, to save register values. We can extend the register-machine language to include a stack by adding two kinds of instructions: Values are placed on the stack using a `save` instruction and restored from the stack using a `restore` instruction. After a sequence of values has been saved on the stack, a sequence of `restores` will retrieve these values in reverse order.[6]

With the aid of the stack, we can reuse a single copy of the factorial machine's data paths for each factorial subproblem. There is a similar design issue in reusing the controller program that operates the data paths. To reexecute the factorial computation, the controller program cannot simply loop back to the beginning, as with an iterative process, because after solving the $(n-1)!$ subproblem the machine must still multiply the result by n. The controller must suspend its computation of $n!$, solve the $(n-1)!$ subproblem, then continue its computation of $n!$. This view of the factorial computation suggests the use of the subroutine mechanism described in section 5.1.3, which has the controller program use a `continue` register to transfer to the part of the program that solves a subproblem and then continue where it left off on the main problem. We can thus make a factorial subroutine that returns to the entry stored in the `continue` register. Around each subroutine call, we save and restore `continue` just as we do the n register, since each "level" of the factorial computation will use the same `continue` register. That is, the factorial subroutine must put a new value in `continue` when it calls itself for a subproblem, but it will need the old value in order to return to the place that called it to solve a subproblem.

Figure 5.10 shows the data paths and controller for a machine that implements the recursive `factorial` procedure. The machine has a stack and three registers, called `n`, `val`, and `continue`. To simplify the data-path diagram, we have not named the register-assignment buttons, only the stack-operation buttons (`sc` and `sn` to save registers, `rc` and `rn` to restore registers). To operate the machine, we put in register n the number whose

[6] We can define a stack as an abstract data structure by specifying that `save` and `restore` satisfy the following conditions: If the stack is in state s_1 and register `x` has contents c, then executing (`save x`) will put the stack into state s_2. If when the stack is in state s_2 we execute (`restore x`), the contents of register `x` reverts to c and the stack reverts to state s_1. In section 5.4 we will see how to implement a stack in terms of more primitive operations.

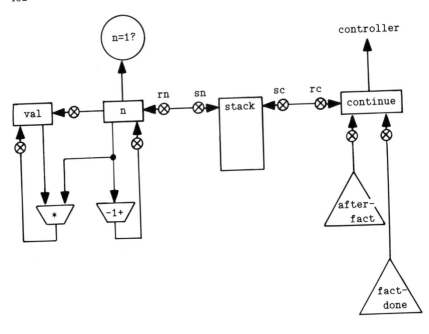

```
(define-machine factorial
  (registers n val continue)
  (controller
      (assign continue fact-done)          ;set up final return address
    fact-loop
      (branch (=1? (fetch n)) base-case)
      ;; Here we set up for the recursive call, saving n and continue.
      ;; We then set up continue so that the computation will
      ;; continue at after-fact when the subroutine returns.
      (save continue)
      (save n)
      (assign n (-1+ (fetch n)))
      (assign continue after-fact)
      (goto fact-loop)
    after-fact
      (restore n)
      (restore continue)
      (assign val
              (* (fetch n) (fetch val)))    ; val now contains n(n − 1)!
      (goto (fetch continue))               ;return to caller
    base-case
      (assign val (fetch n))                ;base case: 1! = 1
      (goto (fetch continue))               ;return to caller
    fact-done))
```

Figure 5.10
A recursive factorial machine.

factorial we wish to compute and start the machine. When the machine reaches fact-done, the computation is finished and the answer will be found in the val register. In the controller program, n and continue are saved before each recursive call and restored upon return from the call. Returning from a call is accomplished by branching to the location stored in continue. Continue is initialized when the machine starts so that the last return will go to fact-done. The val register, which holds the result of the factorial computation, is not saved before the recursive call, because the old contents of val is not useful after the subroutine returns. Only the new value, which is the value of the subcomputation, is needed.

Although in principle the factorial computation requires an infinite machine, the machine in figure 5.10 is actually finite except for the stack, which is potentially unbounded. Any particular physical implementation of a stack, however, will be of finite size, and this will limit the depth of recursive calls that can be handled by the machine. This implementation of factorial illustrates the general strategy for realizing recursive algorithms as ordinary register machines augmented by stacks. When a recursive subproblem is encountered, we save on the stack the registers whose current values will be required after the subproblem is solved, solve the recursive subproblem, then restore the saved registers and continue execution on the main problem. The continue register must always be saved. Whether there are other registers that need to be saved depends on the particular machine, since not all recursive computations need the original values of registers that are modified during solution of the subproblem (see exercise 5.4).

A double recursion

Let us examine a more complex recursive process, the tree-recursive computation of the Fibonacci numbers, which we introduced in section 1.2.2:

```
(define (fib n)
  (if (< n 2)
      n
      (+ (fib (- n 1)) (fib (- n 2)))))
```

Just as with factorial, we can implement the recursive Fibonacci computation as a register machine with registers n, val, and continue. The machine is more complex than the one for factorial, because there are two places in the controller program where we need to perform recursive calls—once to compute $\text{Fib}(n-1)$ and once to compute $\text{Fib}(n-2)$. To set up for each of these calls, we save the registers whose values will be needed later, set the n register to the number whose Fib we need to compute recursively

$(n - 1$ or $n - 2)$, and assign to continue the entry in the main program to which to return (after-fib-n-1 or after-fib-n-2, respectively). We then go to fib-loop. When we return from the recursive call, the answer is in val. Figure 5.11 shows the controller program for this machine.

Exercise 5.4

Specify register machines that implement each of the following procedures. Assume that machine registers can hold list data, and that the list operations cons, car, cdr, atom?, eq?, and null? are available as primitives to be used in the machines. For each machine, write a machine definition and draw a diagram showing the data paths.

a. Recursive exponentiation:

```
(define (expt b n)
  (if (= n 0)
      1
      (* b (expt b (- n 1)))))
```

b. Iterative exponentiation:

```
(define (expt b n)
  (define (exp-iter counter product)
    (if (= counter 0)
        product
        (exp-iter (- counter 1) (* b product))))
  (exp-iter n 1))
```

c. Recursive countatoms:

```
(define (countatoms tree)
  (cond ((null? tree) 0)
        ((atom? tree) 1)
        (else (+ (countatoms (car tree))
                 (countatoms (cdr tree))))))
```

d. Recursive countatoms:

```
(define (countatoms tree)
  (define (count-iter tree n)
    (cond ((null? tree) n)
          ((atom? tree) (1+ n))
          (else (count-iter (cdr tree)
                            (count-iter (car tree) n)))))
  (count-iter tree 0))
```

Exercise 5.5

Hand-simulate the factorial and fib machines, using some nontrivial input (requiring execution of at least one recursive call). Show the contents of the stack at each significant point in the execution of the program.

```
(define-machine fib
  (registers n val continue)
  (controller
     (assign continue fib-done)
   fib-loop
     (branch (< (fetch n) 2) immediate-answer)
     ;; Set up to compute Fib(n − 1).
     (save continue)
     (assign continue afterfib-n-1)
     (save n)                       ;save old value of n
     (assign n (- (fetch n) 1))     ;clobber n to n − 1
     (goto fib-loop)                ;perform recursive call
   afterfib-n-1                     ;upon return, val contains Fib(n − 1)
     (restore n)
     (restore continue)
     ;;Set up to compute Fib(n − 2).
     (assign n (- (fetch n) 2))     ; n now contains n − 2
     (save continue)
     (assign continue afterfib-n-2)
     (save val)                     ;save Fib(n − 1)
     (goto fib-loop)
   afterfib-n-2                     ;upon return, val contains Fib(n − 2)
     (assign n (fetch val))         ; n now contains Fib(n − 2)
     (restore val)                  ; val now contains Fib(n − 1)
     (restore continue)
     (assign val                    ; val now contains Fib(n − 1) + Fib(n − 2)
            (+ (fetch val) (fetch n)))
     (goto (fetch continue))        ;return to caller, answer is in val
   immediate-answer
     (assign val (fetch n))         ;base case: Fib(n) = n
     (goto (fetch continue))
   fib-done))
```

Figure 5.11
Controller program for a machine to compute Fibonacci numbers.

Exercise 5.6

Ben Bitdiddle observes that the fib machine's controller program has an extra
save and an extra restore, which can be removed to make a faster program.
Where are these instructions?

Exercise 5.7

Exercise 3.12 of section 3.3.1 presented an append procedure that appends two
lists to form a new list and an append! procedure that splices two lists together.
Design a register machine to implement each of these procedures. Assume that
cons, car, cdr, and null? are available as primitive operations. Note that
although nested expressions can be written in Lisp (e.g., (null? (cdr x))), they
must be broken into separate stages in a register machine, because the inputs
to a machine operation must come from registers (not from functions) and the
outputs of functions must go to registers. For the append! machine, assume that
set-cdr! is a primitive action that can be invoked using perform.

5.1.5 A Register-Machine Simulator

We now have all the mechanisms we need to implement any Lisp program
as a register machine. In order to gain a good understanding of the design
of register machines, we must test the machines we design to see if they
perform as expected. One way to test a design is to hand-simulate the
operation of the controller, as in exercise 5.5. But this is extremely tedious
for all but the simplest machines. In this section we construct a simulator
for machines described in the register-machine language. The simulator is
a Lisp program with four interface procedures. The first uses a description
of a register machine to construct a model of the machine (a data structure
whose parts correspond to the parts of the machine to be simulated), and
the other three allow us to simulate the machine by manipulating the
model:

(build-model ⟨registers⟩ ⟨controller⟩) constructs and returns a model of
the machine with the given registers and controller.

(remote-assign ⟨machine-model⟩ ⟨register-name⟩ ⟨value⟩) stores a value in a simulated register in the given machine.

(remote-fetch ⟨machine-model⟩ ⟨register-name⟩) returns the contents
of a simulated register in the given machine.

(start ⟨machine-model⟩) simulates the execution of the given machine,
starting from the beginning of the controller program and stopping when
it reaches the end of the program.

For compatibility with the define-machine syntax we have been using, let us assume that there is some syntactic sugar that transforms a define-machine expression into a call to the model builder. For example, the gcd machine definition in section 5.1.1 would become

```
(define gcd
  (build-model '(a b t)
               '(test-b
                 (branch (zero? (fetch b)) gcd-done)
                 (assign t (remainder (fetch a) (fetch b)))
                 (assign a (fetch b))
                 (assign b (fetch t))
                 (goto test-b)
                 gcd-done)))
```

This defines a Lisp variable gcd whose value is a model of the gcd machine. To compute GCDs with this machine, we set the input registers, start the machine, and examine the result when the simulation terminates:

```
==> (remote-assign gcd 'a 206)
done

==> (remote-assign gcd 'b 40)
done

==> (start gcd)
done

==> (remote-fetch gcd 'a)
2
```

This computation will run much more slowly than a gcd procedure written in Lisp, because we will simulate low-level machine instructions, such as assign, by much more complex operations.

Constructing a machine model
Build-model begins by using the procedure make-new-machine to construct the parts of the machine model that are common to all register machines (such as a stack). It then extends this basic machine to include the registers and the controller of the particular machine being defined. This is accomplished by calling procedures that modify the machine-model data structure. Build-model returns as its value the modified machine model.

```
(define (build-model registers controller)
  (let ((machine (make-new-machine)))
    (set-up-registers machine registers)
    (set-up-controller machine controller)
    machine))
```

For each name in the given list of registers, `set-up-registers` adds a register with that name to the given machine model:

```
(define (set-up-registers machine registers)
  (mapc (lambda (register-name)
          (make-machine-register machine register-name))
        registers))
```

Set-up-registers iterates through the register list by using the higher-order procedure `mapc`, which applies a given procedure to each item in a given list.[7]

Set-up-controller scans the controller list and constructs a model of the controller by adding the labels and instructions to the machine model. It uses `make-machine-instruction` to construct a model of each instruction in the list, and it forms a list of these modeled instructions. Each label in the controller list is declared as an entry point to the instruction sequence. The label itself is not retained in the instruction sequence; rather, the declaration associates the label with the portion of the instruction sequence that follows it. In addition, a special entry point called `*start*` is created to specify the beginning of the controller sequence.

```
(define (set-up-controller machine controller)
  (build-instruction-list machine
                          (cons '*start* controller)))
```

```
(define (build-instruction-list machine op-list)
  (if (null? op-list)
      '()
      (let ((rest-of-instructions
             (build-instruction-list machine (cdr op-list))))
        ;; continued on next page
```

---

7 Mapc could be defined as

```
(define (mapc proc l)
  (if (null? l)
      'done
      (sequence (proc (car l))
                (mapc proc (cdr l)))))
```

```
(if (label? (car op-list))
    (sequence
     (declare-label machine
                    (car op-list)
                    rest-of-instructions)
     rest-of-instructions)
    (cons (make-machine-instruction machine
                                    (car op-list))
          rest-of-instructions)))))
```

According to the syntax of our register-machine language, a label is an atomic symbol in the controller sequence:

```
(define (label? expression)
  (symbol? expression))
```

The machine model: registers, labels, and stacks

Our method of modeling a machine must include some way to associate names with values. We will need this ability, for example, to identify the data structure that models a given register so that we can simulate execution of an instruction that refers to the register by name. We will assume that we have three procedures available for manipulating name-value associations in a model:

(remote-define ⟨*machine-model*⟩ ⟨*name*⟩ ⟨*value*⟩) adds to the machine model an association between the given name and the given value.

(remote-get ⟨*machine-model*⟩ ⟨*name*⟩) returns the value associated with the given name in the given machine model.

(remote-set ⟨*machine-model*⟩ ⟨*name*⟩ ⟨*value*⟩) changes the value associated with an existing name in the machine model.

Using these procedures, we can add registers and labels to a machine model. Make-machine-register adds a register with a specified name to a machine model. It uses make-register to create a data structure to represent the register, then uses remote-define to add to the machine model an association between this register model and the specified register name.

```
(define (make-machine-register machine name)
  (remote-define machine name (make-register name)))
```

A register is an object with state. We will represent a register as a dispatch procedure with local state, using the techniques developed in chapter 3. The procedure make-register creates a register that holds a value that can be accessed or changed:

```
(define (make-register name)
  (define contents nil)
  (define (get) contents)
  (define (set value)
    (set! contents value))
  (define (dispatch message)
    (cond ((eq? message 'get) (get))
          ((eq? message 'set) set)
          (else (error "Unknown request -- REGISTER"
                       name
                       message))))
  dispatch)
```

The following procedures are used to access registers:

```
(define (get-contents register)
  (register 'get))
```

```
(define (set-contents register value)
  ((register 'set) value))
```

To process a label declaration, we use remote-define to add to the machine model an association between the label name and the portion of the controller instruction sequence following the label. This association will enable us to find out what instructions to execute after we execute a branch or goto instruction that contains a label. First, however, we check to make sure that a label with the same name has not already been defined in the machine. To keep track of what labels have been seen, we associate a list of the names of declared labels with the name *labels* in the machine model. (The name *labels* is predefined with the empty list as its value by make-new-machine, which is called by build-model to create the initial machine model.)

```
(define (declare-label machine label labeled-entry)
  (let ((defined-labels (remote-get machine '*labels*)))
    (if (memq label defined-labels)
        (error "Multiply-defined label" label)
        (sequence
          (remote-define machine label labeled-entry)
          (remote-set machine
                      '*labels*
                      (cons label defined-labels))))))
```

Before we decide how to actually represent a machine or how to model the machine instructions, we will show how to model a machine's stack. We can represent a stack as an object with local state in the same way we represented a register. The procedure `make-stack` creates a stack whose local state consists of a list of the items on the stack. A stack accepts requests to push an item onto the stack, to pop the top item off the stack and return it, and to `initialize` the stack to empty.

```
(define (make-stack)
  (define s '())
  (define (push x)
    (set! s (cons x s)))
  (define (pop)
    (if (null? s)
        (error "Empty stack -- POP")
        (let ((top (car s)))
          (set! s (cdr s))
          top)))
  (define (initialize)
    (set! s '()))
  (define (dispatch message)
    (cond ((eq? message 'push) push)
          ((eq? message 'pop) (pop))
          ((eq? message 'initialize) (initialize))
          (else (error "Unknown request -- STACK" message))))
  dispatch)
```

The following procedures are used to access stacks:

```
(define (pop stack)
  (stack 'pop))
```

```
(define (push stack value)
  ((stack 'push) value))
```

The machine model: machines and instructions

We still need to design a data structure to represent the machine as a whole. The choice of this data structure is closely bound up with the design of a mechanism for simulating the execution of instructions, because it is during execution of an instruction that we use the name-object associations in the machine model. We need to implement an interpreter that "evaluates" the instructions of our register-machine language. One way to do this would be to design a `machine-instruction-eval` procedure similar in spirit to the eval and qeval procedures of chapter 4. However, there is another strategy we can pursue in "evaluating" machine instructions.

In our register-machine language, an instruction (which is a data object from the simulator's point of view) has the same form as a Lisp expression. If we can somehow arrange things so that evaluating the instruction as a Lisp expression simulates the instruction's effect, we will not have to write a special instruction interpreter to analyze and simulate instructions. All we will have to do is select the right instruction to execute and have Lisp evaluate it for us.

In order for this approach to work, the instruction must be evaluated in an environment that defines all the symbols that appear in it. For instance, the instruction (branch (zero? (fetch b)) gcd-done) cannot be evaluated without appropriate bindings for branch, zero?, fetch, b, and gcd-done. In general, we will need the following bindings:

• There must be a procedure to simulate fetch and each kind of instruction (assign, branch, goto, save, restore, and perform). These procedures will be defined by the simulator, since they are common to all register machines and their implementation depends on the simulator's representation of registers, stacks, and labels.

• There must be a procedure to simulate each primitive operation (test, function, or action) of the machine. In our gcd, factorial, and fib machines, most of the machine's operations were in fact also Lisp primitives. The machine designer must define Lisp procedures to simulate other operations, such as =1? in the factorial machine.

• There must be a binding for each register and label name. The value of each of these variables must be an appropriate argument to the procedures that implement instructions containing register names and labels. For example, the value of a register name must be the associated register model, so that assign, fetch, save, or restore can manipulate the register. The simulator will set up these bindings when it builds the machine model.

The bindings of register and label names must be local to the machine, so that the simulator can build models of more than one machine. We will thus represent a machine as an environment, and our machine constructor will use make-environment (section 4.3).

```
(define (make-new-machine)
  (make-environment
   ⟨contents of the initial machine environment⟩))
```

We can implement the manipulation of name-value associations in a machine by using relative evaluation (evaluation with respect to the environment that represents the machine), as described in section 4.3, to define and access local variables in the machine environment.

```
(define (remote-get machine variable)
  (eval variable machine))

(define (remote-set machine variable value)
  (eval (list 'set! variable (list 'quote value))
        machine))

(define (remote-define machine variable value)
  (eval (list 'define variable (list 'quote value))
        machine))
```

In order to associate an instruction with a machine environment, so that the symbols in it will be evaluated in that environment when the instruction is executed, we model an instruction as a procedure (of no arguments) constructed in the machine environment. The body of the procedure is the instruction expression.

```
(define (make-machine-instruction machine exp)
  (eval (list 'lambda '() exp) machine))
```

The initial machine environment
When a new machine is created, it is initialized to contain procedures and data structures that are common to every register machine, such as a stack and procedures to simulate the various kinds of instructions. We have already seen how the machine-specific registers, labels, and instructions are defined in this environment. The rest of this section describes the contents of the initial environment. All of the following definitions should be included within the make-environment expression in make-new-machine.

The initial machine environment includes the special variable *labels*, which is used during construction of the machine model:

```
(define *labels* '())
```

There is also a special variable to designate the stack, which is created when the machine is created:

```
(define *the-stack* (make-stack))
```

We provide a primitive action that a register machine can use to reinitialize the stack by means of the instruction (perform (initialize-stack)):

```
(define (initialize-stack)
  (*the-stack* 'initialize))
```

We can model fetching the contents of a register as follows:

```
(define fetch get-contents)
```

To see how this works, consider an instruction containing (fetch a). First the operator, fetch, is evaluated; this yields the procedure get-contents. Then the operand, a, is evaluated; this yields the register object that was constructed and associated with the name a by make-machine-register. Get-contents is thus called with a register object as argument.

In order to model the sequencing of instructions, the simulator, as it executes instructions, must keep track of where the register machine is in the controller sequence. We use a variable called *program-counter* to hold the sequence of instructions to be executed next:

```
(define *program-counter* '())
```

The procedure execute takes a sequence of instructions to be executed and stores this in the program counter. It then executes the instruction indicated by the program counter. Recall that each instruction in the controller sequence is represented as a procedure with no parameters. This procedure will have been defined (by make-machine-instruction) in the machine environment, so that free variables in the procedure body (the register names and labels in the instruction) will refer to the correct values in the simulated machine. Execute calls the procedure at the head of the list pointed to by *program-counter*. This evaluates the procedure body in the machine environment. When the list runs out, the simulation stops and returns the symbol done.

```
(define (execute sequence)
  (set! *program-counter* sequence)
  (if (null? *program-counter*)
      'done
      ((car *program-counter*)))))
```

An instruction that branches will call execute directly with the new sequence to execute. Each nonbranching instruction calls normal-next-instruction to get to the next instruction. This calls execute with the rest of the sequence designated by *program-counter*:

```
(define (normal-next-instruction)
  (execute (cdr *program-counter*)))
```

Finally, we define the procedures that implement the various kinds of instructions. Assign changes the value of the designated register and then tells the controller to execute the next instruction in the sequence:

```
(define (assign register value)
  (set-contents register value)
  (normal-next-instruction))
```

Save and restore manipulate the stack and registers as appropriate, then proceed to the next instruction:

```
(define (save reg)
  (push *the-stack* (get-contents reg))
  (normal-next-instruction))

(define (restore reg)
  (set-contents reg (pop *the-stack*))
  (normal-next-instruction))
```

Goto continues execution with a new sequence. Branch either proceeds with the next instruction in the sequence or executes an alternative sequence, depending on the result of a test. The argument to goto or branch is an instruction sequence (the value resulting from evaluating the instruction's label operand—a label name or a register fetch—in the machine environment).

```
(define (goto new-sequence)
  (execute new-sequence))

(define (branch predicate alternate-next)
  (if predicate
      (goto alternate-next)
      (normal-next-instruction)))
```

Perform simply proceeds with the next instruction. Since the action to be performed is the operand of the perform expression, it is evaluated by Lisp when the perform procedure is called.

```
(define (perform operation)
  (normal-next-instruction))
```

This completes the declarations of the initial machine environment, which are included as the body of the make-environment expression in the procedure make-new-machine.

Using the simulator

The procedures that allow us to interact with a simulated machine are defined as follows. To access a register, we use remote-get to get the register object that is associated with the register name in the machine environment.

```
(define (remote-fetch machine register-name)
  (get-contents (remote-get machine register-name)))

(define (remote-assign machine register-name value)
  (set-contents (remote-get machine register-name) value)
  'done)
```

To start a machine, we execute a goto instruction to the start of the controller sequence:

```
(define (start machine)
  (eval '(goto *start*) machine))
```

Exercise 5.8

Use the simulator to test each of the machines you designed in exercise 5.4.

Exercise 5.9

Our model builder is not very careful about whether the machine being defined is in fact a legitimate register machine. For example, it does not check that the only registers used are the ones declared or that instructions use registers only in correct ways. Add error checking to the model-construction process to verify the following:

a. Every instruction is one of the following kinds: assign, branch, goto, save, restore, perform.

b. The only symbols used in a fetch, an assign, a save, or a restore are ones that are declared as registers. (You may want to add a list of declared registers, analogous to the list of declared labels, to the machine model.)

c. No declared register is used except in the appropriate context of a fetch, an assign, a save, or a restore.

d. The targets of goto instructions are declared labels or fetches from registers. The targets of branch instructions are declared labels.

e. If the target of a goto instruction is a fetch from a register, then there is an instruction that assigns a declared label to that register.

f. All arguments in the test part of each branch and the action part of each perform are constants or fetches from registers. The value assigned to a register is a fetch from a register, a constant, or a function whose arguments are constants or fetches from registers. A constant must be an atom or an expression of the form (quote ⟨exp⟩). (Although we have seen only atomic constants so far, we will use quoted constants later in this chapter.)

Exercise 5.10

Alyssa P. Hacker has been using the simulator to help with the design of a "fifth-generation machine" for high-speed execution of the query language. Unfortunately, the simulator takes so long to do even simple operations that the debugging of the new machine is very slow and painful. Ben Bitdiddle suggests that one problem is that the simulator represents registers of the simulated machine as procedures with local state. Access to a register thus requires several procedure calls rather than a simple data-structure operation. Ben proposes that a register be represented as a simple list whose car is the value of the register. Thus, get-contents could be car and set-contents could be set-car!. Implement the register abstraction as Ben's suggests and use the resulting simulator to simulate some of your machines. Use Scheme's runtime primitive (see exercise 1.17) to compare the speed of Ben's version of the simulator with that of the simulator you started with.

Exercise 5.11

The simulator can be used to help determine the data paths required for implementing a machine with a given controller. Extend build-model to produce the following information:

a. a list of all instructions, with duplicates removed, sorted by instruction type (assign, goto, and so on);

b. a list (without duplicates) of the registers used to hold entry points (these are the registers referenced by goto instructions);

c. a list (without duplicates) of the registers that are saved or restored;

d. for each register, a list (without duplicates) of the sources from which it is assigned (for example, the sources for register val in the factorial machine of figure 5.10 are (fetch n) and (* (fetch n) (fetch val))).

These lists should be stored in the machine model, in four new variables that you can call *all-instructions*, *label-registers*, *stack-registers*, and *register-sources*. To test your analyzer, define the fib machine from figure 5.11 and use remote-get to examine the lists you have constructed.

Exercise 5.12

Our simulator maintains local names for registers and labels by representing machines as environments. Another way to handle this is to represent a machine as a table (see section 3.3.3). Reimplement the simulator to use this organization. Note that you will no longer be able to simulate instructions by evaluating them as Lisp expressions, so you will have to write an instruction interpreter.

Monitoring machine performance

Simulation is useful not only for verifying the correctness of a proposed machine design but also for measuring the machine's performance. For example, we can install in our simulation program a "meter" that measures the number of stack operations used in a computation. To do this, we modify our simulated stack to keep track of the number of times registers are saved on the stack and the maximum depth reached by the stack:

```
(define (make-stack)
  (define s '())
  (define number-pushes 0)
  (define max-depth 0)
  (define (push x)
    (set! s (cons x s))
    (set! number-pushes (1+ number-pushes))
    (set! max-depth (max (length s) max-depth)))
  (define (pop)
    (if (null? s)
        (error "Empty stack -- POP")
        (let ((top (car s)))
          (set! s (cdr s))
          top)))
  (define (initialize)
    (set! s '())
    (set! number-pushes 0)
    (set! max-depth 0))
  (define (print-statistics)
    (print (list 'total-pushes: number-pushes
                 'maximum-depth: max-depth)))
  (define (dispatch message)
    (cond ((eq? message 'push) push)
          ((eq? message 'pop) (pop))
          ((eq? message 'initialize) (initialize))
          ((eq? message 'print-statistics)
           (print-statistics))
          (else (error "Unknown request -- STACK" message))))
  dispatch)
```

We will also modify the initialize-stack operation so that it prints the statistics before initializing the stack:

```
(define (initialize-stack)
  (*the-stack* 'print-statistics)
  (*the-stack* 'initialize))
```

Exercise 5.13

Measure the number of pushes and the maximum stack depth required to compute $n!$ for various small values of n using the factorial machine of section 5.1.4. From your data determine formulas in terms of n for the total number of push operations and the maximum stack depth used in computing $n!$ for any $n > 1$.

Note that each of these is a linear function of n and is thus determined by two constants.

In order to get the statistics printed, you will have to augment the machine with an instruction to initialize the stack. You may want to also modify the factorial machine so that it repeatedly reads a value for n, computes the factorial, and prints the result (as we did for the gcd machine in figure 5.4), so that you will not have to repeatedly invoke remote-fetch, remote-assign, and start.

Exercise 5.14

When we introduced save and restore in section 5.1.4, we didn't specify what would happen if you tried to restore a register that was not the last one saved, as in the sequence

```
(save y)
(save x)
(restore y)
```

There are several reasonable possibilities for the meaning of restore:

a. (Restore y) puts into y the last value saved on the stack, regardless of what register that value came from. This is the way our simulator behaves. Show how to take advantage of this behavior to eliminate one instruction from the fib machine of section 5.1.4.

b. (Restore y) puts into y the last value saved on the stack, but only if that value was saved from y; otherwise, it signals an error. Modify the simulator to behave this way. You will have to change save to put the register name on the stack along with the value.

c. (Restore y) puts into y the last value saved from y regardless of what other registers were saved after y and not restored. Modify the simulator to behave this way. You will have to associate a separate stack with each register. You should make the initialize-stack operation initialize all the register stacks.

Exercise 5.15

Alyssa P. Hacker needs a *breakpoint* feature in the simulator to help her debug her design for a machine to execute the query language. You have been hired to install this feature for her. She wants to be able to specify a place in the controller program where the simulator will stop and allow her to examine the state of the machine. You are to implement a procedure

```
(set-breakpoint ⟨machine⟩ ⟨label⟩ ⟨n⟩)
```

that sets a breakpoint just before the nth instruction after the given label. For example,

```
(set-breakpoint gcd 'test-b 2)
```

installs a breakpoint in the gcd machine just before the assignment to register a. When the simulator reaches the breakpoint it should print the label and the offset of the breakpoint and stop executing instructions. Alyssa can then use remote-

`fetch` and `remote-assign` to manipulate the state of the simulated machine. She should then be able to continue execution by saying

`(proceed-machine` ⟨*machine*⟩`)`

She should also be able to remove a specific breakpoint by means of

`(cancel-breakpoint` ⟨*machine*⟩ ⟨*label*⟩ ⟨*n*⟩`)`

or to remove all breakpoints by means of

`(cancel-all-breakpoints` ⟨*machine*⟩`)`

In order to install a breakpoint, you must construct a procedure to handle the breakpoint and splice it into the controller instruction sequence in such a way that the execution of other instructions and the use of labels are not affected.

5.2 The Explicit-Control Evaluator

In section 5.1 we saw how to transform simple Lisp programs into descriptions of register machines. We will now perform this transformation on a more complex program, the metacircular evaluator of section 4.1, which shows how the behavior of a Lisp interpreter can be described in terms of the procedures `eval` and `apply`. The *explicit-control evaluator* that we develop in this section shows how the underlying procedure-calling and argument-passing mechanisms used in the evaluation process can be described in terms of operations on registers and stacks. In addition, the explicit-control evaluator can serve as an implementation of a Lisp interpreter, written in a language that is very similar to the native machine language of conventional computers. The evaluator can be executed by the register-machine simulator of section 5.1.5. Alternatively, it can be used as a starting point for building a machine-language implementation of a Lisp evaluator, or even a special-purpose machine for evaluating Lisp expressions. Figure 5.12 shows such a hardware implementation: a silicon chip that acts as an evaluator for the Scheme dialect of Lisp. The chip designers started with the data-path and controller specifications for a register machine similar to the evaluator described in this section and used design automation programs to construct the integrated-circuit layout. (See Batali 1981 for more information on the chip and the method by which it was designed.)

Registers and operations

In designing the explicit-control evaluator, we must specify the operations to be used in our register machine. We described the metacircular evaluator in terms of abstract syntax, using procedures such as `quoted?` and `make-procedure`. In implementing the register machine, we could expand these syntax procedures into sequences of elementary list-structure operations.

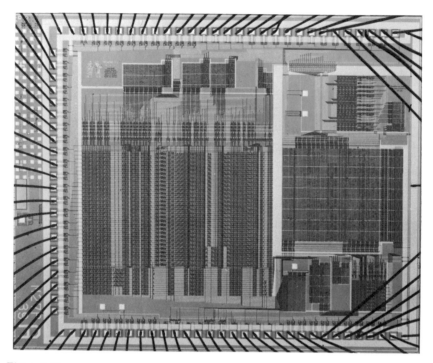

Figure 5.12
A silicon-chip implementation of an evaluator for Scheme.

However, this would make our evaluator program very long, obscuring the basic structure with details. To clarify the presentation, we will include as primitive operations of the register machine the environment-manipulation and syntax procedures given in sections 4.1.2, 4.1.3, and 4.1.4. In order to completely specify an evaluator that could be programmed in a low-level machine language or implemented in hardware, we would replace these operations by more elementary list-structure operations. In section 5.4 we will discuss the implementation of the lowest-level list-structure primitives (such as car, cdr, cons, eq?, and atom?) and show how we can arrange the representation of list structure in memory so that registers can hold pointers to list structure.

Our Lisp evaluator register machine includes a stack and seven registers: exp, env, val, continue, fun, argl, and unev. Exp is used to hold the expression to be evaluated, and env contains the environment in which the evaluation is to be performed. At the end of an evaluation, val contains the value obtained by evaluating the expression in the designated environment. The continue register is used to implement recursion, as explained in section 5.1.4. (The evaluator needs to call itself recursively, since evaluating an expression requires evaluating its subexpressions.) The registers fun, argl, and unev are used in evaluating combinations.

We will not provide a data-path diagram to show how the registers and operations of the evaluator are connected. The data paths are implicit in the evaluator's controller, which will be presented in detail.

5.2.1 The Core of the Explicit-Control Evaluator

The central element in the evaluator is the sequence beginning at eval-dispatch. This corresponds to the eval procedure of the metacircular evaluator described in section 4.1.1. When the program starts at eval-dispatch, it evaluates the expression specified by exp in the environment specified by env. When evaluation is complete, the program will go to the entry stored in continue, and the val register will hold the value of the expression. As with the metacircular eval, the structure of eval-dispatch is a case analysis on the syntactic type of the expression to be evaluated.[8] One minor difference between this evaluator and the metacircular eval is that we distinguish applications of procedures with no arguments from other applications. (We will see later how this leads to increased efficiency.)[9]

```
eval-dispatch
    (branch (self-evaluating? (fetch exp)) ev-self-eval)
    (branch (quoted? (fetch exp)) ev-quote)
    (branch (variable? (fetch exp)) ev-variable)
    (branch (definition? (fetch exp)) ev-definition)
    (branch (assignment? (fetch exp)) ev-assignment)
    (branch (lambda? (fetch exp)) ev-lambda)
    (branch (conditional? (fetch exp)) ev-cond)
    ;; continued on next page
```

8 In our program, the dispatch is written as a sequence of branch instructions. Alternatively, it could have been written in a data-directed style (and in a real system it probably would have been) to avoid the need to perform sequential tests and to facilitate the definition of new expression types. A machine designed to run Lisp would probably include a dispatch-on-type instruction that would efficiently execute such data-directed dispatches.

9 We add a no-args? predicate to the collection of syntax procedures taken from section 4.1.2 and also modify the application? predicate to check that arguments are present:

```
(define (no-args? exp)
  (if (atom? exp)
      nil
      (null? (cdr exp))))

(define (application? exp)
  (if (atom? exp)
      nil
      (not (null? (cdr exp)))))
```

```
(branch (no-args? (fetch exp)) ev-no-args)
(branch (application? (fetch exp)) ev-application)
(goto unknown-expression-type-error)
```

Evaluating simple expressions

Simple expressions—numbers, variables, quotations, and **lambda** expressions—have no subexpressions to be evaluated. For these, the evaluator simply places the correct value in the **val** register and continues execution at the entry point specified by continue. Evaluation of simple expressions is performed by the following controller code:

```
ev-self-eval
  (assign val (fetch exp))
  (goto (fetch continue))
ev-quote
  (assign val (text-of-quotation (fetch exp)))
  (goto (fetch continue))
ev-variable
  (assign val
          (lookup-variable-value (fetch exp) (fetch env)))
  (goto (fetch continue))
ev-lambda
  (assign val (make-procedure (fetch exp) (fetch env)))
  (goto (fetch continue))
```

Evaluating procedure applications

A procedure application is specified by a combination containing an operator and operands. The operator is a subexpression whose value is a procedure, and the operands are subexpressions whose values are the arguments to which the procedure should be applied. The metacircular **eval** handled applications by calling itself recursively to evaluate each element of the combination, and then passing the results to **apply**, which performs the actual procedure application. The explicit-control evaluator does the same thing; these recursive calls are implemented by goto instructions, together with use of the stack to save registers that will be restored after the recursive call returns. Before each call we will be careful to identify which registers must be saved (because their values will be needed later).[10]

10 This is an important but subtle point in translating algorithms from a procedural language, such as Lisp, to a register-machine language. As an alternative to saving only what is needed, we could save all the registers (except **val**) before each recursive call. This is called a *framed-stack* discipline. The resulting program would work but might save more registers than necessary; this could be an important consideration in a system where stack operations are expensive.

We start by considering the case of an operator with no operands. The operator must be evaluated to produce a procedure, which will then be applied to no arguments. To evaluate the operator, we move it to the exp register and go to eval-dispatch. The environment in the env register is already the correct one in which to evaluate the operator. We do not need to save env, because there are no more parts of the original expression that must be evaluated in this environment before the procedure can be applied. Nor do we need to save the old value of exp. We set up continue so that eval-dispatch will resume at the entry point setup-no-arg-apply after the operator has been evaluated. First, however, we save the old value of continue, which tells the controller where to continue after applying the procedure.

```
ev-no-args
  (assign exp (operator (fetch exp)))
  (save continue)
  (assign continue setup-no-arg-apply)
  (goto eval-dispatch)
```

When the operator expression of a no-argument combination has been evaluated, execution continues at setup-no-arg-apply with the value of the operator (i.e., the procedure to be applied) in val. We move this to the fun register and initialize argl, the list of arguments, to be empty. Then we transfer to apply-dispatch (whose details we will see below) to perform the actual application.

```
setup-no-arg-apply
  (assign fun (fetch val))
  (assign argl '())
  (goto apply-dispatch)
```

The operand-evaluation loop

Next we consider the case of a general combination. Here, in addition to the operator to be evaluated to obtain the procedure, there are also operands to be evaluated to obtain the arguments. Thus, before we go to eval-dispatch to evaluate the operator, we save env, since we will need this environment for evaluating the operands. We also set up the unev register to contain the unevaluated operand parts of the expression, and save this on the stack. When we finish evaluating the operator, execution is to continue at eval-args.

```
ev-application
  (assign unev (operands (fetch exp)))
  (assign exp (operator (fetch exp)))
  (save continue)
  (save env)
  (save unev)
  (assign continue eval-args)
  (goto eval-dispatch)
```

Upon returning from evaluating the operator subexpression of a general combination, we proceed to evaluate the operands of the combination and to accumulate the resulting arguments in a list, held in argl. First we restore the environment and the unevaluated operands. Then we assign to the fun register the procedure that was produced by evaluating the operator, save this on the stack, and initialize argl to an empty list. We then start the argument-evaluation loop:

```
eval-args
  (restore unev)
  (restore env)
  (assign fun (fetch val))
  (save fun)
  (assign argl '())
  (goto eval-arg-loop)
```

In each cycle of the argument-evaluation loop, we evaluate an operand from the list in unev and accumulate the result into argl. To evaluate an operand, we place the operand in the exp register and go to eval-dispatch, setting continue so that execution will resume with the argument-accumulation phase. But first we save the arguments accumulated so far (in argl), the environment (in env), and the remaining operands to be evaluated (in unev). A special case is made for the evaluation of the last operand, which is handled at eval-last-arg.[11]

11 To enable the evaluator to test for the last operand in a combination, we add the following syntax procedure to the collection given in section 4.1.2:

```
(define (last-operand? args)
  (null? (cdr args)))
```

We could be somewhat more efficient in the evaluation loop if we made evaluation of the first operand a special case too; we could postpone initializing argl until after evaluating the first operand, so as to avoid saving argl in this case. The compiler in section 5.3 performs this optimization and others.

```
eval-arg-loop
  (save argl)
  (assign exp (first-operand (fetch unev)))
  (branch (last-operand? (fetch unev)) eval-last-arg)
  (save env)
  (save unev)
  (assign continue accumulate-arg)
  (goto eval-dispatch)
```

When an operand has been evaluated, the value is accumulated into the list held in argl. The operand is then removed from the list of unevaluated operands in unev, and the argument-evaluation loop continues.

```
accumulate-arg
  (restore unev)
  (restore env)
  (restore argl)
  (assign argl (cons (fetch val) (fetch argl)))
  (assign unev (rest-operands (fetch unev)))
  (goto eval-arg-loop)
```

Evaluation of the last argument is handled differently. There is no need to save the environment or the list of unevaluated operands, since they will not be required after the last operand is evaluated. Thus, we return to a special entry point accumulate-last-arg, which restores the argument list, accumulates the new argument, restores the saved procedure, and goes off to perform the application.

```
eval-last-arg
  (assign continue accumulate-last-arg)
  (goto eval-dispatch)
accumulate-last-arg
  (restore argl)
  (assign argl (cons (fetch val) (fetch argl)))
  (restore fun)
  (goto apply-dispatch)
```

The details of the argument-evaluation loop determine the order in which the interpreter evaluates the operands of a combination (e.g., left to right or right to left—see exercise 3.6). This order is not determined by the metacircular evaluator, which inherits its control structure from the underlying Lisp in which it is implemented.[12] If the first-operand selector (used in

---

12 The order of operand evaluation in the metacircular evaluator is determined by the order of evaluation of the arguments to cons in the else clause of the procedure list-of-values of section 4.1.1.

eval-arg-loop to extract successive operands from unev) is implemented as car and the rest-operands selector is implemented as cdr, then the explicit-control evaluator will evaluate the operands of a combination in left-to-right order. Since we assemble argl by successively consing items onto the front of the list, the evaluated arguments appear in the argl list in the reverse of the order in which they were extracted from unev. We must implement the procedure-application phase of the evaluator so that it expects the arguments to appear in this order.[13]

Procedure application

The entry apply-dispatch corresponds to the apply procedure of the metacircular evaluator. By the time we get to apply-dispatch, the fun register contains the procedure to apply and argl contains the list of evaluated arguments to which it must be applied (in reverse order from how they appeared in the combination). The saved value of continue (originally passed to eval-dispatch and saved at ev-application or ev-no-args), which tells where to return with the result of the procedure application, is on the stack. When the application is complete, the program transfers to the entry point specified by the saved continue, with the result of the application in val. As with the metacircular apply, there are two cases to consider. Either the procedure to be applied is a primitive or it is a compound procedure.

```
apply-dispatch
  (branch (primitive-procedure? (fetch fun)) primitive-apply)
  (branch (compound-procedure? (fetch fun)) compound-apply)
  (goto unknown-procedure-type-error)
```

We assume that each primitive is implemented so as to obtain its arguments from argl and place the result in val. To specify how the machine handles primitives, we would have to provide a sequence of controller instructions to implement each primitive and make primitive-apply dispatch to the primitive identified by the contents of fun. Since we are interested in the structure of the evaluation process rather than the details of the primitives, we will instead just use an apply-primitive-procedure operation that applies the procedure in fun to the arguments in argl. For the purpose of simulating the evaluator with the simulator of section 5.1.5, we use the procedure apply-primitive-procedure, which calls on the

---

13 The metacircular evaluator did not reverse the order of the arguments. The order is different here because we have transformed the recursive argument-accumulation process given in section 4.1.1 into an iterative process. We cons each argument as we evaluate it rather than saving it until the rest of the arguments have been accumulated.

underlying Lisp system to perform the application, just as we did for the metacircular evaluator in section 4.1.4.[14]   After computing the value of the primitive application, we restore continue and go to the designated entry point.

```
primitive-apply
  (assign val
          (apply-primitive-procedure (fetch fun)
                                     (fetch argl)))
  (restore continue)
  (goto (fetch continue))
```

To apply a compound procedure, we proceed just as with the metacircular evaluator. We construct a frame that binds the procedure's parameters to the actual arguments, use this frame to extend the environment carried by the procedure, and evaluate in this extended environment the sequence of expressions that forms the body of the procedure. Eval-sequence, described below in section 5.2.2, handles the actual evaluation of the sequence.

```
compound-apply
  (assign env (make-bindings (fetch fun) (fetch argl)))
  (assign unev (procedure-body (fetch fun)))
  (goto eval-sequence)
```

Compound-apply is the only place in the interpreter where the env register is ever assigned a new value. The new environment is constructed from the environment carried by the procedure, together with the argument list and the corresponding list of variables to be bound. We assume that our register machine contains a data-manipulation operation make-bindings that accomplishes this. In terms of our basic environment-manipulation procedures (section 4.1.3), we could describe make-bindings as follows. (Note the reversal of the arguments to account for the reverse order of argl.)[15]

---

14 We can use the procedure

```
(define (apply-primitive-procedure p args)
  (apply (eval (primitive-id p) user-initial-environment)
         (reverse args)))
```

where apply and eval are the primitive apply and eval in the underlying Lisp. (The arguments must be reversed to account for the fact that argl lists the arguments in reverse order.) Alternatively, we can use the definition of apply-primitive-procedure given in section 4.1.4, modified to account for the argument reversal.

15 Make-bindings could directly call extend-environment instead of using the additional procedure extend-binding-environment. We defined it this way because we will need extend-binding-environment for the compiler in section 5.3.

```
(define (make-bindings proc args)
  (extend-binding-environment (parameters proc)
                              args
                              (procedure-environment proc)))

(define (extend-binding-environment vars args env)
  (extend-environment vars (reverse args) env))
```

Exercise 5.16

Ben Bitdiddle suggests that, for the purposes of simulating the explicit-control evaluator in Lisp, it would be better to modify the procedure constructor make-procedure so that it builds the parameter list of a procedure in reverse order, and to eliminate the call to reverse in extend-binding-environment. How would this change affect the performance of the evaluator?

5.2.2 Sequence Evaluation and Tail Recursion

The evaluation of sequences of expressions is handled by eval-sequence. This entry, together with eval-sequence-continue, forms a loop that successively evaluates each expression in a sequence. The list of unevaluated expressions is kept in unev. Before evaluating each expression, we check to see if there are additional expressions to be evaluated in the sequence. If so, we save the rest of the unevaluated expressions (held in unev) and the environment in which these must be evaluated (held in env) and call eval-dispatch to evaluate the expression. The two saved registers are restored upon the return from this evaluation, at eval-sequence-continue.

The final expression in the sequence is handled differently, at the entry point last-exp. Since there are no more expressions to be evaluated after this one, we need not save unev or env before going to eval-dispatch. The value of the whole sequence is the value of the last expression, so after the evaluation of the last expression there is nothing left to do except continue at the entry currently held on the stack. (It has been there all through the procedure-application phase, ever since it was saved by ev-application or ev-no-args.) Instead of setting up continue to make eval-dispatch return here and then restoring continue from the stack and continuing at that entry, we restore continue from the stack before going to eval-dispatch, so that eval-dispatch will continue at that entry after evaluating the expression.

```
eval-sequence
  (assign exp (first-exp (fetch unev)))
  (branch (last-exp? (fetch unev)) last-exp)
  (save unev)
  (save env)
  (assign continue eval-sequence-continue)
  (goto eval-dispatch)
eval-sequence-continue
  (restore env)
  (restore unev)
  (assign unev (rest-exps (fetch unev)))
  (goto eval-sequence)
last-exp
  (restore continue)
  (goto eval-dispatch)
```

Tail recursion

In chapter 1 we said that the process described by a procedure such as

```
(define (sqrt-iter guess radicand)
  (cond ((good-enough? guess radicand) guess)
        (else (sqrt-iter (improve guess radicand)
                         radicand))))
```

is an iterative process. Even though the procedure is syntactically recursive (defined in terms of itself), it is not logically necessary for an evaluator to save information in passing from one call to sqrt-iter to the next.[16] An evaluator that can execute a procedure such as sqrt-iter without requiring increasing storage as the procedure continues to call itself is called a *tail-recursive* evaluator. The metacircular implementation of the evaluator in chapter 4 does not specify whether the evaluator is tail-recursive, because that evaluator inherits its mechanism for saving state from the underlying Lisp. With the explicit-control evaluator, however, we can trace through the evaluation process to see when procedure calls cause a net accumulation of information on the stack.

Our evaluator is tail-recursive, because in order to evaluate the final expression of a sequence (at last-exp) we transfer directly to eval-dispatch without saving any information on the stack. Hence, evaluating the final

---

16 We saw in section 5.1 how to implement such a process with a register machine that had no stack; the state of the process was stored in a fixed set of registers.

expression in a sequence—even if it is a procedure call (as in sqrt-iter)—will not cause any information to be accumulated on the stack.[17]

If we did not think to take advantage of the fact that it was unnecessary to save information in this case, we might have implemented eval-sequence by treating all the expressions in a sequence uniformly—saving the registers, evaluating the expression, returning to restore the registers, and repeating this until all the expressions have been evaluated:[18]

```
eval-sequence
  (branch (no-more-exps? (fetch unev)) end-sequence)   ;***
  (assign exp (first-exp (fetch unev)))                ;***
  (save unev)
  (save env)
  (assign continue eval-sequence-continue)
  (goto eval-dispatch)
eval-sequence-continue
  (restore env)
  (restore unev)
  (assign unev (rest-exps (fetch unev)))
  (goto eval-sequence)
end-sequence
  (restore continue)
  (goto (fetch continue))                              ;***
```

This may seem like a minor change to our previous code for evaluation of a sequence: Only the starred lines are changed, so that we go through the save-restore cycle for the last expression in a sequence as well as for the others. The interpreter will still give the same value for any expression. But this change is fatal to the tail-recursive implementation, because we must now return after evaluating the final expression in a sequence in order to undo the (useless) register saves. These extra saves will accumulate during a nest of procedure calls. Consequently, processes such as sqrt-iter will require space proportional to the number of iterations rather than requiring constant space. This difference can be significant. For example, with tail

---

17 This implementation of tail recursion in eval-sequence is one variety of a well-known optimization technique used by many compilers. In compiling a procedure whose final instruction is another procedure call, one can replace the second procedure call by a jump to the second procedure's entry point. Building this strategy into the interpreter, as we have done in this section, provides the optimization uniformly throughout the language.

18 We can define no-more-exps? as follows:

```
(define no-more-exps? null?)
```

recursion, an infinite loop can be expressed using only the procedure-call mechanism:

```
(define (count n)
  (print n)
  (count (1+ n)))
```

Without tail recursion, such a procedure would eventually run out of stack space, and expressing a true iteration would require some control mechanism other than procedure call.

5.2.3 Conditionals and Other Special Forms

As with the metacircular evaluator, special forms are handled by selectively evaluating fragments of the expression. For a conditional expression, we evaluate the predicate part of the first clause. We then decide, based on the value of that predicate, whether to evaluate the action sequence of the clause or to consider the next clause.

The first thing we do upon encountering a conditional is to save the continue register, because we will need it later in order to return to the evaluation of the expression that is waiting for the value of the conditional. Internal to the conditional evaluation, the continuation will be evcond-decide—the section of the code that receives the value of the predicate and decides whether to evaluate the action sequence. We initialize the unev register to the list of pending clauses. We then begin the part of the code (at evcond-pred) that evaluates the predicate of the first clause of the conditional. If there are no clauses, we simply return nil (by going to the original continuation with nil in the val register). Otherwise, unless the clause is an else clause, we save the environment and the list of pending clauses (in unev) and go to eval-dispatch to evaluate the predicate.

```
ev-cond
  (save continue)
  (assign continue evcond-decide)
  (assign unev (clauses (fetch exp)))
evcond-pred
  (branch (no-clauses? (fetch unev)) evcond-return-nil)
  (assign exp (first-clause (fetch unev)))
  (branch (else-clause? (fetch exp)) evcond-else-clause)
  (save env)
  (save unev)
  (assign exp (predicate (fetch exp)))
  (goto eval-dispatch)
```

```
evcond-return-nil
  (restore continue)
  (assign val nil)
  (goto (fetch continue))
```

After it has evaluated the predicate, `eval-dispatch` returns to `evcond-decide`, which restores the environment and the list of unevaluated clauses. We now test whether the predicate was true. If the predicate was true, we set things up to evaluate the action sequence of the clause. If the predicate was false, we remove the first clause from the `unev` list and go back to `evcond-pred` to examine the next clause.

```
evcond-decide
  (restore unev)
  (restore env)
  (branch (true? (fetch val)) evcond-true-predicate)
  (assign unev (rest-clauses (fetch unev)))
  (goto evcond-pred)
```

For a true predicate or an `else` clause, the associated action sequence of the clause must be evaluated and the value of the last expression in the sequence must be returned as the value of the conditional expression. To evaluate this sequence, we go to `eval-sequence`. First, however, we set things up for `eval-sequence` by placing in `unev` the sequence of expressions to be evaluated. The environment is already in the `env` register, and the continuation to return to after evaluating the conditional is already saved on the stack, as is required for `eval-sequence`.

```
evcond-true-predicate
  (assign exp (first-clause (fetch unev)))
evcond-else-clause
  (assign unev (actions (fetch exp)))
  (goto eval-sequence)
```

Assignments and definitions

Assignments are handled by `ev-assignment`, which is reached from `eval-dispatch` with the assignment expression in `exp`. Ev-assignment first evaluates the value part of the expression and then installs the new value in the environment. Set-variable-value! is assumed to be a primitive machine operation.

```
ev-assignment
  (assign unev (assignment-variable (fetch exp)))
  (save unev)
  (assign exp (assignment-value (fetch exp)))
  (save env)
  (save continue)
  (assign continue ev-assignment-1)
  (goto eval-dispatch)
ev-assignment-1
  (restore continue)
  (restore env)
  (restore unev)
  (perform (set-variable-value! (fetch unev)
                                (fetch val)
                                (fetch env)))

  (goto (fetch continue))
```

Definitions are handled in a similar way:[19]

```
ev-definition
  (assign unev (definition-variable (fetch exp)))
  (save unev)
  (assign exp (definition-value (fetch exp)))
  (save env)
  (save continue)
  (assign continue ev-definition-1)
  (goto eval-dispatch)
ev-definition-1
  (restore continue)
  (restore env)
  (restore unev)
  (perform
   (define-variable! (fetch unev) (fetch val) (fetch env)))
  (assign val (fetch unev))        ;return as value
                                   ;the symbol being defined

  (goto (fetch continue))
```

Exercise 5.17

Extend the evaluator to handle if as a special form. You will need to install
some additional syntax procedures. (Compare exercise 4.2.)

---

19 This implementation of **define** ignores a subtle issue in the handling of internal
definitions, although it works correctly in most cases. We will see what the problem is
and how to solve it in section 5.2.5.

Exercise 5.18

By adapting the method discussed in section 4.2.1, modify the evaluator so that it uses normal-order evaluation.

5.2.4 Running the Evaluator

We will install a driver loop in our evaluator machine, as we did for the gcd machine in figure 5.4. This plays the role of the `driver-loop` procedure of section 4.1.4. The evaluator will repeatedly print a prompt, read an expression from the terminal, evaluate the expression by going to `eval-dispatch`, and print the result. The following instructions form the beginning of the explicit-control evaluator's controller sequence:

```
read-eval-print-loop
  (perform (initialize-stack))
  (perform (newline))
  (perform (princ "EC-EVAL==> "))
  (assign exp (read))
  (assign env the-global-environment)
  (assign continue print-result)
  (goto eval-dispatch)
print-result
  (perform (user-print (fetch val)))
  (goto read-eval-print-loop)
```

We have chosen the prompt `EC-EVAL==>` to keep from being confused about when we are typing at the explicit-control evaluator that is being simulated and when we are typing at the underlying Lisp that is running the simulation. In order to avoid printing environments (which may be circular lists) we use `user-print`, just as we did with the metacircular evaluator in section 4.1.4. We assume that `read` and all the printing operations are primitive.

When we encounter an error in a procedure (such as the "unknown procedure type error" indicated at `apply-dispatch`), we print an error message and return to the driver loop:

```
unknown-procedure-type-error
  (assign val 'unknown-procedure-type-error)
  (goto signal-error)
```

```
unknown-expression-type-error
  (assign val 'unknown-expression-type-error)
  (goto signal-error)
```

```
signal-error
  (perform (user-print (fetch val)))
  (goto read-eval-print-loop)
```

We initialize the stack before each evaluation, since it won't be empty after an error interrupts an evaluation.[20]

If we take all the code fragments presented in the previous sections and include them within a define-machine construct, we can create an evaluator machine that we can run using the register-machine simulator of section 5.1.5. Before starting the simulation, we must define Lisp procedures to simulate the syntax and environment operations used as primitives by the evaluator. These are the same procedures we used for the metacircular evaluator in sections 4.1.2, 4.1.3, and 4.1.4, along with the apply-primitive-procedure, make-bindings, last-operand?, no-args?, and application? procedures described in section 5.2.1 and no-more-exps? from section 5.2.2. Once these procedures have been defined, we can define the constant the-global-environment using setup-environment from the metacircular evaluator in section 4.1.4, and start the register machine:

```
(define the-global-environment (setup-environment))
(define-machine explicit-control-evaluator
  (registers exp env val continue fun argl unev)
  (controller
    ⟨body of the controller as given in this section⟩))

(start explicit-control-evaluator)

EC-EVAL==> (define (append x y)
              (cond ((null? x) y)
                    (else (cons (car x)
                                (append (cdr x) y)))))
append

EC-EVAL==> (append '(a b c) '(d e f))
(a b c d e f)
```

Of course, evaluating expressions in this way will take much longer than if we had directly typed them into Lisp, because of the multiple levels of

---

20 We could perform the initialization only after errors, at signal-error, but doing it in the driver loop will be convenient for monitoring the evaluator's performance, as described below.

simulation involved. Our expressions are evaluated by the explicit-control-evaluator register machine, which is being simulated by a Lisp program, which is itself being evaluated by the Lisp interpreter.

Monitoring the performance of the evaluator

A simulation such as the one we designed in section 5.1.5 can be a powerful tool to guide the implementation of evaluators. The simulation makes it easy not only to explore variations of the register-machine design but also to monitor the performance of the simulated evaluator. For example, one important factor in performance is how efficiently the evaluator uses the stack. If we define the evaluator register machine with the version of the simulator that collects statistics on stack use, we can observe the number of stack operations required to evaluate various expressions:

```
EC-EVAL==> (define (factorial n)
             (cond ((= n 1) 1)
                   (else (* (factorial (- n 1)) n))))
```
factorial
(total-pushes: 3 maximum-depth: 3)

```
EC-EVAL==> (factorial 5)
```
120
(total-pushes: 144 maximum-depth: 28)

Note that the driver loop of the evaluator reinitializes the stack on each interaction, so that the statistics printed will refer only to stack operations used to evaluate the previous expression.

Exercise 5.19

Use the analyzer you added to build-model in exercise 5.11 to determine the data paths of the explicit-control evaluator machine. Are there any registers that are never saved or restored? What are the sources for assignment to the env register?

Exercise 5.20

Use the monitored stack to explore the tail-recursive property of the evaluator (section 5.2.2). Start the evaluator and define the iterative factorial procedure from section 1.2.1:

```
(define (factorial n)
  (define (iter product counter)
    (cond ((> counter n) product)
          (else (iter (* counter product)
                      (+ counter 1)))))
  (iter 1 1))
```

Run the procedure with some small values of n. Record the maximum depth and the number of pushes required to compute $n!$ for each of these values.

a. You will find that the maximum depth required to evaluate $n!$ is independent of n. What is that depth?

b. Determine from your data a formula in terms of n for the total number of push operations used in evaluating $n!$ for any $n > 1$. Note that the number of operations used is a linear function of n and is thus determined by two constants.

Exercise 5.21

For comparison with exercise 5.20, define the following procedure for computing factorials recursively:

```
(define (factorial n)
  (cond ((= n 1) 1)
        (else (* (factorial (- n 1)) n)))))
```

By running this procedure with the monitored stack, determine, as a function of n, the maximum depth of the stack and the total number of pushes used in evaluating $n!$ for $n > 1$. (Again, these functions will be linear.) Summarize your experiments by filling in the following table with the appropriate expressions in n:

	Maximum depth	Number of pushes
Recursive factorial		
Iterative factorial		

The maximum depth is a measure of the amount of space used by the evaluator in carrying out the computation, and the number of pushes correlates well with the time required.

Exercise 5.22

Monitor the stack operations in the tree-recursive Fibonacci computation:

```
(define (fib n)
  (cond ((= n 0) 0)
        ((= n 1) 1)
        (else (+ (fib (- n 1)) (fib (- n 2))))))
```

a. Give a formula in terms of n for the maximum depth of the stack required to compute Fib(n) for $n > 2$. Hint: In section 1.2.2 we argued that the space used by this process grows linearly with n.

b. Give a formula for the total number of pushes used to compute Fib(n) for $n > 2$. Recall that the number of pushes corresponds to the time used, and hence should grow exponentially. Hint: Let $S(n)$ be the number of pushes used in computing Fib(n). You should be able to argue that there is a formula that expresses $S(n)$ in terms of $S(n-1)$, $S(n-2)$, and some fixed "overhead" constant k that is independent of n. Give the formula, and say what k is. Use your formula to express $S(n)$ in terms of the Fibonacci numbers.

Exercise 5.23

Modify the definition of the evaluator by changing the instructions at `eval-sequence` as described in section 5.2.2 so that the evaluator is no longer tail-recursive. Rerun your experiments from exercises 5.20 and 5.21 to demonstrate that both versions of the `factorial` procedure now require space that grows linearly with their input.

5.2.5 Internal Definitions

With the implementation of the explicit-control evaluator we come to the end of a development, begun in chapter 1, in which we have explored successively more precise models of the evaluation process. We started with the relatively informal substitution model, then extended this in chapter 3 to the environment model, which enabled us to deal with state and change. In the metacircular evaluator of chapter 4, we used Lisp itself as a language for making more explicit the environment structure constructed during evaluation of an expression. Now, with register machines, we have taken a close look at the evaluator's mechanisms for argument passing and control. At each new level of description, we have had to raise issues and resolve ambiguities that were not apparent at the previous, less precise treatment of evaluation.

One such ambiguity is the evaluation of `define` expressions, as this relates to block structure and internal definitions. Although we have waited until now to address this issue, the problem could have been raised in the context of the metacircular evaluator. Our evaluation model and the evaluators we have implemented execute definitions in sequence, extending the environment frame one definition at a time. This is particularly convenient for interactive program development, in which the programmer needs to freely mix the evaluation of procedures with the definition of new procedures. On the other hand, if we think carefully about the internal `define` expressions used to implement block structure (introduced in section 1.1.8), we will find that name-by-name extension of the environment is not the correct way to define local variables. In fact, our implementation of `define` contradicts the requirement that, in block structure, the scope of a local name is the entire procedure in which the `define` is evaluated.

To see why this is the case, consider a procedure with internal definitions, such as

```
(define (f x)
  (define (g y) (h (+ x y)))
  (define (h z) ... )
  ⟨rest of body of f⟩)
```

Our intention here is that the name h in the body of the procedure g should refer to the procedure h that is defined on the next line after g. The scope of the name h is the entire body of f, not just the portion of the body of f starting at the point where the define for h occurs. Indeed, when we consider that h might itself be defined in terms of g—so that g and h are mutually recursive procedures—we see that the only satisfactory interpretation of the two defines is to regard them as if the names g and h were being added to the environment simultaneously.

As it happens, our interpreter will evaluate calls to f correctly, but for an "accidental" reason: Since the definitions of the internal procedures come first, no calls to these procedures will be evaluated until all of them have been defined. Hence, h will have been defined by the time g is executed. On the other hand, this "lucky accident" would not have saved us if we had intermixed internal definitions with other expressions in the body of a procedure.[21] What we need is a mechanism that will cause internally defined names to have truly simultaneous scope.

We can achieve such a scope rule for internal definitions by creating all local variables that will be in the current environment before actually evaluating any of the value expressions. One way to do this is by a syntax transformation on lambda expressions. Before evaluating the body of a lambda expression, we "scan out" and eliminate all the internal definitions in the body. The internally defined variables will be created with a let and then set to their values by assignment. For example, the procedure

```
(lambda ⟨vars⟩
  (define u ⟨e1⟩)
  (define v ⟨e2⟩)
  ⟨e3⟩)
```

---

21 This is the reason for the "management is not responsible" remark in footnote 23 of chapter 1. By insisting that internal procedure definitions come first, the language implementor reserves the right to be ambiguous about the actual mechanism used to evaluate these definitions. The choice of one evaluation rule rather than another here may seem like a small issue, affecting only the interpretation of "badly formed" programs. However, we will see in section 5.3.7 that moving to a model of simultaneous scoping for internal definitions avoids some nasty difficulties that would otherwise arise in implementing a compiler.

would be transformed into

```
(lambda ⟨vars⟩
  (let ((u '*unassigned*)
        (v '*unassigned*))
    (set! u ⟨e1⟩)
    (set! v ⟨e2⟩)
    ⟨e3⟩)))
```

where *unassigned* is a special object that causes lookup-variable-value to signal an error if an attempt is made to use the value of the not-yet-assigned variable.

Exercise 5.24

In this exercise we implement the method just described for interpreting internal definitions.

a. Implement let for the explicit-control evaluator by transforming it to the equivalent lambda combination, as was done in exercise 4.3.

b. Change lookup-variable-value (section 4.1.3) to signal an error if the value it finds is the *unassigned* object.

c. Write a procedure scan-out-defines that takes a lambda expression and returns an equivalent one that has no internal definitions, by making the transformation described above.

d. Install your scan-out-defines in the interpreter either in make-procedure or in procedure-body (see section 4.1.2). Which is a better place? Why?

Exercise 5.25

Draw diagrams of the environment in effect when evaluating the expression ⟨e3⟩ in the procedure in the text, comparing how this will be structured when definitions are interpreted sequentially with how it will be structured if definitions are scanned out as described. Why is there an extra frame in the transformed program? Explain why this difference in environment structure can never make a difference in the behavior of a correct program. Design a way to make the interpreter implement the "simultaneous" scope rule for internal definitions without constructing the extra frame.

Exercise 5.26

Consider an alternative strategy for scanning out definitions that translates the example in the text to

```
(lambda ⟨vars⟩
  (let ((u '*unassigned*)
        (v '*unassigned*))
    (let ((a ⟨e1⟩)
          (b ⟨e2⟩))
      (set! u a)
      (set! v b))
    ⟨e3⟩))
```

Here a and b are meant to represent new variable names, created by the interpreter, that could not be part of a user's program. Comment on the relative merits of the two translations of internal definitions.

Exercise 5.27

Ben Bitdiddle, Alyssa P. Hacker, and Eva Lu Ator are arguing about the desired result of evaluating the expression

```
(let ((a 1))
  (define (f x)
    (define b (+ a x))
    (define a 5)
    (+ a b))
  (f 10))
```

Ben asserts that the result should be obtained using the sequential rule for define: b is defined to be 11, then a is defined to be 5, so the result is 16. Alyssa objects that mutual recursion requires the simultaneous scope rule for internal procedure definitions, and that it is unreasonable to treat procedure names differently from other names. Thus, she argues for the mechanism implemented in exercise 5.24. This would lead to a being unassigned at the time that the value for b is to be computed. Hence, in Alyssa's view the procedure should produce an error. Eva has a third opinion. She says that if the definitions of a and b are truly meant to be simultaneous, then the value 5 for a should be used in evaluating b. Hence, in Eva's view a should be 5, b should be 15, and the result should be 20. Which (if any) of these viewpoints do you support? Can you devise a way to implement internal definitions so that they behave as Eva prefers?[22]

5.3 Compilation

Almost every contemporary computer is a register machine whose primitive instructions constitute a *native language* that is organized in terms of

---

[22] The MIT implementors of Scheme support Alyssa on the following grounds: Eva is in principle correct—the definitions should be regarded as simultaneous. But it seems difficult to implement a general, efficient mechanism that does what Eva requires. In the absence of such a mechanism, it is better to generate an error in the difficult cases of simultaneous definitions (Alyssa's notion) than to produce an incorrect answer (as Ben would have it).

operations on the contents of registers. There are two common strategies for bridging the gap between such register-machine languages and higher-level languages that are structured in terms of expressions and procedures. The explicit-control evaluator of section 5.2 illustrates the strategy of interpretation. An interpreter written in the native language of a machine configures the machine to execute programs written in a language (called the *source language*) that may differ from the native language of the machine performing the evaluation. The primitive operators of the source language are implemented as a library of subroutines written in the native language of the given machine. A program to be interpreted (called the *source program*) is represented as a data structure. The interpreter traverses this data structure, analyzing the source program. As it does so, it simulates the intended behavior of the source program by calling appropriate primitive operators from the library.

In this section, we explore the alternative strategy of *compilation*. A compiler for a given source language and machine translates a source program into an equivalent program (called the *object program*) written in the machine's native language. The compiler that we implement in this section translates programs written in the Scheme dialect of Lisp into sequences of instructions for the explicit-control evaluator machine described in section 5.2. Compared with interpretation, compilation can provide a great increase in the efficiency of program execution. This is because with an interpreter the analysis of a source program and reduction to equivalent machine-language operations is performed each time the program is interpreted, whereas with a compiler the program analysis is performed only once (when the object program is constructed), and the resulting object program can be run repeatedly in different contexts and with different inputs. On the other hand, an interpreter provides a more powerful environment for interactive program development and debugging, because the source program being executed is available at run time to be examined and modified. In addition, because the entire library of primitive operators is present, new programs can be constructed and added to the system during debugging.

In view of the complementary advantages of compilation and interpretation, modern program-development environments pursue a mixed strategy. Lisp interpreters are generally organized so that interpreted procedures and compiled procedures can call each other. This enables a programmer to compile those parts of a program that are assumed to be debugged, thus gaining the efficiency advantage of compilation, while retaining the interpretive mode of execution for those parts of the program that are in the flux of interactive development and debugging. In section 5.3.6, after we have implemented the compiler, we will show how to interface it with our interpreter to produce an integrated interpreter-compiler development system.

An overview of the compiler

A compiler is much like an interpreter, both in its structure and in the function it performs. Accordingly, the mechanisms used by the compiler for analyzing expressions will be similar to those used by the interpreter. Moreover, to make it easy to interface compiled and interpreted code, we will design the compiler to generate code that obeys the same conventions of register usage as the interpreter: The environment will be kept in the env register, argument lists will be accumulated in argl, and so on. Compiled code will also obey the interpreter's conventions for procedure application: When a procedure is to be applied, a continuation will be saved on the stack, the procedure will be in fun, and the arguments will be in argl; the procedure call will restore and return to the saved continuation with the answer in val. In general, the compiler translates a source program into an object program that performs essentially the same register operations as would the interpreter in evaluating the same source program.

This description suggests a strategy for implementing a rudimentary compiler: We traverse the expression in the same way as does the interpreter. When we encounter a register instruction that the interpreter would perform in evaluating the expression, we do not execute the instruction but instead accumulate it into a sequence. The resulting sequence of instructions will be the object code. Observe the efficiency advantage of compilation over interpretation. Each time the interpreter evaluates an expression—for example, (f $\langle arg_1 \rangle$ $\langle arg_2 \rangle$)—it performs the work of classifying the expression (discovering that this is a procedure application) and testing for the end of the operand list (discovering that there are two operands). With a compiler, analysis of the expression is done only once, when the instruction sequence is generated at compile time. The object code produced by the compiler contains only the instructions that evaluate the operator and the two operands, assemble the argument list, and apply the procedure (in fun) to the arguments (in argl).

There are further opportunities to gain efficiency in compiled code. As the interpreter runs, it follows a process that must be applicable to any expression in the language. In contrast, a given segment of compiled code is meant to execute some particular expression. This can make a big difference, for example in the use of the stack to save registers. When the interpreter evaluates an expression, it must be prepared for any contingency. Before evaluating a subexpression, the interpreter saves all registers that will be needed later, because the subexpression might require an arbitrary evaluation. A compiler, on the other hand, can exploit the structure of the particular expression it is processing to generate code that avoids unnecessary stack operations.

As a case in point, consider the combination (f $\langle arg_1 \rangle$ $\langle arg_2 \rangle$). Before the interpreter evaluates the operator of the combination, it prepares for this evaluation by saving the registers exp and env, whose values will be needed later. The interpreter then evaluates the operator to obtain the result in val, restores exp and env, and finally moves the result from val to fun. However, in the particular expression we are dealing with, the operator is the symbol f, whose evaluation is accomplished by the primitive operation lookup-variable-value, which does not alter any registers. The compiler that we implement in this section will take advantage of this fact and generate code that evaluates the operator using the instruction

```
(assign fun (lookup-variable-value 'f (fetch env)))
```

This code not only avoids the unnecessary saves and restores but also assigns the value of the lookup directly to fun, whereas the interpreter would obtain the result in val and then move this to fun.

A compiler can also optimize access to the environment. Having analyzed the code, the compiler can in many cases know in which frame a particular variable will be located and access that frame directly, rather than performing the lookup-variable-value search. We will discuss how to implement such variable access in section 5.3.7. Until then, however, we will focus on the kind of register and stack optimizations described above. There are many other optimizations that can be performed by a compiler, such as coding primitive operations "in line" instead of using a general apply mechanism; but we will not consider these here. Our main goal in this section is to illustrate the compilation process in a simplified (but still interesting) context.

5.3.1 Structure of the Compiler

Our compiler processes an expression by classifying it and dispatching to a procedure that serves as a *code generator* for that type of expression. A code generator *meta-evaluates* a designated expression. That is, rather than evaluating the expression at the moment, the code generator produces a sequence of instructions that, when run, has the effect of evaluating the expression.

The procedure compile-expression is the central element in the compiler, corresponding to the eval procedure of the metacircular evaluator and to the eval-dispatch entry of the explicit-control evaluator. Compile-

expression performs a case analysis on the syntactic type of the expression
to be compiled. For each type of expression, it dispatches to a specialized
code generator:

```
(define (compile-expression exp c-t-env target cont)
  (cond ((self-evaluating? exp)
         (compile-constant exp c-t-env target cont))
        ((quoted? exp)
         (compile-constant (text-of-quotation exp)
                           c-t-env target cont))
        ((variable? exp)
         (compile-variable-access exp c-t-env target cont))
        ((assignment? exp)
         (compile-assignment exp c-t-env target cont))
        ((definition? exp)
         (compile-definition exp c-t-env target cont))
        ((lambda? exp)
         (compile-lambda exp c-t-env target cont))
        ((conditional? exp)
         (compile-cond (clauses exp) c-t-env target cont))
        ((no-args? exp)
         (compile-no-args exp c-t-env target cont))
        ((application? exp)
         (compile-application exp c-t-env target cont))
        (else
         (error "Unknown expression type -- COMPILE" exp)))))
```

Targets, continuations, and compile-time environments

Compile-expression and the code generators it calls take several arguments in addition to the expression to be compiled. There is a *target*, which
specifies the register in which the compiled code is to return the value of the
expression. There is also a *continuation descriptor*, which describes how
the code resulting from the compilation of the expression should proceed
when it has finished its execution. The continuation descriptor can require
that the code do one of the following three things:

• continue at the next instruction in sequence (this is specified by the
continuation descriptor next),

• return from the procedure being compiled (this is specified by the continuation descriptor return),

• jump over some instructions to a named entry point (this is specified by
using the designated label as the continuation descriptor).

In addition to a target and a continuation descriptor, each code generator takes as argument a *compile-time environment*, which is a data structure that contains information about the environment that will be in effect when the code is run. In section 5.3.7 we will see how a compile-time environment can be used to optimize references to variables in compiled code. Until then, we will not actually use the compile-time environment in generating code; however, we will make sure that it is maintained by the compiler (when the entry to a procedure body is compiled), so that it will be available for subsequent use.[23]

Instruction sequences and stack discipline
Each code generator returns an *instruction sequence* containing the object code it has generated for the expression. Code generation for a compound expression is accomplished by combining the output from simpler code generators for the components of the expression, just as evaluation of a compound expression is accomplished by evaluating the component expressions. The simplest instruction sequences are created by calling generators for primitive register instructions, such as `make-register-assignment`. The primitive code generators form an abstraction barrier, isolating the organization of the compiler from the format of the object-code instructions to be generated. By using different sets of primitive code generators, we could compile code for a variety of machines.

There are two procedures used throughout the compiler to combine instruction sequences. `Append-instruction-sequences` takes as arguments any number of instruction sequences that are to be executed sequentially; it appends them and returns the combined sequence. `Preserving` takes three arguments: the name of a register and two instruction sequences that are to be executed sequentially. It appends the sequences in such a way that the contents of the designated register is preserved over the execution of the first sequence, if this is needed for the execution of the second sequence. If the first sequence modifies the register and the second sequence actually needs the register's original contents, then `preserving` wraps a `save` and a `restore` of the register around the first sequence before appending the sequences. Otherwise, `preserving` simply returns the appended instruction sequences.

---

23 In examining the compiler, be careful not to confuse the compile-time environment (which is referred to in the procedures as c-t-env) with the **env** register of the machine on which the compiled code is to run (which sometimes appears as a symbol in the instructions generated by the compiler). Similarly, do not confuse the continuation descriptor (usually referred to by the compiler as cont) with the **continue** register of the machine. The compiler procedures also refer to the expression to be compiled as **exp**. This should not cause confusion with the **exp** register of the interpreter machine, since compiled code does not reference the **exp** register at all. The compiled code does not look at an expression to be evaluated; rather, it embodies the evaluation of a particular expression. For the same reason, compiled code does not use the **unev** register.

```
(define (preserving reg seq1 seq2)
  (if (and (needs-register seq2 reg)
           (modifies-register seq1 reg))
      (append-instruction-sequences
       (wrap-save-restore seq1 reg)
       seq2)
      (append-instruction-sequences seq1 seq2)))
```

Thus, (append-instruction-sequences ⟨ seq1 ⟩ ⟨ seq2 ⟩) produces the sequence

⟨ seq1 ⟩
⟨ seq2 ⟩

whereas (preserving ⟨ reg ⟩ ⟨ seq1 ⟩ ⟨ seq2 ⟩) produces either the same sequence or

(save ⟨ reg ⟩)
⟨ seq1 ⟩
(restore ⟨ reg ⟩)
⟨ seq2 ⟩

depending on how ⟨ seq1 ⟩ and ⟨ seq2 ⟩ use ⟨ reg ⟩.

By using preserving whenever it must worry about preserving the contents of a register, the compiler avoids unnecessary stack operations. The only stack instructions that are generated explicitly are those dictated by our procedure-calling convention, which requires that the continuation be on the stack. The detailed representation of instruction sequences and the implementation of the procedures for sequence manipulation will be described in section 5.3.3.

Exercise 5.28

In evaluating a procedure application, the interpreter always saves and restores the env register around the evaluation of the operator, saves and restores env around the evaluation of each operand (except the final one), saves and restores argl around the evaluation of each operand, and saves and restores fun around the evaluation of the operand sequence. For each of the following combinations, say which of these save and restore operations are superfluous and thus could be eliminated by the compiler's preserving mechanism:

(f 'x 'y)

((f) 'x 'y)

(f (g 'x) y)

(f (g 'x) 'y)

Exercise 5.29

Using the `preserving` mechanism, the compiler will avoid saving and restoring env around the evaluation of the operator of a combination in the case where the operator is a symbol. We could also build such optimizations into the evaluator. Indeed, the explicit-control evaluator of section 5.2 already performs such an optimization, by treating combinations with no operands as a special case.

a. Extend the explicit-control evaluator to recognize as a separate class of expressions combinations whose operator is a symbol, and to take advantage of this fact in evaluating such expressions.

b. Alyssa P. Hacker suggests that by extending the evaluator to recognize more and more special cases we could incorporate all the compiler's optimizations, and that this would eliminate the advantage of compilation altogether. What do you think of this idea?

5.3.2 Compiling Expressions

In this section we implement the code generators to which the procedure `compile-expression` dispatches. These code generators use primitive code generators to generate the actual instructions and instruction fragments. (Primitive code generators, which have names beginning with `make-`, will be described in section 5.3.4.) They also use `compile-expression` (to recursively compile subexpressions) and the instruction-sequence combiners discussed in section 5.3.1.

Given a continuation descriptor, the compiler can construct the appropriate instructions with which to terminate the code for an expression by using the procedure `compile-continuation`:

```
(define (compile-continuation continuation)
  (cond ((eq? continuation 'return) (compile-return))
        ((eq? continuation 'next)
         (empty-instruction-sequence))
        (else (make-jump continuation))))
```

This procedure uses the primitive code generator `make-jump`, as well as a procedure `empty-instruction-sequence` that generates a sequence with no instructions (see sections 5.3.3 and 5.3.4). `Compile-return` will be shown, along with compilation of procedure calls, later in this section.

Simple expressions

The code generators for constants and variables construct instruction sequences that assign the required value to the target register and then continue with the designated continuation:

```
(define (compile-constant constant c-t-env target cont)
  (append-instruction-sequences
   (make-register-assignment target (make-constant constant))
   (compile-continuation cont)))

(define (compile-variable-access var c-t-env target cont)
  (append-instruction-sequences
   (make-register-assignment target
                       (make-variable-access var
                                             c-t-env))
   (compile-continuation cont)))
```

Each of these two code generators constructs its result by appending two simpler instruction sequences. The first sequence (constructed by primitive code generators) assigns the appropriate value to the target register, and the second sequence continues as required after the assignment. If the continuation descriptor is next, then (compile-continuation cont) will produce an empty instruction sequence.

Evaluating the elements of an application

The essence of the compilation process is the compilation of procedure applications. The instruction sequence to be constructed for an application must evaluate the operator of the combination and assign the result to the fun register. It must also evaluate the operands and accumulate the results into argl. Then it must apply the procedure in fun to the arguments in argl. The procedure application should return to the continuation that was specified for this combination. The registers env, fun, and argl may have to be saved and restored during evaluation of the operator and operands.

The required code is generated by the procedure compile-application, which uses preserving to append two instruction sequences. The first sequence is formed by recursively calling compile-expression to compile the operator of the combination with the target fun and the continuation next. The second sequence will perform the operand evaluation and procedure application. Since evaluation of the operator may destroy the contents of the env register (which is needed for operand evaluation), the two code sequences are appended preserving env.[24] The second code sequence is generated by appending the instruction sequence produced by the procedure compile-operands (which handles the operands) and the sequence

---

24 Note the contrast with the interpreter. The interpreter would save env unconditionally before evaluating the operator. The compiler uses preserving so that env will be saved only if this is actually necessary.

produced by `compile-call` (which generates the procedure application).
Since the operand evaluation might modify the `fun` register (which is needed
for the application), these sequences are appended preserving `fun`. The
object code will thus have the form shown in the top part of figure 5.13.
In the figure, the code in brackets will be generated only if necessary.

```
(define (compile-application app c-t-env target cont)
  (preserving
    'env
    (compile-expression (operator app) c-t-env 'fun 'next)
    (preserving 'fun
                (compile-operands (operands app) c-t-env)
                (compile-call target cont)))))
```

Compiling the evaluation of the operands is a bit tricky, because the first
operand and the last operand must be treated specially. The first operand is
evaluated before there is an argument list in `argl`. Thus, the code sequence
for the first argument must evaluate the operand and then construct the
initial `argl`. The rest of the operands, which are to be evaluated and
accumulated into the existing argument list, must be evaluated with `argl`
preserved. Each operand evaluation except the last must also preserve
`env` for use by subsequent operand evaluations. The general form of the
operand evaluation will be as shown in the bottom part of figure 5.13.

The `compile-operands` procedure takes as arguments the operands of
the combination and the compile-time environment, which is passed along
so as to be available in recursive calls to `compile-expression`. Compile-
operands begins by compiling the first operand. If that is the only operand,
then the resulting instruction sequence is returned. If not, we append the
instruction sequence to the result of compiling the rest of the operands,
using `preserving` to protect the `env` register for these operands.

```
(define (compile-operands rands c-t-env)
  (let ((first-operand-code
         (compile-first-operand rands c-t-env)))
    (if (last-operand? rands)
        first-operand-code
        (preserving
         'env
         first-operand-code
         (compile-rest-operands (rest-operands rands)
                                c-t-env)))))
```

[(save env)]
⟨evaluate operator, put result into fun⟩
[(restore env)]
[(save fun)]
⟨evaluate operands into argl—expansion shown below⟩
[(restore fun)]
⟨apply procedure in fun to arguments in argl⟩

[(save env)]
⟨evaluate first operand into val⟩
⟨put first argument (from val) into argl⟩
[(restore env)]

[(save env)]
[(save argl)]   This block of code
⟨evaluate next operand into val⟩   is repeated for each
[(restore argl)]   argument except the
⟨add next argument (from val) into argl⟩   first and the last.
[(restore env)]

[(save argl)]
⟨evaluate last operand into val⟩
[(restore argl)]
⟨add last argument (from val) into argl⟩

Figure 5.13
Compilation of a procedure application. The top of the figure shows the overall structure
of the code. The bottom shows details of the operand evaluation.

Compilation of the first operand is targeted to the val register with
the continuation next. The argl (the list of evaluated arguments) is then
initialized to the singleton of the result that appears in val as the value of
the first operand.

```
(define (compile-first-operand rands c-t-env)
  (append-instruction-sequences
   (compile-expression (first-operand rands)
                       c-t-env 'val 'next)
   (make-register-assignment
    'argl
    (make-singleton-arglist (make-fetch 'val)))))
```

The additional operands are compiled in succession with compile-next-
operand. In each case, env is preserved around the evaluation only if there
are additional operands.

```
(define (compile-rest-operands rands c-t-env)
  (let ((next-operand-code
          (compile-next-operand rands c-t-env)))
    (if (last-operand? rands)
        next-operand-code
        (preserving
         'env
         next-operand-code
         (compile-rest-operands (rest-operands rands)
                                c-t-env)))))
```

We compile each operand (other than the first), preserving the argl register, and accumulate the result into argl. The primitive code generator make-add-to-arglist generates the actual instruction that will perform the accumulation.

```
(define (compile-next-operand rands c-t-env)
  (preserving
   'argl
   (compile-expression (first-operand rands)
                       c-t-env 'val 'next)
   (make-register-assignment
    'argl
    (make-add-to-arglist (make-fetch 'val)
                         (make-fetch 'argl)))))
```

Combinations with no operands are treated specially, as they are in the interpreter. All that is required is to compile the operator with the result targeted to fun, initialize argl to the empty argument list, and call the procedure:

```
(define (compile-no-args app c-t-env target cont)
  (append-instruction-sequences
   (compile-expression (operator app) c-t-env 'fun 'next)
   (make-register-assignment 'argl (make-empty-arglist))
   (compile-call target cont)))
```

Applying a procedure

After evaluating the elements of a combination, the compiled code must call the evaluated operator, which is located in the fun register. The instruction sequence that handles the procedure call, generated by compile-call, depends on the target of the procedure value. All procedures in our system return their values in the val register. Thus, if we want the value of a procedure application to be in some other register, we must follow the procedure call with an instruction that assigns the contents of val to the designated target register after the procedure returns.

```
(define (compile-call target cont)
  (if (eq? target 'val)
      (compile-call-result-in-val cont)
      (append-instruction-sequences
       (compile-call-result-in-val 'next)
       (make-register-assignment target (make-fetch 'val))
       (compile-continuation cont))))
```

The basic procedure call (which returns the result in val) is compiled differently depending upon the kind of continuation. There are three cases:

• If the continuation descriptor is return, the value of the procedure in which this combination appears is the value of the procedure we are about to call. The compiler generates a call that will not return here (as indicated by calling compile-call-return-to with an argument of nil for the return address); instead, the call will return directly to the pending continuation. This results in a tail-recursive implementation.

• If the continuation is to a named entry point, the compiler generates a call that will return to that entry point.

• If the continuation descriptor is next, the procedure application should return to whatever instruction directly follows the call. The compiler constructs a label to indicate this entry point and generates a call that will return to this named entry point. It puts the label into the generated instruction sequence following the code for the call.

```
(define (compile-call-result-in-val cont)
  (cond ((eq? cont 'return)
         (compile-call-return-to nil))
        ((eq? cont 'next)
         (let ((after-call (make-new-label 'after-call)))
           (append-instruction-sequences
            (compile-call-return-to after-call)
            (make-entry-point-designator after-call))))
        (else
         (compile-call-return-to cont))))
```

The primitive code generator make-new-label constructs a new label whose name begins with the characters of a given symbol. The label is used as a continuation for the generation of the actual call. `Make-entry-point-designator` generates an "instruction" (suitable for inclusion in the compiled code) consisting of the label.

We will adopt the convention that a procedure returns to the continuation it finds on the stack. `Compile-return`, called by `compile-continuation` when code for a `return` continuation is to be compiled, generates code to restore the continuation from the stack and calls on the primitive code generator `make-return-from-procedure` to generate the actual return to that continuation:

```
(define (compile-return)
  (append-instruction-sequences
   (make-restore 'continue)
   (make-return-from-procedure)))
```

`Compile-call-return-to` generates the code to call a procedure such that it will return to the designated `return-entry`. If we want the called procedure to return to our own caller (`return-entry` is `nil`), then it should return to the continuation we were given, which is already on the stack. We thus transfer directly to the procedure. To accomplish a procedure call that returns to a designated entry point, we place the entry in the continue register and save continue on the stack before transferring to the procedure.

```
(define (compile-call-return-to return-entry)
  (if (null? return-entry)
      (make-transfer-to-procedure)
      (append-instruction-sequences
       (make-register-assignment 'continue return-entry)
       (make-save 'continue)
       (make-transfer-to-procedure))))
```

Conditional expressions
The object code for a conditional expression will have the form shown in figure 5.14 for the expression

```
(cond (⟨p₁⟩ ⟨e₁⟩)
      (⟨p₂⟩ ⟨e₂⟩)
      (else ⟨e₃⟩))
```

Code in brackets will be generated only if necessary. This illustrates the general way that conditionals are handled. (A conditional with no `else` clause is treated as if it ended with (`else nil`).)

```
[(save env)]
⟨evaluate ⟨p₁⟩ (predicate for first clause), result in val⟩
[(restore env)]
⟨branch to first consequent if val is true⟩

[(save env)]
⟨evaluate ⟨p₂⟩, result in val⟩
[(restore env)]
⟨branch to second consequent if val is true⟩

⟨evaluate ⟨e₃⟩ (consequent of the else clause) –
continues at the continuation of the cond
with result in the target of the cond⟩

⟨label for second consequent⟩
⟨evaluate ⟨e₂⟩ (consequent of second clause) –
continues at the continuation of the cond
with result in the target of the cond⟩

⟨label for first consequent⟩
⟨evaluate ⟨e₁⟩ –
continues at the continuation of the cond
with result in the target of the cond⟩
```

Figure 5.14
Compilation of a conditional expression.

Since the value of a conditional is the value of whichever consequent is executed, each consequent puts its result into the target register specified for the conditional and goes to the continuation specified for the conditional. If the continuation descriptor for the conditional is next, then compile-cond must generate a label to identify the next instruction after the conditional, use that label as the continuation when compiling the clauses, and place the label after the end of the code for the conditional. If the clauses were compiled with next, each consequent would fall through to the physically next instruction, which is the code for another consequent.

```
(define (compile-cond clauses c-t-env target cont)
  (if (eq? cont 'next)
      (let ((end-of-cond (make-new-label 'cond-end)))
        (append-instruction-sequences
          (compile-clauses clauses c-t-env target end-of-cond)
          (make-entry-point-designator end-of-cond)))
      (compile-clauses clauses c-t-env target cont)))
```

To compile a list of clauses, we first check whether the list is empty. If so, we have come to the end of the conditional without encountering an else clause, so we generate an instruction that returns nil. If not, we compile the first clause, considering the remaining clauses as the alternative to be evaluated if the first predicate is false.

```
(define (compile-clauses clauses c-t-env target cont)
  (if (no-clauses? clauses)
      (compile-constant nil c-t-env target cont)
      (compile-a-clause (first-clause clauses)
                        (rest-clauses clauses)
                        c-t-env target cont)))
```

For an else clause, all that is required is to compile the consequent. We view any other clause as an if whose consequent is the consequent of the clause and whose alternative is the conditional composed of the rest of the clauses. That is, we view

```
(cond ((⟨p₁⟩ ⟨e₁⟩)
       (⟨p₂⟩ ⟨e₂⟩)
       (else ⟨e₃⟩)))
```

as

```
(if ⟨p₁⟩
    ⟨e₁⟩
    (cond (⟨p₂⟩ ⟨e₂⟩)
          (else ⟨e₃⟩)))
```

We compile the predicate, consequent, and alternative of the clause and put them together with a newly generated label as follows:

```
[(save env)]
⟨evaluate predicate, result in val⟩
[(restore env)]
⟨branch to new label if val is true⟩
⟨code for alternative⟩
⟨new label⟩
⟨code for consequent⟩
```

We must preserve env around the evaluation of the predicate, since this will in general be needed for evaluating the consequent and the alternative.

```
(define (compile-a-clause clause rest c-t-env target cont)
  (let ((consequent (compile-sequence (actions clause)
                                      c-t-env target cont)))
    (if (else-clause? clause)
        consequent
        (let
          ((alternative (compile-clauses rest
                                         c-t-env target cont))
           (pred (compile-expression (predicate clause)
                                     c-t-env 'val 'next))
           (true-branch (make-new-label 'true-branch)))
          (let ((alternative-and-consequent
                 (parallel-instruction-sequences
                  alternative
                  (append-instruction-sequences
                   (make-entry-point-designator true-branch)
                   consequent))))
            (preserving
             'env
             pred
             (append-instruction-sequences
              (make-branch (make-test 'val) true-branch)
              alternative-and-consequent)))))))
```

When we combine the instruction sequences for the alternative and the consequent, we are constructing an instruction sequence that is not intended to be executed sequentially. Only one of the two branches will be traversed in any particular evaluation of the conditional. These sequences are therefore not appended with the usual append-instruction-sequences. (We will see in section 5.3.3 why a special combiner is needed.)

Sequences

The compilation of sequences (from the consequent of a conditional or from a lambda body) parallels their evaluation. Each expression of the sequence except the last is compiled, with env (needed for the rest of the sequence) preserved, with continuation next (to execute the rest of the sequence), and with target nil (because only the value of the last expression is retained).[25] The final expression is compiled with the target and the continuation specified for the sequence. The instruction sequences for the individual expressions are appended to form a single instruction sequence.

---

25 Throughout the compiler, we use a target of nil to mean that we don't care about the value being returned. The primitive code generator make-register-assignment (section 5.3.4) will avoid generating an assign instruction if the target is nil.

```
(define (compile-sequence seq c-t-env target cont)
  (if (last-exp? seq)
      (compile-expression (first-exp seq)
                          c-t-env target cont)
      (preserving
       'env
       (compile-expression (first-exp seq) c-t-env nil 'next)
       (compile-sequence (rest-exps seq) c-t-env target cont)
       )))
```

Here we see another optimization resulting from the use of a compiler. An interpreter, when evaluating a sequence, must continually check to see if it has reached the final expression. This must be done each time it proceeds to the next expression in the sequence and each time the sequence is encountered. The compiler needs to do this only once for each expression when compiling the sequence. The resulting object code "knows" when it has reached the final expression and thus need not perform explicit tests at run time.

Assignments and definitions

Assignments and definitions are handled much as they are in the interpreter. We compile instructions that will compute the value to be assigned to the variable and append the instruction that actually sets or defines the variable. In the appending the env register must be preserved, since the environment is needed when the variable is to be set.

A register is needed to hold the computed value so that it can be accessed by the operations that modify the environment. We use the val register to hold the computed value unless a target register was specified, in which case we use the target. (The target is usually nil because assignments and definitions are usually done for their effect, not their value. Scheme does not specify what the value of an assignment will be.)

```
(define (compile-assignment exp c-t-env target cont)
  (let ((hold-value (if (null? target) 'val target)))
    (preserving
     'env
     (compile-expression (assignment-value exp)
                         c-t-env hold-value 'next)
     (append-instruction-sequences
      (make-variable-assignment (assignment-variable exp)
                                c-t-env
                                (make-fetch hold-value))
      (compile-continuation cont)))))
```

One difference between definitions and assignments is that a definition is supposed to return the name of the defined variable as its value, so we include an instruction in the compiled code that assigns the variable name to the specified target.[26]

```
(define (compile-definition exp c-t-env target cont)
  (let ((hold-value (if (null? target) 'val target))
        (var (definition-variable exp)))
    (preserving
     'env
     (compile-expression (definition-value exp)
                         c-t-env hold-value 'next)
     (append-instruction-sequences
      (make-variable-definition var
                                c-t-env
                                (make-fetch hold-value))
      (make-register-assignment target (make-constant var))
      (compile-continuation cont)))))
```

Lambda expressions

The only special form we have not yet considered is lambda, the constructor for procedures. The object code for a lambda expression must have the form

⟨ *construct procedure object and assign it to target register* ⟩
⟨ *go to appropriate continuation* ⟩

When we compile the lambda expression, we also generate the code for the procedure body. Although the body won't be executed at the time of procedure construction, it is convenient to insert it into the object code near the code for the lambda expression as follows:

⟨ *construct procedure object and assign it to target register* ⟩
⟨ *go to appropriate continuation* ⟩
⟨ *procedure body* ⟩

---

26 Definitions also differ from assignments in that they create new bindings rather than change existing bindings. Recall that we are maintaining a compile-time environment, which is supposed to mirror the structure of the run-time environment that will be in effect when the compiled code is executed. Since running the compiled definition will add a binding to the run-time environment, we might consider also augmenting the compile-time environment at the time a definition is compiled, to reflect the modification to the run-time environment. While it is possible to follow such a strategy, there are complex issues that arise in trying to account at compile time for modifications to the environment that may happen at run time. See section 5.3.7, which discusses the compile-time environment and the issues raised by define.

If the continuation descriptor for the lambda compilation is a label or return, this is fine. But if the continuation is next, the above sequence will enter the procedure body after constructing the procedure object, because the continuation code (generated by compile-continuation) will be empty. The trouble is that the logically next instruction is no longer physically next; it is necessary to skip the procedure body in order to reach the instruction that is really next in the object program. If the original continuation is next, we thus generate a new label to use as the continuation instead of next, and we place the new label after the procedure body as follows:

⟨construct procedure object and assign it to target register⟩
⟨go to new label⟩
⟨procedure body⟩
⟨new label⟩

```
(define (compile-lambda exp c-t-env target cont)
  (if (eq? cont 'next)
      (let ((after-lambda (make-new-label 'after-lambda)))
        (append-instruction-sequences
         (compile-lambda-2 exp c-t-env target after-lambda)
         (make-entry-point-designator after-lambda)))
      (compile-lambda-2 exp c-t-env target cont)))
```

Compile-lambda-2 generates the code just described. It uses the primitive code generator make-procedure-constructor to generate the instruction that constructs the procedure object. The procedure object will be constructed at run time by combining the current environment (the environment at the point of definition) with the entry point to the compiled procedure body (a newly generated label).

```
(define (compile-lambda-2 exp c-t-env target cont)
  (let ((proc-entry (make-new-label 'entry)))
    (tack-on-instruction-sequence
     (append-instruction-sequences
      (make-register-assignment
       target
       (make-procedure-constructor proc-entry))
      (compile-continuation cont))
     (compile-lambda-body exp c-t-env proc-entry))))
```

Compile-lambda-2 uses tack-on-instruction-sequence (rather than append-instruction-sequences) to append the procedure body to the lambda expression code, because the body is not part of the sequence of instructions that will be executed when the combined sequence is entered; rather, it is in the sequence only because that was a convenient place to put it. We will see in section 5.3.3 why a special combiner is needed.

The compiled body of the procedure begins with a designator for the entry point. Next come instructions (created by the primitive code generator make-environment-switch) that will cause the run-time evaluation environment to switch to the correct environment for evaluating the procedure body—namely, the definition environment of the procedure, extended to include the bindings of the formal parameters to the arguments with which the procedure is called. After this comes the actual procedure body, which is a sequence of expressions.[27] The sequence is compiled with continuation descriptor return and target val so that it will end by returning from the procedure with the result of calling the procedure in val. The procedure body is compiled with a compile-time environment that is the extension of the original compile-time environment by the procedure's formal parameters, so that the compile-time environment for compilation of expressions in the body will mirror the run-time environment in which the corresponding code will be executed. (The compile-time environment will be discussed in section 5.3.7.)

```
(define (compile-lambda-body exp c-t-env proc-entry)
  (append-instruction-sequences
   (make-entry-point-designator proc-entry)
   (make-environment-switch (lambda-parameters exp)))
  (compile-sequence
   (lambda-body exp)
   (extend-compile-time-env (lambda-parameters exp) c-t-env)
   'val
   'return)))
```

5.3.3 Compiler Data Structures

We have said that our code generators produce and combine instruction sequences. Assuming that we have a representation for individual instructions (and labels), we could represent an instruction sequence as a list

---

[27] In order to extract the relevant pieces of the lambda expression, we need two new syntax procedures, in addition to the syntax procedures used in the interpreter (section 4.1.2):

```
(define (lambda-parameters exp) (cadr exp))
(define (lambda-body exp) (cddr exp))
```

of instructions. Append-instruction-sequences could then combine instruction sequences by performing an ordinary list append. However, the needs-register and modifies-register predicates used by preserving (section 5.3.1) would be very complex operations, because they would have to analyze an instruction sequence to determine how it uses a given register. Preserving would be inefficient as well as complex, because it would have to analyze an entire instruction sequence, even though the sequence might itself have been constructed by a call to preserving, in which case its parts would already have been analyzed. The key to avoiding this repetitious analysis is to associate with each instruction sequence information about its register use. The primitive code generators will provide this information explicitly, and the procedures that combine instruction sequences will derive register-use information for the combined sequence from the information associated with the component sequences.

An instruction sequence will thus contain three pieces of information:

• the actual instructions (also called *statements*) in the sequence,

• the set of registers whose values are modified by the instructions in the sequence, and

• the set of registers that must be initialized before the instructions in the sequence are executed (these registers are said to be *needed* by the sequence).

We will represent an instruction sequence as a list of its three parts. The constructor for instruction sequences is thus

```
(define (make-instruction-sequence needs modifies statements)
  (list needs modifies statements))
```

The corresponding selectors are

```
(define (registers-needed s) (car s))
```

```
(define (registers-modified s) (cadr s))
```

```
(define (statements s) (caddr s))
```

and the predicates used by preserving are

```
(define (needs-register seq reg)
  (element-of-set? reg (registers-needed seq)))
```

```
(define (modifies-register seq reg)
  (element-of-set? reg (registers-modified seq)))
```

We will also use a constructor `make-instruction` that forms an instruction sequence containing a single statement (instruction), and a constructor `empty-instruction-sequence` that produces a sequence with no statements. Sequences of statements are represented as lists.

```
(define (make-instruction needed modified statement)
  (make-instruction-sequence needed
                             modified
                             (list statement)))

(define (empty-instruction-sequence)
  (make-instruction-sequence empty-set empty-set '()))
```

Combining instruction sequences

`Append-instruction-sequences` takes as arguments an arbitrary number of instruction sequences that are to be executed sequentially and returns the instruction sequence whose statements are the statements of all the sequences appended together. The resulting sequence modifies those registers that are modified by any of the sequences; it needs those registers that must be initialized before the first sequence can be run, together with those registers needed by any of the other sequences that are not initialized by sequences preceding it. The sequences are appended two at a time by `append-2-sequences`, which takes two instruction sequences `seq1` and `seq2` and returns the instruction sequence whose statements are the statements of `seq1` followed by the statements of `seq2`. The set of modified registers for the resulting sequence consists of those registers that are modified by either sequence. The registers needed by the compound sequence are the registers needed by `seq1`, together with those registers needed by `seq2` that are not initialized by `seq1`. (That is, the new set of needed registers is the union of the set of registers needed by `seq1` with the set difference of the registers needed by `seq2` and the registers modified by `seq1`.) Thus, the basic means of combination for instruction sequences is implemented as follows:

```
(define (append-instruction-sequences . seqs)
  (define (append-2-sequences seq1 seq2)
    (make-instruction-sequence
     (union-set (registers-needed seq1)
                (difference-set (registers-needed seq2)
                                (registers-modified seq1)))
     (union-set (registers-modified seq1)
                (registers-modified seq2))
     (append (statements seq1) (statements seq2))))
  ;; continued on next page
```

```
(define (append-seq-list seqs)
  (if (null? seqs)
      (empty-instruction-sequence)
      (append-2-sequences (car seqs)
                          (append-seq-list (cdr seqs)))))
(append-seq-list seqs))
```

This uses dot notation (explained in section 4.3.2 for the make generic operator) to bind the parameter seqs to a list containing all the arguments.[28]

Compile-lambda used a special combiner called tack-on-instruction-sequence to append a procedure body to another sequence. Because the procedure body is not "in line" to be executed as part of the combined sequence, its register use has no impact on the register use of the sequence in which it is embedded. We thus ignore the procedure body's sets of needed and modified registers when we tack it onto the other sequence.

```
(define (tack-on-instruction-sequence seq body-seq)
  (append-instruction-sequences
   seq
   (make-instruction-sequence empty-set
                              empty-set
                              (statements body-seq))))
```

Compile-cond used a special combiner called parallel-instruction-sequences to append the consequent and the alternative of a cond clause. The two sequences will never be executed sequentially; for any particular evaluation of the conditional, one sequence or the other will be entered. Because of this, the registers needed by the second sequence are still needed by the combined sequence, even if these are modified by the first sequence.

```
(define (parallel-instruction-sequences seq1 seq2)
  (make-instruction-sequence
   (union-set (registers-needed seq1)
              (registers-needed seq2))
   (union-set (registers-modified seq1)
              (registers-modified seq2))
   (append (statements seq1) (statements seq2))))
```

----

28 If instead we were to write

```
(define (append-instruction-sequences seqs)
  ⟨same body as above⟩)
```

then callers of append-instruction-sequences would have to combine the arguments into a list.

Sets of registers
We will represent sets as unordered lists, as described in section 2.2.5, and
use the following set operations:

```
(define (union-set s1 s2)
  (cond ((null? s1) s2)
        ((memq (car s1) s2) (union-set (cdr s1) s2))
        (else (cons (car s1) (union-set (cdr s1) s2)))))

(define (difference-set s1 s2)
  (cond ((null? s1) '())
        ((memq (car s1) s2) (difference-set (cdr s1) s2))
        (else (cons (car s1) (difference-set (cdr s1) s2)))))

(define (element-of-set? x s) (memq x s))

(define (singleton x) (list x))

(define (make-set list-of-elements) list-of-elements)

(define empty-set '())
```

The procedure `singleton` constructs a set with a single element, and `make-
set` constructs a set from a given list of elements.[29]  `Difference-set`
returns the set of elements of s1 that are not in s2.

Value specifiers
The simplest things the compiler must generate are not complete instructions but rather fragments that appear as "values" specifying the source
of data for an instruction. These represent constants (generated by `make-
constant`), labels (generated by `make-label`), access to the contents of a
register (generated by `make-fetch`), or the use of a primitive operation of
the machine (generated by `make-operation`). We will call such fragments
value specifiers. We will include as part of a value specifier a set of needed
registers, which will be used in determining the registers needed by the
instruction for which the value specifier is a fragment. We do not include
a set of modified registers for a value specifier, since a value specifier does
not modify any registers. We will represent a value specifier as a list containing the specifier expression itself and the set of registers needed by

---

29 **Make-set** is the identity operation, since we are using the unordered-list representation
for sets. We include it here explicitly so as to maintain the abstraction barrier around
the set representation.

the expression. We have the following constructor and selectors for value specifiers:

```
(define (make-val-spec registers-needed expression)
  (list registers-needed expression))

(define (val-spec-registers-needed value)
  (car value))

(define (val-spec-expression value)
  (cadr value))
```

5.3.4 Primitive Code Generators

In this section we present the primitive code generators that construct the actual instructions that make up the compiled program. The primitive code generators form an abstraction barrier that isolates our compiler's analysis of expressions from the details of the machine for which we are compiling. By relying on these primitive generators, the compiler in effect compiles code for an abstract register machine. The implementation of the primitive code generators makes the abstract machine concrete. By changing these procedures we can compile code for different machines. For example, our machine performs register assignments with instructions of the form

(assign ⟨register⟩ ⟨value⟩)

If instead we needed to generate

(store ⟨value⟩ in ⟨register⟩)

or even

(access-value ⟨value⟩)
(store-accessed-value ⟨register⟩)

all we would have to change in the compiler is the primitive generator `make-register-assignment`.

First we will present the code generators that can be used for any register machine of the type we have been using. All knowledge of the form of our machine language is embodied in these procedures. Then we will present the code generators that are specific to the evaluator machine—that is, the code generators that make use of the primitive operations of the evaluator machine's data paths.

Generators for any register machine

The simplest kind of value specifier is a constant, which has no needed registers. Note the explicit quote that is included when the value-specifier expression is constructed.[30]

```
(define (make-constant c)
  (make-val-spec empty-set (list 'quote c)))
```

Labels are represented as symbols. The make-label procedure takes a symbol as argument and generates a value specifier that consists of that symbol (and no needed registers):

```
(define (make-label symbol)
  (make-val-spec empty-set symbol))
```

The compiler often needs to generate a new label. This is done by calling make-label with a new symbol as argument.

```
(define (make-new-label name)
  (make-label (make-new-symbol name)))
```

The procedure make-new-symbol takes a symbol as argument and returns a new symbol whose initial characters are the characters of the given symbol.[31] (For example, (make-label 'after-call) might return after-call147.)

Fetch expressions are also constructed as value specifiers. The set of needed registers is the one-element set containing the register to be accessed.

```
(define (make-fetch reg)
  (make-val-spec (singleton reg) (list 'fetch reg)))
```

The value specifier for use of a primitive operation of the machine, constructed by make-operation, needs all the registers needed by any

---

30 To understand why the quote is needed, consider constructing the instruction (assign val 'apple), which is actually the list (assign val (quote apple)). The instruction fragment (quote apple) is created by evaluating the expression (make-constant 'apple), which applies make-constant to the symbol apple. If the body of make-constant were simply (make-val-spec empty-set c), then the generated instruction would be (assign val apple), which is not what we want.

31 Lisp dialects standardly supply this facility, either as a primitive or as a procedure written in terms of character-manipulation primitives. When we say that the procedure generates a "new" symbol, we mean that the resulting symbol is guaranteed to not be eq? to any existing symbol. In the MIT implementation of Scheme, make-new-symbol is equivalent to a primitive procedure called generate-uninterned-symbol:

(define make-new-symbol generate-uninterned-symbol)

The designation "uninterned" refers to the *intern* operation, by means of which character strings input to Lisp are transformed into (pointers to) symbols. See section 5.4.1.

of the inputs to the operation. Make-operation is used by the machine-specific code generators below, not by the abstract parts of the compiler we have seen already. Make-operation takes an operation name and value specifiers for an arbitrary number of inputs (since different operations have different numbers of inputs).

```
(define (make-operation operation . inputs)
  (make-val-spec  '
    (union-all-sets (mapcar val-spec-registers-needed inputs))
    (cons operation (mapcar val-spec-expression inputs)))))
```

Like append-instruction-sequences (section 5.3.3), this uses dot nota-tion—in this case to bind the parameter inputs to a list containing all but the first argument. We also use mapcar (see exercise 2.20) to apply a selector to each element of a list and return a list of the results, and the following procedure to find the union of all the sets in a list:

```
(define (union-all-sets sets)
  (if (null? sets)
      empty-set
      (union-set (car sets) (union-all-sets (cdr sets)))))
```

Using value specifiers as fragments, we can now represent the basic in-structions to be generated by the compiler. A register-assignment instruc-tion assigns to a register the value indicated by a value specifier. The result-ing instruction needs the registers that are needed by the value specifier and modifies the register that is the target of the assign operation. The compiler uses the convention that if the target register is nil, there is no need to do the assignment. (We saw in section 5.3.2 that all expressions in a sequence except the last are compiled with target nil since their values are not used.)

```
(define (make-register-assignment reg val-spec)
  (if (null? reg)
      (empty-instruction-sequence)
      (make-instruction
       (val-spec-registers-needed val-spec)
       (singleton reg)
       (list 'assign reg (val-spec-expression val-spec)))))
```

Goto instructions are generated for two reasons. Make-transfer-to-procedure and make-return-from-procedure use make-nonlocal-goto to generate a transfer of control from the code sequence of one procedure to the code sequence of another. In our simple compiler we have no way of knowing what registers are modified by a procedure, so we assume that a procedure modifies all the machine registers. That is, if execution gets to this goto, any machine register can be modified. We do know what registers are needed by the code to which we are transferring; a list of these registers is supplied in the cont-needs argument.

```
(define (make-nonlocal-goto continuation cont-needs)
  (make-goto continuation (make-set cont-needs) all))
```

```
(define all (make-set '(fun env val argl continue)))
```

All is the set of all the registers used at run time.

The only other gotos are generated by compile-continue, via calls to make-jump, when it is given a label as the continuation. This arises when the code for an expression needs to go to the next expression, but some other code from the current expression (for example, a procedure body or some other part of a conditional) is in the way. The code to which the goto transfers will be appended to the sequence containing the goto, so the goto does not need or modify any registers that are not known about for other reasons.

```
(define (make-jump continuation)
  (make-goto continuation empty-set empty-set))
```

A goto instruction transfers to a continuation given by some value specifier (a specifier for a label or a register access). The instruction modifies whatever registers it is told will be modified at that entry; it needs any registers needed by the continuation value specifier (if the continuation is fetched from a register, that register is needed) as well as whatever registers it is told will be needed at the destination entry.

```
(define (make-goto cont cont-needs cont-modifies)
  (make-instruction
    (union-set (val-spec-registers-needed cont) cont-needs)
    cont-modifies
    (list 'goto (val-spec-expression cont))))
```

A branch instruction is built out of value specifiers that specify the predicate and the continuation to be used if the predicate is true. The branch instruction needs all the registers needed by either of the two value specifiers, and modifies no registers.

```
(define (make-branch predicate true-branch)
  (make-instruction
   (union-set (val-spec-registers-needed predicate)
              (val-spec-registers-needed true-branch))
   empty-set
   (list 'branch
         (val-spec-expression predicate)
         (val-spec-expression true-branch)))))
```

Save needs the register whose contents it saves on the stack, and restore modifies the register whose contents it restores from the stack.

```
(define (make-save reg)
  (make-instruction (singleton reg)
                    empty-set
                    (list 'save reg)))
```

```
(define (make-restore reg)
  (make-instruction empty-set
                    (singleton reg)
                    (list 'restore reg)))
```

The instruction to perform a primitive action of the machine is constructed from a value specifier (constructed by make-operation) for the operation to be performed. An action cannot modify registers.

```
(define (make-perform action)
  (make-instruction
   (val-spec-registers-needed action)
   empty-set
   (list 'perform (val-spec-expression action))))
```

In our register-machine language, an entry point into a sequence of instructions is indicated by a label at the appropriate point in the instruction sequence. The compiler generates an entry-point designator as an "instruction" whose "statement" is the label expression provided by make-label:

```
(define (make-entry-point-designator label-val-spec)
  (make-instruction empty-set
                    empty-set
                    (val-spec-expression label-val-spec)))
```

Preserving (section 5.3.1) uses the following procedure to preserve the contents of a register across execution of a sequence that modifies the register:

```
(define (wrap-save-restore seq reg)
  (make-instruction-sequence
   (registers-needed seq)
   (difference-set (registers-modified seq) (singleton reg))
   (append (statements (make-save reg))
           (statements seq)
           (statements (make-restore reg)))))
```

In forming the new instruction sequence, wrap-save-restore takes account of the fact that wrapping seq within save and restore instructions removes reg from the set of modified registers.

Generators for the evaluator machine

The compiler must also generate code that uses the operations of the specific machine. For instance, the compiled code uses the primitive function lookup-variable-value of the evaluator machine in such instructions as

```
(assign val (lookup-variable-value 'x (fetch env)))
```

The following procedure (used by compile-variable-access) takes a variable name as argument and generates a value specifier for a lookup-variable-value operation:[32]

```
(define (make-variable-access var c-t-env)
  (make-operation 'lookup-variable-value
                  (make-constant var)
                  (make-fetch 'env)))
```

The following procedure (used in the compilation of conditionals) generates a value specifier for a true? test of the value in the given register:

```
(define (make-test reg)
  (make-operation 'true? (make-fetch reg)))
```

Variable assignments and definitions use the primitive set-variable-value! and define-variable! actions of the evaluator machine. The following code generators take as arguments a variable name and a value specifier for the variable's new value:

---

32 In compiling variable accesses, assignments, and definitions, we have passed the compile-time environment to the primitive code generators; however, we do not use this environment. In section 5.3.7 we discuss how to modify these code generators to make the compiler take advantage of the compile-time environment.

```
(define (make-variable-assignment var c-t-env value)
  (make-perform
   (make-operation 'set-variable-value!
                   (make-constant var)
                   value
                   (make-fetch 'env))))
```

```
(define (make-variable-definition var c-t-env value)
  (make-perform
   (make-operation 'define-variable!
                   (make-constant var)
                   value
                   (make-fetch 'env))))
```

Lambda expressions compile into code that constructs procedures. A procedure object is constructed from compiled code by a new primitive function make-compiled-procedure that we must add to the evaluator machine. Make-compiled-procedure takes as inputs the current environment (in env) and the entry point for the body of the compiled procedure. We will provide a procedure to simulate this machine function in section 5.3.6. The code generator make-procedure-constructor takes a value specifier for the entry point of the compiled procedure body, as produced by compile-lambda (section 5.3.2), and generates a value specifier for the make-compiled-procedure operation:

```
(define (make-procedure-constructor entry)
  (make-operation 'make-compiled-procedure
                  entry
                  (make-fetch 'env)))
```

When a compiled procedure is entered, it is necessary to assign to the env register the environment in which the procedure body should be executed. This is accomplished by first assigning to env the environment that is packaged with the procedure (which at run time will be held in the fun register) and then extending this environment by a frame that binds the formal parameters to the actual arguments. The code that performs this environment switch is constructed by a code generator (called by compile-lambda-body, section 5.3.2) that takes as its argument a list of the formal parameters of the procedure to be applied. We add to our machine a primitive operation compiled-procedure-env, which extracts the environment part of a procedure object constructed by make-compiled-procedure. (A procedure to simulate this primitive is given in section 5.3.6.) The environment is extended by the evaluator machine primitive `extend-binding-environment` (defined in section 5.2.1), which takes as inputs the list of parameters, the list of arguments to which these should be bound, and the environment to be extended.

```
(define (make-environment-switch formals)
  (append-instruction-sequences
   (make-register-assignment
    'env
    (make-operation 'compiled-procedure-env
                    (make-fetch 'fun)))
   (make-register-assignment
    'env
    (make-operation 'extend-binding-environment
                    (make-constant formals)
                    (make-fetch 'argl)
                    (make-fetch 'env)))))
```

When a procedure is to be applied at run time, we need to construct the list of arguments and assign it to `argl`. The compiled code, like the evaluator, constructs the list using cons, starting from the empty list.

```
(define (make-singleton-arglist first-arg-spec)
  (make-operation 'cons first-arg-spec (make-constant '())))
```

```
(define (make-add-to-arglist next-arg-spec rest-args-spec)
  (make-operation 'cons next-arg-spec rest-args-spec))
```

When a procedure application has no arguments, `argl` is assigned the empty list.

```
(define (make-empty-arglist)
  (make-constant '()))
```

Our compiled code will run in the evaluator machine. It will apply procedures by transferring to the `apply-dispatch` entry of the evaluator (which will be augmented in section 5.3.6 to handle compiled procedures). This enables compiled code to call primitive procedures and interpreted procedures as well as other compiled procedures. The instructions at `apply-dispatch` need fun in order to know what procedure to call. Argl is also needed, as it contains the arguments to be bound to the procedure's parameters.

```
(define (make-transfer-to-procedure)
  (make-nonlocal-goto (make-label 'apply-dispatch)
                      '(fun argl)))
```

A compiled procedure will return by transferring to the entry point stored in the `continue` register. The instructions at that entry expect to find the procedure's result in `val`, so that register is needed for proper execution of this transfer.

```
(define (make-return-from-procedure)
  (make-nonlocal-goto (make-fetch 'continue)
                      '(val)))
```

5.3.5 An Example of Compiled Code

Now that we have seen all the elements of the compiler, let us examine an example of compiled code to see how all the elements fit together. We will compile a recursive `factorial` procedure by calling `compile-expression`:

```
(compile-expression
 '(define (factorial n)
    (cond ((= n 1) 1)
          (else (* (factorial (- n 1)) n))))
 initial-c-t-env
 'val
 'next)
```

The call to `compile-expression` specifies an initial compile-time environment, which we can take to be the empty list for now.[33] We have specified that the value of the `define` expression should be placed in the `val` register. We don't care what the compiled code does after executing the `define`, so our choice of `next` as the continuation descriptor is arbitrary.

`Compile-expression` discovers that the expression is a definition, so it compiles code to compute the value to be assigned (targeted to `val`), then code to install the definition, then code to put the value of the `define` into the target register, and finally the continuation code. The compilation of the value is done preserving `env`, which we will need in order to install the definition. Because the continuation descriptor is `next`, there is no continuation code in this case. The skeleton of the compiled code is thus

⟨*compilation of value, target* `val`, *preserving* `env`⟩
```
(perform
 (define-variable! 'factorial (fetch val) (fetch env)))
(assign val 'factorial)
```

---

33 In order to actually run the compiler, we must define `extend-compile-time-env`. This definition is provided in section 5.3.7. For now, since we are not making any use of the compile-time environment, we can define this as a dummy procedure that simply returns the empty list.

The expression that is to be compiled to produce the value for the variable factorial is a lambda expression whose value is the procedure that computes factorials. Compile-expression dispatches to compile-lambda, which compiles the procedure body, labels it as a new entry point, and generates the instruction that will combine the procedure body with the run-time environment and assign the result to val. The sequence then skips around the compiled procedure code, which is inserted at this point. The procedure code itself begins by extending the procedure's definition environment by a frame that binds the procedure argument to the formal parameter n. Then comes the actual procedure body. The skeleton for the compiled code is now

```
(assign val (make-compiled-procedure entry76 (fetch env)))
(goto after-lambda77)
entry76
(assign env (compiled-procedure-env (fetch fun)))
(assign env (extend-binding-environment '(n)
                                        (fetch argl)
                                        (fetch env)))
```
⟨compilation of procedure body⟩
```
after-lambda77
(perform
 (define-variable! 'factorial (fetch val) (fetch env)))
(assign val 'factorial)
```

A procedure body is always compiled (by compile-lambda-body) as a sequence with target val and continuation return. The sequence in this case consists of a single conditional expression:

```
(cond ((= n 1) 1)
      (else (* (factorial (- n 1)) n)))
```

The compiler generates code that first computes the predicate for the first clause (targeted to val), then checks the result and branches around the alternative if the predicate is true:

⟨compilation of predicate for first clause, target val⟩
```
(branch (true? (fetch val)) true-branch78)
```
⟨compilation of else clause⟩
```
true-branch78
```
⟨compilation of consequent for first clause⟩

Because the conditional is the last expression in the sequence making up the procedure body, its target is `val` and its continuation is `return`, so both the `else` clause and the consequent will be compiled with target `val` and continuation descriptor `return`. (That is, the value of the conditional, which is the value computed by any one of its clauses, is the value of the procedure.) The consequent of the first clause, which is the constant 1, thus compiles to

```
(assign val '1)
(restore continue)
(goto (fetch continue))
```

The code for the `else` clause is the code for its consequent, which is a procedure call. The predicate of the first clause is also a procedure call. These compile to code that will set up `fun` and `argl` and then transfer to `apply-dispatch`. Figure 5.15 shows the full compilation of the `factorial` definition.

Exercise 5.30

Consider the following definition of a factorial procedure, which is slightly different from the one given above:

```
(define (factorial-alt n)
  (cond ((= n 1) 1)
        (else (* n (factorial-alt (- n 1))))))
```

Compile this procedure and compare the resulting code with that produced for `factorial`. Explain any differences you find. Does either program execute more efficiently than the other?

Exercise 5.31

Compile the iterative factorial procedure

```
(define (factorial-iter n)
  (define (iter product counter)
    (cond ((> counter n) product)
          (else (iter (* counter product) (+ counter 1)))))
  (iter 1 1))
```

Annotate the resulting code, showing the essential difference between `factorial-iter` and `factorial` or `factorial-alt` that makes `factorial-iter` generate iterative processes while the other two procedures generate recursive processes.[34]

---

34 When we extend the compiler to incorporate lexical addressing in section 5.3.7, we will require that internal definitions such as `iter` be eliminated by scanning them out, as explained in section 5.2.5. For now, since we are not using the compile-time environment, the compiler will perform adequately by treating the internal definition of `iter` as an ordinary definition, using `compile-definition`.

```
;;construct the procedure and skip over the code for the procedure body
(assign val (make-compiled-procedure entry76 (fetch env)))
(goto after-lambda77)
entry76                         ;calls to factorial will enter here
(assign env (compiled-procedure-env (fetch fun)))
(assign env (extend-binding-environment '(n)
                                        (fetch argl)
                                        (fetch env)))
;;begin actual procedure body—compilation of (= n 1)
(save env)
(assign fun (lookup-variable-value '= (fetch env)))
(assign val (lookup-variable-value 'n (fetch env)))
(assign argl (cons (fetch val) '()))
(assign val '1)
(assign argl (cons (fetch val) (fetch argl)))
(assign continue after-call79)
(save continue)                ;set up return from apply-dispatch
(goto apply-dispatch)          ;to apply =
after-call79
(restore env)                  ; val now contains (= n 1)
(branch (true? (fetch val)) true-branch78)
;;compilation of (* (factorial (- n 1)) n)
(assign fun (lookup-variable-value '* (fetch env)))
(save fun)
(save env)
(assign fun (lookup-variable-value 'factorial (fetch env)))
(save fun)
(assign fun (lookup-variable-value '- (fetch env)))
;; continued on next page
```

Figure 5.15
Compilation of the factorial procedure (continued on next page).

Exercise 5.32

Our compiler will sometimes produce extra goto instructions—for example, to branch to a label that immediately follows the goto.

a. Find an example of a program that compiles into code with such a useless goto.

b. Fix the compiler so that the useless goto you found is not generated. Explain why your change will not cause the compiler to produce incorrect code for other programs, and test your change on several examples.

c. Compilers often produce code that is locally suboptimal, as in the case above. There are often very simple sequences of a few instructions that can profitably be transformed into more efficient sequences. This kind of transformation is usually done by a *peephole optimizer* that is passed over the compiler's output repeatedly until it can find no changes worth making in the object code. Write a peephole optimizer for our compiler that removes the useless goto described

```
(assign val (lookup-variable-value 'n (fetch env)))
(assign argl (cons (fetch val) '()))
(assign val '1)
(assign argl (cons (fetch val) (fetch argl)))
(assign continue after-call181)
(save continue)
(goto apply-dispatch)      ;to apply -
after-call181
(assign argl (cons (fetch val) '()))
(restore fun)
(assign continue after-call180)
(save continue)
(goto apply-dispatch)      ;to apply factorial recursively
after-call180
(assign argl (cons (fetch val) '()))
(restore env)
(assign val (lookup-variable-value 'n (fetch env)))
(assign argl (cons (fetch val) (fetch argl)))
(restore fun)
(goto apply-dispatch)      ;to apply *. Return will be to caller of factorial
;;consequent of first cond clause
true-branch78
(assign val '1)
(restore continue)
(goto (fetch continue))
;;assignment of the procedure to the variable factorial
after-lambda77
(perform (define-variable! 'factorial (fetch val) (fetch env)))
(assign val 'factorial)
```

Figure 5.15 (continued)

above and makes any other improvements in the object code that you think are appropriate. Is there a good way to perform these general-purpose optimizations while the object code is being constructed instead of examining the complete object code produced for an expression?

Exercise 5.33

Our compiler is very clever about avoiding unnecessary stack operations, but it is not clever at all when it comes to compiling the primitive procedures of the language in terms of the primitive operations supplied by the machine. For example, consider how much code is compiled to compute (+ a 1): The code sets up an argument list in argl, puts the primitive addition procedure (which it finds by looking up the symbol + in the environment) into fun, preserves all the registers (since a procedure potentially modifies all registers), and transfers to apply-dispatch, which dispatches to the controller instructions that implement addition. We have not shown the part of the controller that implements primitives, but we presume that these instructions make use of primitive arithmetic operations in the machine's data paths. Consider how much less code would be generated if the compiler could *open-code* primitives—that is, if it could generate code to directly use these primitive machine operations. The expression (+ a 1) might be compiled into as few as two instructions (if the machine has an instruction to assign to val the result of adding a constant to the contents of val):[35]

```
(assign val (lookup-variable-value 'a (fetch env)))
(assign val (+ (fetch val) '1))
```

In this exercise we will extend our compiler to support open coding of selected primitive operators. Special-purpose code will be generated for calls to these primitive operators instead of the general procedure-application code. In order to support this, we will augment our machine with special argument registers arg1 and arg2. The primitive arithmetic operations of the machine will take their inputs from arg1 and arg2. The results may be put into val, arg1, or arg2.

The compiler must be able to recognize the application of an open-coded primitive in the source program. We will augment the dispatch in compile-expression to recognize the names of these primitives in addition to the reserved words (the special forms) it currently recognizes.[36] For each special form our compiler has a code generator. In this exercise we will construct a family of code generators for the open-coded primitives.

a. The open-coded primitives, unlike the special forms, all need their operands evaluated. Write a code generator (spread-arguments ⟨*operand list*⟩ ⟨*c-t-env*⟩) that all the open-coding code generators can call to compile the given operand list with the operands targeted to successive argument registers. Note that an operand may contain a call to an open-coded primitive operator, so argument registers will have to be preserved during operand evaluation.

b. For each of the primitive operators =, *, -, and +, write a code generator that takes the expression, the compile-time environment, the target, and the continuation, spreads the arguments into the registers, and then produces the code to perform the operation targeted to the given target with the given continuation. You need only handle operators with two operands. Make compile-expression dispatch to these code generators.

c. Try your new compiler on the factorial example. Compare the resulting code with that produced without open coding.

---

35 We have used the same symbol + here to denote both the source-language operator and the machine operation. In general there will not be a one-to-one correspondence between primitives of the source language and primitives of the machine.

36 Making the primitives into reserved words is in general a bad idea, since a user cannot then rebind these names to different procedures. Moreover, if we add reserved words to a compiler that is in use, existing programs that define procedures with these names will stop working. See exercise 5.40 for ideas on how to avoid this problem.

d. Extend your code generators for + and * so that they can handle expressions with arbitrary numbers of operands. An expression with more than two operands will have to be expanded into a sequence of operations, each with only two operands.

5.3.6 Interfacing Compiled Code to the Evaluator

The code generated by our compiler relies on the evaluator's mechanism for applying procedures. The code generated to call a procedure simply executes a branch to apply-dispatch. In order to make compiled code run in our evaluator machine, we must therefore modify apply-dispatch (section 5.2.1) so that it can handle compiled procedures. To apply a compiled procedure, the machine should simply transfer control directly to the entry point of the compiled code:

```
apply-dispatch
  (branch (primitive-procedure? (fetch fun)) primitive-apply)
  (branch (compound-procedure? (fetch fun)) compound-apply)
  (branch (compiled-procedure? (fetch fun)) compiled-apply)
  (goto unknown-procedure-type-error)

compiled-apply
  (assign val (compiled-procedure-entry (fetch fun)))
  (goto (fetch val))
```

These instructions use a new operation compiled-procedure? to recognize a compiled procedure object, and a new operation compiled-procedure-entry to get the entry point of a compiled procedure. Two other operations on compiled procedure objects were introduced in section 5.3.4: The code generated by make-procedure-constructor to implement lambda expressions used make-compiled-procedure to construct a compiled procedure object, and the code generated by make-environment-switch to bind a procedure's parameters used compiled-procedure-env to get the environment of a compiled procedure. These four operations can be implemented as follows:

```
(define (make-compiled-procedure entry env)
  (list 'compiled-procedure entry env))

(define (compiled-procedure? proc)
  (if (atom? proc)
      nil
      (eq? (car proc) 'compiled-procedure)))
```

```
(define (compiled-procedure-entry proc)
  (cadr proc))

(define (compiled-procedure-env proc)
  (caddr proc))
```

Because all procedure applications (whether invoked from interpreted procedures or from compiled procedures) are handled by `apply-dispatch`, which knows how to apply any kind of procedure, compiled and interpreted procedures can call each other. Our machine should be able to execute a program containing compiled procedures (by directly executing them) and procedures that have not been compiled (by interpreting them).

Using the compiler

We have not yet explained how to load compiled code into the evaluator machine or how to run it. We will assume that the `explicit-control-evaluator` machine has been defined as in section 5.2.4. We will implement a procedure `compile-and-go` that compiles a Lisp expression, loads it into the `explicit-control-evaluator` machine, runs the resulting compiled code in the evaluator global environment, and causes the machine to print the result and enter the evaluator's driver loop. We can then put a compiled procedure into the machine and use the evaluator to call it:

```
==> (compile-and-go
      '(define (factorial n)
         (cond ((= n 1) 1)
               (else (* (factorial (- n 1)) n)))))
factorial

EC-EVAL==> (factorial 5)
120
```

We can accomplish this as follows. Our compiler generates its object code as a list of expressions that represent machine instructions. In order to transform this list of expressions into executable instructions for the evaluator register machine, we use the procedure `build-instruction-list` from the register-machine simulator program (section 5.1.5). We then place the list of instructions in the `val` register and start the evaluator at a special entry point `external-entry` (instead of its normal `read-eval-print-loop` entry). This dispatches to the instructions in `val` after saving on the stack a continuation that will cause execution to resume at the `print-result` entry in the evaluator (section 5.2.4) when the compiled code returns.

```
(define (compile-and-go expression)
  (remote-assign
   explicit-control-evaluator
   'val
   (build-instruction-list explicit-control-evaluator
                           (compile expression)))
  (eval '(goto external-entry)
        explicit-control-evaluator))
```

In order to accommodate this, the following code should be added to the explicit-control evaluator:

```
external-entry
    (perform (initialize-stack))
    (assign env the-global-environment)
    (assign continue print-result)
    (save continue)
    (goto (fetch val))
```

Print-result is at the end of the evaluator's driver loop. It prints the value in val, then goes to the beginning of the loop.[37]

To compile an expression, we extract the statements from the instruction sequence produced by calling compile-expression (section 5.3.1). Because we want the compiled code to return to the saved continuation, with its result in val, we specify a target of val and a return continuation descriptor. We must also provide an initial compile-time environment.[38]

```
(define (compile expression)
  (statements (compile-expression expression
                                  initial-c-t-env
                                  'val
                                  'return)))
```

---

[37] Since a compiled procedure is an object that the system may try to print, we also modify the system print operation user-print (from section 4.1.4) so that it will not attempt to print the components of a compiled procedure:

```
(define (user-print object)
  (cond ((compound-procedure? object)
         (print (list 'compound-procedure
                      (parameters object)
                      (procedure-body object)
                      '[procedure-env])))
        ((compiled-procedure? object)      ;new clause
         (print '[compiled-procedure]))
        (else (print object))))
```

[38] For now, we are not using the compile-time environment, so we can specify an arbitrary value (such as the empty list) for initial-c-t-env.

If we have set up the simulator to use a metered stack, we can monitor the number of stack operations used to evaluate expressions:

```
==> (compile-and-go
       '(define (factorial n)
          (cond ((= n 1) 1)
                (else (* (factorial (- n 1)) n)))))
factorial
(total-pushes: 1 maximum-depth: 1)


EC-EVAL==> (factorial 5)
120
(total-pushes: 35 maximum-depth: 15)
```

Compare this example with the evaluation of (factorial 5) using the interpreted version of the same procedure, shown at the end of section 5.2.4. The interpreted version required 144 pushes and a maximum stack depth of 28. This illustrates the optimization that results from our compilation strategy, which attempts to eliminate unnecessary stack operations.

Exercise 5.34

Exercise 5.21 asked you to determine, as a function of n, the number of pushes and the maximum stack depth needed to compute $n!$ using the recursive factorial procedure given above. Now perform the same analysis using the compiled factorial procedure. The ratios of the results obtained with the compiled and interpreted versions indicate the extent to which the compiler optimizes use of the stack, both in speed (reducing the total number of stack operations) and in space (reducing the maximum stack depth). Since the number of operations used to compute $n!$ is linear in n, each of these ratios will approach a constant as n becomes large. What are these constants? In addition, determine the number of stack operations required to compute $n!$ using the special-purpose factorial machine defined in section 5.1.4, if you have not already done so (see exercise 5.13). Summarize these results by filling in the following chart with ratios to the performance of the interpreted factorial:

	Speed-up	Space-saving
Compiled code		
Special-purpose machine		

You should find that the special-purpose machine does much better than the compiled version, since the "hand-tailored" controller code should be much better than what is produced by our rudimentary general-purpose compiler. Can you suggest improvements to the compiler that would help it generate code that would come closer in performance to the hand-tailored version?

Exercise 5.35

Carry out an analysis like the one in exercise 5.34 to determine the efficiency gained by compilation in computing Fib(n) via the tree-recursive fib procedure of exercise 5.22. Also compare this efficiency gain with that of the special-purpose fib machine of section 5.1.4. For fib, the time resource used is not linear in n; hence the ratio of compiled to interpreted stack operations will not approach a limiting value that is independent of n.

Exercise 5.36

The compile-and-go interface implemented above is somewhat awkward, since the compiler can only be called once (when the evaluator machine is started). Redesign the compiler-interpreter interface to provide a compile-and-run operation that can be called from within the explicit-control evaluator as follows:

```
EC-EVAL==> (compile-and-run
            '(define (factorial n)
               (cond ((= n 1) 1)
                     (else (* (factorial (- n 1)) n)))))
factorial

EC-EVAL==> (factorial 5)
120
```

5.3.7 Lexical Addressing

One of the most common optimizations performed by compilers is the optimization of variable lookup. Our compiler, as we have implemented it so far, generates code that uses the lookup-variable-value operation of the evaluator machine. This searches for a variable by comparing it with each variable that is currently bound, working frame by frame outward through the run-time environment. This search can be expensive if the frames are deeply nested or if there are many variables. For example, consider the problem of looking up the value of x while evaluating the expression (* x y z) in an application of the procedure that is returned by

```
(let ((x 3) (y 4))
  (lambda (a b c d e)
    (let ((y (* a b x))
          (z (+ c d x)))
      (* x y z))))
```

Since a let expression is just syntactic sugar for a lambda combination, this expression is equivalent to

```
((lambda (x y)
   (lambda (a b c d e)
     ((lambda (y z) (* x y z))
      (* a b x)
      (+ c d x)))))
 3
 4)
```

Each time lookup-variable-value searches for x, it must determine that the symbol x is not eq? to y or z (in the first frame), nor to a, b, c, d, or e (in the second frame). We will assume, for the moment, that our programs have no define expressions—that variables are bound only with lambda. Because our language is lexically scoped, the run-time environment for any expression will have a structure that parallels the lexical structure of the program in which the expression appears.[39] Thus, the compiler can know, when it analyzes the above expression, that each time the procedure is applied the variable x in (* x y z) will be found two frames out from the current frame and will be the first variable in that frame.

We can exploit this fact by inventing a new kind of variable-lookup operation, lexical-address-lookup, that takes as arguments an environment and a *lexical address* that consists of two numbers: a *frame number*, which specifies how many frames to pass over, and a *displacement number*, which specifies how many variables to pass over in that frame. Lexical-address-lookup will produce the value of the variable stored at /that lexical address relative to the current environment. If we add the lexical-address-lookup operation to our machine, we can make the compiler generate code that uses lexical-address-lookup instead of the lookup-variable-value operation used by the interpreter. Similarly, our compiled code can use a new lexical-address-set! operation instead of set-variable-value!.

In order to generate such code, the compiler must be able to determine the lexical address of a variable it is about to compile a reference to. The lexical address of a variable in a program depends on where one is in the code. For example, in the following program, the address of x in expression

---

39 This is not true if we allow incremental internal definitions, interactive definition and redefinition, and relative evaluation of definitions. We are thus outlawing define for the time being. We will treat define separately below.

$\langle e1 \rangle$ is (2,0)—two frames back and the first variable in the frame. At that point y is at address (0,0) and c is at address (1,2). In expression $\langle e2 \rangle$, x is at (1,0), y is at (1,1), and c is at (0,2).

```
((lambda (x y)
   (lambda (a b c d e)
     ((lambda (y z) ⟨e1⟩)
      ⟨e2⟩
      (+ c d e)))))
 3
 4)
```

Now we see what the compile-time environment is for: It is the compiler's mechanism for keeping track of which variables will be at which positions in which frames in the run-time environment when a particular variable-access operation is executed. The compile-time environment is a list of frames, each containing a list of variables. (There will of course be no values bound to the variables, since values are not computed at compile time.) When a lambda body is compiled (by compile-lambda-body), the compile-time environment is extended by a frame containing the parameters of the procedure.

```
(define (extend-compile-time-env params c-t-env)
  (cons params c-t-env))
```

Exercises 5.37 through 5.39 describe how to complete this sketch of the lexical-addressing strategy in order to incorporate lexical lookup into the compiler for programs that do not use define. Exercise 5.40 describes another use for the compile-time environment.

Exercise 5.37

Write a procedure lexical-address-lookup to simulate the new lookup operation. It should take two arguments—a run-time environment and a lexical address—and return the value of the variable stored at the specified lexical address. Lexical-address-lookup should signal an error if the value of the variable is the *unassigned* object.[40] Also write a procedure lexical-address-set! to simulate the operation that changes the value of a variable at a specified lexical address.

---

40 This is the modification to variable lookup required if we implement the scanning method to eliminate internal definitions. (Compare exercise 5.24.) As we will see below, we will need to eliminate these definitions in order for lexical addressing to work.

Exercise 5.38

Write a procedure find-variable that takes as arguments a variable and a compile-time environment and returns the lexical address of the variable with respect to that environment. For example, in the program fragment that is shown above, the compile-time environment during the compilation of expression ⟨e1⟩ is ((y z) (a b c d e) (x y)). Find-variable should produce

```
==> (find-variable 'c '((y z) (a b c d e) (x y)))
(1 2)

==> (find-variable 'x '((y z) (a b c d e) (x y)))
(2 0)

==> (find-variable 'w '((y z) (a b c d e) (x y)))
nil
```

Exercise 5.39

Using find-variable from exercise 5.38, rewrite the compiler's primitive code generators make-variable-access and make-variable-assignment to output lexical-address instructions. In cases where find-variable returns nil (that is, where the variable is not in the compile-time environment), you should have the code generators use the evaluator operations, as before. (For example, the variable may be in the global environment, which would be part of the run-time environment but is not part of the compile-time environment. This strategy of using the evaluator operations is critical to our handling of define, as discussed below.) Test the modified compiler, first on a few simple cases (such as the nested lambda combination at the beginning of this section) and then by compiling the following application of an iterative factorial procedure and running the resulting code:[41]

```
((lambda (n)
   ((lambda (fact-iter)
      (fact-iter fact-iter 1 1))
    (lambda (f-i product counter)
      (cond ((> counter n) product)
            (else (f-i f-i
                       (* counter product)
                       (+ counter 1)))))))
 4)
```

[41] The programming trick used in this example shows how one can evaluate recursive procedures without resorting to the use of define. The most famous trick of this sort is the Y operator, which can be used to give a "pure λ-calculus" implementation of recursion. See Stoy 1977 for details.

Exercise 5.40

In this section we have focused on the use of the compile-time environment to produce lexical addresses. But there are other uses for compile-time environments. For instance, in exercise 5.33 we increased the efficiency of compiled code by open-coding primitive operators. Our implementation treated the names of open-coded operators as reserved words. If a program were to rebind such an operator, the mechanism described in exercise 5.33 would still open-code it as a primitive, ignoring the new binding. For example, consider the procedure

```
(lambda (+ * a b x y)
  (+ (* a x) (* b y)))
```

which computes a linear combination of x and y. We might call it with arguments +matrix, *matrix, and four matrices, but the open-coding compiler would still open-code the + and the * in (+ (* a x) (* b y)) as primitive + and *. Modify the open-coding compiler to consult the compile-time environment in order to compile the correct code for expressions involving the names of primitive operators.

Compiling define expressions

Our lexical addressing scheme is based on the assumption that environment structures are invariant—if a variable is found at a particular lexical address at compile time, it will also be at that lexical address at run time. The interactive use of define is in direct conflict with this assumption, because lexical addresses of variables in a frame may change as a result of the addition of new variables at run time. Coping with the unrestricted use of define requires a much more complex approach to lexical addressing. However, the simple mechanism introduced above can still serve well in many cases. In order to discuss these issues, it is useful to distinguish three categories of define expressions: internal definitions (used to implement block structure), definitions entered interactively by the user in the global environment, and other uses of define.

We argued in section 5.2.5 that internal definitions for block structure should not be considered "real" defines. Rather, a procedure body should be interpreted as if the internal variables being defined were installed as ordinary lambda variables initialized to their correct values using set!. Details of a method to accomplish this are given in section 5.2.5 and in exercise 5.24. Thus, we can solve the problem of define for internal definitions by simply assuming that such definitions have been scanned out of the program before it is compiled.

Compilations of definitions that will create new variables in the global environment also do not cause difficulties. Our compiler does not enter defined names in the compile-time environment, and when a variable is not found in the compile-time environment the compiled code will use the interpreter's ordinary lookup-variable-value mechanism to search for the binding. (This is the technique explained in exercise 5.39.) Thus, lexical addresses will never be used to access variables in the global environment.

The real troubles with lexical addressing arise with the other uses of define, such as using eval to define a variable relative to an existing environment. Consider an environment created by make-environment:

```
(define env
  (make-environment
   ⟨ body of environment ⟩))
```

Suppose that we compile the code that forms the body of env. Later on, at run time, we could use eval to install a new definition in env. (This is precisely how we used remote-define in the register-machine simulator of section 5.1.5.) Although our new definition might invalidate the lexical addresses computed at compile time, the actual define that invalidates the addresses does not appear as part of the definition of env, so there is no way that the compiler can know about it. In general, there is no way to deal with such situations using the simple method of lexical addressing outlined above.[42]

Exercise 5.41

Exercise 5.24 showed how to modify the metacircular interpreter and the explicit-control evaluator so that they scan out internal definitions. Modify the compiler to perform the same transformation.

Exercise 5.42

One approach to dealing with the "difficult cases" for define is to make the compiler keep a "dependency structure" that describes how the code already compiled depends on assumptions made by the compiler. Changes that are incompatible with those assumptions should cause the compiler to automagically[43] recompile the code whose assumptions have been violated. Build a compiler and an interpreter that keep track of changes in the assumptions about environment structure and recompile as necessary. This is a major design project that involves original research.

---

42 The MIT implementation of Scheme incorporates a lexical-addressing algorithm that successfully copes with remote-define, and other uses of define, such as definitions entered interactively by the user in environments other than the global environment. This lexical-addressing algorithm is a much more complex mechanism than the one we have discussed in this section. The basic idea is to combine lexical addressing with "violation notices" generated at run time to warn the interpreter that certain lexical addresses may no longer be valid and must be recomputed.

43 Automagically: "Automatically, but in a way which, for some reason (typically because it is too complicated, or too ugly, or perhaps even too trivial), the speaker doesn't feel like explaining." (Steele 1983)

5.4 Storage Allocation and Garbage Collection

We have seen in this chapter how expressions in a high-level, procedural language such as Lisp can be evaluated by register machines. However, we have regarded list-structure operations as primitive data operations. In effect, we have assumed that our register machines are equipped with a *list-structured memory*, in which the basic operations for manipulating list-structured data are primitive. Postulating the existence of such a memory is a useful abstraction when one is focusing on the mechanisms of control in a Lisp interpreter, but this does not reflect a realistic view of the actual primitive data operations of contemporary computers. To obtain a more complete picture of how a Lisp system operates, we must investigate how list structure can be represented in a way that is compatible with conventional computer memories.

There are two considerations in implementing a list-structured memory. The first is purely an issue of representation: how to represent the "box-and-pointer" structure of Lisp pairs, using only the storage and addressing capabilities of typical computer memories. The second issue concerns the management of memory as a computation proceeds. The operation of a Lisp system depends crucially on the ability to continually create new data objects. These include objects that are explicitly created by the Lisp procedures being interpreted as well as structures created by the interpreter itself, such as environments and argument lists. Although the constant creation of new data objects would pose no problem on a computer with an infinite amount of rapidly addressable memory, computer memories are available only in finite sizes (more's the pity). Lisp systems thus provide an *automatic storage allocation* facility to support the illusion of an infinite memory. When a data object is no longer needed, the memory allocated to it is automatically recycled and used to construct new data objects. There are many different techniques for providing such automatic storage allocation. The method we shall discuss in this section is called *garbage collection*.

5.4.1 Memory as Vectors

A conventional computer memory can be thought of as an array of cubbyholes, each of which can contain a piece of information. Each cubbyhole has a unique name, called its *address* or *location*. Typical memory systems provide two primitive operations: one that fetches the data stored in a specified location and one that assigns new data to a specified location. Memory addresses can be incremented to support sequential access to some set of the cubbyholes. More generally, many important data operations require that memory addresses be treated as data, which can be stored in memory locations and manipulated in machine registers. The representation of list structure is one application of such *address arithmetic*.

To model computer memory, we introduce into Scheme a new kind of data structure called a *vector*. Abstractly, a vector is a compound data object whose individual elements can be accessed by means of an integer index in an amount of time that is independent of the index.[44] In order to describe memory operations, we introduce two primitive Scheme procedures for manipulating vectors:

(vector-ref ⟨vector⟩ ⟨n⟩) returns the nth element of the vector.

(vector-set! ⟨vector⟩ ⟨n⟩ ⟨value⟩) sets the nth element of the vector to the designated value.

For example, if v is a vector, then (vector-ref v 5) gets the fifth entry in the vector v and (vector-set! v 5 7) changes the value of the fifth entry of the vector v to 7.[45] For computer memory, this access can be implemented through the use of address arithmetic to combine a *base address* that specifies the beginning location of a vector in memory with an *index* that specifies the offset of a particular element of the vector.

Representing Lisp data

We can use vectors to implement the basic pair structures required for a list-structured memory. Let us imagine that computer memory is divided into two vectors: the-cars and the-cdrs. We will represent list structure as follows: A pointer to a pair is an index into the two vectors. The car of the pair is the entry in the-cars with the designated index, and the cdr of the pair is the entry in the-cdrs with the designated index. We also need a representation for objects other than pairs (such as numbers and symbols) and a way to distinguish one kind of data from another. There are many methods of accomplishing this, but they all reduce to using *typed pointers*, that is, to extending the notion of "pointer" to include information on data type.[46] The data type enables the system to distinguish a pointer

---

44 We could represent vectors as lists of items. However, the access time would then not be independent of the index, since accessing the nth element of a list requires $n - 1$ cdr operations.

45 For completeness, we should specify a make-vector operation that constructs vectors. However, in the present application we will use vectors only to model fixed divisions of the computer memory.

46 This is precisely the same "typed data" idea we introduced in chapter 2 for dealing with generic operators. Here, however, the data types are included at the primitive machine level rather than constructed through the use of lists.

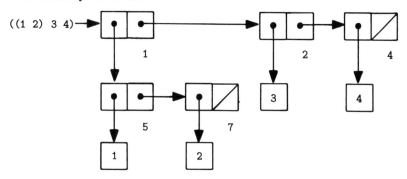

Index	0	1	2	3	4	5	6	7	8	...
the-cars		p5	n3		n4	n1		n2		...
the-cdrs		p2	p4		e0	p7		e0		...

Figure 5.16
Box-and-pointer and memory-vector representations of the list ((1 2) 3 4).

to a pair (which consists of the "pair" data type and an index into the memory vectors) from pointers to other kinds of data (which consist of some other data type and whatever is being used to represent data of that type). Two data objects are considered to be the same (eq?) if their pointers are identical.[47] Figure 5.16 illustrates the use of this method to represent the list ((1 2) 3 4), whose box-and-pointer diagram is also shown. We use letter prefixes to denote the data-type information. Thus, a pointer to the pair with index 5 is denoted p5, the empty list is denoted by the pointer e0, and a pointer to the number 4 is denoted n4. In the box-and-pointer diagram, we have indicated at the lower right of each pair the vector index that specifies where the car and cdr of the pair are stored. The blank locations in the-cars and the-cdrs may contain parts of other list structures (not of interest here).

The details of data representations are highly implementation-dependent. A pointer to a number, such as n4, might consist of a type indicating

[47] Type information may be encoded in a variety of ways, depending on the details of the machine on which the Lisp system is to be implemented. The execution efficiency of Lisp programs will be strongly dependent on how cleverly this choice is made, but it is difficult to formulate general design rules for good choices. The most straightforward way to implement typed pointers is to allocate a fixed set of bits in each pointer to be a *type field* that encodes the data type. Important questions to be addressed in designing such a representation include the following: How many type bits are required? How large must the vector indices be? How efficiently can the primitive machine instructions be used to manipulate the type fields of pointers? Machines that include special hardware for the efficient handling of type fields are said to have *tagged architectures*.

numeric data together with the actual representation of the number 4.[48] To deal with numbers that are too large to be represented in the fixed amount of space allocated for a single pointer, we could use a distinct *bignum* data type, for which the pointer designates a list in which the parts of the number are stored.[49]

A symbol might be represented as a typed pointer that designates a list of the characters that form the symbol's printed representation. This list is constructed by the Lisp reader when the character string is initially encountered in input. Since we want two instances of a symbol to be recognized as the "same" symbol by eq? and we want eq? to be a simple test for equality of pointers, we must ensure that if the reader sees the same character string twice, it will use the same pointer (to the same list of characters) to represent both occurrences. To accomplish this, the reader maintains a table, traditionally called the *obarray*, of all the symbols it has ever encountered. When the reader encounters a character string and is about to construct a symbol, it checks the obarray to see if it has ever before seen the same character string. If it has not, it uses the characters to construct a new symbol (a typed pointer to a new character list) and enters this pointer in the obarray. If the reader has seen the string before, it returns the symbol pointer stored in the obarray. This process of replacing character strings by unique pointers is called *interning* symbols.

Implementing the primitive list operations

Given the above representation scheme, we can replace each primitive list operation of a register machine with one or more primitive vector operations. We will use two registers, the-cars and the-cdrs, to identify the memory vectors, and will assume that vector-ref and vector-set! are available as primitive operations. We also assume that numeric operations on pointers (such as incrementing a pointer, using a pair pointer to index a vector, or adding two numbers) use only the index portion of the typed pointer. Thus, the register-machine instructions

```
(assign ⟨reg₁⟩ (car (fetch ⟨reg₂⟩)))
```

```
(assign ⟨reg₁⟩ (cdr (fetch ⟨reg₂⟩)))
```

---

48 This decision on the representation of numbers determines whether eq?, which tests equality of pointers, can be used to test for equality of numbers. If the pointer contains the number itself, then equal numbers will have the same pointer. But if the pointer contains the index of a location where the number is stored, equal numbers will be guaranteed to have equal pointers only if we are careful never to store the same number in more than one location.

49 This is just like writing a number as a sequence of digits, except that each "digit" is a number between 0 and the largest number that can be stored in a single pointer.

are implemented, respectively, as

```
(assign ⟨reg₁⟩ (vector-ref (fetch the-cars) (fetch ⟨reg₂⟩)))
```

```
(assign ⟨reg₁⟩ (vector-ref (fetch the-cdrs) (fetch ⟨reg₂⟩)))
```
and the instructions
```
(perform
 (set-car! (fetch ⟨reg₁⟩) (fetch ⟨reg₂⟩)))
```

```
(perform
 (set-cdr! (fetch ⟨reg₁⟩) (fetch ⟨reg₂⟩)))
```
are implemented as
```
(perform
 (vector-set! (fetch the-cars) (fetch ⟨reg₁⟩) (fetch ⟨reg₂⟩)))
```

```
(perform
 (vector-set! (fetch the-cdrs) (fetch ⟨reg₁⟩) (fetch ⟨reg₂⟩)))
```
Cons is performed by allocating an unused index and storing the arguments to cons in the-cars and the-cdrs at that indexed vector position. We presume that there is a special register, free, that always holds a pair pointer containing the next available index, and that we can increment the index part of that pointer to find the next free location.[50] Thus, the operation
```
(assign ⟨reg₁⟩ (cons (fetch ⟨reg₂⟩) (fetch ⟨reg₃⟩)))
```
is implemented as the following sequence of vector operations:[51]
```
(perform
 (vector-set! (fetch the-cars) (fetch free) (fetch ⟨reg₂⟩)))
(perform
 (vector-set! (fetch the-cdrs) (fetch free) (fetch ⟨reg₃⟩)))
(assign ⟨reg₁⟩ (fetch free))
(assign free (1+ (fetch free)))
```

---

[50] There are other ways of finding free storage. For example, we could link together all the unused pairs into a *free list*. Our free locations are consecutive (and hence can be accessed by incrementing a pointer) because we are using a compacting garbage collector, as we will see in section 5.4.2.

[51] This is essentially the implementation of cons in terms of set-car! and set-cdr!, as described in section 3.3.1. The operation get-new-pair used in that implementation is realized here by the free pointer.

The predicate

```
(eq? (fetch ⟨reg₁⟩) (fetch ⟨reg₂⟩))
```

simply tests the equality of all fields in the registers, and predicates such as atom?, null?, symbol?, and number? need only check the type field.

Although our register machines use stacks, we need do nothing special here, since stacks can be modeled in terms of lists. The stack can be a list of the saved values, pointed to by a special register the-stack. Thus, (save ⟨reg⟩) can be implemented as

```
(assign the-stack (cons (fetch ⟨reg⟩) (fetch the-stack)))
```

Similarly, (restore ⟨reg⟩) can be implemented as

```
(assign ⟨reg⟩ (car (fetch the-stack)))
(assign the-stack (cdr (fetch the-stack)))
```

and (perform (initialize-stack)) can be implemented as

```
(assign the-stack '())
```

These operations can be further expanded in terms of the vector operations given above. In conventional computer architectures, however, it is usually advantageous to allocate the stack as a separate vector. Then pushing and popping the stack can be accomplished by incrementing or decrementing an index into that vector.

Exercise 5.43

Draw the box-and-pointer representation and the memory-vector representation (as in figure 5.16) of the list structure produced by

```
(define x (cons 1 2))
(define y (list x x))
```

with the free pointer initially p1. What is the final value of free? What pointers represent the values of x and y?

5.4.2 Maintaining the Illusion of Infinite Memory

The representation method outlined in section 5.4.1 solves the problem of implementing list structure, provided that we have an infinite amount of memory. With a real computer we will eventually run out of free space in which to construct new pairs.[52] However, most of the pairs generated in a

---

[52] This may not be true eventually, because memories may get large enough so that it would be impossible to run out of free memory in the lifetime of the computer. For example, there are about 3×10^{13} microseconds in a year, so if we were to cons once

typical computation are used only to hold intermediate results. After these results are accessed, the pairs are no longer needed—they are *garbage*. For instance, if we perform the computation

```
(accumulate + 0 (filter odd? (enumerate-interval 0 n)))
```

we construct two lists: the enumeration and the result of filtering the enumeration. When the accumulation is complete, these lists are no longer needed, and the allocated memory can be reclaimed. Moreover, if we use streams to perform this computation, we can reclaim most of that memory even sooner, because we need not finish enumerating before we begin to filter and accumulate. If we can arrange to collect all the garbage periodically, and if this turns out to recycle memory at about the same rate at which we construct new pairs, we will have preserved the illusion that there is an infinite amount of memory.

In order to recycle pairs, we must have a way to determine which allocated pairs are not needed (in the sense that their contents can no longer influence the future of the computation). The method we shall examine for accomplishing this is known as *garbage collection*. Garbage collection is based on the observation that, at any moment in a Lisp interpretation, the only objects that can affect the future of the computation are those that can be reached by some succession of car and cdr operations starting from the pointers that are currently in the machine registers.[53] Any memory cell that is not so accessible may be recycled.

There are many ways to perform garbage collection. The method we shall examine here is called *stop-and-copy*. The basic idea is to divide memory into two halves: "working memory" and "free memory." When cons constructs pairs, it allocates these in working memory. When working memory is full, we perform garbage collection by locating all the useful pairs in working memory and copying these into consecutive locations in free memory. (The useful pairs are located by tracing all the car and cdr pointers, starting with the machine registers.) Since we do not copy the garbage, there will presumably be additional free memory that we can use to allocate new pairs. In addition, nothing in the working memory

---

per microsecond we would need about 10^{15} cells of memory to build a machine that could operate for 30 years without running out of memory. That much memory seems absurdly large by today's standards, but it is not physically impossible. On the other hand, processors are getting faster and a future computer may have large numbers of processors operating in parallel on a single memory, so it may be possible to use up memory much faster than we have postulated.

53 We assume here that the stack is represented as a list as shown in section 5.4.1, so that items on the stack are accessible via the pointer in the stack register.

is needed, since all the useful pairs in it have been copied. Thus, if we interchange the roles of working memory and free memory, we can continue processing; new pairs will be allocated in the new working memory (which was the old free memory). When this is full, we can copy the useful pairs into the new free memory (which was the old working memory).[54]

Implementation of a stop-and-copy garbage collector

We now use our register-machine language to describe the stop-and-copy algorithm in more detail. We will assume that there is a register called root that contains a pointer to a structure that eventually points at all accessible data. This can be arranged by storing the contents of all the interpreter registers in a pre-allocated list pointed at by root just before starting garbage collection.[55] We also assume that, in addition to the current working memory, there is free memory available into which we can copy the useful data. The current working memory consists of vectors whose base addresses are in registers called the-cars and the-cdrs, and the free memory is in registers called new-cars and new-cdrs.

Garbage collection is triggered when we exhaust the free cells in the current working memory, that is, when a cons operation attempts to increment the free pointer beyond the end of the memory vector. When the garbage-collection process is complete, the root pointer will point into the new memory, all objects accessible from the root will have been moved to the new memory, and the free pointer will indicate the next place in the new memory where a new pair can be allocated. In addition, the roles of working memory and new memory will have been interchanged—new pairs

54 This idea was invented and first implemented by Minsky, as part of the implementation of Lisp for the PDP-1 at the MIT Research Laboratory of Electronics. It was further developed by Fenichel and Yochelson (1969) for use in the Lisp implementation for the Multics time-sharing system. Later, Baker (1978) developed a "real-time" version of the method, which does not require the Lisp computation to stop during garbage collection. An alternative commonly used garbage-collection technique is the *mark-sweep* method. This consists of tracing all the structure accessible from the machine registers and marking each pair we reach. We then scan all of memory, and any location that is unmarked is "swept up" as garbage and made available for reuse. A full discussion of the mark-sweep method can be found in Allen 1978. The Minsky-Fenichel-Yochelson algorithm is the dominant algorithm in use for large-memory systems because it examines only the useful part of memory. This is in contrast to mark-sweep, in which the sweep phase must check all of memory. A second advantage of stop-and-copy is that it is a *compacting* garbage collector. That is, at the end of the garbage-collection phase the useful data will have been moved to consecutive memory locations, with all garbage pairs compressed out. This can be an extremely important performance consideration in machines with virtual memory, in which accesses to widely separated memory addresses may require extra paging operations.

55 The interpreter registers do not include the registers used by the storage-allocation system—root, the-cars, the-cdrs, and the other registers that will be introduced in this section.

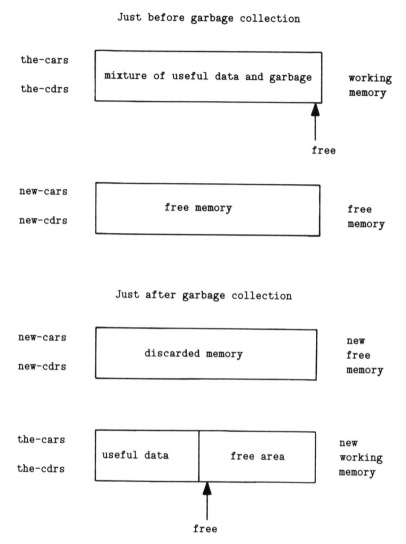

Figure 5.17
Reconfiguration of memory by the garbage-collection process.

will be constructed in the new memory, beginning at the place indicated by free, and the (previous) working memory will be available as the new memory for the next garbage collection. Figure 5.17 shows the arrangement of memory just before and just after garbage collection.

The state of the garbage-collection process is controlled by maintaining two pointers: free and scan. These are initialized to point at the beginning of the new memory. The algorithm begins by relocating the pair pointed at by root to the beginning of the new memory. The pair is copied, the root pointer is adjusted to point to the new location, and the free pointer is incremented. In addition, the old location of the pair is marked to show that its contents have been moved. This marking is done as follows: In the car position, we place a special tag that signals that this is an already-moved object. (Such an object is traditionally called a *broken heart*.)[56]   In the cdr position we place a *forwarding address* that points at the location to which the object has been moved.

After relocating the root, the garbage collector enters its basic cycle. At each step in the algorithm, the scan pointer (initially pointing at the relocated root) points at a pair that has been moved to the new memory but whose car and cdr pointers still refer to objects in the old memory. These objects are each relocated, and the scan pointer is incremented. To relocate an object (for example, the object indicated by the car pointer of the pair we are scanning) we check to see if the object has already been moved (as indicated by the presence of a broken-heart tag in the car position of the object). If the object has not already been moved, we copy it to the place indicated by free, update free, and update the pointer to the object (in this example, the car pointer of the pair we are scanning) to point to the new location. If the object has already been moved, its forwarding address (found in the cdr position of the broken heart) is substituted for the pointer in the pair being scanned. Eventually, all accessible objects will have been moved and scanned, at which point the scan pointer will overtake the free pointer and the process will terminate.

We can specify the stop-and-copy algorithm as a program for a register machine. The basic step of relocating an object is accomplished by a subroutine relocate-old-result-in-new. This subroutine gets its argument, a pointer to the object to be relocated, from a register named old. It relocates the designated object, puts a pointer to the relocated object into a register called new, and returns by branching to the entry stored in the register relocate-continue. To begin garbage collection, we invoke this subroutine to relocate the root pointer, after initializing free and scan. When the relocation of root has been accomplished, we install the new pointer as the new root and enter the main loop of the garbage collector.

```
begin-garbage-collection
    (assign free 0)
    (assign scan 0)
    (assign old (fetch root))
    (assign relocate-continue reassign-root)
    (goto relocate-old-result-in-new)
```

---

56 The term *broken heart* was coined by David Cressey, who wrote a garbage collector for MDL, a dialect of Lisp developed at MIT during the early 1970s.

```
reassign-root
  (assign root (fetch new))
  (goto gc-loop)
```

In the main loop of the garbage collector we must determine whether there are any more objects to be scanned. We do this by testing whether the scan pointer is coincident with the free pointer. If the pointers are equal, then all accessible objects have been relocated, and we branch to gc-flip, which cleans things up so that we can continue the interrupted computation. If there are still pairs to be scanned, we call the relocate subroutine to relocate the car of the pair (by placing the car pointer in old). The relocate-continue register is set up so that the subroutine will return to update the car pointer.

```
gc-loop
  (branch (= (fetch scan) (fetch free)) gc-flip)
  (assign old (vector-ref (fetch new-cars) (fetch scan)))
  (assign relocate-continue update-car)
  (goto relocate-old-result-in-new)
```

At update-car, we modify the car pointer of the pair being scanned, then proceed to relocate the cdr of the pair. We will return to update-cdr when that relocation has been accomplished. After relocating and updating the cdr, we are finished scanning that pair, so we continue with the main loop.

```
update-car
  (perform
   (vector-set! (fetch new-cars) (fetch scan) (fetch new)))
  (assign old (vector-ref (fetch new-cdrs) (fetch scan)))
  (assign relocate-continue update-cdr)
  (goto relocate-old-result-in-new)
```

```
update-cdr
  (perform
   (vector-set! (fetch new-cdrs) (fetch scan) (fetch new)))
  (assign scan (1+ (fetch scan)))
  (goto gc-loop)
```

The subroutine relocate-old-result-in-new relocates objects as follows: If the object to be relocated (pointed at by old) is not a pair, then we return the same pointer to the object unchanged (in new). (For example, we may be scanning a pair whose car is the number 4. If we represent the car by n4, as described in section 5.4.1, then we want the "relocated" car pointer to still be n4.) Otherwise, we must perform the relocation. If the car position of the pair to be relocated contains a broken-heart tag, then the pair has in fact already been moved, so we retrieve the forwarding address (from the cdr position of the broken heart) and return this in new. If the pointer in old points at a yet-unmoved pair, then we move the pair to the first free cell in new memory (pointed at by free) and set up the broken heart by storing a broken-heart tag and forwarding address at the old location. We use a register oldcr to hold the car or the cdr of the object pointed at by old.

```
relocate-old-result-in-new
  (branch (pointer-to-pair? (fetch old)) pair)
  (assign new (fetch old))
  (goto (fetch relocate-continue))


pair
  (assign oldcr (vector-ref (fetch the-cars) (fetch old)))
  (branch (broken-heart? (fetch oldcr)) already-moved)
  (assign new (fetch free))              ;new location for pair
  (assign free (1+ (fetch free)))        ;update free pointer


  ;;Copy the car and cdr to new memory.
  (perform
   (vector-set! (fetch new-cars) (fetch new) (fetch oldcr)))
  (assign oldcr (vector-ref (fetch the-cdrs) (fetch old)))
  (perform
   (vector-set! (fetch new-cdrs) (fetch new) (fetch oldcr)))


  ;;Construct the broken heart.
  (perform
   (vector-set! (fetch the-cars) (fetch old) broken-heart))
  (perform
   (vector-set! (fetch the-cdrs) (fetch old) (fetch new)))
  (goto (fetch relocate-continue))


already-moved
  (assign new (vector-ref (fetch the-cdrs) (fetch old)))
  (goto (fetch relocate-continue))
```

At the very end of the garbage-collection process, we interchange the role of old and new memories by interchanging pointers: interchanging

the-cars with new-cars, and the-cdrs with new-cdrs. We will then be
ready to perform another garbage collection the next time memory runs
out.

```
gc-flip
  (assign temp (fetch the-cdrs))
  (assign the-cdrs (fetch new-cdrs))
  (assign new-cdrs (fetch temp))
  (assign temp (fetch the-cars))
  (assign the-cars (fetch new-cars))
  (assign new-cars (fetch temp))
```

Exercise 5.44

Show how to integrate the storage-allocation and garbage-collection scheme discussed in this section with the explicit-control evaluator of section 5.2. How
should the need for garbage collection be triggered? Where in the interpreter
code should the appropriate code be installed?

References

Allen, John. 1978. *Anatomy of Lisp*. New York: McGraw-Hill.

Arvind, and J. Dean Brock. 1983. Streams and managers. In *Proceedings of the 14th IBM Computer Science Symposium*, Lecture Notes in Computer Science (New York: Springer-Verlag).

Backus, John. 1978. Can programming be liberated from the von Neumann style? *Communications of the ACM* 21(8):613–641.

Baker, Henry G., Jr. 1978. List processing in real time on a serial computer. *Communications of the ACM* 21(4):280–293.

Batali, John, Neil Mayle, Howard Shrobe, Gerald Jay Sussman, and Daniel Weise. 1982. The Scheme-81 architecture—System and chip. In *Proceedings of the MIT Conference on Advanced Research in VLSI*, edited by Paul Penfield, Jr. (Dedham, Mass.: Artech House).

Borning, Alan. 1977. ThingLab—An object-oriented system for building simulations using constraints. In *Proceedings of the 5th International Joint Conference on Artificial Intelligence*.

Borodin, Alan, and Ian Munro. 1975. *The Computational Complexity of Algebraic and Numeric Problems*. New York: American Elsevier.

Chaitin, Gregory J. 1975. Randomness and mathematical proof. *Scientific American* 232(5): 47–52.

Church, Alonzo. 1941. *The Calculi of Lambda-Conversion*. Princeton, N.J.: Princeton University Press.

Clark, Keith L. 1978. Negation as failure. In *Logic and Data Bases* (New York: Plenum Press), pp. 293–322.

Clinger, William. 1982. Nondeterministic call by need is neither lazy nor by name. In *Proceedings of the ACM Symposium on Lisp and Functional Programming*, pp. 226–234.

Colmerauer A., H. Kanoui, R. Pasero, and P. Roussel. 1973. Un system de communication homme-machine en français. Technical report, Groupe Intelligence Artificielle, Université d'Aix Marseille, Luminy.

Darlington, John, Peter Henderson, and David Turner. 1982. *Functional Programming and Its Applications*. New York: Cambridge University Press.

deKleer, Johan, Jon Doyle, Guy Steele, and Gerald J. Sussman. 1977. AMORD: Explicit control of reasoning. In *Proceedings of the ACM Symposium on Artificial Intelligence and Programming Languages*, pp. 116–125.

Feller, William. 1957. *An Introduction to Probability Theory and Its Applications*, volume 1. New York: John Wiley & Sons.

Fenichel, R., and J. Yochelson. 1969. A Lisp garbage collector for virtual memory computer systems. *Communications of the ACM* 12(11):611–612.

Friedman, Daniel P., and David S. Wise. 1976. CONS should not evaluate its arguments. In *Automata, Languages, and Programming: Third International Colloquium*, edited by S. Michaelson and R. Milner, pp. 257–284.

Goldberg, Adele, and David Robson. 1983. *Smalltalk-80: The Language and Its Implementation*. Reading, Mass.: Addison-Wesley.

Gordon, Michael, Robin Milner, and Christopher Wadsworth. 1979. *Edinburgh LCF*. Lecture Notes in Computer Science, volume 78. New York: Springer-Verlag.

Green, Cordell. 1969. Application of theorem proving to problem solving. In *Proceedings of the International Joint Conference on Artificial Intelligence*, pp. 219–240.

Green, Cordell, and Bertram Raphael. 1968. The use of theorem-proving techniques in question-answering systems. In *Proceedings of the ACM National Conference*, pp. 169–181.

Griss, Martin L. 1981. Portable Standard Lisp, a brief overview. Utah Symbolic Computation Group Operating Note 58, University of Utah.

Guttag, John V. 1977. Abstract data types and the development of data structures. *Communications of the ACM* 20(6):397–404.

Hamming, Richard W. 1980. *Coding and Information Theory*. Englewood Cliffs, N.J.: Prentice-Hall.

Hardy, Godfrey H. 1921. Srinivasa Ramanujan. *Proceedings of the London Mathematical Society* XIX(2).

Hardy, Godfrey H., and E. M. Wright. 1960. *An Introduction to the Theory of Numbers*, fourth edition. New York: Oxford University Press.

Hearn, Anthony C. 1969. Standard Lisp. Technical report AIM-90, Artificial Intelligence Project, Stanford University.

Henderson, Peter. 1980. *Functional Programming: Application and Implementation*. Englewood Cliffs, N.J.: Prentice-Hall.

Hewitt, Carl E. 1969. PLANNER: A language for proving theorems in robots. In *Proceedings of the International Joint Conference on Artificial Intelligence*, pp. 295–301.

Hewitt, Carl E. 1977. Viewing control structures as patterns of passing messages. *Journal of Artificial Intelligence* 8(3):323–364.

Hoare, C. A. R. 1972. Proof of correctness of data representations. *Communications of the ACM* 1(4):271–281.

Hofstadter, Douglas R. 1979. *Gödel, Escher, Bach: An Eternal Golden Braid.* New York: Basic Books.

Knuth, Donald E. 1969. *Seminumerical Algorithms.* Volume 2 of *The Art of Computer Programming.* Reading, Mass.: Addison-Wesley.

Kowalski, Robert. 1973. Predicate logic as a programming language. Technical report 70, Department of Computational Logic, School of Artificial Intelligence, University of Edinburgh.

Kowalski, Robert. 1979. *Logic for Problem Solving.* New York: North-Holland.

Lampson, Butler, J. J. Horning, R. London, J. G. Mitchell, and G. K. Popek. 1981. Report on the programming language Euclid. Technical report, Computer Systems Research Group, University of Toronto.

Landin, Peter. 1965. A correspondence between Algol 60 and Church's lambda notation: Part I. *Communications of the ACM* 8(2):89–101.

Liskov, Barbara H., and Stephen N. Zilles. 1975. Specification techniques for data abstractions. *IEEE Transactions on Software Engineering* 1(1):7–19.

McCarthy, John. 1960. Recursive functions of symbolic expressions and their computation by machine. In *Communications of the ACM* 3(4):184–195.

McCarthy, John. 1978. The history of Lisp. In *Proceedings of the ACM SIGPLAN Conference on the History of Programming Languages.*

McCarthy, John, P. W. Abrahams, D. J. Edwards, T. P. Hart, and M. I. Levin. 1965. *Lisp 1.5 Programmer's Manual,* second edition. Cambridge, Mass.: MIT Press.

Moon, David. 1978. MacLisp reference manual, Version 0. Technical report, MIT Laboratory for Computer Science.

Moon, David, and Daniel Weinreb. 1981. Lisp machine manual. Technical report, MIT Artificial Intelligence Laboratory.

Morris, J. H., Eric Schmidt, and Philip Wadler. 1980. Experience with an applicative string processing language. In *Proceedings of the 7th Annual ACM SIGACT/SIGPLAN Symposium on the Principles of Programming Languages.*

Pitman, Kent. 1983. The revised MacLisp Manual (Saturday evening edition). Technical report 295, MIT Laboratory for Computer Science.

Rivest, Ronald, Adi Shamir, and Leonard Adelman. 1977. A method for obtaining digital signatures and public-key cryptosystems. Technical memo LCS/TM82, MIT Laboratory for Computer Science.

Robinson, J. A. 1965. A machine-oriented logic based on the resolution principle. *Journal of the ACM* 12(1):23.

Robinson, J. A. 1983. Logic programming—Past, present, and future. *New Generation Computing* 1:107–124.

Software Arts, Inc., 1982. TK!Solver(TM) Program. Wellesley, Mass.: Software Arts.

Solovay, Robert, and Volker Strassen. 1977. A fast Monte Carlo test for primality. *SIAM Journal on Computing* (March 1977):84–85.

Steele, Guy Lewis, Jr. 1977. Debunking the "expensive procedure call" myth. In *Proceedings of the National Conference of the ACM,* pp. 153–62.

Steele, Guy Lewis, Jr. 1982. An overview of Common Lisp. In *Proceedings of the ACM Symposium on Lisp and Functional Programming,* pp. 98–107.

Steele, Guy Lewis, Jr., and Gerald Jay Sussman. 1975. Scheme: An interpreter for the extended lambda calculus. Memo 349, MIT Artificial Intelligence Laboratory.

Steele, Guy Lewis, Jr., Donald R. Woods, Raphael A. Finkel, Mark R. Crispin, Richard M. Stallman, and Geoffrey S. Goodfellow. 1983. *The Hacker's Dictionary.* New York: Harper & Row.

Stoy, Joseph E. 1977. *Denotational Semantics.* Cambridge, Mass.: MIT Press.

Sussman, Gerald Jay, and Richard M. Stallman. 1975. Heuristic techniques in computer-aided circuit analysis. *IEEE Transactions on Circuits and Systems* CAS-22(11):857–865.

Sussman, Gerald Jay, and Guy Lewis Steele Jr. 1980. Constraints—A language for expressing almost-hierachical descriptions. *AI Journal* 14:1–39.

Sussman, Gerald Jay, Terry Winograd, and Eugene Charniak. 1971. Microplanner reference manual. Memo 203A, MIT Artificial Intelligence Laboratory.

Sutherland, Ivan E. 1963. SKETCHPAD: A man-machine graphical communication system. Technical report 296, MIT Lincoln Laboratory.

Teitelman, Warren. 1974. Interlisp reference manual. Technical report, Xerox Palo Alto Research Center.

Turner, David. 1981. The future of applicative languages. In *Proceedings of the 3rd European Conference on Informatics*, Lecture Notes in Computer Science, volume 123 (New York: Springer-Verlag), pp. 334–348.

Wand, Mitchell. 1978. Continuation-based program transformation strategies. *Journal of the ACM* 27(1):164–180.

Waters, Richard C. 1979. A method for analyzing loop programs. *IEEE Transactions on Software Engineering* 5(3):237–247.

Winograd, Terry. 1971. Procedures as a representation for data in a computer program for understanding natural language. Technical report AI TR-17, MIT Artificial Intelligence Laboratory.

Zippel, Richard. 1979. Probabilistic algorithms for sparse polynomials. Ph.D. dissertation, Department of Electrical Engineering and Computer Science, MIT.

List of Exercises

Index

Page numbers for definitions are in italics